European University Studies

Europäische Hochschulschriften
Publications Universitaires Européennes

Series XIV
Anglo-Saxon Language and Literature

Reihe XIV   Série XIV
Angelsächsische Sprache und Literatur
Langue et littérature anglo-saxonnes

Vol./Bd. 458

PETER LANG

Frankfurt am Main · Berlin · Bern · Bruxelles · New York · Oxford · Wien

Hanne Bewernick

The Storyteller's Memory Palace

A Method of Interpretation Based on the Function of Memory Systems in Literature

Geoffrey Chaucer, William Langland,
Salman Rushdie, Angela Carter,
Thomas Pynchon and Paul Auster

PETER LANG
Internationaler Verlag der Wissenschaften

Bibliographic Information published by the Deutsche Nationalbibliothek
The Deutsche Nationalbibliothek lists this publication in the Deutsche Nationalbibliografie; detailed bibliographic data is available in the internet at http://dnb.d-nb.de.

Zugl.: Flensburg, Univ., Diss., 2008

FI 3
ISSN 0721-3387
ISBN 978-3-631-60470-0

© Peter Lang GmbH
Internationaler Verlag der Wissenschaften
Frankfurt am Main 2010
All rights reserved.

www.peterlang.de

Acknowledgements

I would like to thank Dr. Charles Moseley for his inspirational tutorials on medieval literature which set me on this journey, and for the generosity and grace with which he shares his knowledge. I was very fortunate that Prof. Dr. Werner Reinhart trusted my concept and gave me the opportunity to write this thesis. Without the study grant from Universität Flensburg, my thoughts would have remained a jumble of ideas in my unstructured memory. Dansk Centralbibliotek for Sydslesvig eased my research by their efficient and friendly assistance, and particularly Rita Jakobsen proved invaluable in getting hold of elusive texts. I would especially like to thank family and friends for smiling and nodding encouragingly, even after their eyes had glazed over while enduring yet another of my extended enthusiastic ramblings about literature and memory.

Contents

Introduction

Imagine, you are entering a lofty cathedral. The air is cool, it is quiet. Distant footsteps echo in the large nave of the church, dappled light floats in through the elongated stained-glass windows and gently illuminates the various architectural features. As you walk slowly up the central aisle, you notice the tomb of a famous poet in a niche to your right. You walk on and pass the eagle-shaped lectern where the notes for last Sunday's sermon still lie. You arrive at the altar: an illuminated manuscript lies open on a colourful page. Looking up at the central stained-glass window, you see the figure of Mnemosyne (the personification of Memory) depicted there, surrounded by her nine daughters, the Muses. Memory's right arm points to the left where discarded objects stand half hidden behind a partly drawn curtain. You walk towards it and discover a dilapidated statue of Lesmosyne (the personification of Forgetting: Memory's sister). You walk past the half-forgotten objects back to the main door. On leaving, you look up and discover a large rose-window which shows scenes from the Last Judgment: a reminder that the inspiration contained within the building is a guide to everyday life.

Storytelling and remembering rely on similar practices: they both arrange images in an ordered structure. The brief description above is a combination of these two processes. It tells the story of a visit to a church where images in their particular order give meaning to the narrative. It is also an example of an ancient artificial memory aid: the memory palace. The memory palace is a mental structure originally created by orators to aid the ancient art of public speaking. Items to be remembered for a speech are placed in a three-dimensional imagined building which, at the required time, can be traversed in the mind, thus revealing each memorised item in the correct order.

If you have followed me into my imaginary cathedral above, you will be imagining a church that is nothing like the one I see in my mind's eye, but I will, hopefully, have made you follow my train of thought and introduced images that help to convey my meaning. This brazen and exaggerated approach – asking you directly to imagine, and guiding you through the actual building – is, of course, not common practice amongst writers. It is usually taken as a given that the reader will recreate the imaginary space that the author invents, thereby automatically entering the fictional world.

I have chosen this particular situation (the church and images) for three reasons. First, I want to introduce the topic of memory and storytelling. Each item either symbolises how narrative is stored in the memory: a tomb (history), a poet, speech notes, a book, a stained-glass window; or relates to the concept behind it: remembering and forgetting, memory as the mother of creative inspiration. It highlights the role of memory in literary fiction. Secondly, I want to show how memory systems work by creating the experience of entering an imaginary location rather than by merely explaining the theory. Finally, I chose this setting because it employs the memory palace – the most common memory system in mnemonics and the foundation upon which my theory of interpretation is built.

I propose to offer a new method of literary interpretation based on the compatible mental functions of memorising and creative writing. My theory is that by visualising the imaginary landscape contained within the words of a text, the reader gains more direct access to the underlying ideas of a story. The process of creative writing requires an initial period where the story exists only in the imagination of the author. The narrative is placed in space and time in some form of architectural framework or landscape, a type of memory palace that the author sees in his mind's eye. It is lodged in the memory in a three-dimensional space and is then transferred to the page. A story that is written down is a manifestation of creative memory at work because the memory structures of the author's thoughts are revealed in the text. The author's memory processes are embedded in the story's structure and in the visual aspects of the language; for example, in the use of location, backgrounds, images and in the sequence of events. By looking out for these building bricks in the text, readers can attempt to rebuild and enter the memory palace which the author has used as his blueprint for the story. By engaging the imagining faculty and the memory which feeds it, it is possible to approximate the picture, landscape and fictional world which originally only existed in the mind of the author, and thereby deduce meaning from the words.

The question of meaning in literature remains a contentious topic. A brief look at the discussion will explain how the term is used in my investigation and why I still deem it relevant to modern literary criticism. E.D. Hirsch aims to elucidate the term by distinguishing between 'meaning' and 'significance' in *Validity in Interpretation* (1967).[1] He clarifies the differentiation in *The Aims of Interpretation* (1976):

The term 'meaning' refers to the whole verbal meaning of a text, and 'significance' to textual meaning in relation to a larger context, i.e., another mind, another era, a wider subject matter, an alien system of values, and so on. In other words, 'significance' is textual meaning as related to some context, indeed any context, beyond itself.[2]

He borrows the definition from Gottlob Frege, who already in 1892 coined the phrase *Sinn und Bedeutung*, in order to explain why interpretations of the same text vary over time. In Hirsch's words: "the meaning of the text has remained the same while the significance of that meaning has shifted".[3] What T.S. Eliot

---

1   See in particular "The two horizons of textual meaning", pp.212–24.
2   pp.2–3.
3   *Validity in Interpretation*, p.213.

attributed to the changing of literary tradition,[4] phenomenological relativists have argued changes with each reader and their individual angle on the text. Hirsch develops his own definition with recourse to Husserl's ideas of an inner and outer horizon, saying that the "permanent meaning" of the text "is, and can be, nothing other than the author's meaning",[5] independent of whether the author is aware of his intention, and whether the reader is able to discover this meaning or not. "The interpreter's aim, then, is to posit the author's horizon and carefully exclude his own accidental associations."[6] Only when an inner horizon has been established, when some form of limitation has been applied to the possible author meaning or intention, can an interpretation take place. This will vary according to reader, literary tradition or cultural background but will nevertheless be founded on a permanent 'meaning': extant, even if not definable.

Terry Eagleton questions what he terms "Hirsch's defence of authorial meaning". He argues that "[m]eanings are not as stable and determinate as Hirsch thinks, even authorial ones – and the reason they are not is because, as he will not recognize, they are the products of language which always has something slippery about it."[7] He asks why Hirsch is so fearful of the indeterminacy of meaning.

That it is impossible to pin down the author's meaning with absolute certainty is undeniable; that every reader attempts to make sense of what is read, and therefore searches for meaning, is also a given. What interests me with regard to my investigation is how these two types of meaning can be made to approach each other. The two opposite views – either that there is one exact authorial meaning or that there are as many meanings as there are reader interpretations (as suggested by Barthes in his provocatively entitled essay "Death of the Author") – need not be mutually exclusive.

If there is only the one meaning, then, as Hirsch argues, "[t]he reader should try to reconstruct authorial meaning, and he can in principle succeed in his attempt".[8] A search for 'the one true meaning', however, limits the range of interpretation and denies the multiple functions that literature has. Any interpretation assumes that it will yield a result: this result is what I term the text's meaning. Therefore, the word 'meaning' will be used as a general term, both for the possible author meaning and for the meaning the reader extrapolates from the text. It is ultimately a combination of both that makes up the reading experience. When author and reader approach each other, when their thought processes are aligned, that is when an intense exchange of ideas becomes possible.

---

4   "Tradition and the individual talent".
5   *Validity in Interpretation*, p.216.
6   Ibid., p.222.
7   *Literary Theory*, p.60.
8   *The Aims of Interpretation*, p.8.

Literature is a form of communication between author and reader and as such underlies the natural limitations of conveying ideas: it is impossible to grasp an idea exactly as the creator of the idea imagined it. However, one way of bridging the gap between the words used to explain ideas and the ideas themselves when attempting to convey a story is to go beyond the words and see how they were put together in the first place. The memory is paramount in this process: from the initial invention to the resulting creation of images and the final communication of ideas. The Roman orator and writer Cicero's five steps of rhetoric express this concept and emphasise memory as the most important step.[9]

In the German language there are two strictly distinguished meanings of the word 'memory': *Gedächtnis* and *Erinnerung* (translatable as memorisation and remembrance). My interest lies in the *Gedächtnis*, or memorisation: not the involuntary memory that calls up past memories as we are accidentally reminded of them, but the artificial memory that is employed on purpose to store and retrieve information, whether for mere fact remembrance or for creative thinking.

The natural and the artificial memory differ in one point only: the second requires a conscious application and effort. Although I will focus on the artificial memory, it is understood throughout that it relies entirely on the natural function, merely enhancing what is already there; the natural processes of involuntary memory are exactly the same as for voluntary (artificial) memory, only in the latter case they are encouraged and strengthened. It is exactly this interplay between natural and artificial memory which lays the foundation for my theory. Since the memory is always engaged in creative thinking, natural memory processes will have been involved in the invention of a story and therefore will follow specific patterns of creation. By becoming aware of these patterns and comparing them to patterns of known artificial memory systems, we can gain an insight into the workings of the mind, exactly because the natural and artificial memories follow the same rules.

Research into the interaction between memory and literature has emphasised cultural memory to the detriment of artificial memory. It has neglected the practical use of memory systems as an interpretative tool. Although scholars such as Mary Carruthers (*The Book of Memory*, 1990) and Aleida Assmann (*Erninnerungsräume*, 1999) refer to mnemonics, they very much treat it as an inferior topic. Recent research, when dealing with the mnemonic aspect of memory at all, has concentrated on how memories are stored; the alternative employment of memory systems as the foundation for creative and original thinking has been overlooked or else cast aside as a fanciful by-product of Neoplatonic mysticism.

---

9   Cicero's five steps of rhetoric are: Invention (getting the idea), disposition (organising all parts of the idea into an orderly sequence), elocution (finding the right words to express these parts), memory (storing the words in the right order in the memory) and pronunciation (speaking the words in order to make the meaning as clear as possible). See *De Inventione, I, vii, 9.*

However, writers from Antiquity, such as Aristotle, had previously encouraged the more fluent adaptation of memorised material to move a debate forward: the progressive interaction between thinkers is the main function of memory and *not* the wading through facts or concepts in search of the one correct answer. Memory is a tool whereby a complex question may be seen in its fullness by compounding as many ideas as possible, thus creating a new, more inclusive view – it is not a mere retainer of facts, as expressed in the modern metaphor that equates memory with a computer.

This investigation uses the more expansive appreciation of the memory faculty as a springboard into hermeneutics. It argues that memory systems, as employed by the orators of ancient Rome, can be used as interpretative literary tools. I will employ examples from the medieval and modern periods to show that memory systems from Antiquity were still known and employed with great success in medieval secular writing and, furthermore, have remained an integral part of literature until today. In medieval and modern texts these simple systems help to structure, hold together and explain the concepts behind a text, thereby helping the reader to follow the story.

The current discussion about memory systems in literature was initiated by Frances A. Yates in her seminal work *The Art of Memory* (1966). She raises the question whether mnemonic aids can be ascertained in medieval literature to the extent that she has proven their presence in Renaissance texts. This question is taken up and developed or modified by various scholars, notably by Carruthers (*The Book of Memory*, mentioned above, and *The Craft of Thought*, 1998). Their approach is guided by a different interest than mine: Yates specialises in complex memory systems of the Renaissance, using ancient and medieval memory treaties as historical background; Carruthers follows the development and application of the systems in, mainly, rhetorical and theological writings. My theory, instead, concentrates on memory systems in literary fiction and how these can be used in order to interpret the text by approaching the thought processes of the author.

Another seminal text, to which I am indebted for the connection between iconography and text as an interpretative tool, is A.V. Kolve's *Chaucer and the Imagery of Narrative* (1984). Kolve identifies particular images used in Chaucer's stories and specifies their significance. He, for example, publishes pictures in his volume that would have been familiar to Chaucer's contemporaries, thereby suggesting what images the author's words would have inspired in his medieval reader's mind. In other words, Kolve investigates the iconography of cultural memory in the Middle Ages, even calling for a dictionary of images. Kolve's historical approach to images – attempting to reproduce the actual items from which images were created – proves that visualisation and ordered placement of items and events in a story were a conscious part of the medieval writer's art, an intentional aid to the imagination.

The words of modern-day authors pose less of an obstacle to the reader's imagination, but these, too, benefit from detailed analysis. To the emphasis placed on images by Kolve, I add an emphasis on backgrounds: by distinguishing between the settings and the events played out against them, the story gains depth and perspective so that the original imaginary landscape can be recreated.

Memory systems, the very basic ones that I will deal with, have hardly changed over time and are so closely linked with human perception and understanding that an awareness of the part they play in storytelling can offer direct access to complex texts. With the help of mnemonic aids, readers can tap into often unconscious modes of communication familiar to everyone by experience if not by name, purely through years of listening to and telling stories. By clarifying these patterns of communication that link ideas, concepts and events together, a framework is created that can become a fundamental tool in secular hermeneutics.

Chapter one (Ancient and Medieval Memory Techniques) provides the basis for all further chapters. It elucidates the principles of a number of memory systems as they were taught and used in Antiquity and appropriated in the Middle Ages. Among them is the memory palace – the most comprehensive system and the one upon which my system of interpretation is founded.

Chapter two (Medieval Literature) shows by example that the ancient memory system, which places images against backgrounds in order to enhance the memory, has a striking correlation with the presentation of narrative in works of fiction in the Middle Ages.

Chapter three (Modern Memory Concepts) brings the concept from the Middle Ages to the modern day in preparation for chapters four and five on modern literature. It asks how classical and medieval memory psychology compare to modern neuropsychology, determining whether memory systems are still relevant in our modern perception of how the memory functions.

In chapters four and five I apply my method of interpretation to modern literature, analysing chosen texts from England and the US, to show how memory systems can be applied as literary tools. The modern novels under investigation were not chosen for their presumed conformity to my approach, but because they are well-known texts by established authors: their familiarity enables me to focus on my particular approach to literature.[10]

---

10   The possibility of an unconscious tendency towards choosing particularly appropriate texts cannot be entirely disregarded, but it was not consciously done. The chosen texts do appeal to me personally, and this may partly be due to the fact that they are very visually engaging and therefore lend themselves to the kind of interpretative method I propose. Had there been space, it would have been enlightening to undertake an interpretation of a text that lacks much description and imagery and is more factual than the ones I have chosen. I strongly believe that also such a text would benefit from an interpretation based on images placed in a three-dimensional setting.

14

The conclusion draws together the information gathered from my analysis of medieval and modern texts and outlines a practical method of interpretation in four steps that is based on the concept of the memory palace from the ancient art of memory:

1. The general concept of memory
2. The particular type of background
3. The structural connection of backgrounds
    a. the alphabet- and number-systems
    b. the journey method
    c. the memory map
    d. the memory building
4. The significance of images

Chapter 1

Ancient and Medieval Memory Techniques
Entering the Memory Palace

The method of interpretation developed over the following five chapters is derived from artificial memory systems that lie at the heart of the classical art of memory. The art of memory is said to have been invented by Simonides. Cicero, amongst others, recounts the story of the poet Simonides who was employed by the nobleman Scopas to compose a poem and recite it to his guests at a sumptuous dinner. After the recital Simonides is called outside; shortly afterwards the dining hall's roof caves in and crushes everyone beneath it. Simonides, having escaped the accident, returns to the ruined dining hall and is able to identify the disfigured bodies, because he can remember *where* each guest was sitting at the table.

Simonides did not stop to imprint on his memory which guest sat where, but when asked, he is able to visualise each person in his place. This capacity for visualisation by the natural memory is the basis of the artificial memory that uses architectural structures. The story above describes how the natural memory uses backgrounds and images: objects (here persons) are situated in a designated spot (at the table) in an exact, unchanging order (in a chair next to somebody else) against a specific background (in the dining hall), thereby creating an organising space for the memory. Cicero concludes that persons who want to train their memory must consciously employ these visualisation aids:

[They] must select [backgrounds] and form mental images of the facts they wish to remember and store those images in the [backgrounds], with the result that the arrangement of the [backgrounds] will preserve the order of the facts and the images of the facts will designate the facts themselves.[1]

In other words, the architectural memory system is based on the principle of backgrounds and images (*locis et imaginibus*) which says that an item to be remembered will be retained more easily if it is placed against a specific background. This involves a visualisation of the interior of a particular building that offers a number of clearly distinguished backgrounds (corners, doorways, windows, alcoves, pillars, etc.) in which images of objects representing the things to be memorised can be situated. These architectural backgrounds are organised and arranged in sequence inside the building which the memoriser can then enter in the mind and inspect, as if walking through an actual building. Each image is encountered in its particular background, in its predetermined order which links the images together and thereby aids recall.[2]

---

1   Cicero, *De Oratore*, II, lxxxvi, 354.
2   The word *loci* is variously translated. Thus Sutton and Rackham's translation of Cicero's *De Oratore* uses 'localities' (here replaced by the word 'backgrounds' for continuity and clarity), Yates translates it as 'places' and Carruthers as 'architectural backgrounds'. Russell uses 'sites'

The oldest extant text that describes this process is the anonymous *Rhetorica ad Herennium*. Written in the first century BC, for many years it was falsely attributed to Cicero. It is an instruction on the art of rhetoric that contains a section on memory as the fourth part of rhetoric. Having made the distinction between natural and artificial memory, the author sets out the latter as follows:

The artificial memory includes backgrounds and images. By backgrounds I mean such scenes as are naturally or artificially set off on a small scale, complete and conspicuous, so that we can grasp and embrace them easily by the natural memory – for example, a house, an intercolumnar space, a recess, an arch, or the like. An image is, as it were, a figure, mark, or portrait of the object we wish to remember; for example, if we wish to recall a horse, a lion, or an eagle, we must place its image in a definite background.[3]

Having established what is meant by '*locis et imaginibus*', the author gives instructions on how these backgrounds and images are best chosen and which buildings (or palaces) are best suited to contain them.

The rules governing BACKGROUNDS are: a large number of backgrounds ought to be memorised in order to facilitate a large number of memorisable items; the backgrounds should be arranged in an unalterable sequence, so that the items placed in this determined order can be accessed from any point – from the beginning, the end or even the middle, enabling the memoriser to work backwards and forwards along the items as required; each fifth background should be marked by a symbol representing its place in the sequence (e.g., a hand for the fifth) which serve as orientational signposts along the way. The backgrounds should be situated in a deserted rather than a populated region – too much activity would weaken the impact of the images placed against the backgrounds; backgrounds should differ from each other to ease the distinction between them; they should be of moderate size; be adequately lit – neither too dark nor too bright; and they should be placed about thirty feet apart. Finally, the backgrounds can either be chosen from amongst buildings with which the memoriser is already familiar, or they can be entirely fictional ones, constructed to house a larger number of items.

All the rules governing the choice of IMAGES emphasise that they should be chosen according to their impact on the mind: the more striking and novel the image, the longer it will remain in the memory. This can be achieved in several ways: by making the image do something; by investing the image with great beauty or great ugliness; by dressing it with distinctive objects like a crown or a purple robe; by disfiguring it or by creating a comic effect. When describing the

---

and 'localities' when translating Quintilian's reference to the practice in *Institutio Oratoria* while Caplan translates the original source for the concept, the *Rhetorica ad Herennium*, as 'backgrounds'. In order to distinguish between an architectural site or building which frames the entire system and the individual places chosen within it, I will throughout refer to *loci* as 'backgrounds'. Any reference to 'backgrounds and images' therefore designates the entire architectural system contained within an architectural structure – such as the memory palace.

3   *Rhetorica ad Herennium*, III, xvi, 29.

kind of image that is most effective, the author distinguishes between images for things (*rerum*) and images for words (*verborum*). The practice of memorising texts word for word is extremely useful as an exercise for training and improving the artificial memory, but is of less practical use to orators, who benefit more from creating images for things.

The author emphasises that artificial memory is an extension of the natural memory: it "reinforces and develops the natural advantages". Images used in the artificial memory, therefore, should be chosen according to their natural effectiveness; for, what naturally adheres to the memory will be retained most persistently. In accordance with this tenet, the backgrounds should be realistic structures which, even if invented, must follow the guidelines that dictate the effectiveness of natural memory. An imagined building must contain rooms that can be entered, traversed and inspected in the same way as those of an actual building. Just as artificial memory must build on principles of natural memory, so the "inner eye" absorbs images based on principles underlying the function of the "external eye". Circumstances that determine our capacity to see with the physical eye also determine our ability to see with the "inner eye": to create, recognise and store images in the memory.[4]

Unfortunately, the author of the *Rhetorica ad Herennium* does not describe the building he imagines further than saying it could be a house or some parts of it, "an intercolumnar space, a recess, an arch or the like". But Quintilian, who comments on the *Rhetorica ad Herennium*'s architectural system in his work the *Institutio Oratoria* (*c.*AD 95), presents his interpretation of the system by suggesting a traditional Roman house as the blueprint for a memory building. He describes how those practising this memory technique place the individual images throughout a large house divided into many separate areas (*domum [...] magnam et in multos diductam recessus*):

They place the first idea [...] in the vestibule, the second, let us say, in the atrium, and then they go round the open areas, assigning ideas systematically not only to bedrooms and bays, but to statues and the like. This done, when they have to revive the memory, they begin to go over these Sites from the beginning, calling in whatever they deposited with each of them, as the images remind them. Thus, however many things have to be remembered, they become a single item, held together as it were by a sort of outer shell [...][5]

Here we have a practical application of the system. Quintilian takes a realistic, familiar building as his setting (Roman houses were commonly designed on the same basic ground-plan) and explains how one should run through the entire order, giving later centuries an insight into the process. Indeed, Frances Yates comments that "[t]he perplexed student of the art of memory is grateful to Quintilian. Had it not been for his clear directions about how we are to go through

---

4   Ibid., 30–37.
5   Quintilian, *Institutio Oratoria*, XI, ii, 20.

the rooms of a house [...] we might never have understood what 'rules for places' were about."[6] Although a little exaggerated, it is true that the *Rhetorica ad Herennium* author leaves the reader to imagine many particulars as to how to apply the system.

The concept of backgrounds and images was taken up again in the Middle Ages, having lost popularity in later Antiquity (going on its lack of incorporation into texts on rhetoric and memory treatises). However, the medieval application was an altered form, mainly because those concerned with the question of memory were no longer orators and rhetoricians, but theologians and schoolmasters.

Through the influence of Neoplatonic ideas of memory (which suggest that the individual can reach God by 'remembering' where the soul has originated) that merged with Christian ideals of salvation in the writings of St Augustine (AD 354–430) and Proclus (AD 411–85)[7], artificial memory took a back seat to natural memory, or at least to a memory which aided meditation and not oratory, especially in the monastic discipline relating to the *lectio divina*. The *Rhetorica ad Herennium* and the backgrounds and images were referred to by several medieval writers, amongst them Albertus Magnus, Thomas Aquinas, John of Garland, John of Salisbury and Geoffrey of Vinsauf, but with generally no more than a passing reference being made or a general summary of the system being given.

Albertus Magnus, like several other medieval writers, considered memory as a part of prudence rather than of rhetoric. Cicero divided prudence into three parts: memory, intelligence and foresight. Thomas Aquinas extended the number of parts to eight, and he took the description from the *Rhetorica ad Herennium*. But even with the same source, the parts were adapted to support the idea of memory as the faculty with which lessons can be drawn from the past in order to improve the future. Thus Albertus Magnus, when describing the function of using buildings as memory settings in *De Bono* (*c*.1246), interprets the rules governing the right choice of building in the light of his religious background: he writes that the buildings best suited are those most 'solemn and moving' (*solemnis et rarus*), which Yates takes to imply a church.[8]

In time architectural features and associated symbols employed in the memory building were transferred to actual buildings: to medieval churches. Erwin Panofsky compares the structure of the Gothic cathedral to a medieval Summa.[9] This 'cathedral summa' was not only divided and arranged into a logical order in accordance with artificial memory practice; it also had striking images

---

6   Yates, *The Art of Memory*, p.38.
7   The writings of Proclus are best known in their reworked form, disseminated under the name of Dionysius the Aeropagite. An unknown author had rewritten the original texts to combine Proclus' Neoplatonic ideas with Christian dogma, thereby greatly influencing medieval thought. Only in the nineteenth century was their supposed authenticity disproven.
8   Yates, *The Art of Memory*, p.75.
9   Panofsky, *Gothic Architecture and Scholasticism*, pp.44–5.

placed against specific backgrounds in a predetermined order and so followed the rules governing the placement of images in the architectural memory system.

The physical church building and the imaginary memory palace function in very similar ways. As Mary Carruthers points out: "The medieval monastery church is not itself a cryptogram, but rather a tool, a machine for thinking, whose structure and decoration together serve as its functioning parts."[10] The church is a 'tool' that relies on the faculty of memory to engender associations in the mind of those who enter it by reminding them of specific Christian events, texts or tenets through the structure itself and the individual features and images displayed within it.

This is not an incidental connection. Architectural examples from the golden age of cathedral building (especially twelfth-century France) show that mnemonic *picturae* were incorporated into Cistercian oratories under Bernard of Clairvoux – famous for encouraging purity in the decoration of church buildings – and the choirs at St Remi and St Denis were redesigned, so that the windows (in the structure and content of their stained-glass decorations) represented the Heavenly Jerusalem.[11] Entire ground-plans for monasteries were made with the express aim of linking memory processes used for meditation to the structural features. These monasteries were never intended for construction: their measure and structure were taken from the Bible, as in the instance of the ground-plan for the monastery at St Gall which was used solely for reflective and meditational purposes.

What works successfully when we enter an inspirational building, like a church, will also be effective when undertaken in the mind, in an imaginary building like that suggested by the *Rhetorica ad Herennium*. It follows that the same ought to be true for structures described in literature: the various settings described by authors produce backgrounds against which the action can take place, functioning just as memory backgrounds do, and the images placed against them (be they static or active) will be framed and secured by this setting, creating a succession of stages upon which the events are enacted. The 'sister arts' of painting and poetry seem to have a further sibling: that of architecture. The rhetorical device of *ekphrasis* (the vivid description of architectural structures, benefiting from the interaction of painting and poetry in its word-painting capacity) is inverted in that the physical placement and exact location of its parts within architecture gives structure to the word-painting, adding a third dimension.

Alphabet- and Number-Systems

The *Rhetorica ad Herennium* author compares basic mnemonics to the ABC, and the architectural system to the activity of writing and reading. Just as a firm knowledge of the ABC is an absolute requirement for reading and writing (being

---

10   Carruthers, *The Craft of Thought*, p.276.
11   Ibid., p.258. See also Wilson, *The Gothic Cathedral*.

able to identify individual letters, shape words and extract meaning from them), so a firm knowledge of mnemonics is an absolute requirement for using memory techniques (being able to identify each system, understand the symbolic value of their individual parts and make basic links between them to extract meaning).

Letters and numbers are the most basic ingredients in mnemonics. They are involved in all memory systems. This becomes apparent in the two absolutely fundamental techniques within memory: that of division and arrangement, and that of creating visual images through association. Alphabet- and number-systems provide a determined, unchangeable, consecutive order of signs which serve as immovable points in a chain on which items to be remembered are hung.

DIVISION AND ARRANGEMENT

Consultus Fortunatianus (fourth century) asked, "what best helps the memory? Division and composition (*devisio et compositio*); for order most secures the memory".[12] This sentiment is echoed by many of the writers on rhetoric and memory, including Quintilian, Augustine, Geoffrey of Vinsauf, Hugh of St Victor and the author of the *Rhetorica ad Herennium*, all of whom have written influential texts on the uses of artificial memory.

The alphabet- and number-systems are the simplest and commonest forms of memory aid determined by the process of division and arrangement. These include techniques and systems we have learned intuitively from the day of our birth, memorised automatically or acquired in the first years of our lives when we learned the ABC or how to count. We use these memory systems unconsciously every day in almost everything we do: remembering to put the key in our pocket before slamming the door shut (first 1, then 2); consulting a calendar (by date); or looking up a word in the dictionary (in alphabetical order). We use memory techniques on a daily basis without even considering for a second how they work. They make possible a fundamental organisation of activities, both mental and physical, without which we would be unable to function.

The organisational memory structure underlying every text, independent of its quality, falls under this basic form of division and arrangement, and conforms to the three first steps of rhetoric: first collecting the information required to be written down, then dividing this material into manageable segments, and finally arranging these in a logical order to be able to put the ideas down in writing.[13]

Some texts add visual signs of this division on the page in order to facilitate a clearer understanding of the underlying structure. The division of the Bible into chapter and verse is an instance of organisation by number. Although Jerome (*c*.347–420) and Cassiodorus (*c*.490–583) had referred to this division of the Bible, chapter numbers were not routinely copied into manuscripts until the

---

12   Carruthers, *The Book of Memory*, p.86.
13   And I mean *every* text. Even in automatic writing the mind collects, divides and arranges the material in an instant before letting it flow onto the page through the hand that writes.

beginning of the thirteenth century, and notation of verse numbers was not common in Bible manuscripts until the sixteenth century. This suggests that even though the divisions had been undertaken, and were used and referred to, it was not thought necessary to write them down in the manuscripts containing the Scriptures; the numerical aids were held in the memory instead. Hence the divisions initially served as a mental grid wherein the individual narrative could be situated in order to aid memorisation.

Growing numbers of manuscripts and a need for ordering their contents also brought about a growing number of indices. The way they were organised says something about their origins in mnemonic rather than alphabetical thinking. Jerome, for instance, created an index from the Hebrew names in the Scriptures. But instead of organising them alphabetically by each letter of the name, he limited arrangement to the initial letter of each, ignoring the following ones. Thus he lists all names beginning with 'A' under that letter, those beginning with 'B' under that, and so on. But within each category the names appear in the order in which they are mentioned in the text. To the simple alphabetising system, Jerome adds another memory system: he creates an ordered sequence, and thereby a path of memory.[14] This kind of combination of several systems is quite common for numerical and letter systems, as they lend themselves readily to extension by an amalgamation of several forms.

The extent to which the division into segments and organisation of knowledge was popular in the Middle Ages is evident in the proliferation of such collating works as *summae, florilegia* and even bestiaries. But the practice also finds its outlet in works of fiction where a particular subject is accompanied by a list of the different viewpoints regarding that topic, usually listing the author or proponent of each thought as well. Thus Chaucer's extensive exploration in the *Book of the Duchess* of different kinds of dreams may appear to be a deviation, unrelated to the main narrative. But the author is merely following the rhetorical convention of division and arrangement by faithfully listing each part of an argument in order to provide a fuller background to his discussion. A person educated in basic mnemonics would easily follow this diversion, lay out the individual parts in front of his mind's eye and not only be able to memorise the individual items, but also to draw an informed conclusion based on these.

Schools in the Middle Ages taught memory techniques as one of the parts of rhetoric: it was often called the most important of the five parts. "Memory [...] embraces everything which has been brought together to contribute to a speech,"[15] writes Quintilian, and the *Rhetorica ad Herennium* author sets memory up as "guardian" to the other four parts of rhetoric.[16] Simple mnemonics taught in

---

14   Carruthers, *The Book of Memory*, p.115.
15   Quintilian, *Institutio Oratoria*, III, iii, 10.
16   *Rhetorica ad Herennium*, III, xvi, 28.

schools under the section of memory were common knowledge, known as 'puerilia', or "kid's-stuff" as Carruthers translates the term.[17]

In "De tribus maximis circumstantiis gestorum" Hugh of St Victor instructs school children on the importance of creating and practising memory systems, such as the numerical grid, as an educational tool.[18] Once the system is integrated into their thinking, any new piece of information can be added to it. Placed in its correct spot, it can be recalled alongside all the other items lodged there, pertaining to the same field of knowledge. Hugh goes on to explain how this numerical grid is suitable for learning by heart; as an example he uses the 150 psalms. The large number shows that the grid was not a mnemonic aid in the sense it is usually understood today with lists of five, maybe ten items. The storing of such large amounts of information would require a familiarity with the system beyond mere comprehension: it would require constant practice. This the children would get at school every day, and their capacity for memorising would increase with time. The apparent necessity to remind pupils of the importance of constant repetition, mentioned by most writers on artificial memory, shows that not all pupils acquired the skill as fully as their teachers hoped for.

By the time the pupil had reached university level, he was expected to bring with him a proficiency in the application of memory techniques and a collection of memory structures already secured in the mind, to be employed almost instinctively when appropriating new knowledge. These artificial memory systems could be quite extensive and are known to have included complex ones devised by teachers like Thomas Bradwardine, whose work was known to Chaucer,[19] and Raymond Lull, whose "fondness for diagrams in the form of trees" produced extensive memory systems since "[t]heir branches and leaves are decorated with abstract formulae and classifications".[20]

ASSOCIATION AND IMAGE MAKING

Hugh of St Victor's mental list of 150 psalms was to be "extended as it were before the eye of the mind",[21] i.e., it was to be visualised by the students in order for it to be effective. It therefore relies on the second of the two most fundamental mnemonic techniques: creating images through association.

Two steps are involved in creating memory images: 1) finding the appropriate image for the item to be remembered, and 2) linking the image to its memory 'hook' or to the items immediately preceding or following it. The first is simple if a *thing* is to be remembered (a person, an animal or an object) in which case the thing itself is brought before the mind's eye. However, if it is an intangible item

---

17   Carruthers, *The Book of Memory*, p.95.
18   Translated by Carruthers in 'Appendix A' of *The Book of Memory*.
19   Chaucer, *The Nun's Priest's Tale* (line 3242).
20   Yates, *The Art of Memory*, p.187.
21   "De tribus maximus…" in Carruthers, *The Book of Memory*, p.262.

(e.g. justice) or an extensive subject (such as the entire navy or a country), it has to be represented symbolically (e.g., justice as a blindfolded woman holding a pair of scales, a single ship representing the entire fleet or a flag for the country).

In literature figures of speech fulfil this function (like personification or synecdoche employed in the cases above) and are elemental in producing images of things which cannot readily be put into words or would suffer from too clinical a description. Quintilian, in the passage on artificial memory, gives helpful examples of this technique. He writes that the images (which he calls signs, or *signo*) "may be based on the subject as a whole (on navigation or warfare, for example) or on a word [...]". For navigation he suggests the sign could be an anchor; for warfare, a weapon.[22]

The second step, creating links between what is to be remembered and the place in the arrangement where it belongs, requires a little more ingenuity. Straightforward number systems simply divide the material to be memorised into several parts. By remembering how many parts there are, it is easier to place the individual item in relation to the others; for example, the five parts of rhetoric, the Ten Commandments or the Seven Liberal Arts. Listing items by number gives a helpful overview.

However, to aid memory further, the number must represent more than its place in the list of consecutive figures. Robert of Basevorn suggests using lists of numbers that lend themselves as visual guides as well as numerical ones. He suggests one use a familiar list of items made up of the corresponding number to the items required to be memorised: if five items were to be remembered, the five vowels might suffice; for six, the six musical notes (ut, re, mi, fa, so, la); for seven he suggests the seven mercies of God; eight, the eight Beatitudes; nine, the nine orders of Angels; ten, the Ten Commandments; and twelve, the twelve hours of the day.[23] In this way, a (then) very familiar list supplies the images to which the items on the new list can be attached, each image clearly linked to a number. It is easier to tie an item to be remembered to a visual clue than to a number because a bond can be created between the two. For example, ten people are to be remembered. Rather than attach a number to each name, a visual clue is added. Each person could be linked to one of the Ten Commandments – possibly visualising each person breaking a different one to intensify the image and thereby imprint it deeper in the mind.

Letters have the advantage over numbers in that they can form parts of words which contain the image, and no further visual link is necessary to create a connection. Alphabetic mnemonics employ acronyms (for example HOMES for the North American Great Lakes Huron, Ontario, Michigan, Erie and Superior), initials (such as the initials of each word corresponding to the initial of the colours of the rainbow in 'Richard Of York Gave Battle In Vain' – red, orange, yellow,

22   Quintilian, *Institutio Oratoria*, XI, ii, 19.
23   Carruthers, *The Book of Memory*, pp.104–6.

green, blue, indigo, violet) or homophones (such as the modern reminder to turn the clock an hour ahead in the spring and turn it back in the autumn: 'spring forward, fall back').

Wordplay, or punning is one of the commonest techniques used by writers to create tension, either through emphasis or when used as a comic device. In the use of homophony above, this is done by comparing two words similar in sound or spelling, but different in meaning. The homophonic pun on 'sun' and 'son' is one of the commonest in the English language. Thomas Bradwardine even used bilingual puns to increase the possibilities of homophony and homography.[24] Punning is often used mnemonically in order to remember names through homonymy: attaching an image to a name – based on the way the name sounds or is spelled – is a very effective short cut to memory. Statuary representations of Cicero often used homography to aid identification: a chickpea was incorporated amongst his features because the first five letters of his name spell out the Latin word *cicer*, meaning "chickpea". Herwig Blum suggests homonymy played a large part in the popular performances of memory feats in Antiquity, one of which was to astound the audience by remembering immensely long lists of names.[25]

Geoffrey of Vinsauf dissects a name for greater punning effect. In the introduction to his *Poetria Nova* (*c*.1207–14), a text on rhetoric which includes a section on memory, Geoffrey writes about Pope Innocent the third:

Papa stupor mundi, si dixero, Papa Nocenti,
Acephalum nomen tribuam; sed, si caput addam,
Hostis erit metri. Nomen tibi vult similari:
Nec nomen metro, nec vult tua maxima virtus
Claudi mensura. Nihil est quo metiar illam:
Transit mensuras hominum. Sed divide nomen,
Divide sic nomen: "In" praefer, et adde "nocenti,"
Efficiturque comes metri. Sic et tua virtus
Pluribus aequatur divisa, sed integra nulli.[26]

Geoffrey's use of rhetorical terminology relating to poetry (metre and measure) is employed to emphasise how immeasurable the Pope's own goodness is by comparing his virtues to his name, Innocenti. However, by severing the name ('*in*' and '*nocenti*'), Geoffrey also adds unpleasant associations since *nocens* and *nocentis*, respectively, mean 'harmful' and 'criminal' or 'guilty'. Furthermore,

---

24   Ibid., p.135.
25   Blum, *Die antike Mnemotechnik*, pp.24–30.
26   "Pope, marvel of the world, if I were to call you 'Pope Nocent' I would be giving you a headless name; but if I add the prefix, it would spoil the metre. Your name is meant to be similar to you: neither must the name be imprisoned by the metre, nor your great virtue restricted by any measure. There is nothing by which I can measure it, for it surpasses human computation. Rather, divide the name thus: set down "In," and add "nocent," and thus it will fit the metre. Thus also would your virtue, if broken into parts, be equivalent to that of many men; but taken as a whole, it is incomparable." Geoffrey of Vinsauf, *Poetria Nova*, "Dedication", (lines 1–9).

Geoffrey says that the Pope is "equivalent to […] many men" in his individual virtues, two of which are listed as 'harmful' and 'guilty', thus undermining the foundations of the Pope's position. Paired with the visual image created in the first sentence – that of a headless or beheaded Pope – the seemingly innocent pun on the name "Innocenti" (no pun intended) suggests that Geoffrey was not entirely sincere in his adulations, and the dedication to the Pope seems circumstantial rather than heartfelt. Or it may suggest that Geoffrey wasn't as adept at realising the implications of his puns as he was at creating them.

Either way, this is an example of the strong effect a simple literary and mnemonic device like the pun can have on the complexity of a text by merely linking images to words, thereby visualising the situation for the reader through association and image-making.

The concept of *ut pictura poiesis*, explored by both the Roman poet Horace (65–8 BC) and the Greek philosopher and historian Plutarch (*c.* AD 46–*c.* 120), rests on the assumption that painting and poetry are sister arts. In his *Ars Poetica* (in the Middle Ages accepted as a complete guide to the art of poetry) Horace expresses the idea that poetry can imitate the effects which painting has and vice versa. This interchangeability explains the memory technique of creating mental images. When Horace and Plutarch speak of the sister arts and of painting a word poem, they relate it to the field of poetry. However, it relies on a rhetorical concept: *enargeia* – vivid, sensuous word-painting.

Enargeia was used to describe works of art or architecture (*ekphrasis*), for giving vividness to fictive speeches through quality of language (*prosopopeia*) and to paint a word-portrait of a person, whether real or imagined (*ethopoeia*). Quintilian says that *enargeia* "makes us seem not so much to be talking about something as exhibiting it. Emotions will ensue as if we were present at the event itself".[27] This emphasises the well-known instruction to writers to 'show, don't tell' and thereby the importance of being able to visualise words in order to get a stronger sense of them. The involvement of the emotions is a common tenet in natural memory: the more emotionally involved a person is, the greater the impression will be on the memory. And since artificial memory processes build upon natural ones, the sentence applies to memory systems as well.

Extensions of the Memory Palace
Geometric Shapes and Memory Journeys

GEOMETRIC SHAPES

From numerical lists that divide and arrange items to letters that allow creative visualisation and wordplay, the alphabet- and number-systems are the backbone

---

27   Quintilian, *Institutio Oratoria*, VI, ii, 32.

of mnemonic devices whether simple or complex. The memory palace which uses backgrounds and images would disintegrate without the numerically determined order and arrangement of memory-items, while the items themselves would be ineffective unless they were somehow linked associatively to each other and the greater memory structure.

But although fundamental to all memory, the alphabet- and number-systems on their own only have a limited application as memory systems. To memorise anything that goes beyond a mere list of things, more complex systems are required. One development of the numerical system, used extensively by medieval writers, involves geometric shapes.

The medieval predilection for organising and categorising information and knowledge produced a vast amount of *summae*, *florilegia* and other *compendia* that list, enumerate and arrange collated items on various topics. This also had an impact on the presentation of memory systems. To a much greater degree than before, mnemonic systems were schematised. Although memory systems usually were concerned with mental, intangible images, attempts were made to capture the underlying form of a memory system in two-dimensional geometric shapes.

Individual shapes such as circles, squares and triangles, as well as a number of shapes, such as concentric circles or a square inside a circle, produced diagrams that supplied a number of backgrounds onto which memorised items could be projected. Geoffrey of Vinsauf may well be referring to the use of schemata in his *Poetria Nova* when he writes that memory is aided by "loca, tempora, *formae* / Aut aliquae similes notulae". This was translated as "Place, time, appearance, or other similar signs" by Ernest Gallo in his 1971 translation. However, Carruthers convincingly points out that *formae* may be more specifically designating "geometrical shapes" or "outlines", since simple schemata were commonly used to present material in a memorable way to students, and a familiarity with the application of shapes to aid memory already existed.[28]

Geoffrey's list of *loca, tempora* and *formae* refers to the memorisation of something previously seen, heard or thought. He suggests that the natural ability of remembering a past event can be enhanced by visualising the circumstances surrounding it, much as Simonides did following the collapse of the ceiling at Scopas' banquet. In this context *formae* initially seems to lend itself better to Gallo's translation of it as 'appearance', since attempting to recall something seen or heard can be aided naturally by recalling where and when it happened. The 'appearance' of the surroundings would be a logical development of this recreation of the situation. However, taking into account the attention to correspondence of parts of speech in rhetoric in general, and to medieval structural techniques of composing parallel lists of items in particular, *formae* suggests an abstract rather than a practical subject. The relevant passage reads:

---

28   Carruthers, *The Book of Memory*, p.251.

Sic vidi, sic audivi, sic mente revolvi,
Sic egi, vel tunc, vel ibi: loca, tempora, formae
Aut aliquae similes notulae mihi sunt via certa
Quae me ducit ad haec. et [sic.] *in his intelligo signis.*[29]

The triad of 'seeing, hearing, thinking' is paralleled by the triad 'place, time, *formae*'. Sight and sound are clearly relevant to place and time as they convey the sensory impressions of the physical surroundings of an event taking place in the physical world. The activity of thinking, or of 'turning over in the mind' as a more exact translation of the words *sic mente revolvi*, suggests an abstract activity which is somewhat distanced from physical activity, and hence may need a disparate hook for retrieving from the memory, one that goes beyond the physical surroundings. Geoffrey may have chosen the term *formae* on purpose to complement the abstract activity of thinking.

Geoffrey of Vinsauf writes somewhat disparagingly that the author of the *Rhetorica ad Herennium* with his "*imaginibus peregrinis*" (wandering images) is teaching only himself, as the subtlety of the system would please only the man who had invented it. This emphasises how important it is for each person to develop their own system in order to ensure its efficacy, and Geoffrey himself falls back on the system of backgrounds and images. Tellingly, the pejorative comment immediately follows the accreditation of *formae*, which suggests a substitution of the three-dimensional architectural unit with the two-dimensional geometric form – this becomes representative of medieval memory systems.

A number of authors developed their own two-dimensional geometric shapes to depict memory systems, most prominent amongst them was Raymond Lull, who created a complex alphabetical ordering system by placing letters in various schemata in order to give an insight into a variety of topics via the multifarious combinations of letters. His schemes fall back upon basic shapes, like the triangle, the square and the tree-shape which Lull imbued with Christian symbolism.[30]

John of Garland describes a geometrical memory shape when he comments on the *rota Vergiliana* (Virgil's Wheel). The wheel is made out of concentric circles divided up into three equal conical sections, each representing a literary generic form: heroic, georgic and pastoral. Each concentric circle represents a different aspect connected with a specific sphere in human society: a profession (farmer, soldier, shepherd), an animal (cow, horse, sheep), a plant (fruit tree, bay tree, beech), environs (country, city, pasture), an implement (plough, sword, staff) and a human representative (Triptolemus or Coelius, Hector or Ajax, Titirus or Meliboeus). A combination made up of one item from each of the sub-categories describes appropriate components of a given genre; for example, the heroic genre is represented by 'soldier', 'horse', 'bay tree', 'city', 'sword' and Hector or Ajax.

---

29   Geoffrey of Vinsauf, *Poetria Nova*, VIII, (lines 2017–2020).
30   See for example Paolo Rossi, *Logic and the Art of Memory*, esp. pp.32–6 on the Lullian tradition and pp.44–55 on Lull's memorative technique; or *Ramon Lull, Selected Works of...*

If several of these aspects appear in a piece of writing, this indicates that the text in question belongs to the heroic genre.

Alistair Fowler, who reproduces a drawing of the diagram from Edmund Faral's 1962 book on poetic arts, condemns the wheel as "misleading and confusing", and suggests that it would only make sense if it were "redrawn, as John of Garland himself redraws it, in columns".[31] In relation to his discussion about systems of genre being depicted as maps and their serviceability for distinguishing between kinds of literature, he is certainly right to say that the wheel is misleading – genres are no longer as clearly defined as they were in Antiquity. However, if seen as originating in the tradition of geometrical memory *formae*, the wheel functions perfectly: it uses visualisations and linking images that provide memory-shapes; backgrounds that images can be placed against. When Fowler suggests that the wheel's inherent 'confusion' would be avoided if the information were organised in columns, he imitates his medieval predecessors who, concerned with the organisation and definition of genre as well as other subjects, made the same shift from three-dimensional to two-dimensional – moving from memorisation to notation.

Presumably, Virgil's Wheel was originally meant to exist solely in the mind. Only later was it drawn on paper to aid understanding of how it functions, but ultimately it was intended purely as a mental image. After all, when explaining the much more complicated memory structure of Noah's Ark, Hugh of St Victor writes: "I depict as an object, so that you learn outwardly what you ought to do inwardly." The pupil was meant to "imprint the form of this example in [his] heart", and not refer to a visual reproduction of it.[32]

Yates has argued that John of Garland introduced movement to memory systems through his description of Virgil's Wheel, which Garland says he holds in his hands. Yates takes this to mean that he holds in his hands a cut-out version of the wheel that can be manipulated in order to alter the combinations. This may well be true. If this were the case, however, it goes against the original purpose of memory systems and seems to be a later development. Carruthers places the introduction of movement at an even earlier time as several of the simpler geometrical shapes lend themselves to be fashioned as real models. There is certainly evidence of moveable memory diagrams. They may have been connected to the treatises describing the function of physical objects like the astrolabe: a mechanism of circles and diagonals used to determine the position of stars and planets in the sky.[33] These would be based on the manipulatable object, and the drawings used to describe them referred to the movement of the individual parts. The flexibility of moveable objects is compatible with the capacity to

---

31   Fowler, *Kinds of Literature*, p.241.

32   Carruthers and Ziolkowski, *Medieval Craft of Memory*, p.45.

33   An example is Chaucer's *A Treatise on the Astrolabe* which is presented as an educational text to his ten-year-old son, Lewis.

manipulate memory schemata in the mind, 'rotating' ideas (as in Geoffrey of Vinsauf's *sic mente revolvi*), and is the logical step after visualising a system two dimensionally on a page.

The majority of schemata remained two-dimensional in their medieval conception as actual drawings on a page, although there are exceptions. Hugh of St Victor's Noah's Ark combines a great number of memory structures within it. He uses ladders, circles, trees and grids.[34] Even a computer programmer would be challenged to create a convincing three-dimensional reproduction of Hugh's *Arca* – although I wish someone would try…

JOURNEY METHOD

The third dimension, that of space, had already been integrated successfully by the system of backgrounds and images described in the *Rhetorica ad Herennium*. The mnemonic technique of situating the things to be remembered in previously determined places inside a three-dimensional architectural shape, based on realistic measurements, changes the involvement of the memoriser: it places her inside the structure, inside the memory image and makes her an active participant in a three-dimensional mind-picture.

Furthermore, this direct involvement, where a walk through the memory resembles an actual visit to an imaginatively decorated building, adds the concept of time (the fourth dimension). Each image is viewed by itself, consecutively, the order depending on where in the building the 'viewing' is started from. As the memoriser mentally walks through the memory building, each image presents itself automatically as the next sequential background is reached. This concept of backgrounds and images moves from the simpler form of basic patterns, like the alphabet- and number-systems, towards a more plastic, three-dimensional art. But what it loses in simplicity, it gains in accessibility. When memorising a list of items, the list will be a detached unit, held in the mind as an abstract concept. The architectural system integrates its foundation into the actual world of the memoriser, thereby anchoring the concept in natural surroundings, giving it realistic significance and aiding natural memory.

A building is, of course, only one of many 'spaces' available in which to create an imaginative memory background. Already in Antiquity spaces were extended from that of an isolated building to include gardens, cities, long journeys and, occasionally, even an entire world. Quintilian refers to extended memory spaces in *Institutio Oratoria* when he lists alternatives to the architectural method:

Quod de domo dixi, et in operibus publicis et in itinere longo et urbium ambitu et picturis fieri potest.[35]

---

34   Hugh of St Victor, "De arca Noe morali" and "De arca Noe mystica"; see Carruthers, *The Book of Memory*, pp.43–5.

35   "What I said about a house can be done also with public buildings, a long road, a town

31

Examples from literature showing uses of *itinere longo* (long roads) or *urbinum ambitu* (a town perambulation) stem from the Renaissance, but the casual reference by Quintilian (and others) suggests these were already commonly known as alternative memory systems. The final option Quintilian suggests, the picture, is merely the imaginary place aided by a physical shape in a two-dimensional painting – like a geometric shape – and need not interest us here.

Riccio uses the 'long road' as a mnemonic aid. He explains how the buildings, doorways, niches and gardens on the Florentine Via della Scala make up the backgrounds for his memory structure (1595 MS). Grataroli suggests a walk through a town as a memory background: as soon as the city gates are entered in the mind, the various aspects of the town (the streets, the houses of friends or official buildings) will supply a vast amount of backgrounds against which the items to be remembered can be placed (1554 MS).[36]

The journey method uses the same principles as the architectural memory system in that it places objects to be remembered against specific backgrounds and arranges these backgrounds in a fixed order. It differs from it through the linear structure of this ordered arrangement. Architectural buildings confine the memories in an enclosed space of a particular size which allows for 'real time', or 'near-real time' in the memory image: it takes about the same time to walk through the building in the imagination as it would do in its physical equivalent. The journey method can be elongated since its extent is not determined by tangible barriers, i.e., the walls, floors and ceilings of the architectural structure. The extent of the journey is only limited by the experience or imaginative powers of the person using the journey method as a memory aid.

The creation of memory images for the journey method is guided largely by the same rules the *Rhetorica ad Herennium* author sets out for the architectural memory system: the more striking the image, the more memorable. Hence, added movement, extreme beauty or beastliness, symbolic objects, disfigurement and comic aspects will all make the mental images stand out just as much whether placed at points along a journey or throughout a building.

The choice of backgrounds against which these images are to be set must, however, be based on different premises. An extensive number of backgrounds to accommodate a high number of memorisable items and a fixed order are still necessary conditions. A symbol at every fifth place to help keep track could still be helpful, but is not as necessary: the journey is linear and will automatically link one background to the next as they are naturally consecutive.

Desertedness of place, moderate size, adequate lighting and a distance between backgrounds of about thirty feet no longer apply unrestrictedly; it depends on the kind of journey chosen as to what sort of background is most memorable. A

---

perambulation, or pictures." Quintilian, *Institutio Oratoria*, XI, ii, 21.
36 Blum, *Die antike Mnemotechnik*, p.7.

distance of about thirty feet on a train journey (or even in a horse-drawn carriage) would make no sense at all, and a night-time walk through Venice may offer very striking backgrounds despite being cloaked in relative darkness.

Another benefit of choosing backgrounds outdoors is that there is a much larger variety of them than inside a building, and they may therefore be associatively more powerful than a recess or a doorway. If, for example, you come to your sixteenth background inside the architectural structure – despite having gone upstairs to a room with frescoed walls – you may be 'standing' by your third window. It may be difficult to find a new link, to associate something to a window for the third time, no matter how different it is from the first two. In the open you need not repeat the background – unless it aids your memory.

A natural extension of the journey method is the town or cityscape. It owes much to the architectural memory system, as many of the chosen backgrounds will be architectural features seen from the outside: doorways, facades, pediments, stone steps and different types of building all offer backgrounds which in themselves are highly associative. A familiar city has an emotional geography as well as a topographical one. Many places will be invested with feelings created during personal experiences at those spots and, since sensory responses are such strong memory triggers, these places are particularly memorable.

There are two types of memory journeys: the earthly and the heavenly journey. The earthly journey relies on experience. Whether a short journey (the daily trip to work) or a long one (such as a train journey or even a trip abroad), the earthly journey is based on physical experience, is familiar, and the various stations along the way are clearly distinguishable and their sequence is locked securely in the memory. The heavenly journey is a symbolic one, in the sense that it is an advancement in understanding, taken step by step to reach an ultimate goal, sometimes in a symbolic landscape, taking on religious connotations as it was employed in the Middle Ages.

The method of fourfold exegesis is itself frequently compared to a journey comprising the four steps towards understanding (literal, moral, allegorical and anagogical – extended from three to four in the Middle Ages). The transference of memory system techniques from rhetoric and oratory to theology becomes clear in this transference from the earthly to the heavenly spheres in religious medieval English society. The journey of the mind finds echoes in some ecclesiastical ceremonies, particularly in processions and pilgrimages. Both are symbolic acts as well as actual ones which represent man's journey towards God. They resemble the memory journey system in many individual points: the persons involved in either a procession or a pilgrimage are familiar with the 'journey' to be undertaken; during it they pass specific stations with particular images that recall a certain story, often of the life and passion of Christ, conspicuous in medieval passion plays.

The ladder is a common metaphor employed to express this gradual advancement of man towards God. In biblical narrative Jacob's Ladder and the Tower of Babel are implements built by man through which they attempt to reach Heaven. This convention is also employed by Walter Hilton in *The Scale* [Ladder] *of Perfection* (*c.* 1380–96), in which he outlines the individual steps a novice must take to become a nun and obtain the fullest fulfilment of her calling, moving towards 'perfection' and towards Heaven at the same time. John of Salisbury and Bonaventura both use a symbolic reading of Jacob's Ladder as a spiritual advancement taken step by step, probably based on Augustine's description of the seven mental powers necessary to be acquired in order to move from fear to wisdom.[37+38]

The journey has here taken on ethical dimensions and the 'stations' or 'backgrounds' have lost their physical reference. In one sense it is a move back towards a simpler memory system, that of a list mnemonic. The backgrounds are mere 'steps', often numbered to secure a fixed sequence. But the movement on the ladder is a three-dimensional one: we move forwards but also upwards as the greater understanding enables us to take the next step. The greatest difference to the architectural system is that we must begin at the bottom rung in order to make sense of the ladder-concept, and we must continue upwards in the same direction. It would lose its validity if we started at the top (say Augustine's seventh rung) and worked our way backwards from wisdom to fear. The spiritual application of the system, therefore, to some extent limits its capacity as a memory system by introducing the concept of right and wrong; i.e., of prudence.

Direct Literary Appropriation: Allegory

[Allegory] can use almost any external structure or "outside" allegorically, making it the husk or *sens* of an inner *matière* [...][39]

By substituting the word 'allegorically' with 'mnemonically', this description of the function of allegory (here in relation to genre) neatly explains why allegory is, in effect, a memory system: such a system, too, "can use almost any external structure or 'outside'" *mnemonically*, "making it the husk or *sens* of an inner *matière*". When placing memorable items in a precreated storage facility in the mind, this facility is merely the husk (or shell, using Quintilian's word[40]) of an inner sense or *matière*. The system is the means; not the end. Allegories and memory systems function in very similar ways: they are both nothing more than vehicles for the 'true' matter.

---

37   Bundy, *The Theory of Imagination*, Ch.10, "The psychology of the mystics", especially p.184 (Salisbury) and p.207 (Bonaventura).
38   St Augustine, *De Doctrina Christiana*, II, vii.
39   Fowler, *Kinds of Literature*, p.191.
40   Quintilian, *Institutio Oratoria*, XI, ii, 20.

When considering memory systems in literature, allegorical narrative appears like a literary manifestation of the memory process: the reader is constantly drawing parallels, making connections between the two (or more) levels of meaning incorporated in the tale. Backgrounds and images that are typical for allegorical narratives from Antiquity and the Middle Ages, such as the *Iliad*, *Aeneid*, *The Canterbury Tales* or the *Decameron*, greatly resemble the mnemonic backgrounds and mnemonic images used in memory systems, as do the techniques employed in creating them.

Common settings for allegorical narratives are famously the garden, as in the *Romance of the Rose* and Guillaume de Machant's *Dit dou Vergier*, and the castle or palace, as employed in Langland's *Piers Plowman* and Chaucer's *The House of Fame*, or as described in the stage-set for mystery plays like *The Castle of Perseverance*. Architectural variations on the theme include other secular and, prominently, ecclesiastical buildings, as in the allegorical romance *The Abbey of the Holy Ghost*. A variation on the secular garden setting is that of Paradise, the Garden of Eden, more suitable for expounding spiritual concepts symbolically. The word 'garden' in medieval times automatically carried the association of 'Eden', and a romance set in a secular walled garden dealing with questions about the 'love of man' would automatically also be interpreted with regard to questions about the 'love of God': *cupiditas* and *caritas* being conventional analogues in medieval hermeneutics.

With the predilection for pairings, be they consecutive, similar or paradoxical, it is natural that Paradise was set against its opposite, and settings paralleling Heaven and Hell abound – most famously in Dante's *The Divine Comedy*, a text that fits beautifully into several of the memory system definitions given here. It mimics both the geometrical *formae* with its rigorously ordered circles (e.g., of Purgatory with the exactly classified sins) and the journey method as we are guided from station to station, encountering images (persons) symbolic of specific sins and set against varying backgrounds. It is certainly an allegorical poem which very intensively employs techniques common to allegorical literature and the artificial memory systems. Heaven and Hell frequently make up the allegorical background in medieval texts. The clear distinction between the two sides allows for a decisive attribution of qualities to the items placed within each; for example, personified vices and virtues that populate such backgrounds in the psychomachia are described in the tradition of personified memory images.

Maps lend themselves as allegorical backgrounds because they, like Heaven and Hell, invite the creation of symbolical places through which the figures can wander and where they experience insights reflected in the location. This technique was extremely popular with writers of moral treatises.[41] Actual maps of

---

41   A late example and one of the best know pilgrimage texts today is Bunyan's *The Pilgrim's Progress* (1678). Here the protagonist wanders through a world where each new station equals a new confrontation with moral tenets.

the world, as opposed to literary descriptions of places, exemplified in medieval *mappaemundi*, were not primarily interested in representing a geographically and topographically correct plan of the world. Instead, they used schematics, places and visual symbolism to portray a Christian world view, and the maps were intended to be read as such. Without this visual/associative approach, these maps would make little sense. They have to be read on several levels at once to reveal their full significance.[42]

Fowler lists the commonest features of allegorical texts as "personifications, abstraction, metaphorically doubled chains of discourse and of narrative, generated sub-characters, deletion of non significant description and several topics (journey, battle, monster, disease)."[43] All of these are used as tools when creating memory systems as well. The first item on the list, personification – giving human shape to abstract qualities – is fundamental to the creation of memory images. In fact, the *Rhetorica ad Herennium* author clearly suggests the use of human figures as effective images when he describes how their impact can be strengthened by clothing them conspicuously, adding movement, exaggerated beauty or ugliness, etc.[44] The description of characters is an integral part of the narrative when telling stories. Correspondingly, personifications populate the memory palace and are protagonists of memory systems. Personifications, in the architectural memory system as well as in allegorical writing, overcome the difficulty of making intangible concepts concrete. A much-quoted example of allegorical narrative from late Antiquity, in its extensive use of personification, is *De Nuptiis Philologiae et Mercurii* by Martianus Capella, written in the first half of the fifth century. It tells the story of Mercury's wedding to Philology and describes the dowry of seven handmaidens to Philology: personifications of the Seven Liberal Arts. This allegory on the fruitful union between eloquence (Philology) and learning (the Seven Liberal Arts) was extremely popular and still well known during the later Middle Ages for its employment of personifications as a means of visualising an abstract concept.

---

42   The famous Ebstorf map of the world from *c*.1234 is superimposed on the body of Christ (his head, hands and feet depicted at the edges of the map). On this and the Hereford *mappamundi* (*c*.1290) Jerusalem is at the centre and the maps are oriented towards the East (with Asia at the top) in the traditional T and O scheme. Both incorporate the Garden of Eden in the East, while only the Hereford map adds colour as a visual clue: the Red Sea is actually depicted in red. These maps, representative of many others, were drawn according to a signifying schematic, meant to be read symbolically through the use of visual mnemonics. It promulgated the teleological world-view rather than the scientific, natural history one and expected its viewers to understand how to approach it, using "here be monsters" as a pictorial expression of 'the unknown' rather than an actual belief in such creatures. In fact, only one map contains this phrase and the modern myth that medieval cartographers and explorers were fearful and inclined to fantastical imaginings stems from a misapprehension of how these colourful, imaginative phrases and images are to be understood, i.e., associatively or mnemonically.

43   Fowler, *Kinds of Literature*, p.191.

44   Yates, *The Art of Memory*, p.186.

A common literary device within allegorical writing is the use of dreams or visions that function as the connecting structure for two (or more) levels of meaning. The dream or vision supplies an outer framework for the topic which enables multilayered and/or fantastical events to take place. Dreams and visions are historically closely linked to the art of memory, although more often to the natural than to the artificial kind. Macrobius' distinction between five kinds of dreams was well known and frequently employed by medieval writers, and dream poetry became a popular sub-genre. Among other things, it enabled authors to place allegorical characters in imaginary and extraordinary settings, removed from reality, yet bound closely to familiar concerns through its vehicle – the dream – which was commonly understood to work symbolically.

Visions were thought to reveal hidden memories through their spiritual connotation, and both dreams and visions could contain earthly or spiritual insights. The twelfth-century Jewish philosopher Maimonides understood dreams as prophetic visions and describes the way in which these visions occur:

The prophets […] are also shown things [other than allegorical symbols] which do not illustrate the object of the vision, but indicate it by their name through its etymology or homonymity. Thus the imaginative faculty forms the image of a thing, the name of which has two meanings, one of which denotes something different.[45]

Maimonides considers the rhetorical devices of homonymy and etymology as part of the language of visions. When this visual language is translated by the imagination, man is able to reach a higher understanding. This is also the case in the architectural memory system: the images convey the meaning, even when they must be translated using etymology or other rhetorical devices. Maimonides' combination of prophetic vision with their interpretation by rhetorical means indicates that the techniques used in the art of memory were seen as successful tools of interpretation.

Allegory became prominent in the Middle Ages when anagogical and allegorical exegesis were separated into individual points, extending threefold exegesis into four steps of interpretation. Like Maimonides in his visions, allegory seeks connections or correspondences between two realms, e.g., the physical and spiritual, and looks for added layers of meaning. This was adapted seamlessly to secular writings and extended its limits with regard to content. Traditionally, correspondence between the Old and the New Testament might be sought, as depicted in stained-glass windows of many churches. However, in secular literature allegory helped to link seemingly unconnected topics together, frequently using rhetorical devices such as the ones Maimonides refers to.

This correspondence remains the A and O of memory systems: the linking together of seemingly unconnected items; the creation of a combination through

---

45   In Bundy, *The Theory of Imagination*, p.217.

placement and visualisation. The fact that allegorical settings and elements in narratives share many similarities with backgrounds and images in memory systems may be interesting, but is not, in itself, very enlightening. The real reward of this assertion is that it reveals how the memory is at work within an allegorical text. That memory processes and allegorical interpretations use similar techniques when creating the images suggests which feats allegory expects of the reader's memory in order to comprehend the narrative.

One literary technique that is linked directly to memory images rather than to backgrounds, and which expresses the demands on the reader's memory, is the layering of disparate but inherently connected shapes. Placing one shape on top of the other, this technique relates to the idea of over-writing, of adding layer upon layer whilst the previous level is not concealed, but added to instead. It is related to the palimpsest technique referred to in literary theory, which, however, results in the obliteration of earlier layers. In relation to memory processes, this layering results in an amalgamation and combination of several similar structures which may carry each other's symbolism, for example the tree and the cross with their several associated forms. In the religious society of the Middle Ages the cross is clearly one of the, if not *the*, most dominant geometrical symbols. It is linked to the tree both physically and metaphysically: through the wood from which the cross of Christ was made, and because it is the typological equivalent of the Tree of Knowledge, the Tree of the Virgins, the Jesse trees and the genealogical trees that developed from it.[46]

When referring to one of the trees (from now on I include the cross in this plural), the others are automatically integrated in the extended thematics under discussion. Palimpsest writing is an unspoken associative technique. The connection between the trees is taken as a given. An author using this image expects that links between the various associated images will already exist in the memory of the reader, its relevance would otherwise be missed. This implies that a society has a common store of memories which can be tapped into: an unspoken memory chain which is established through time and ensures that one symbol will automatically call forth a related one from the memory. This collective memory is part of what modern critics call cultural memory and has met with much interest. I will restrict my discussion to considering the way in which this common store of linked symbols plays into the comprehension of a text and simply assert that this common store is certainly expected by authors, if not actually present in the memory of all readers.

This type of over-writing, or palimpsest memory is particularly prominent in ecclesiastical writings of the Middle Ages. There are several shapes that lend

---

46   Peter Lombard (*c*.1100–1160/64) even translates the Biblical depiction of the cross – based on *Ephesians* 3:16–19 which speaks about "the breadth, length, depth and height" of it – into a memory shape when he follows conventional practice and attributes specific qualities to each part of the cross. See Smith, *Traditional Imagery of Charity in Piers Plowman*, p.64.

themselves to this kind of interpretation, either as extensions of the tree or as entirely separate images created through association with it. Palimpsest images have become conventional symbols in stained-glass windows through their function in typology; one image carries two meanings, each relating to an Old and a New Testament episode, thereby linking them together. These images also find their way into writings that attempt to increase comprehension of the text by layering the information from the simple to the complex, or from the specific to the all-inclusive, particularly with regard to theological questions.

Techniques of such complexity, requiring skill and application, may well be one of the reasons why allegorical writings have lost popularity: we no longer have the capability to follow the conventions involved in interpreting allegory with ease, because we no longer are trained mentally to cope with the task. In late Antiquity and in medieval times allegories were conventional and taken for granted, in the same way that, today, literary conventions governing, say, the novel are seamlessly integrated into the modern reader's perception. However, allegory, although out of fashion, is a recurring element in modern fiction, as will be seen in chapters four and five.

Memory and the Page

It is not only allegorical writing that lends itself to a comparison with and an interpretation by memory techniques. Literature in general benefits from an investigation into underlying memory systems. These systems affect texts in two ways: internally and externally, through literary devices embedded in the content and by how they are presented on the page.

DESIGN
Under the heading 'design' I group the visual memory aids employed in manuscripts, particularly in medieval ones. This is a disparate group which includes the use of marginalia, symbols, punctuation, decorative figures, colours and layout. These are not memory aids embedded in the text, but marked additionally on the actual page.

During the transition from an oral to a written culture the need for memory aids did not diminish despite the fact that the items were now no longer stored in the mind alone, but could be put down on paper (or papyrus or vellum) instead. The possibility of keeping extensive records within the pages of a manuscript did not make memorisation obsolete; it required an additional form of memory system to aid the reader in finding a way through and an appropriation of the written text.

There are at least two ways in which visual memory aids were helpful in medieval manuscripts: either as markers which eased the relocation of a particular theme or item in the text, or as visual points along the way at which readers could orientate themselves while they were reading the text, enabling them to create hooks in their mental memory structure on which to hang the newly acquired pieces of information. The second application was much more common. Michael Camille's *Mirror in Parchment* is an investigation into, amongst other things, the pictorial marginalia in a fourteenth-century manuscript, the *Luttrell Psalter*. His detailed descriptions and explanations of their various uses – as visual puns, memory triggers and complex associative references to things both in and external to the text – is highly illuminating, and he concludes that "[w]e have to rethink our modern notion that reading is the rapid relay of information and see it as a far more meditative meandering, in which images are not so much illustrations of an already pre-existing text as part of the process of reading itself".[47]

Nowadays the existence of information in a written document *replaces* the need for memorising the material. The book becomes an external memory store which requires the reader to remember *where* to look rather than *what* to look for. Originally, a text was merely the first step of a process that culminates in the mental combination and evaluation of information safely stored in the memory and retrieved from there for the activity of creative thinking. Even if the text was readily available, it would not usually be consulted beyond the initial 'taking in' process of its most valuable contents. Hugh of St Victor writes that the aim is to avoid constantly having to "thumb the pages of books to hunt for rules and reasons" in order to accommodate an argument but, instead, is to memorise the previously read in such a way that "the particulars" are "at once" "ready by heart".[48] Having said this, Hugo's theory represents the ultimate goal, and its practice was probably less widespread, partly because not many people had regular access to texts. The facts might have been available in writing, but manuscripts were expensive, rare and sometimes only in the hands of the reader for a short period of time. So texts often contained visual memory aids that would help to anchor the text in an existing mental memory framework, or to retrieve the things read by supplying hooks, often associations, that would provide the links.

The techniques used for both locating particular passages and for memorising texts on first reading are either based on the principle of division and arrangement or on the principles guiding memory-for-things (*memoria rerum*) mentioned in the *Rhetorica ad Herennium*. Dividing material to be memorised into sections and arranging them in a logical order is inherent in all memory systems, as mentioned

---

47   Camille, *Mirror in Parchment*, p.162. For examples of Camille's in depth investigations, see, e.g., the complex external references contained in the bear baiting scene (pp.67–9) or the detailed explanation of the illuminated spread for Psalm 88 (pp.163–9).

48   *Didascalicon*, III, iv. The entire extract reads: "We read that some men studied these seven [liberal arts] with such zeal that they had them completely in memory, so that whatever writings they subsequently took in hand or whatever questions they proposed for solution of proof, they did not thumb the pages of books to hunt for rules and reasons which the liberal arts might afford for the resolution of a doubtful matter, but at once had the particulars ready by heart." Transladed by J. Taylor.

above, because the memory works by linking individual items together, breaking complex thoughts or arguments down into their constituent parts, which makes them anchorable in the mind. The division of a text into manageable and logically sequential portions takes very different forms on the pages of medieval manuscripts.

The largest design features – divisions into books, parts, chapters or steps (*passus*) – are aided by adding colour, a decorated initial, different sizes of lettering or even pages of pure decoration, like carpet pages, to emphasise 'here starts another section', 'this is a new thought, a further step along the way'. Although this sounds obvious, the implications for memory, and what this kind of division does to the reader's ability to retain the information, are profound. Anyone who has read a book without chapter headings, or other distinctive divisions of the text, often used in post-modernist writing, will know that the 'relationship' with the text is entirely different.

A simple example of visual division in medieval manuscripts is the use of key words written in the margin as the briefest of summaries around which the entire text can be memorised. Petrarch, a great proponent of artificial memory, fills his margins with notes in addition to collating *florilegia*; he urges readers to use marginal notes as memory aids.[49] The symbolic version would offer 'signs', such as a hand with an extended index finger that points to a particularly important section of the text, or even just the word 'nota' in the margin to indicate that here is a thought worth 'noting', making a mental note of,[50] or indicating that this is a good point to stop and 'take note' of the text so far.

In fact, teaching 'by point' (*punctum*) was common practice at the early university of Bologna, where teachers of Roman or canon law (by university statute of 1252) were bound to teach the text to their students at a certain pace:

The *puncta* were literally the 'points' or places in the text where the Bolognese masters should be, at twelve- or fourteen-day intervals through the term; and they appear in Bolognese manuscripts of canon and civil law, either as dots or written out (*punctum i, punctum ii*, etc.), at the appropriate places in the margin of the manuscript.[51]

This division of the text would take into account the content as well as the amount of text required to be taught, since it only makes sense to create sections that are teachable units of the given topic. It seems that this system, which also interlinks with the medieval pecia-system employed at the universities for the copying of manuscripts, leans on the fundamental practice of dividing a text to ease its memorisation.

Dante's *Inferno* also seems to refer to a division of a text by *punctum*, although of a different kind, in a passage concerning the tragic love story of Francesca and

---

49   Carruthers, *The Book of Memory*, p.163.
50   Yates, *The Art of Memory*, p.108.
51   Rouse and Rouse, "The dissemination of texts in pecia…", p.70.

Paolo. Francesca, recounting the tale to Dante, describes how she and Paolo had been reading a text about Lancelot. On reading how Lancelot had finally kissed the woman he loved, they were tempted to imitate the literary hero – they stopped reading at this point and kissed instead – not taking up the book again. It was *solo un punto fu quel che ci vinse* (one point alone it was that mastered us).[52] Had they read on, they would have realised the downfall that awaited them after giving in to temptation, the text seems to imply. But as Carruthers points out, this *punto* may well refer to the customary punctuation of the text: dividing it up into small parts, easy to remember and often seen in medieval manuscripts;[53] points or dots added at frequent intervals between two words to create gaps in a passage which would otherwise run together. In only this point lies their misfortune: had they read on to the next point, they might have averted their misery.

These various types of division – whether large or minute, in the margin or in the text itself – tell the reader when to halt in their perusal and link the recently read to the foregone passages, lines or parts. Some of these have remained integral parts of modern book production (like chapter headings, large initials at the beginning of a new chapter and sometimes even colouring), while others have been lost entirely (the instruction 'nota' – make a note – or the various kinds of *punctum*). The concept of dividing a text is just as relevant today, however, and the necessity of aiding the reader in memorising what has gone before is still as great. But modern authors avail themselves of it very differently than their medieval counterparts.

After visual memory aids related to division of the text, we now come to those based on the principles of *memoria rerum* (memory of things). To recapitulate – this method (mentioned in the *Rhetorica ad Herennium* and repeated many times over by later authors on rhetoric and/or memory) states that to remember 'things' one must create images which relate to the 'thing' to be remembered, either by similarity or contrariness.

The frequent instruction 'nota' refers to this method because it supposedly implies 'a mental note' rather than an additional written one. More conclusive are the marginal instructions by Robert Holcot (1290–1349) which use the word *pictura* rather than *nota* to indicate the importance of a certain passage.[54] *Pictura* – 'make a picture' – refers to an image, and certainly a mental one, to aid the memory by creating in the mind a picture related to the text. Sometimes the image itself is provided in the margin. These visual memory aids are directly linked to the text in that they use key words or themes and create linking images to be drawn on the page nearby to fire up the visual memory. These drawings, often

---

52   Dante, *Inferno*, V (lines 127–138).
53   Carruthers, *The Book of Memory*, p.187.
54   Yates, *The Art of Memory*, pp.105–7.

part of an elaborate decoration, are not necessarily accurate depictions of the things mentioned in the text. Instead, they often rely on wordplay and punning.

According to Thomas Bradwardine, "manuscript decorators [*pictoribus*]" depict "things of extreme size, whether large or small [...] either by means of something contrary to them, similar, or that will in another way match up a related memory of such kinds of things".[55] Bradwardine, a theologian writing a manual for students rather than a treatise on rhetoric, does not base his findings directly on the *Rhetorica ad Herennium*, instead he seems to bring together the helpful advice available to university students at an advanced level. Since Bradwardine's is a collation of common memory aids, his reference to manuscript decorators suggests that their practice of adding drawings, made explicitly to function as visual memory aids, is a common occurrence. The popularity suggests their effectiveness. The frequent crudeness or brutality of these images lies fully within the memory tradition. The example Bradwardine uses when explaining how the sings of the zodiac can be arranged in order to aid memory is particularly harsh in its depiction.[56] It is especially interesting that the example he uses emphasises the importance of linking the individual images through interaction. In doing so, he also prescribes a specific arrangement of the individual parts: the *direction* in which the action spreads.

He begins with an image in the centre and links further images right and left, alternatively one to the right then one to the left, taking great care to create a linking activity between the neighbouring figures. Although this is reminiscent of the linking of visual images, i.e., for pictorial arts, it is also relevant for books that contain a sequence of drawings. The organisation of drawings in a medieval manuscript may confuse the modern reader: we are used to read in a particular direction both horizontally and vertically – in the West words are usually read from left to right and the lines from top to bottom. Picture series in medieval codices do not follow this printing convention and must be approached in a different way.

---

55   Translated by Carruthers in 'Appendix C' of *The Book of Memory*, p.284.

56   Ibid., pp.283–4. An excerpt reads: "Suppose that someone must memorise the twelve zodiacal signs, that is the ram, the bull, etc. So he should make for himself in the front of the first location a very white ram standing up and rearing on his hind feet, with (if you like) golden horns. Likewise one places a very red bull to the right of the ram, kicking the ram with his rear feet; standing erect, the ram then with his right foot kicks the bull above his large and super-swollen testicles, causing a copious infusion of blood. And by means of the testicles one will recall that it is a bull, not a castrated ox or cow.

In a similar manner, a woman is placed before the bull as though labouring in birth, and from her uterus as though ripped open from the breast are figured coming forth two most beautiful twins, playing with a horrible, intensely red crab, which holds captive the hand of one of the little ones and thus compels him to weeping and to such signs, the remaining child wondering yet nonetheless caressing the crab in a childish way."

Bradwardine's description of the arrangement of the zodiac signs is quite representative in that a group of five pictures, with one in the centre and four around it, one at each corner of the central square, is to be read from the centre, then top right and further clockwise. This, however, is not a set rule. In fact, there are several sources that suggest an anti-clockwise movement: upon entering a space, for example a building, one turns first to one's right – as during religious processions in Italy, or indeed in the sports arenas of Antiquity[57] – and then proceeds to moves anti-clockwise through the space. This suggests that pictorial representation follows its own rules. Often direction depends on the circumstances surrounding the presentation of the pictures. Stained-glass windows follow their own guidelines. Some are to be read from bottom to top, especially the monolithic church windows which guide the view from base events of earthly life at the bottom of the window upwards to the elevated events of the heavenly one at the top. When church windows employ typology in their imagery, the pictures will usually be placed in the relevant pairs next to each other, one prefiguring the event depicted in the next.

The human body is another example of a directional frame, as in the depiction of the 'anatomical man' (or better 'astronomical man') in the Duc de Berry's early-fifteenth-century *Très Riches Heures*. Geoffrey of Vinsauf links the twelve zodiac signs to the human body by attributing each sign to a particular body part. Thus the head is Aries, the stomach Virgo, the feet Pisces and so on. Geoffrey's figure is an instructional example of how to use arrangement to aid memory. He begins at the head and moves down the length of the body to the feet, saying, "Thus let beauty descent from the top of the head to the root".[58] The inversion of bottom to top preferred for ecclesiastical windows signifies that the arrangement comes second to the content: as long as it is memorable and makes sense in the given circumstances, the direction is subordinated.

The directional choice for decorative drawings also relies on its effectiveness. But once a direction, an arrangement or a symbol has been chosen, it is important for the reader to stick to it. Both Quintilian and Hugh of St Victor, representative for many others, emphasise the importance of using the same manuscript to memorise from. Manuscripts differ in layout and may confuse the mental image the reader creates in his mind. This could weaken the mental image and thereby obscure it in the ensuing confusion. The pages themselves, here, become the backgrounds for the images placed against them. This is true also today despite the fact that book printing processes and digital publishing methods have conformed the appearance of the text in many editions.

---

57   Blum, *Die antike Mnemotechnik*, p.12.
58   Geoffrey of Vinsauf, *Poetria Nova*, III, (lines 614–5).

Conclusion: Creative Thinking

One of the ways in which artificial memory was used was to stimulate creative thinking. It puts to shame our modern perception of memory feats as the mere filing away of facts. To classical as well as medieval apologists for the art of memory, the collecting of information was merely the beginning or the fundament for the actual process which made the hard mental work of remembering and storing worthwhile. As Carruthers writes: "They would not [...] have understood our separation of 'memory' from 'learning'", since "it was memory that made knowledge into useful experience, and memory that combined these pieces of information-become-experience into [...] 'ideas'".[59] Rather than memorising facts and figures, which we tend to use memory-work for today, they might remember their 'sources': various aspects and viewpoints concerning debates about a given topic which had acquired the status of being authoritative texts. It was not the basis for a regurgitation of the views of others, but provided a mental overview of the topic from which own ideas could be developed.

William of Ockham complains about being refused access to certain books (by papal instruction) when he writes his contribution to an ongoing discussion. This complaint is not made because he has forgotten his sources – those he has stored away safely in his memory. Instead, since he does not have access to the latest documents regarding the topic under discussion, the latest viewpoints cannot be assimilated into his already existing store of arguments and will, hence, be missing from his own contribution: missing bricks in the argument build upon the many different viewpoints which, according to William, will leave the building of his argument a little less secure.[60]

Furthermore, it seems that writers did not necessarily aim to have the final word in an argument. Writing was seen as an ongoing process with new ideas born every time a further angle was added to the topic. When the critic Gaunilo comments on Anselm's *Proslogion* in very critical terms, the author thanks him and adds the criticism to the next manuscript, taking pleasure in the fact that his thesis has engender an earnest response – showing that the worth of writing lies in the continuation of the debate.[61]

This continuous development shows that no finite number of memory items can ever be found, for with every new development a further item must be added. The memory structures employed cannot have a finite number of places either, as they require constant extension. This also means that the activity involved when using the ancient and medieval art of memory is an organic one where structures are constantly growing, and which requires an active and open mind. Even with the increase of written material, the collation in the memory continued because, as

---

59   Carruthers, *The Book of Memory*, p.1.
60   Ibid., pp.156–7.
61   Ibid., p.212.

Hugh of St Victor says above, one does not have the time to keep searching through books in order to seek out all the relevant points for an argument.

Many a time I've envied Hugh's ability to have all the relevant information available in his memory (and not at his fingertips!), as I trawl through my many notes to relocate items I half-remember but can't straightaway find amongst my notes. I have also miserably failed in following Quintilian's advice to "never write out anything which we do not intend to commit to memory."[62] Since no structures to receive all the information and arguments I found during my research exist in my memory, a reliance on my natural memory would have been fatal for the outcome of this thesis! Therefore, every time I write about a new subject I first collect together the relevant bits from various external memory storage facilities (books, notes, computer files…), then, based on the accumulated additional notes, I fill my mind with the various ideas, build an outline for the topic and finally begin writing. In Quintilian's time, as in Hugh's, the aim was clearly to place the stage of note-taking almost entirely in the mind. But, furthermore, and far more importantly, Quintilian's instruction also shows that the ultimate storage facility is not a written text, but the memory itself. Write things down ONLY IN ORDER TO MEMORISE THEM. The visual page is the memory aid which helps anchor the items in the memory, for the real work happens here once all items have been remembered. Not the items themselves, but what is done with them matters. What artificial memory trains above all else is creative thinking.

It is this aspect of the artificial memory which makes it imminently suitable as a tool for literary hermeneutics, both with regard to the author and the reader. The rules and processes that govern the artificial memory contain structures and functions which correspond to the ways in which texts are both created by the author and received by the reader. The author must use his artificial memory to tell a story because he consciously selects, divides and organises the individual parts of the story, deciding which images are most relevant, carry most 'meaning' in each case, which words are most forceful and how best to convey the resulting chain of images to the reader. Each reader, in turn, must engage their individual natural memory, aided by the artificial one, linking the images created by the author's words with extant pictures already lodged in the memory, often creating unusual combinations as inspired by the writer.

In practical terms this means that all texts contain aspects of the processes of artificial memory. I will show by examples how these can be revealed.

---

62   Ibid., p.206.

Chapter 2

Medieval Literature
Geoffrey Chaucer and William Langland

There is no evidence that either Chaucer or Langland knew directly the memory treatises from Antiquity, such as the *Rhetorica ad Herennium*, Cicero's *De Oratore* or Quintilian's *Institutio Oratoria*. That they knew of the rhetorical subject of memory and their Roman exponents, however, is certain: the medieval authors who described the ancient memory systems were familiar to both.

Chaucer mentions prominent medieval writers on memory like Geoffrey of Vinsauf and Thomas Bradwardine – to name only two – and adds Tullius (Cicero), Macrobius and other classical writers. He clearly refers to their texts, not merely their reputation. For example, he draws on Martianus Capella's depiction of the seven liberal arts in *De Nuptiis Philologiae et Mercurii*, a text which also contains a brief exposition on the art of memory. Although little is known about Chaucer's schooling, his position as a merchant's son in central London and his poetry suggest a good education, possibly at the acclaimed St Paul's Cathedral School, which would have given him a thorough grounding in the subject of rhetoric.[1] His poems, which provide the only certain proof of Chaucer's acquaintance with classical subjects, show that he was widely read – not only in English, French and Italian literature, but also in the Latin classics. It was Chaucer's elevation of the English language through eloquence and rhetoric which won him most acclaim from fifteenth-century writers such as William Caxton, William Dunbar and John Lydgate, the latter honouring him in this well-known passage, saying that Chaucer was the one

> That made firste to distille and reyne
> The golde dewe droppis of speche and eloquence
> In-to oure tongue thourg his excellence
> And founde the flourys first of rethoryk
> Oure rude speche oonly to enlumyne.[2]

However, the terminology used – the golden drops of rain and fresh flowers which so enlighten the 'rude' English language – spring from the aureate poetry of Lydgate's generation, visible in poems by Dunbar and John Skelton, amongst others, with their extensive use of amplification to suit the fashionable 'high style' of poetry. Lydgate's praise is a reflection of his own time and its preferences rather than an objective evaluation of Chaucer's poetry. David Wallace calls Lydgate's perception of the poet's work "a radical departure from Chaucer's own

---

1   For a brief life of Chaucer, see the introduction to *The Riverside Chaucer*.
2   From "The Life of Our Lady" by John Lydgate, in Clemens, *Chaucer's Early Poetry*, p.7.

agenda" which Wallace interprets as his wish "to liberate and organize those natural rhythms and energies which were peculiar to his own native tongue".[3] I will show that both the eloquence and rhetoric so admired by Lydgate and the liberation of the native tongue are merely symptoms. Chaucer's main aim in employing them is to enhance the underlying concerns of a story. Any classical techniques or figurative or aureate language applied to his poetry ultimately help the reader to gain a better, more comprehensive understanding of the text.

In the case of Langland, there is no documentation about his life, except what can be gleaned from the text itself,[4] and this must be treated with caution. However, the topics under consideration in *Piers Plowman* show an intensive involvement in the great questions of the day which came from the universities and new scholasticism – questions of doctrinal import such as predestination, free will and salvation. Thomas Bradwardine (mentioned in *Piers Plowman*) and Robert Holcot took an active part in these discussions, to which Ramon Lull had also contributed. All three were seminal exponents of the memory treatises adapted for medieval uses. If Langland was familiar with their writings on the debate, he was probably aware of other aspects of their writings, too.

There was once disagreement between scholars whether Langland was a highly educated man who created a complex, profound and highly original epic poem or merely a clerk who wrote one poem rather badly. Farther, did Langland get a university education, as M.W. Bloomfield suggests,[5] or did he merely pick up disparate aspects of a topic during his work as a psalter-clerk (saying prayers for the dead in return for payment from the relatives) and from copying legal and other documents?[6] Robert Worth Frank suggests that Langland was not widely read on predestination and that his knowledge was based on the catch-as-catch-can principle[7] while Janet Coleman writes that he was thoroughly versed in all aspects of the complex question.[8] Based on the quotations used in *Piers Plowman*, John A. Alford deduces that Langland uses only those most commonly known and the ones which could be expected – concluding that Langland need not have been widely read to supply them. In fact, he finds that the commentaries and a preaching manual, possibly the *Ars Praedicandi*, a standard text book for

---

3 "Chaucer's Continental inheritance: the early poems and *Troilus and Cryside*", p.25.
4 Especially from the apparently autobiographical scene added to the C-text (passus V) as well as the punning anagram in the B-text on Langland's name (passus XV, 152) and a possible identification of the protagonist Will with the author (e.g. in passus III).
5 *Piers Plowman as a Fourteenth Century Apocalypse*, p.163.
6 Schmidt, "Introduction" to his translation of *Piers Plowman*, p.xiv.
7 Frank, *Piers Plowman and the Scheme of Salvation*, p.2.
8 Coleman, *Piers Plowman and the "Moderni"*. The book investigates the various scholastic, ecclesiastical and rhetorical subjects which must have been known and comprehended by Langland in order to write about "the pros and contras, the variety of solutions to the overwhelming issues of how to achieve salvation", p.190.

preachers in the twelfth and thirteenth centuries, would have provided the majority of the quotations.[9]

In the end the texts themselves will have to indicate the extent of both Langland and Chaucer's acquaintance with particular topics and texts. But this chapter will show that, despite a lack of direct references to memory treatises, both Langland in *Piers Plowman* and Chaucer in *The House of Fame* and *Troilus and Criseyde* employ memory structures as frameworks for the entire poem, and as integral parts and literary devices within the story itself.

In Chaucer's texts direct references to memory exist, but only in the simplest form, i.e., when a character 'remembers' something or 'recalls' another as a purely physical act of storytelling. However, the terminology surrounding these usages exposes their origin in artificial memory. Thus experiences or things are frequently "ymarked" (*HF* 1103) or "prenten" (*Tr.* 900) in the "herte" (*Tr.* 900) or the "mynde" (*Tr.* 521) in the same way that items retained by the artificial memory are marked or imprinted in the memory, as in Plato's famous metaphor of memory as a wax tablet upon which things to be remembered are inscribed.[10] The heart and mind as interchangeable storage spaces for memories goes back to the ancient concept taken over by the Middle Ages that memories are created via the senses: sense-experiences produce the items to be remembered – and since emotions and feelings were said to be situated in the heart, this was often the symbolic seat of their creation.

The reason for locating the act of memorising in the mind (or 'head') is conventional, and today scientifically proven. The medieval mapping of the mind, however, is very specific. In medieval descriptive psychology, conventional tripartite sectioning of the head placed imagination in the front part or cell of the head, reason in the middle, and memory in the back or third part or cell of the head.[11] Memories were thought to be created by the imagination which fashions an image for the new experience or thought. Reason, using common sense, then relates this new 'idea' to reality (madness was thought to be a result of the reason not being able to judge which 'ideas' were rational and which not). Finally, the 'inspected' images move to the last cell in the head where they are stored in the

---

9   Alford, "The role of quotations in *Piers Plowman*", p.99; and Salter, *Piers Plowman, An Introduction*, p.26 ff.

10   All references to Chaucer's texts follow divisions and line-numbers in *The Riverside Chaucer*. The individual texts are abbreviated as follows: *HF* – *The House of Fame*, *Tr.* – *Troilus and Criseyde*, *CT* – *The Canterbury Tales*, *GP* – *The General Prologue*.

11   A later architectural example of the tripartite system appears in Edmund Spencer's *The Faerie Queene* from 1596 where the 'heavenly tower' of a castle contains three rooms, each filled with images and persons representative of the three cells of the head with memory situated in the traditional "hindmost roome of three": it is a vividly allegorical, three-dimensional recreation and derivative of the medieval psychological classifications of memory functions. Book II, Canto IX, verses 47–58.

memory for future reference.[12] In medieval texts (as in literature today) the heart and the head are the most commonly depicted memory receptacles.

The metaphors of head and heart can be mixed. When Troilus sits down to consider how best to describe his suffering to Criseyde in writing (*Tr.* V, 1313–14), he "rolleth in his herte to and fro / How he may best descryven hire his wo." Here the still familiar phrase of 'turning over in the mind' (used by Geoffrey of Vinsauf in his *Poetria Nova*, see Ch.1) is altered. Thus 'turning over', 'revolving' becomes 'rolling' in Middle English, and the mind is replaced by the heart as the organ creating descriptive images because the topic here is feelings, and an emotional (heart-led) rather than a logical (mind-led) Troilus is composing a letter. The extension of the term from merely 'rolling' to 'rolling back and forth' is an example of Chaucer's ability to paint word-pictures in a minimal space by using extant images and contorting or adding to them: the sleepless Troilus rolling back and forth in his bed occasioned by his yearnings for Criseyde is called to the mind's eye by this phrase, while he is sitting down, pen in hand, to express just this misery. In fact, the heart is called the "brestez yë" (*Tr.* I, 453) and is another adaptation of a mental function: that of the mind's eye which can visualise things not present by recalling images stored in the memory.

When Chaucer refers to the topic of memory, it is often through a character's application of it in order to sketch their person. As noted by Carruthers[13] and others, these instances, however, also tell us something about Chaucer's affinity with artificial memory. Thus when talking about learning by rote, i.e., by heart, Chaucer does not overlay the term with any prejudice, but uses it simply to describe the action. In the case of the Sergeant of Law it seems to be an acknowledgment of the sergeant's legal skills when it is stated that "every statut koude he pleyn by rote" (*CT* I, 327), although it also implies that he may be rather a dry conversationalist. The Pardoner, on the other hand, is clearly criticised when he boasts about his ability to perform to his audience in church where he can concentrate on the delivery rather than the content because, as he says, "I kan al by rote that I telle". This is emphasised by the following line in which the Pardoner states: "My theme is alwey oon, and evere was – / *Radix malorum est Cupiditas*" (*CT* VI (C), 332–4). The quotation taken from I *Timothy* 6:10, which says that greed is the root of all evil, is repeated in line 426 to emphasise that the Pardoner has learned his Bible text 'by rote' out of greed alone: it enable him to bully his listeners into buying a pardon from him.

What Chaucer condemns outright is the mere parroting of phrases for the benefit of self-aggrandisement, as is the case with the Summoner who liberally employs two or three helpful phrases he has picked up at the ecclesiastical courts. Chaucer comments that even a jay can repeat the word "Watte" (Walter) as well

---

12   See for example Kolve, *Chaucer's Imagery of Narrative*, Ch.1, "Audience and image", pp.20-23; Bundy, *The Theory of Imagination*, Ch.9, "Medieval descriptive psychology", p.179.
13   Carruthers, *The Book of Memory*, p.20.

as the Pope (*CT, GP* I (A), 637–46). Since animals were thought to have no memory, this comparison of the Summoner to the bird suggests that Chaucer does not attribute this kind of 'memorising' to actual memory work. It may even indicate that 'learning by rote' to him means more than simply learning a few phrases off by heart; it means the systematic imprinting on the memory of long, complex texts, using artificial memory techniques as they were taught at schools as a fundamental principle of rhetoric in Chaucer's time. Carruthers goes even further and puts forward the possibility that the phrase 'by rote' may in fact be an adaptation of the Latin word for 'wheel'. She links the concept of memorising by heart to that of memorising using a wheel, a geometrical figure such as the *rota Virgili*, Virgil's wheel.[14] This would explain, quite neatly, the providence of the phrase 'learn by rote' that has not yet been conclusively established.

Even if Chaucer was not deliberately referring to the techniques of artificial memory, the terminology he uses is firmly grounded in that specific field and urges the assumption that a fourteenth-century writer, particularly one honoured for his success at refining the English language through his eloquence and rhetorical skills (both highly valued aspects of classical rhetoric), was immersed at least in the remaining conventions surrounding the memory topic, if not consciously imitating his predecessors from Antiquity.

Certainly, although the artificial memory always remained part of the trivium (as the fourth part of rhetoric) and hence a scholastic topic, it had its roots and most practical application in the oratory of legal and philosophical matters. An adaptation to the secular and popular genres of dream-poetry and allegorical texts meant that memory changed its function. The terms to describe it remained the same, but the actual application was altered. Even when considering that Chaucer's was a largely oral culture, and many of its literary texts were performed orally, they nevertheless had a physical text as their source and their means of transmission. Thus the kind of memory techniques employed by writers of the Middle Ages aided the composition of a text in the first place – and only secondly became a mnemonic framework for the 'performance' of it in front of an audience, although this certainly would have played a part.

As Elizabeth Salter points out, the famous depiction of Chaucer 'reading' from *Troilus and Criseyde* to a courtly audience shows him without a book placed on the lectern in front of him, suggesting that he knew his stories 'by rote'.[15] Furthermore, Thomas Occleve's portrait of Chaucer also shows the poet without a book and gesticulating (as in the Ellesmere portrait), suggesting a free flow of words rather than a reading. The case for a writing implement which hangs around his neck clearly identifies him as a writer, but stance and gesture depict the poet as

---

14   Ibid., p.252.
15   Elizabeth Salter's introduction to the facsimile of the Corpus MS (1978).

a storyteller rather than a writer, equating the two activities: the writing and the consequent performing of the text.[16]

I will proceed to show that Chaucer was aware of artificial memory systems developed from the ancient backgrounds-and-images system described in the *Rhetorica ad Herennium* and, moreover, that he used them in his texts.[17] I will approach two of Chaucer's poems, using structures from artificial memory as guides to discover whether this releases inherent concerns of the text. I am using these texts to break down the backgrounds-and-images memory concept into its individual parts to clarify the separate devices and to show how they can be linked to literature, and then can be used to aid an interpretation of the text. Since I am starting with the simple building-blocks, the following is a somewhat fragmented approach. It will, however, provide the basis for an interpretation of more complex adaptations of memory structures to literature, i.e., in texts that use a combination of systems, such as Langland's *Piers Plowman*.

The House of Fame lends itself to an interpretation through architectural structures – the be all and end all of the backgrounds-and-images system – the main plot taking place in the Temple of Venus, the House of Fame and the House of Rumours, while *Troilus and Criseyde* and its setting in the town of Troy invites an application of the journey and town map method.

Chaucer – *The House of Fame*

Chaucer's poem *The House of Fame* recounts the protagonist Chaucer's dream in which he visits three very different places: a temple in the desert in which is depicted the love story of Dido and Aeneas, a palace of Fame on a block of ice and a twirling house of twigs where rumours are made. Chaucer is transported from one location to the next by an eagle who explains that the journey is a gift from Jupiter. The god means it to be an education for the love-poet, Chaucer, who has no direct knowledge of the subject. Upon entering the final destination and encountering an enigmatic man, the poem suddenly breaks off.

The three very different buildings Chaucer visits in his dream form the basis for my discussion. I will examine whether these more or less fantastical buildings yield any meaning when compared to imaginary buildings suggested for use in the art of memory. I will concentrate on the structure itself, on how the individual

---

16   Thomas Occleve, "De regis principium", British Museum Harley MS 4866, f.88. For pictorial representations of Chaucer, see Loomis, *A Mirror of Chaucer's World*.
17   I am interested in themes, images and structures rather than in words because etymology is backwards-looking and confirms convention rather than giving information about the semantic field they describe or stem from – in this case that of memory. I am aiming to establish Chaucer's source to uncover what he uses the words for, not what memory-aspects they convey or may already contain.

backgrounds are ordered inside the structure and on what is displayed against them. To remind ourselves: according to the *Rhetorica ad Herennium*, places used for memory work should be "deserted and solitary, for crowds of people tend to weaken the impression";[18] should be of moderate size (too large and the images placed there become vague, too small and it will be overcrowded); should not be too brightly lit (or it will dazzle), not too dark (shadows will obscure the image).[19]

Central to *The House of Fame* is Chaucer the poet/narrator's journey to Fame's Palace where he witnesses the fickleness with which Fame wields her power to grant or refuse oblivion or renown. The main setting of Fame's palace is framed by two further architectural structures. All three buildings have very definite symbolic values and strong figurative associations. The subject of fame is put in a different perspective in each structure. Fame relies on events and persons being remembered, i.e., kept alive by being lodged in the memories of people or, alternatively, in external storage facilities which retain memorable items, retrievable at will. I argue that the three buildings are all examples of memory storage facilities, in this case memory palaces, and will look at how effectual these three building work as memory storage spaces.

THE TEMPLE OF VENUS

The first architectural structure providing the background for the topic of fame is the temple of Venus, described as "a temple ymad of glas" (I, 190). It is not entirely clear from the terminology how this building is constructed. Is it literally made wholly from glass? Or is it a reference to the enormous stained-glass windows installed in medieval cathedrals from the twelfth century onwards through which the dimmed light floats into the interior of the building, giving the appearance that the only building material used is glass? If Chaucer did visit St Chapelle in Paris on one of his trips to France, it seems likely that this small palatine chapel with its extraordinarily large percentage of stained glass – making the Upper Chapel appear as though it were made almost entirely of that material – was the inspiration for the temple of Venus. If we take Chaucer literally, the space employed for the depiction of the story, that is, the space employed to contain the images in an arranged order, is very bright and magical in appearance. Apart from being very light, Chaucer's temple is also solitary (as far as we know, no other person shares the space with Chaucer the protagonist) and of moderate size (since Chaucer can move effortlessly from one image placed on the wall to the next). Hence all three conditions for being a helpful memory palace are given, although

---

18   Yates, *The Art of Memory*, p.23.
19   The *Rhetorica ad Herennium* author does not distinguish between the entire space (such as a building) and individual backgrounds (a recess, a doorway, etc.); therefore, guidelines appear to apply to both. I've chosen only those relevant for the entire space: buildings, in the case of the text under discussion.

the very light interior seems to be in danger of being too dazzling and is not a realistic representation of light broken through stained-glass windows.

As Chaucer walks through the temple, he comes across the opening lines of Virgil's *Aeneid* "writen on a table of bras" (142) and goes on to describe the images that follow. The verbs describing how the story of Troy is incorporated into the structure of the temple are not conclusive either. Most common is "grave" or "graven" (seven times in 123 lines) while "peynted" appears only once; and is also the only reference of it being applied to a wall. So uncertainty is incorporated into the description of the building which makes the visualisation of the space a little difficult. However, the images certainly have an impact on the visitor of the temple. The frequent references to the sense of seeing emphasise the visualisation which takes place as Chaucer wanders through the temple. In the same 123 lines mentioned above, describing the *Aeneid*, the visitor "sawgh" or "saugh" (saw) what was depicted no less than thirteen times.

In the architectural memory system each item to be remembered is placed against its own background and by walking through the building these images are linked. The narrator's physical movement through the building is communicated when each new image or incident is introduced by a phrase akin to "after this", "next I saw" and "ther I saw". This is a technique Chaucer uses repeatedly; for example, the temple of *The Knight's Tale* and the garden in *The Parliament of Fowls* both include aspects highly reminiscent of the art of memory. In *The House of Fame* the narrator is pacing around the room, stopping at each station to take in the new image revealing itself before his eyes. The images themselves do only partly adhere to the guidelines given by the *Rhetorica ad Herennium* author: in the telling they are made to do something; they are not static pictures, but actively perform their part in the story in accordance with the rules of artificial-memory. However, they are rarely invested with great beauty or ugliness, dressed with distinctive items, disfigured or comic. Chaucer adopts only one of the five main devices for creating effective memory images. He is not interested in creating lasting memory pictures for the reader to retain for future reference. Chaucer expects his audience to be familiar with the tale and able to activate the images already stored in the memory from previous encounters – one of these possibly Chaucer's own treatment of it in *The Legend of Good Women*. This changes when we come to the description of Fame herself in the next memory palace where a new image is meant to be added to those already existing in the reader's mind.

Before going on, it makes sense to look at a logical forerunner for Chaucer's Temple of Venus: Virgil's Temple of Juno in the *Aeneid*. This temple, also depicting the story of Troy (up to Aeneas' arrival in Carthage where he views it) is placed in the Libyan desert, just like Chaucer's Temple of Venus. On its facade Aeneas notices "a series of frescoes depicting the Trojan War" (I, 456) which move him to tears, recalling the hardship and struggle of his people's flight from

Troy.[20] He even recognises himself amongst the "insubstantial figures" (I, 464), recalling his own experiences. To him these figures are not made from physical materials, but relate to the "insubstantial figures" who populate his memory; that is, the images lodged there and activated by their representation on the facade of the temple. For Aeneas this frescoed facade is an exterior memory aid.

The external facade of the temple of Juno in the *Aeneid*, which reanimates memories of the actual events in Aeneas' memory, is transposed to the inside of the temple in *The House of Fame*, where the emotion expressed is second-hand compassion for those depicted. Juno (the goddess of Marriage) worshipped by Dido in the erection of the temple in Carthage is tellingly replaced by Venus (the goddess of Love and Beauty) in *The House of Fame* where the theme is worldly love and infatuation rather than the 'hallowed love' between man and wife. Virgil's aim by choosing to have Dido dedicate a temple to the goddess of marriage is surely to indicate Dido's wish: the mourning widow who in her meeting with Aeneas sees a future husband, while Chaucer's Temple of Venus indicates the topic of love, more relevant to the popular courtly-love stories in the Middle Ages and the theme of worldly renown.

THE PALACE OF FAME

The first of the three architectural settings in *The House of Fame* sets the scene for women made famous through their experience of tragic love. The second one, the house (or palace) of Fame, is an unexpected plot development because it neither seems to extend the topic of love, nor seems to form the link in a logical progression from one topic to another.[21]

The house of Fame is extensively, almost garishly decorated from the outside with a multitude of turrets, pinnacles, statues and carvings – in keeping with contemporary fashion, if the buildings depicted in manuscripts like *Les Très Riches Heures* are to be believed. Although it is clearly a secular building, many of its features are reminiscent of church architecture, such as the row of statutes carved into the facade, reminiscent of the twenty-eight Kings of Israel positioned on the front of medieval churches (e.g., on Notre Dame in Paris – which was

---

20   Translated by C. Day Lewis, p.20.

21   Koonce in *Chaucer and the Tradition of Fame* makes the distinction between charity and cupidity the crux of his interpretation, linking it with that between earthly and heavenly fame. He suggests that the "tydynges" so eagerly awaited in the poem are the words of Christ which make this distinction. He therefore identifies the "man of gret auctorite" in the final line with Jesus Christ (pp.265–6). However, to my mind his interpretation sits uncomfortably with the overtly hilarious comedy of the poem and does not explain the movement from one building to the next, which I see as fundamental to the comprehension of the theme. Bennett in *Chaucer's Book of Fame* argues that "any attempt to unriddle [the unidentified figure] is supererogatory", both because the poet himself states that this is a person unknown to him, and because the main action of the poem has already taken place. Bennett suggests that this enigmatic man is representative of the great storytellers, those feeding the rumours created in the house of twigs (p.184).

under construction about the time Chaucer visited France). The interior also echoes church architecture. For one thing, Fame is placed on a throne at the end of the hall in mock-imitation of the Last Judgment scene depicted in many apocalypse windows of medieval churches to remind churchgoers that their actions will ultimately be judged by the highest authority. Similarly, Fame is enthroned in front of the supplicants who come to get their final judgment: whether they and their deeds will be remembered or forgotten.

Furthermore, on either side of Fame's hall are rows of pillars supporting sculptures which help carry the weight of the ceiling. In Chaucer's palace these prominent positions are given to famous men who uphold the memory of the past. They are historians, mentioned by name, whereas statues on pillars in churches often depict the twelve apostles (as in St Chapelle) or the Church Fathers. There they carry the weight of the heavens on their shoulders, supporting Christian faith and keeping the memory of Biblical events alive. In comparison, the historians on the pillars in Fame's palace promote the remembrance of worldly events and are not necessarily selected due to the truthfulness of their works. Tellingly, the list diminishes in grandeur as we near the poet's own time.[22] The historians mentioned in Chaucer's poem are not only secularised, but also mock their ecclesiastical counterparts. The aggrandisement of Fame to the position of Christ at the Last Judgment clearly shows an intended cutting satirical look at the power of Fame – she doles out favours and disfavours indiscriminately like her sister Fortune does good and bad luck (mentioned in line 1547), presenting herself as the ultimate authority and superior to all worldly affairs. She represents the vanity and fickleness that lies in trusting in worldly renown.

A large part of Christian church architecture carries mnemonic value which makes churches entirely appropriate as blueprints for memory palaces: the line of rulers or churchmen on the facade of churches are reminders of the passing of time, of a teleological development towards the final judgment; the apocalyptic windows of the Last Judgment imprints on the memory the necessity of taking responsibility for one's actions in order to be amongst the elect on Judgment Day; while the pillars (in churches often the number of pillars rather than actually carved statues set into them) are memory cues helping the visitor to recall Bible stories and, if twelve pillars, to follow the example of the twelve disciples in order to uphold the protection that Christian faith can provide. A walk through a church has been likened to a journey through the most important tenets of the Christian religion: at specific points within its structure certain areas (or backgrounds)

---

22   It includes Geoffrey of Monmouth whose *History of the Kings of Britain* in the Middle Ages supported the proposition of renaming London Troynovant (New Troy), because the book promoted the idea that Aeneas' heirs came to London from Troy and settled there, bringing with them their renown and grand history – another form of fame – taken entirely seriously until the sixteenth century.

contain symbolic objects (or images) which remind the visitor of his or her faith (see Ch.1).[23]

The memory palace depicted in *The House of Fame* is certainly a receptacle of memories in that everything that is said (or written down) arrives here to have its fate decided. Words appear in the guise of the person who spoke (or wrote) them or, as Carruthers points out, in the red or black ink in which they were written.[24] Thus 'dead' words come alive, dressed up as a record of their 'pronouncer'. The words, in this instance, are the signs by which the memory of the thing is activated.[25]

But these words, or memories, are not ordered or structured in any way. They arrive in droves and are haphazardly admitted to the palace (remembered) or dismissed (forgotten). In this respect the house of fame is very much like the natural memory, for not everything we hear or see sticks in the mind. This can be trained in the artificial memory, but it is not what Chaucer is interested in. He is more concerned with the moral aspect of memory. It is not the most important, the most worthy supplicant that receives a place in the memory palace. Sometimes feckless, useless or callous men are remembered and an image of them retained amongst the features of the building, while wise, gracious and courageous persons are dismissed and forgotten.

The natural memory is not a moral faculty, but an impressionable one. As we know from artificial memory, the most extreme, vivid and grotesque images lodge themselves most securely in the memory; thus, the selection is not made by a judgment based on the worth of the item, but on coincidence, on whatever affects the senses most strongly and leaves the most intense sense-impression behind. In Chaucer's poem Fame, and the palace where she is enthroned, portray many attributes of the natural (immoral) memory. Thus the constantly changing size of the palace (1494–7) makes it an unreliable memory storage building: it keeps changing its structure, altering the distances between the backgrounds, disturbing their visual clarity, thereby confusing who enters and distracting the mind from the activity of memorising. This may also be one of the reasons why Chaucer says that no man alive "Ne han the kunnynge to descrive / The beauty of that ylke

---

23   See, for example, Mâle, *Religious Art in France*; Burckhardt, *Chartres and the Birth of the Cathedral*; Durandus, *The Symbolism of Churches and Church Ornaments.*

24   *The Book of Memory*, p.225. And not symbolically clad in black or red to signify carnal lust and cupidity as Koonce suggests (p.175), which enables him to contrast the coloured garments to the white ones said to be worn by the elect who gather around the throne at the Last Judgment.

25   Carruthers' essay on *The House of Fame* emphasises the Italian influence on Chaucer. This explains Chaucer's inclusion of 'speaking images' that are not mentioned in the *Rhetorica ad Herennium*, but which appear in Bono Giamboni's translation of the Latin text; hence, Dante and Chaucer share the same literary background. Carruthers makes a strong case to suggest that Chaucer knew the architectural memory system from the Italian dissemination of it, rather than from the English one (which had taken a change in direction with the subcategorisation of memory under prudence rather than rhetoric). "Italy, *ars memorativa*, and Fame's house", p.184.

place, ne coude casten no compace [draw no design]" of the palace (1168–1170). It is both too inconstant in its structure and too overwhelming in its decorations. This metamorphosis of a highly mnemonic church building into a confusing, disorganised, chaotic place redirects the view from the impressive scenario (suitable for the topic of fame) to the unstable, unpleasant and unjust reality which lies beneath the glamorous surface.

THE HOUSE OF RUMOURS

The third architectural setting takes another step into the chaos: it is the twirling house of twigs where rumours are born and from where they advance out into the world. Tellingly, there is no classical reference for the twirling house, but it did appear in medieval romances. Chaucer has come from the supposedly respectable setting of the pagan temple, through the medieval church that was then discredited through its false appearance, and has arrived at the contemporary 'cage of twigs' where all pretence of order or morality has disappeared. The reader has followed Chaucer on the inspirational journey: from Dido's love story that is embedded in the tale of Troy – possibly *the* most famous story of all – to the house of Fame where many other stories gather, old and new, waiting to be judged worthy or unworthy of obtaining fame, based on no solid foundation at all (ice, destined to melt, in fact), and finally to the whirling house of twigs which shows an entirely different function: that of rumour in the making.

This is not a progressively more detailed evaluation of fame, but a gradual devaluation of it from the seemingly elevated classical structure (the temple), through the extravagant, false, worldly palace, to the simple, common cage of mere branches. This cage, viewed from the outside as Chaucer does initially, reveals its dizzying lack of steadfastness through its constant movement, and upon entering, when it seems to stop spinning, through a false sense of grounding. The interior of this setting is not described, only the numerous open doors, windows and gaps in the ceiling through which true and false rumours escape, and the great number of people present who produce them through their gossiping. This building is the exact opposite to what would constitute a helpful memory palace. Nothing is fixed, there is no order, no way to distinguish between individual places and no striking images to be locked into place. Gossip produced whips about and escapes without sense or system – yet this, too, is fame, possibly in its most honest embodiment. Here it has reached its utmost disintegration and has come a long way from the seemingly respectable form it took in relation to Dido and Aeneas. But with hindsight even this story, through the judgmental comments by the narrator, gives a disreputable fame to the "hero" Aeneas and shows how it was the fear of adverse fame that drove Dido to her suicide – maybe the temple "ymad of glas" was so brightly lit that we as readers, along with Chaucer the protagonist, were dazzled by the light and did not see the dark side of fame, as it was undoubtedly present in the uncertainties underlying the scene.[26]

The three buildings imagined and described by Chaucer are telling in the extent to which they can serve as memory palaces. If the building's structure is confusing and its contents disorganised, it represents an unsuitable memory palace that will convey confused and disorganised images to the reader. If, instead, a building adheres to the rules of artificial memory (its contents placed against its backgrounds), the story set within its walls will be more memorable and therefore better comprehensible. Chaucer's aim to portray the fickleness of fame is aided by the structures he has chosen to present it in. He may not have based them directly on the principles stated in the *Rhetorica ad Herennium*, but there is a close link between how and why authors choose particular settings to express particular ideas and how the memory works to take in, store and retrieve these images created by the author. Great writers like Chaucer are able to incorporate into their texts those devices which will influence the reader's memory function in such a way that they are guided towards an almost automatic processing of the images and ideas in the text which most enhance the story.

Chaucer – *Troilus and Criseyde*

Troilus and Criseyde tells the tragic love-story of the eponymous heroes: the long wooing process which brings about Criseyde's acquiescence and how it was orchestrated by the intervention of Troilus' uncle Pandarus within the town walls of besieged Troy. The union is abruptly ended when Criseyde is moved to the Greek enemy-camp to join her father Calkas. Here she is given as wife to the Greek hero Diomede. Troilus is killed in battle after hearing of her new union.

There is a direct reference in *Troilus and Criseyde* to the link between a building structure and artificial memory, expressed in the common metaphor that compares the poet to a master-builder who first makes a mental plan of an object before manifesting it in a physical sense. When Troilus first reveals his secret love for Criseyde to Pandarus, seeing no hope of ever winning her heart and blaming Fortune for playing him such a cruel trick, Pandarus chides Troilus for the inactive part he plays and promises to contrive a meeting between the two which will provide the impetus for a love affair. But before rushing off to speak to Criseyde he must lay a plan:

---

26   Bennett makes the point that "any Renaissance iconologist would recognize" that a temple made of glass denotes insubstantial love. He says, "[w]e should therefore be the less surprised if 360 lines later this temple vanishes like a phantom – or if, still later, the house of fickle Fame is built on ice (and the home of Rumour made of brittle twigs)", making the type of building and its description intrinsic to an understanding of the entire poem. *Chaucer's Book of Fame*, p.11.

For everi wight that hath an hous to founde
Ne renneth naught the werk for to bygynne
With rakel hond, but he wol bide a stounde,
And sende his hertes line out fro withinne
Aldirfirst his purpos for to wynne.
Al this Pandare in his herte thoughte,
And caste his werk ful wisely or he wroughte.

(I, 1065–71)

This metaphor – Pandarus halting to form a mental design ("caste") before executing his intent, compared to a masterbuilder's mental preparation and planning preceding the building of a house – is taken almost word for word from Geoffrey of Vinsauf's *Poetria Nova*. Indeed, it makes up the first six lines after the dedication, inaugurating the entire discussion about rhetoric, including that of memory.[27] This metaphor is therefore the concept underlying all that follows.

Vinsauf does not compare the master-builder to a scheming uncle interfering in young people's affairs, but to the writer of 'poesis' (*PN*, line 48): just as the master-builder makes a mental plan of the building before erecting the physical structure, the writer makes a plan in his mind – draws an outline in his imagination of the object to be expressed – before putting it on paper or presenting it in a speech. Vinsauf actually goes on to point out that it *is* a metaphor for the process of 'poesis'. He writes: "[i]n this mirror [i.e., this metaphor] let poetry itself see what law must be given to poets", and goes on to emphasise the importance of organising one's thoughts before letting "your hand be too swift to grasp the pen, nor your tongue too eager to utter the word".[28] This metaphor equates the master-builder with a poet, and the description of this poet is that of a person using artificial memory, drawing an outline (possibly of a building) in his mind before employing this mental design to tell his story.[29]

---

27   The original Latin reads:
Si quis habet fundare domum, non currit ad actum
Impetuosa manus: intrinseca linea cordis
Praemetitur opus, seriemque sub ordine certo
Interior praescribit homo, totamque figurat
Ante manus cordis quam corporis; et status ejus
Est prius archetypus quam sensilis …
Bk 1, p.16 (lines 43–8).

28   *Poetria Nova*, I, (lines 48–51).

29   This metaphor was not limited to writers and orators, as in Vinsauf's treatise on rhetoric, but had also been used to explain the mental activity of meditation. Hrabanus Maurus (ninth century) writes: "always in the interior of our breast the holy sweetness of heavenly sayings and of gospel praise should resonate in memory. [… T]hese [are] the foundations of a wise master builder" (Carruthers, *The Craft of Thought*, p.275). Hrabanus clearly links heart, mental image and memory in the early medieval *memoria* tradition; in this case "diagramme-like pictures [are] created mentally, which serve as the site for a meditational *collatio*". Carruthers, *The Book of Memory*, p.123.

The inclusion of this metaphor in the text of *Troilus and Criseyde* in such close adherence to Vinsauf's text (practically a direct translation) suggests that Chaucer refers directly to the art of creative thinking, based on the skill of artificial memory, but here transferred to making a plan of action. Pandarus is linked to the concept of the writer because he thinks of himself as the author of Troilus' story (see below).

Earlier in the same encounter between Troilus and Pandarus (I, 749) Chaucer has already used the verb "caste" (to form a design or shape) in relation to the mental activity described in the master-builder metaphor. When Troilus thinks about his situation, before confiding in Pandarus, all the aspects are outlined mentally: "Al this gan Troilus in his herte caste". Again, the shape is formed in the heart – traditionally the seat of memories created through sense-impressions – before it is spoken aloud, in this case to Pandarus.

Furthermore, the building metaphor is continued in Pandarus' reference to Troilus being "the beste post [...] / Of [Love's] lay" (I, 1000–1001). Troilus, who previously jeered at love-sick friends, is now himself the strongest pillar in the church of Love. Here is another imaginary building, the individual parts of which (here the pillar) take on symbolic meaning. In the mouth of Pandarus they take on a satirical meaning. In this instance the conventional comparison of worldly and heavenly love, of charity and cupidity, emphasises that Pandarus' church of Love is certainly a worldly one. Chaucer returns to the building metaphor in book III as Pandarus, once again, instigates the lovers' meeting. At this stage the "tymbur is al redy up to frame" (530): planning the trysts is equal to planning the process of building a house.

None of these instances that use building metaphors appear in the source for Chaucer's text, the *Filostrato* by Giovanni Boccaccio. In fact, when Pandarus initially takes it upon himself to organise the first meeting between the two young people in the *Filostrato*, he does not pause to think, but immediately springs into action, going to Criseyde to work on her. In *Troilus and Criseyde* the metaphor is sustained throughout the book, and its repeated incorporation suggests its great relevance for the story-line. It serves the fundamental question about providence and free will which becomes the main theme in the last two of *Troilus and Criseyde*'s five books: to which extent can we plan anything in our lives in order to influence our future?

THE JOURNEY METHOD

Although buildings in *Troilus and Criseyde* are linked to memory techniques, it is the journey method as memory system which is particularly helpful as a literary device. After Criseyde has left Troy to join her father Calkas in the Greek camp, Troilus rides through the town, reminding himself of their shared time by revisiting places of past encounters:

Fro thennesforth he rideth up and down,
And every thyng com hym to remembraunce
As he rood forby places of the town
In which he whilom hadde al his plesaunce.
"Lo, yonder saugh ich last my lady daunce;
And in that temple, with hire eyen cleere,
Me kaughte first my righte lady dere.

"And yonder have I herd ful lustyly
My dere herte laugh; and yonder pleye
Saugh ich hire ones ek ful blisfully;
And yonder ones to me gan she seye,
'Now goode swete, love me wel, I preye';
And yond so goodly gan she me biholde
That to the deth myn herte is to hire holde.

"And at that corner, in the yonder hous,
Herde I myn alderlevest lady deere
So wommanly, with vois melodious,
Syngen so wel, so goodly, and so cleere
That in my soule yet me thynketh ich here
The blisful sown; and in that yonder place
My lady first me took unto hire grace."
                    (V, 561–81)

Now that Criseyde is no longer present, Troilus visits the backgrounds against which her 'actions' were displayed, in that way calling forth images of her from his memory. By seeking out the actual places where he experienced Criseyde 'in action', he provides an extra impetus for the memory to restore the filed-away images to his mind's eye. This is the work of the natural memory: no act of will is necessary, no conscious effort has to be made for the memories to come flooding back. However, Troilus *seeks out* these places on his ride through Troy, willingly encouraging his natural memory to supply those images. Mark Lambert writes that Troilus "ritualizes his grief by returning to the things associated with his time of joy".[30] Troilus 'ritualizes' them first by intensifying his grief through seeking out reminders of his foregone happiness – the comparison of shared joy increasing his sense of isolation and loss – and secondly by imitating a religious procession in his journey through town. He is like a pilgrim making his way from one station of Christ's passion to another.

Ironically, the 'stations' he visits are all filled with happy memories, suggesting that this activity, although highly appropriate for a knight of courtly love poetry, is also a criticism of Troilus' inclination towards self-pity. Instead of choosing to take charge and do something about his situation, Troilus turns to the past, to something that cannot be altered or rectified.

---

30   Lambert, "Telling the story in *Troilus and Criseyde*", p.71.

Troilus has considered whether he has any influence on shaping his and Criseyde's future in the famous 'necessitee'-passage (IV, 958–1078). He has run through the arguments surrounding destiny and free will (taken from Boethius' *The Consolation of Philosophy*) but ends up with the coward's stand: he chooses not to choose. "The greatest fallacy of [*Troilus and Criseyde*] criticism," writes Alan T. Gaylord, "is to assume that Troilus has no alternatives, or could not discover what they were."[31] The necessity-speech is often seen as the turning point of the story. Much speaks for this because it is the point at which Troilus could have learned from his experience (after all, Criseyde has been manipulated – though not very unwillingly – into accepting Troilus as her lover) and could have taken steps towards reaching a conclusion he wished for. Instead, he revisits places of past happiness, going to the city wall and looking out at the spot where he took his leave of Criseyde. This is very becoming for a romantic, tragic hero, but not, Chaucer seems to say, for a man of philosophical circumspection.

The memorial ride through Troy may be based on the functions of natural memory, but as soon as Chaucer consciously chooses to employ it as a character-descriptive device, it takes the shape of an artificial memory system. To look at this in detail, it is necessary to consider the same scene as it appears in the *Filostrato* to see how much of it is Chaucer's own invention and how much has been taken from Boccaccio's text. In the *Filostrato* Troilo also rides through the town of Troy, visiting places that remind him of his beloved Chryseis. The greatest difference between the two scenes lies in their interpretation, made clear in a few lines inserted in amongst this ride in the form of an address to Cupid/Amor. Chaucer writes:

> "O blisful lord Cupide,
> Whan I the proces have in my memorie
> How thow me hast wereyed on every syde,
> Men myght a book make of it, lik a storie.
>
> (V, 583–85)

The 'proces' Troilus has in his 'memorie' is, of course, the sequence of his love-story with Criseyde. He breaks off the list of memorable incidents in order to take stock of his own situation and returns to his journey of remembrance after the insertion. It is clear that the ride through town is a physical manifestation of the memory process taking place in his mind which, in turn, is the basis for the story, *his* story, of which men might make a book. In these four lines Chaucer gives us concise instructions on how to write stories. First the individual steps arranged in the correct order (the 'proces') must be securely anchored in the memory, then it can be written down in a book to be told to, or read by, the world at large. The underlying thought is here twofold: one, that Troilus sees the entire experience of his love affair spread out in front of him, realising that it would make a good story

---

31   Gaylord, "The lesson of the *Troilus*", p.32.

as a tragic tale of love (again suggesting the tragic courtly-love hero) and two, that Chaucer draws attention to the fact that this is exactly what has happened – he made a book of this tale and the reader is holding it in his hands (or the listener partaking of the contents) at that very moment. Underneath this lies the assertion that memory, and a good memory, is the basis for all storytelling. In the *Filostrato* the passage reads as follows:

> "Long hast thou made the story of me, O Love,
> if I would not hide me from myself,
> and if memory well reports to me the truth of it."
>
> (V, st 56)[32]

The suffering hero whose tragic tale makes a good love-story remains the theme, but the points about memory and written testimony, which stand out in Chaucer's text, have a very different emphasis. In Boccaccio it is the god of Love who has turned Troilo into a story: there is no mention of mortal man producing written evidence of it. Chaucer's transference of the creative power from the god of Love unto the writer to some extent diminishes the fatalistic aspect of the scene. Boccaccio's hero fully sees himself as a plaything of the god of Love, who is responsible for the development of his love-story. Although Chaucer's Troilus also attests that he is "holly in" Cupid's "wille", he nevertheless is worldly enough to consider that it would make a 'good read'. Although the necessity speech should have shown him why free will plays a part in a world of predestination (had he understood Boethius rightly), he makes no attempt to influence his life, but rather aims at prolonging the misery he is in by storing the details of his suffering in another memory retainer: the book.[33]

With regard to memory it is the little word 'if' that makes all the difference. In Chaucer's text there is no question whether Troilus' memories are true or false, merely that they need to be secured: "whan I the proces have in my memorie": when; then the story can be told. Memory is here clearly a practical tool of storytelling, and Troilus is strengthening the individual parts by reviving them in his mind when he revisits the various scenes in Troy. The *Filostrato* is more ambiguous about the powers of memory, saying *if* his memory well reports the truth of it. This line in the original, taken together with its previous line, reads: "*s'io non mi voglio a me gir nascondendo / e 'l ver ben mi ridice la memoria*"...

---

32   Translated from Boccaccio's *Filostrato* by Rossetti, in *Chaucer's Troilus and Criseyde Compared with Boccaccio's Filostrato.*

33   Criseyde, too, anticipates how she will be remembered in books. But hers is an apprehension of the negative representation of her character since she does choose Diomede in the end, acknowledging the consequences of her action by commenting on the effectiveness of books as stores of memories (v, 1058–85). The theme of books as keys to remembrance is a common one in Chaucer's writing and appears in more detail in the prologue to *The Legend of Good Women*, the content of which relies entirely on the information from old books. Chaucer writes, "And if that olde bokes weren aweye, / Yloren were of remembrance the keye" (lines 25–6).

(V, st 56, 3–4).[34] The word 'if' (se) at the beginning of line three (se io elided to s'io) is carried over in meaning to the fourth line and gives it its doubtful quality. Not only is Boccaccio's Troilo not certain whether he can trust his own memory, he also implies that he has not been entirely truthful with himself. This gives an impression of a main character who is confused and uncertain of himself and the meaning of what he has experienced in his infatuation with Chryseis – it makes him rather more sympathetic, as though he were saying, 'I have been a fool and have refused to see the truth, hiding (nascondendo) it from myself, so now I don't even know whether I can trust my own memory'. He doesn't say that the events did not occur as stated, rather that the overwhelming grief for the loss of Chryseis has opened his eyes and made him question himself.

Interestingly, this third line (about hiding it from himself) has been left out by Chaucer. It could be argued that it was simply offered up to accommodate the shorter seven-line stanza-form he was writing in (Boccaccio used an eight-line stanza), but the fifth line didn't make it into translation either, and this, too, contains the powerful little word 'if'. More likely is the conclusion that Chaucer did not want the sentiment of the line in his version of the story. He removes the 'if' from the fourth line by ignoring the third (the se only appearing in line three), and also the aspect of self-deception which would suggest that Troilus had finally learned something from his experiences. Chaucer's Troilus has clearly not learned anything: he bemoans rather than tries to change his situation and he rails against the odds rather than really trying to understand them. The philosophical debate about necessity is an entirely original addition to Chaucer's Troilus and Criseyde; it does not appear at all in the Filostrato. A passage of twenty stanzas on destiny and free will with no reference in the source at all suggests that it was a key issue for Chaucer which also changed the original intent of the entire work. Troilus and Criseyde turns the last two books into a question about predestination, and what started as an entertaining courtly love-story becomes a philosophical discussion about destiny and free will expressed in the actions of the characters.[35]

---

34   Original Italian from Boccaccio's Filostrato in Tutte le opere, ed. V. Branca.

35   As Jill Mann points out in "Chaucer and destiny in Troilus and Criseyde and the Knight's Tale", Chaucer goes out of his way to show that, indeed, Pandarus may think he is the 'author' of the tale, whereas he is as caught up in destiny and free will as are the two other main characters. Where Troilus chooses not to choose and Criseyde uses her powers of free will to the extent that circumstances allow, Pandarus clearly believes that he can influence the outcome by using his free will to manipulate powers around him. In the Filostrato, where the character of Pandarus is sketched much more two dimensionally, this case could be argued, but in Chaucer's Troilus and Criseyde the comparison of the two ride-bys past Criseyde's open window, undertaken by Mann, clearly shows that providence does have the upper hand, although Pandarus, sometimes by pure coincidence, may have attempted to enforce a situation that would have occurred without his assistance anyway. Thus the first instance, when Troilus passes Criseyde's window after Pandarus has told Criseyde of his love for her, is a pure coincidence. Only the second ride-past is instigated by Pandarus, and by then Criseyde has already succumbed to his charm. The Filostrato has only one of these scenes which is brought about by Pandarus' interference. Chaucer's "doubling"

65

Troilus, despite his keen appreciation of the various aspects of the discussion, is incapable of active intervention, while Criseyde again and again makes decisions of free will within the framework given her: in the end her difficult and dangerous position as a single woman in the enemy's camp with a Trojan lover who has no power to protect her. Her decision to accept Diomede earned her the epithet 'false', but Chaucer's version allows for circumstances which cast a more favourable, if not wholly appreciative light upon her character. The spotlight, here, is not on the characters themselves, they are merely the vehicles for the topic, animated and made palpable through their actions, for example in Troilus' memorial ride through town. Thus within this 'journey', seen as an exponent of the memory function, lies a clue to the underlying concerns of the work.

THE TOWN MAP

The town itself, seen in the light of the memory topic as a memory map, reveals further aspects about the poem. Other journeys through town are not so much memory aids as instances being played out against the map of Troy, which is being drawn quite clearly in front of the reader's or listener's mind's eye. The description of the walled city, through which the river Symois runs like an arrow (or "arwe", IV, 1548), lends itself beautifully to an intensive visualisation of its topography. There is much coming and going between palaces, to temples and the town wall that gives the impression of a lively, civilised and pleasant town. Lambert calls the fourteenth-century Troy of Chaucer's invention "one of the great *cittá invisibili* of English literature, one of the wonderful places of our imagination". He also adds that it is "the city of kindliness and friendship".[36] This, of course, stands in stark contrast to the situation it is in: Troy is a besieged city, having to lock its gates at night and sending its male inhabitants of the fighting estate outside the town walls into the field of battle on an almost daily basis. This contrast highlights the atmosphere within the walls of loving kindness amongst which the love-story of Troilus and Criseyde unfolds, only moving outside the safe confines of the city walls when their love, also, is besieged by outside forces. This contrast is emphasised on many occasions and intensifies the intimate atmosphere of the love-story throughout the first three books.

The topography of Troy, with its many architectural features, is often contrasted by interiors which provide the background to a scene. The geographical map of Troy works metaphorically through the opposition of interior/exterior, and by revisiting particular settings for particular topics, for example the garden or the street. Furthermore, the town and its associations help to express the various characters and is a central metaphor for the description of Troilus and Criseyde's

---

[Mann, p.77] of the situation shows a conscious wish to reduce the strength of Pandarus' influence over the development of the scene and thereby clears the way for the more philosophical discussion of predestination and free will that follows.

36   Lambert, *"Troilus*, books I–III: A Criseydan reading", p.109.

love. Buildings, particularly many small/narrow rooms in which a large part of the amorous action takes place, are contrasted by the streets of bustling activity and the garden of contemplation. In the tradition of courtly love poetry the garden is also here the place where the subject of love is confronted (Pandarus happens upon Troilus talking of his secret love in his sleep in a garden, Antigone sings her love-song there and Pandarus hands Troilus' love-letter to Criseyde in a garden) while the actual confrontation between the lovers takes place in enclosed spaces, in accordance with the secretive and hidden state of their affair.

There is also the obvious contrast between the Greeks and the Trojans, firmly located in each their space (outside and inside the town walls), and a further comparison is made in the frequent references to Thebes, another besieged town. The story of Thebes is told to Criseyde and her friends as they sit in the 'paved parlour', inside, in a besieged town (II, 81–4). This is a joyous occasion because Thebes freed itself and won the war – presenting a hopeful prospect to the citizens of Troy. As readers, however, we know that Troy will fall, and within the positive atmosphere the optimistic outlook is shown to instil false hope, introducing a false note into the harmonious setting.

Not only the physical manifestation of Troy, but also its symbolic value plays a large part in the poem. The town is incorporated into similes and comparisons on a regular basis and almost becomes a fourth main character, even being addressed directly by Troilus when he says goodbye to town, king and kin, in that order, while preparing to take his own life (IV, 1205). Hector is said to be the town wall, i.e., the protector of the town and its inhabitants (II, 154) while his brother, Troilus, is Criseyde's "wal / Of stiel" (III, 479–80) through which Love "hadde opened hire the yate". Pandarus, in typical hyperbole, declares to Criseyde that the news he is about to tell her (Troilus' love) is five times better than the news would be had Troy won the war (II, 126) and exclaims that for all the treasures of Troy would he not want to see Troilus in such distress for even one day (III, 874). Troilus does not fall far behind Pandarus in his exaggerations and says that the love of Criseyde would be better than a thousand Troys (II, 977). Furthermore, Pandarus swears on Troy that he means well (II, 1146), the hours of the day are described by the sun's position in relation to Troy (III, 1441 and 1145) and all the bells in Troy seem to ring out as Troilus and Criseyde kiss for the first time (III, 187), to name but a few instances. The love of Troilus and Criseyde is hereby linked linguistically to the town and its fate. But where Troilus is always centring his love on Criseyde, she in turn seems to identify the town itself with Troilus. She makes this exchange when she views the town from the Greek camp. Speaking to Diomede, she transfers the love she feels for Troilus, and which she cannot openly name, to the town: "I love that ilke place" (V, 956). Diomede, however, realises that Criseyde has "a love in Troie" (V, 779) and urges her to "lat Troie and Troian fro youre herte pace!" – even he considers the love of town and man as being inseparable.

As readers, we are given a large number of visualisation aids throughout the text, many related to the memory function. The map of Troy provides the background for the story, but also the emotional blueprint for the two main characters, while actions played out against it are memorable through their movements between clearly defined stations, particularly in Troilus' journey through town. Throughout it runs the master-builder metaphor which says that any good writer must have a plan before setting down his ideas on paper. And the clearly defined structures added to the text through Chaucer's spatial awareness show that he is a master-builder of mental images, and a great rhetorician who knows how to convey these images to his readers.[37]

Langland – *Piers Plowman*

From the physical aspects of backgrounds and images as they appear in medieval texts in the form of buildings (*The House of Fame*) or journeys and maps (*Troilus and Criseyde*), I now pass on to the adaptation of these in allegorical writing where the physical journey becomes an inner or heavenly journey: both apply to Langland's poem *Piers Plowman*. This is also a move from memory devices integrated into the story to memory systems as framework for an entire tale. The journey, particularly a pilgrimage as the underlying structure for a long narrative, is familiar from *The Canterbury Tales*, its mnemonic application fully developed in *Piers Plowman*, as will be seen.[38]

Piers Plowman is a tale of pilgrimage. Will, the dreamer, sets out on his journey in search of "Truth" to discover how to follow the Christian tenet of 'doing good' in its three progressive stages of doing well, better and best. He encounters various personifications of mental faculties which represent stages towards an understanding of this tenet. His most important encounter is with Piers the Plowman, a Christ-figure who aids him on his way and who in the latter part of the poem becomes the main protagonist in a recreation of the passions of

---

37   Many others of Chaucer's poems, if not all, lend themselves to interpretation through the investigation of spatial visualisations, encouraged by the texts themselves. Particularly *The Parliament of Fowls* and *The Knight's Tale* contain clear indications hereof. For an example of the latter, see Kolve, *Chaucer and the Imagery of Narrative*, Ch.3, "*The Knight's Tale* and its settings".

38   The concept of a memory journey is strongly linked to that of pilgrimage in religious thought, and is also the underlying structure of *Piers Plowman*. The vast topic of pilgrimage and memory is far too extensive to be dealt with sufficiently in the short space available. For literature on the concept, see for example the following texts that relate to the subject through history, literature and art-history, and that are relevant for the topic of memory: Martin Robinson, *Sacred Places, Pilgrim Paths*, a collection of pilgrimage texts; Mary Carruthers, "The place of the tabernacle" in *The Craft of Thought* for the concept of linking memory with movement; Richard Foster, *Patterns of Thought: The hidden meaning of the great pavement of Westminster Abbey* for an example of the relationship between church interiors and processions; M.D. Anderson, *Drama and Imagery in English Medieval Churches* for the importance of staging in English passion plays.

Christ. The poem ends with an attack on the Barn of Christianity, or the Christian Church, and therefore concludes with an unexpected sense of uncertainty about the outcome of the pilgrimage.

It is important to distinguish between four kinds of memory at work in the text of *Piers Plowman*: 1) natural memory, created from sense-impressions without a conscious effort, 2) artificial memory, created by a conscious effort using structures and images, 3) *memoria*, the medieval ecclesiastical act of remembering the dead, and 4) the Neoplatonic concept of a dormant memory of God accessible through prayer and meditation. For this discussion of *Piers Plowman* I will set aside 3 and 4. *Memoria* touches upon the person of Will alone and is secondary to my discussion while Neoplatonic ideas, although pervading the text and to some extent creating the atmosphere in which the concerns of the poem can flourish, do not directly interfere with the craft of writing and the techniques employed by Langland in order to communicate his story.

Natural and artificial memory (1 and 2) are closely woven together. As their functions are so similar, it can sometimes be difficult to decide whether one or the other is at work at any given time. However, this comes to the aid of Langland's argument that only in the interaction of all mental faculties is an elevation in perception possible. The function of the memory, whether natural or artificial, is divided (most commonly) into three phases in medieval psychology: take in (or encoding), storage, and retrieval (or decoding). Confusingly, both the storage facility (the memory) and its activities (the three phases) are often covered by the term 'memory', and particular care must be taken to distinguish between them.

Langland consciously employs artificial memory structures, from the very basic to the extremely complex, building up their intensity with the progress of the story in order to lend a structure, a framework to his tale which mirrors the development of the mental capacity to comprehend far-reaching ideas on a spiritual rather than merely a logical plane. Langland expects the reader to bring both a functioning natural and artificial memory-faculty to the text; hence, the memory he (as most authors) is concerned with is that engaged by the reader while perusing the text.

MEMORY REFERENCES
There are few direct references to memory in *Piers Plowman*.[39] When they occur, they usually refer to the ecclesiastic institution of *memoria*: saying prayers for the

---

39   There are three versions of *Piers Plowman*: the unfinished A-text (*c*.1370), the completed B-text (*c*.1378–9) and the revised and completed C-text (*c*.1386). Furthermore, a text has been discovered, called the Z-text, which is thought to be a draft version written even before the A-text. I follow convention in using the B-text, which is generally held to contain the best writing ("the best poetry" as Schmidt says). All references are therefore to, and all quotations taken from, the B-text, unless stated otherwise. The Middle-English text is quoted from William Langland, *The Vision of Piers Plowman*, while the translation into modern English is quoted from William

dead – possibly the profession of Langland, and certainly that of the narrator. Even Anima, when listing his various names, calls himself *memoria* "when facing God in prayer and meditation" (XV, 26). Hence the actual word 'memory' has strong religious connotations for Langland and tends towards the Neoplatonic concept of the memory of God which resides dormant in every human being.

The spiritual connotations are contrasted to the many instances of artificial memory in Langland's prolific use of mnemonics: the use of acronyms (for example, *DEUS: Dans Eternam Uitam Suis* (XII, 290), 'giving eternal life to his own; that is, to the faithful' – not Langland's invention, but an existing acronym presumably well known in Langland's time[40]); the numerous instances of numerical lists (seven deadly sins, seven virtues, five senses, four evangelists, the Trinity, three estates, Ten Commandments, seven liberal arts, etc.); and extensive use of punning. Examples of the latter are homophony: 'heathen/heaven' (XV, 456–60); homography: 'fulling' (XV, 450) used both to describe the cleaning of cloth and for baptism; and visual puns such as the linking of the Cross of Christ to the cross imprinted on a coin (XV, 348–9). The subject of these mnemonics is also primarily religious, but the techniques are traditionally rhetorical and draw on classical memory treatises.

Conventional memory metaphors are frequently used, such as the instruction to place something to be remembered in the heart, mention of the treasure(chest) and book as memory storage facilities and the engraving of memorable names in church windows. On the three-dimensional plane of memory systems there are several instances of buildings, maps and journeys. However, since *Piers Plowman* is an allegorical text, these instances are related to the spiritual aspects of an inner journey, rather than to physical places. The Castle of Caro or flesh (IX, 49–59), for instance, uses symbol-allegory to portray the human body and its mental and spiritual functions; the castle (body) is owned by God (nature) who created it, its resident is Anima (the soul) who is guarded by Inwit (the five internal senses, listed by Frank as will, reason, mind, imagination and thought[41]), etc.

The positioning of individual concepts within a physical framework to express intangible ideas is even more strongly linked to the architectural memory system in the description of the Castle of Truth (V, 560–608) where the drawbridge is prayer, the moat is mercy, the walls are wisdom, the gatekeeper is grace, the buttresses are belief and the crenellations are Christian faith. Each aspect which brings the seeker closer to truth is linked to a specific part of the castle. Truth is protected by mercy, wisdom and Christian faith, it is upheld by belief, and to find truth, i.e., to enter into the castle, one must cross the bridge through prayer and only the grace of God can let one enter. To reach the castle, a journey must be undertaken. The map of the landscape to be traversed is described by Piers the

---

Langland, *Piers Plowman*, both edited by A.V.C. Schmidt.
40   Schmidt, *Piers Plowman*, p.136 and fn. p.308.
41   *Piers Plowman and the Scheme of Salvation*, p.51.

Plowman and contains eight of the Ten Commandments, turned into the names of geographical and natural features (such as a stream, a place, a field, two tree stumps and a hill). Hence the journey to truth is a spiritual one and as the pilgrim passes each station he is reminded, by the name of each place, of what is required of him if he wishes to obtain truth. Incidentally, all the sins the commandments forbid are situated on the left – traditionally the evil side – and is hence another mnemonic aid to make a directional division and thereby place each aspect clearly on the mental map.

The buildings and journeys described in *Piers Plowman* strongly distinguish themselves from those presented in Chaucer's texts looked at above. Their allegorical symbolism makes no pretence at resembling realistic buildings or journeys. Also Chaucer's journey in *The House of Fame* is an inward journey, indicated both through the sub-genre of dream-vision and the flight with the eagle which symbolises a flight of imagination, i.e., a journey in the mind rather than in the physical world. However, it clearly anchors its symbolism in physical manifestations which to a large degree can be related to existing things and places – even if the combination is unusual or original (like a temple in a desert, a palace on a block of ice or a swirling house). Troilus' journey through Troy, likewise, is safely anchored in the realistic townscape, related to natural memory in that physical places may unbidden recall experiences stored in the memory.

Langland largely avoids such realistic manifestations of symbol-allegory in the second and much longer part of the poem (the vita). This, also, provides him with the greatest challenge in writing the poem: how to frame the long tale without binding it to earthly matter which might distract from its spiritual meaning? His solution was one familiar to medieval audiences, but never before (or since) achieved on such a high plane: he uses a combination of, what Schmidt calls, personification-allegory and figural-allegory[42] to give his poem a structure that allows him to situate his journey in the mind without much recourse to physical representation of the stations along the journey.[43]

I suggest that the various personifications function as backgrounds for the individual stations of the inner journey, marking each progression along the way, while the figura are linked to the images placed against these backgrounds and retain the 'true meaning' of the poem – that which is actually to be remembered.

---

42   "Langland's figurative modes", in the introduction to his translation of *Piers Plowman*, p.xxxvi.

43   Although Langland does from time to time refer to actual physical places, frequently places of pilgrimage like Walsingham in Norfolk, Compostella, Jerusalem or Canterbury, or worldly centres like London, Rome or Avignon (although these are also great ecclesiastical centres), these serve as sites on a map that is symbolic rather than geographical, aiming to clarify a theme or a point being made rather than locating an action to a specific spot. The places all carry symbolic or figural meaning and initiate strong associations that point to concepts as well as actual locations. It is another mental map that is meant to help clarify the internal journey, being an externalisation of the spiritual concerns.

This relates to memory systems where the images contain the meaning while the backgrounds are the vehicles that present the individual images within an ordered structure, linking all aspects of a topic together.

It may seem odd that so much has been written about the structure of *Piers Plowman*, and so much contentious analyses as well, when several structural forms are provided in the text, dividing it into logical sections. There is the division into eight visions which suggest there ought to be eight separate, self-contained ideas; or the prologue and the twenty following passus, indicating that twenty steps are to be taken along the way (*passus* = step); or even the basic division into the *visio* and the *vita*, the latter containing the quest for Dowel, Dobet and Dobest, which provides the two-part development of 'seeing' and then 'living' whatever is told. These divisions, however, are not necessarily part of Langland's own scheme, since no autograph manuscript or indeed any manuscript from his own lifetime is still extant.

However, none of these divisions of the text offer a helpful ordering structure for individual ideas or progressive concepts. They merely seem to be practical markers, dividing the text into manageable and semi-logical parts. Nevertheless, they all suggest that a certain progress is taking place rather than a mere listing of events: the passus suggests the medieval steps towards a higher understanding (as in the seven steps to wisdom of St Augustine or Isodore of Seville); the visions indicate that an elevated plane of insight is reached in these passages (as visions and dreams could be regarded as conveyors of messages from God in symbolic form); and the progress from the *visio* (the insight) to the *vita* (the life) supposes that visions can produce guidelines to follow in real life.

Whenever an attempt has been made to fit this progress into an exact numerical form, it has failed. Although Langland uses endless numerical structures (as listed under the mnemonics above) and often repeats them over and over again (the seven deadly sins appear in various guises at least seven times, the five senses at least five times, and the Trinity over and over again, and so on), no numerically limiting structure seems to apply to the text as a whole although many are part of its intricacy.[44]

Where numerical frameworks fail, the personifications succeed because they can represent the individual stages of the progress: not by symbolising each stage; but by expressing its function. For as Bloomfield writes, personifications "can

---

[44] The study of numerology, although highly relevant to this discussion, is too extensive to be sufficiently investigated here. Its influence in the Middle Ages is not disputed and certainly contributes to the highly organised schemes of memory systems. For general information about the topic, see for example, MacQueen, *Numerology: Theory and outline history of a literary mode* and Hopper, *Medieval Number Symbolism: Its sources, meaning, and influence on thought and expression*.

convey, with a directness not matched by concrete description, meaning and psychological states. [Furthermore, the author] can thus avoid unnecessary *amplificatio*".[45] The latter is also a guideline for memory work: in order to aid the function of memory, make the images simple in their appearance.

The stages travelled in the poem are those reached by a person who is on a journey of self-discovery within his own mind (the psychological states). The poem is an allegory of the process of learning, of how we can achieve knowledge and understanding. The castle of Truth is the symbol-allegory which most clearly presents a microcosm to the macrocosm of the entire poem's premise. But Langland not only narrates the process of learning, he also integrates the instruction on how to learn in the structure. Langland doesn't write a manual, as so many of his contemporaries did, but instead implements a heuristic teaching method. As the reader follows each passus, each vision, he must build up his own knowledge, must store in his memory each new step he takes, must appropriate the mental tools necessary for following the teaching. This approach not so much dictates as encourages the reader to play an active part in the reading of the text. The reader is asked to take in new pieces of information so as to get a more insightful understanding of existing knowledge: a delayed understanding of what is already known.

How this works is best described through the memory function necessary to obtain any kind of learning. As mentioned in chapter one, memory training was an unquestioned part of education in schools of the Middle Ages, from simple mnemonics to visualisations of complex memory systems. Langland consciously taps into this form of education in his poem, relying heavily on the readers' ability to create structures in their minds and attach images to them, often cross-referencing extensively between the individual structures. This would be one of the reasons why *Piers Plowman* has few enthusiastic readers today – we are not equipped to uphold such complex structures in our minds because we are not trained to do so. However, there are certain indications, both inside and outside the text, that suggest Langland's complexity was too expectant of the memory-skills of his contemporaries as well, as I shall explain below.

The function of the various personifications – which include Reason, Conscience, Thought, Study, Clergy, Scripture, Wit and Patience – within the process of learning has often been discussed, with various interpretations. I will concentrate on three which seem most closely linked to the memory function: Thought, Imaginative and Anima, although I would argue that all the others are also related to memory since memory is a necessary element in any form of mental activity – also as it was understood in medieval psychology.

The protagonist Will, who goes on the inner journey alongside the reader, meets Thought early on in the proceedings. The *visio* section has concluded with Piers'

---

45   *Piers Plowman as a Fourteenth Century Apocalypse*, p.22.

tearing of the pardon 'for pure tene' / in sheer anger (VII, 115), and with Will's comment on waking that this incident has made him 'studie' / ponder (VII, 144) the dream (the poem so far) and that it has made him 'pencif' / thoughtful (VII, 146). But Will acknowledges that he has 'no savour in songewarie' / no taste for interpreting dreams (VII, 149) because he so often sees these interpretations fail. Yet he continues to roam about searching for Dowel, as suggested by Piers, and meets two friars from whom he expects enlightenment. Instead, they enter into a dispute, initiated by Will, which ends with the friars using a 'forbisne' / parable (VIII, 29) to explain how even a faithful friar can sin the proverbial seven times a day and yet have Dowel as a constant companion, referring to *Proverbs* 24:16 which says that "a just man falleth seven times, and riseth up again: but the wicked shall fall into mischief". One of the friars gives a detailed interpretation of the parable in the simplest of terms, but at the end of it Will admits he has 'no kynde knowynge [...] to conceyve' / no natural understanding by which to take in (VIII, 57) what the meaning is. But he will continue looking (or in his words: 'live and look' – reminiscent of the vita/visio division in inverted order) to see whether he cannot find Dowel somewhere.

He comes to a pleasant spot, promptly falls asleep and instantly meets Thought, a tall man who looks just like Will and says he's been following him for seven years. When asked by Will to explain Dowel, Dobet and Dobest, Thought does so in straightforward, non-symbolic language, giving examples from actual life and hardly using figurative language. Although Will seems to have understood what is meant at a basic level, he is now dissatisfied with the explanation because Thought's words 'savoreth' him 'noght' / don't appeal to him (VIII, 109). He wants a more 'kynde knowyng / a more direct understanding (VIII, 110) of it, so Thought suggests Wit may be able to help. Will and Thought continue together for three days until they meet Wit, who takes over the instruction of Will.

I have described Passus VIII and the immediately preceding section extensively because it is in the details and wording of this part that the function of Thought is made explicit. As John Lawlor rightly points out, Langland here "gives us thinking rather than thought", the function rather than the faculty.[46] In simple terms: in this section Will is thinking about how to live in accordance with the Christian tenet that says one should 'do well'. Will is using his faculty of thought to try to answer this question and Langland is showing us the process of thinking with its aspirations and limitations: Will cannot *interpret* his dreams because he does not believe they are always truthful – or at least this is his excuse, although he, contradictorily, gives examples of successful dream interpretation from Scripture in the same passage. Will cannot *take in* the meaning of the parable, he doesn't have the knowledge required to understand it. And he is not satisfied with his own thoughts' simple description because it doesn't *appeal* to him. What Will lacks at this moment are both the mental tools with which to work out metaphors,

---

46   *Piers Plowman: An essay in criticism*, p.11.

or even images of the simplest kind, and the true commitment to apply them. However, he does have the will (as his name implies) to go on the journey to try to recover both, as is shown in the length of time stated (three days – another recurring numerical mnemonic) which Will spends with Thought (*in* thought) considering what he has heard.

Will, here, is right at the start of the mental journey of discovery and growing understanding. Up to this point the poem has dealt with its theme of how to gain salvation, how to live the right kind of life in accordance with the laws of God, on a general level. Now begins the education of the individual, and Will is the representative of the reader, who needs must go on the same mental journey if he wishes to comprehend what Langland is aiming to communicate.

What *are* the tools, then, that Will lacks and must obtain on his quest to a higher understanding? Each new mental faculty he meets will offer new ones, but already at the beginning, during the encounter with Thought, there are strong suggestions what they might be: the tools required to *interpret* symbolical images, to *take in* their meanings and to make the images that represent them *appealing* to the mind. All three are skills closely related to artificial memory processes and to the three phases of natural memory described in medieval psychology (take in, storage and retrieval). Whatever is to be remembered must first be *taken in* through sensory perception, but it will only stick in the mind, i.e., remain in storage, if the image is *appealing* (either because it is a visually stimulating image or a clear symbol of the thing itself) and finally, in order to make any sense of it at all, the ability to *interpret* the encoded signs and symbols is necessary if the memorised images are to be decoded and made useful when recalled.

So far Will has merely used his memory involuntarily to store whatever experiences happened to befall him. He now seeks to add to it, but is not sure what and how. Hence his following encounters with for example Wit, Clergy and Scripture all give him more material to store in his memory, but it is not until he meets Imaginative that Will's comprehension moves up another level. As Carruthers writes, Imaginative even scolds Will for filling up his mind with "extraneous and meaningless lore":[47] he has learned facts and methods, but not their application to his own life. In order to take this step, Will needs to employ his imagination and "Imaginatif, as the keeper of images, is the key to figural understanding".[48] Again, and more clearly because integrated into the name of the personification itself, we here have the function of imagining rather than the faculty of imagination. It is the action that must take place for Will to progress; the capacity to do so is already present.

Compared to the encounter with Thought, it is apparent that Will has changed in his attitude towards his own engagement and effort necessary to improve his understanding. When Imaginative walks away, having scolded him for being too

---

47   *The Search for St Truth*, p.102.
48   Ibid., p.104.

argumentative (too intent on scholastic debate) and therefore speaks when he should listen, Will acknowledges his own failing: not listening to Reason (whom he has just met in a dream within the dream). He even follows Imaginative and requests to know his name. Will is now taking an active part in his own education, making a physical effort to obtain the abilities which will further his search. In other words, he is artificially enhancing his ability to comprehend.

There is no description of Imaginative, but he, like Thought, has been following Will for years, forty-five in fact. Where Thought's seven years were equated with the first age of man by A.V.C. Schmidt, he now takes these forty-five to mean middle age,[49] and Nevill Coghill defines Imaginative as "the power of man in middle age, to see the images of memory in their true perspective".[50] Will has arrived at a time in his life when he must take stock and make changes if he wishes to guide his existence in the right direction. To express this, Langland uses an implicit reference to Augustine and Isodore of Seville's seven steps to wisdom, both of whom he mentions by name during the later encounter with Anima. Augustine emphasises that fear, and particularly the fear of death, the contemplation of one's own end, is a great impetus for questioning one's own spiritual achievements so far. It is the first step of a spiritual development which moves on through piety, knowledge, strength, counsel, purification of the eyes and finally to wisdom. It would be tempting to try to fit Langland's description of Will's mental progress into this shape because he emphasises intellect and wisdom in this passus and talks about the cleansing of the eyes necessary for perceiving higher wisdom. He also refers to several of the steps to wisdom, as well as making references to Augustine, Isodore and Gregory the Great, all of whom have written famous passages on these seven steps. However, as with any other classifying order, it does not fit very well. Aspects of it apply exactly to steps along the way, and the general idea is carried over into *Piers Plowman*, but Langland uses the conventional development only as another layer to add depth to his complex allegory.

In order to clarify this complex allegory, I return to my concept of the personifications as backgrounds and the images placed against them as carrying the real 'meaning'. Thought, the first background considered here, provides a "state preliminary to understanding", as James Simpson puts it.[51] The images placed against this background, both the encounter with Will and the explanation by Thought, state clearly the concerns of the poem in terms that are very simple, yet are not able to convey the full meaning. At this point the perplexing problem is formulated – thought of, in fact. It is the first step towards understanding. And the question, almost a cliché at this stage, is straightforward: 'how to be good?'

---

49   Translation of *Piers Plowman*, fn p.285 and p.302.
50   "The pardon of Piers Plowman", p.347.
51   *Piers Plowman: An introduction to the B-text*, p.101.

A definition of Imaginative has baffled critics for years. Its direct equation with memory, explained in 1914 by Jones by the fact that "memory is often synonymous with imagination",[52] fuelled the discussion of its exact allegorical significance, and descriptions vary from memory to "spokesman for reason" (R.W. Chambers and Joseph A. Longo) and from "a prophetic faculty" (Bloomfield) to "creative reflection" (Randolf Quirk).[53]

If considering the function rather than the faculty it represents, its meaning becomes clearer. Imaginative is "the mind's power for making similitudes" as Britton J. Harwood writes,[54] "the mind's image-making faculty," according to A.C. Spearing.[55] In Frank's words it is "the vertue imaginative" of Aristotle's definition "which organises and combines the images perceived by the outer senses, 'remembers' these sense impressions, and passes them on to reason for judgment".[56] Imaginative is therefore comparable to the first step of the memory process, the 'take in' (encoding) phase whether for creative thinking or the imagining of concepts. If Thought allows the question to be formulated, Imaginative enables the visualisation of the question in a more abstract form, prepares it for speculation and, according to Frank, for playing a fundamental role in the ability to make decisions. It is, therefore, imperative for the forming of a higher understanding.

THE IMAGES: METAPHORS AND FIGURES

The images placed against the backgrounds (the personifications) are expressed in the metaphors and the figurative language employed. With the encounter of Imaginative, and thereby the introduction of the making of images, we can take another step toward answering the question of 'how to be good', now using our imaginative faculty. In fact, Imaginative straight away challenges the reader's figural understanding by introducing himself in the form of a riddle: "I am Ymaginatif," he says, "ydel was I nevere, / Though I sitte by myself, in siknesse ne in helthe" (XII, 1–2).

Imaginative's answer to the question 'who are Dowel, Dobet and Dobest' is the simplest and most straightforward imaginable, and it is phrased without circumstance: they are Faith, Hope and Charity, the greatest of which is Charity. Will is chided for wasting his life on such a search because the answer is so simple and to be found in "bokes ynowe" / enough books (XII, 17) while Will "medlest thee with makynge" / dabbles in verse-making (XII, 16) when he could be saying his Psalter. Will is asking the wrong question, for each new character he

---

52   "Imaginatif in *Piers Plowman*", p.586, fn.8.
53   For lists of various definitions, see Wittig, "*Piers Plowman* B, Passus IX–XII", p.264 on *Piers Plowman* critics; and Chambers, *Man's Unconquerable Mind*, p.139, on imagination in Antiquity and in the Middle Ages.
54   "Imaginative in *Piers Plowman*", p.249.
55   *Medieval Dream-Poetry*, p.155.
56   *Piers Plowman and the Scheme of Salvation*, fn. to p.62 on 'Imaginatif'.

meets has a new explanation – but what they all have in common is that they are well-established tenets of the same thing. Hence Will knows the answer already, but he does not have the wherewithal to comprehend what lies behind these definitions. Therefore Imaginative, the faculty which allows us to make images and thereby holds "the key to figural understanding", does not go on to use images, complex figures and extensive metaphors as one might expect, because Will is not capable of understanding them yet. Instead, Imaginative goes back to basics, explaining the ground from which imaginative thinking can grow. In order to do so, he clarifies the distinction between book learning (Clergy) and natural knowledge (Kynde wit) and thereby indirectly that between artificial memory and natural memory: until Will understands this distinction, he won't understand Faith, Hope and Charity.

After Will has been left by Imaginative, he wanders "as a freke that fey were" / like a man sentenced to death (XIII, 2),[57] at his wits end, thinking about his dream. Imaginative has initiated the process that Will must undergo if he really wants to reach an understanding. He has taken the first of the seven steps towards wisdom which Augustine calls "the fear of death", the contemplation of one's own end which opens our minds to consider the wider questions about ourselves. Imaginative is a catalyst in the process of Will's mental development: he shows him what is lacking. Imaginative uses more imaginative language than Thought because it is in his nature, but it is not highly figurative or complex, as some critics would have it, to fit neatly with the definition of imagination. In fact, the language he uses is rather disappointing if we expect a visual spectacle. However, Imaginative is merely the station against which Will's progress is placed. The images express his true status: he is still very much at the beginning of his mental journey, but is slowly engaging the new tools he has been made aware of.

Imaginative's metaphor of the two men thrown in the Thames – one who has learned to swim, the other who hasn't – with which he explains the importance of learning to Will, has been criticised for its inappropriateness for the theme. Malcolm Godden even calls the swimming analogy "somewhat unconvincing (the ability is singularly unlike theological knowledge) and some of the other examples are nearly as dubious".[58] He may be right in so far that there are better analogies to communicate the concept of theological knowledge. But what if theological knowledge is not the concept Langland wants to convey? Imaginative is trying to teach a person who has little aptitude for figural or creative thinking, so he keeps his subject matter simple. He merely means to give a lifelike example to show how consciously acquired knowledge – learning by exercising a mental skill – can be extremely valuable, sometimes even life-saving. And he does so, induced by Will's pejorative attitude towards learning. The man who has learned how to swim will survive the fall into the Thames while the other one, who relies

---

57   In Schmidt's translation.
58   *The Making of Piers Plowman*, p.97.

on natural knowledge alone, will drown. At this stage Will must understand that learning, as well as natural knowledge, is invaluable. Individually, learning and natural understanding can be powerful, but together they can lead to the next level of comprehension, just as the training of artificial memory heightens the ability of the natural one.

However, they are merely tools, not the end in themselves, and Will must employ them both to gain better self-understanding. To express this, the figural symbol of the mirror is introduced. Again, this is not a complex example, for Will (and the reader) is being introduced gently to the possibilities of figural thinking. Imaginative urges Will to love both learning and natural knowledge, "[f]or bothe as mirours ben to amenden oure defautes" (XII, 95). So the true lesson to be learned through the encounter with Imaginative is not to think in images as might be expected, but to use book learning and physical experience as mirrors to reflect on ourselves. This is the next step towards 'doing well', this is the meaning contained within the images placed against the background of the imaginative skills which will allow this step to be taken.

It is not until Will meets Anima that the real explaining begins. Anima is a very different type of background to match the complexity of the images put against it. Anima is described as a fine substance without tongue or teeth, i.e., without any physical features, and no time span is given for his accompaniment of Will as was the case with Thought and Imaginative. The soul (Anima) is timeless, spaceless, it is eternal and the appropriate background for a spiritual question. Although this is the most abstract personification so far, it is probably the easiest to fathom. Possibly because it incorporates within it most of the personifications encountered previously in the text and does not rely on a detailed definition. Rather, Anima is a combination of the individual parts that the reader has already been acquainted with and which together make up the faculties of the human mind.[59] Langland again employs the seven steps to wisdom (plus one) to describe the function of Anima, with whom we have reached the highest form of understanding: wisdom. Again, this is the background for the next step in Will's development, and the images he is shown are meant to guide him towards this wisdom.

The central image placed against the background of the Anima-personification is the Tree of Charity, the final and most comprehensive figurative description of Dowel. (We remember, Charity was Imaginative's definition of the greatest of the 'Do's and the goal of Will's journey.) Passus XVI opens with Will thanking Anima for his 'faire shewyng' / magnificent discourse (XVI, 1), but he admits that he is still very confused about exactly what Charity really means (XVI, 3). Anima explains that Charity is a very special tree, its root is mercy, its trunk compassion and its name Patience. When Anima mentions Piers Plowman's name, under

---

59   Anima lists his names, i.e., his component parts, as Animus (intent), Mens (mind), Memoria (recollection), Ratio (reason), Sensus (understanding), Conscience, Amor (faithful love) and Spiritus (spirit) (XV, 23–36).

whose authority the tree is tended by *Liberum Arbitrium* (Free Choice), Will swoons and falls into a dream within the dream: he finds himself in the garden where the Tree of Charity grows. Here he meets Piers who takes over Anima's instruction of Will, explaining to him in detail the symbolism of the garden, the tree and its leaves and fruits and the three props (the Trinity) that uphold the tree, and with which Piers defends it from the Devil, who continuously attempts to steal its fruit. During one of these attacks Piers takes the prop that represents the Son of God and 'for pure tene' / in sheer rage (XVI, 86) – mirroring the words spoken by Piers as he tore the pardon in Passus VII – attacks the Devil with it. Both the repetition of the words and the use of the inner dream show that this is a climactic moment, and the scene metamorphises into a brief recounting of the life of Christ, starting with the annunciation and ending with a medievalised Christ jousting with the Devil and defeating him as he dies on the Cross.

One way that Langland has prepared the reader for this climactic moment is the constant revisiting of systems, concepts and ideas, each time on a higher level. These repetitions emphasise the spiral structure of the poem: just as Will asks the same question over and over again, each time with a greater understanding of the subject, so the poem revisits situations, symbolic images and topics, presenting them in ever more complex manifestations. These constant internal references are strongly linked to the figural-allegory technique. The Tree of Charity is one such figure which links the various layers of interpretation. From this point onwards the style changes to a highly spiritual level, moving amongst scenes from Scripture and other spiritual writings, not to be comprehended with one faculty alone, but requiring a combination of all foregone (collected in Anima) to allow interpretation. To the basic moral and allegorical reading of fourfold exegesis comes extensive use of typology (as part of the anagogical reading), and a four-dimensional setting is presented where past, present and future are melted into one time-frame through the figura of Piers, combining the Old and New Testament with the fourteenth-century plowman figure.[60]

The tree allegory is intricate and works on all levels of fourfold exegesis, but it is not difficult to interpret. The labels used to explain each detail are obvious and the relationship between the individual parts is clear. I won't go into them here as it would be too space-consuming and as the specific symbolism is not necessary to demonstrate the literary technique employed by Langland. Instead, I will look at *how* this image works. Why is it so significant and what makes it seem so difficult, even though its component parts are very straightforward? The answer lies in its mnemonic function which facilitates an interpretation that reaches beyond the text itself.

Margaret E. Goldsmith's comment that "this part of the poem is not to modern taste"[61] may be explained by the fact that we simply don't understand it. The tree

---

60   "Piers and the image of God in man", pp.153–5 and p.176.
61   *The Figure of Piers Plowman*, p.58.

figura "leads the reader's imagination in a number of different directions, which for the medieval reader would be largely controlled by the traditional associations of the figure", writes Ben H. Smith,[62] and thereby explains why it is so difficult for the modern reader to comprehend. He refers to the various trees that instantly were associated with any symbolic tree in the Middle Ages: the Tree of Knowledge, the Tree of the Virtues, the genealogical Tree of Jesse, the tree of Adam's descendants and the Tree of life or the Cross of Christ. Not all of these are activated in Langland's allegory, but they are all available to the medieval reader, who can build up a palimpsest picture in his mind. And this picture is created through "associations" in the "imagination". What clearly is required here is a well-functioning memory. We, as readers, must recall items stored in our memory and linked by association to a particular topic, brought to our attention through visualisation (image-making). And this is where the modern reader usually fails. At the same time, this presents the greatest challenge to Langland.

To be able to convey meaning through symbols and allegory in the text, an author presupposes that a specific image will initiate a certain chain of thought. We can see that Langland expects the reader to bring a specific fount of knowledge to the text, a store of linking images which can be accessed, relatively automatically, when certain keywords/symbols are produced. When Mercy says, "that was tynt thorugh tree, tree shal it wynne" / a tree would be the means of regaining what was lost because of a tree (XVIII, 140), he uses the keyword 'tree' to activate the chain of tree images. But here the Tree of Charity, seemingly an original concept created by Langland, is added to this conventional chain of trees, so that we get the tree in Eden, the tree of Charity and the cross of Christ. The Tree of Charity is thus the combining link between the commonplace comparison of the Fall and the Crucifixion. 'Combining' in the sense that two physical events unite to express the elevated meaning – namely the intangible and fundamental Christian quality of charity; hence, the answer to how to 'do well' is presented by linking it with Scriptural progress, showing the concept of salvation and charity in its active emanation rather than its intellectual sense.

By presenting the Tree of Charity in an inner dream, Langland uses a visual aid, i.e., the division of the text on the page: a practical 'sectioning off' which not only signposts a new episode, but places it at a more central point, going inwards. This is an indirect instruction from Langland to the reader to peel back another layer of meaning – to follow the chain of memory one step further. From the simple cognitive action of linking one tree image to another in a way that was familiar, he is now asking the reader to attach a new image to this chain: the Tree of Charity. And this is possible because it relates to the existing images in several ways. Obviously the basic tree image makes this possible, but is in itself not enough to engender a new, separate memory item. So Langland creates a three-dimensional plane (the garden) into which the image is positioned and to which

---

62   *Traditional Imagery of Charity in Piers Plowman*, p.59.

many related concepts, like the Trinity (the props), the moral reading (the fruit) and the allegorical reading (the tree planted in the heart of man), are integrated to strengthen this new link in the chain of trees similarly related to these topics.

MNEMONIC STRUCTURES

The Tree of Charity is only one of many figural instances which bind the various layers of the tale, the individual spirals of the structure, to each other, emphasising the movement upwards as well as forwards. The simplest technique employed by Langland to strengthen the structure is the repetition of basic symbols/images. Even words have an "architectural function" according to Bernard F. Huppé.[63] Each time these recur, a further layer of meaning is added. This is where the lists, the basic mnemonic structures, come into their own. As mentioned above, they recur in several places – like the seven deadly sins – but each time with a more complex symbolism attached.

Also the Trinity is mentioned repeatedly, reaching its culmination of profundity in the two metaphors of the hand and the torch in Passus XVII when we as readers must use the highest skills of interpretation, a kind of decoding and a skill acquired during the active reading of the text.[64] Another instance is the building: from the two castles of respectively Flesh and Truth to the Barn of Christianity, even the earliest contains the potential for the full interpretation of the final instance. And, on a tangent, the building's spiritual value is revisited in the name of the good Samaritan's horse: "Caro" (xvii) refers back to the Castle of Caro, symbolically expressing the idea that caro (flesh) is the vehicle living creatures have been giving to advance in the physical world (on horseback in the case of the good Samaritan) – but it is the actions, not the flesh that ultimately count.

These forwards- and backwards-looking references are not always easy to follow, but Coghill suggests that "the disorder" we as readers may feel "is often less [Langland's] than ours. Allegorical thinking needs practice".[65] There are indications, though, that not only readers of the following centuries, but also Langland's contemporaries had some difficulty in following his complex ideas. This is indicated by the alterations made to the C-text at the most intricate parts of the poem, like the Tree-of-Charity episode: here Anima is taken out of the scene and replaced by *Liberum Arbitrium* (Free Choice), most of the inner dream is omitted and the change into the inner dream preceding it in the B-text is entirely missing. If we accept that these are in fact Langland's own alterations, they provide a basis for the assumption that Langland was not satisfied with the previous version. I suggest that the reason for his displeasure was that his own

---

63   "Petrus id est Christus", p.164.
64   Particularly the hand is an effective mnemonic image, its different parts supplying individual locations in which the various aspects can be placed, and each location, furthermore, containing the attributes of the item to be remembered.
65   "The pardon of Piers Plowman", p.313.

contemporaries did not react to the text as he had intended, that the text was interpreted entirely contrary to the author's wishes. Langland sensed he had failed to make himself understood – maybe his figural allegories were too challenging for the general reader. And maybe mnemonic systems were less intensely taught by the time Langland was writing.

However, I agree with Schmidt that the alterations in the C-text, where the indication of the onset of an inner dream is excluded, bring with them a fundamental loss of comprehension to the complex structure of the poem.[66] Maybe Langland listened to advice from readers who were incapable of following the step into the inner dream. They couldn't make the implied connections and urged the author to simplify the structure – ill advice which Langland nevertheless might have taken, in his wish for clarity. If this be the case, if contemporaries suggested the second inner dream did not work as a technique for clarification, then we must also conclude that the author possibly expected too much of his readers, and that the creative memory activity necessary for a comprehension of Langland's concepts was not as developed in his readers as he might have expected. Langland's intrinsic thought processes could probably not be followed by all, maybe not even by the majority of his readers. As Goldsmith writes, "the reader requires extrinsic knowledge for full appreciation of what is going on (though some mystification might suit the poet's book). Even in his own time, there must have been many readers who could not follow the hidden sense."[67] What she calls 'extrinsic knowledge' could also be called 'memorised information stored away and available in the reader's memory'. However, a mystification that provides a mystic atmosphere seems to go against the entire grain of the poem where no 'hidden meaning' is meant to remain hidden. Instead, Langland seems to attempt to demystify the topic by showing the reader how to gain access to the meaning which is not easily accessible.[68]

Although memory is not a directly targeted topic in *Piers Plowman*, it is certainly a skill readers *must* bring to the text if they wish to be able to follow it,

---

66   "The inner dream in *Piers Plowman*".
67   *The Figure of Piers Plowman*, p.69.
68   The employment to which the character of Piers was put in the Peasants' Revolt of 1381 may have been an added incentive for Langland to make changes to the text. It is not certain whether the Piers mentioned in John Ball's letter refers to Langland's poem. Although Godden takes Ball's phrase 'do wel and bettre' that relates to the Peres Ploughman mentioned there as a clear indication that "Ball was indeed thinking of Langland's poem" (*The Making of Piers Plowman*, p.17), the figure of Piers the good worker may well have existed before, and therefore independently of Langland's poem. Nevertheless, Schmidt suggests the possibility "that Langland was filled with horror and alarm at the misinterpretation of his work as a call to overthrow the social and religious order by violent means" ("Introduction", p.xv). Were this the case, it would be conceivable that Langland chose to write a new version which emphasised mercy, love and charity, and therefore attempted to make the allegory of the Tree of Charity more accessible to his readers; albeit thereby losing (quite a substantial) part of the underlying structure – and therefore clarity – of the entire poem.

passus by passus. The implicit heuristic seems to teach how one can take the next step by building on the previous one, retaining each step in the memory so as to climb the ladder without losing the foundation it has been placed upon in order to reach heaven, truth, understanding, etc. In a popular phrase of the Middle Ages: if we know more and can see farther than our ancestors, it is because we are dwarfs standing on the shoulders of giants, building on existing knowledge to reach ever greater heights of understanding.

If the reader doesn't remember what went before, she will not be able to make any sense of what follows; therefore, it must have been in Langland's interest, and I argue it was a conscious effort, to make the instances as memorable as possible without becoming extravagant and still suit the memorable images to the subject matter. One of the ways in which Langland aims to aid the reader in following the winding (in fact, spiral) tale is to employ many (then) familiar mnemonic lists, presumably already securely anchored in the mind. To these he adds new lists, for example the personifications which create a fertile ground for innovative thinking. Langland also makes alterations to established mnemonic lists (like the seven steps to wisdom mentioned above) and thereby activates existing memory systems in his reader's mind, but simultaneously extends their significance, freeing the reader from the restraints of limiting conventional thought. The reader must take an active part while reading. This is true of all texts, but particularly of Langland's poem. The creative imagination must be employed in order to follow the story because its structure hinges on the interweaving of images.

J.F. Goodridge practically describes the act of creative thought when he writes that "Langland's form of allegory reorganizes human experience according to new patterns. The cells of the dreamer's thoughts and perceptions keep dividing and coming together again and again around fresh nuclei".[69] And what is true of the dreamer (i.e., Will) is also true for the reader because Langland takes existing patterns (the mnemonics and common religious concepts) and reorganises, rearranges them. However, I would argue that the nucleus always remains the same. The author returns to the same question again and again, but each time from a different angle which allows a fresh view of the matter. Thereby creating what J.S. Wittig calls a "network of perspectives".[70]

The complexity that ensues from such a composite picture has frequently been criticised, claiming that the many asides, deviations and additional information which do not exactly fit into the main line of thought show a disorganisation in the mind of the author. But this, also, can be related to the architectural mnemonic. As Carruthers writes: "[t]he abundance of small sculptures in a cathedral like Chartres never detracts from the logically articulated movement of the building as a whole".[71] Likewise, Langland's structure is secure, the individual

---

69   "Introduction" to Goodridge's translation of *Piers Plowman*, p.16.
70   "*Piers Plowman* B, Passus IX–XII", p.278.
71   *The Search for St Truth*, p.23.

stations obvious despite the very vivid, lively activity which surrounds them. This certainly makes the memorising harder, just as a very crowded memory palace creates distractions in the memory function. But it seems that Langland's aim *is* to distract from the obvious. In his search for a clearer and clearer definition of how to live the right kind of life, he disturbs the established patterns of thought, breaking them open to allow for new thoughts to be added and thereby create a truer perception. This, too, is a definition of creative thinking – the highest aim of artificial memory techniques.

What we may call our modern-day inability to follow sustained allegory could in more rhetorical terms be called our lack of ability in flexing the memory muscle – we have not learned how to engage our storage faculty in such a way that we can easily retrieve relevant bits of information. We have not been taught how to develop automatic activation of memorised elements, for example by linking items together, so that we subconsciously activate and remember corresponding material and combine them with the new impulses we are receiving from a text.

Although Langland's use of images, symbols and personifications are prevalent throughout the text, they are not decidedly chosen to teach us how to use our memory. We, as readers, are supposed to have already acquired the tools whereby we can store information and ideas. Langland is merely being helpful in supplying images that will feed happily into our (supposedly well-functioning) memory systems. The ability to read allegory therefore relies heavily on a developed faculty of memory. Langland requires his reader to think creatively at a very high level. This is what makes him comparable to modern innovative writers, particularly those employing complex systems and seemingly unconventional models and images in their work, such as post-modern writers of magic realism.

The treatment of Langland's poem above demonstrates that the two memory features, the narrative structure and the iconic image, are not mutually exclusive. Rather, they are mutually beneficial and used in combination produce the greatest effect. This is because both features use the technique of delayed decoding. For an image to be comprehended it is required to run through three phases in the memory: taking in, storing and eventually decoding; becoming aware of the image and comparing it to already existing ones, making sense of it by associating it to impressions already stored in the memory. A narrative structure, too, will only reveal its meaning in retrospect, seen as a whole, and one must go through the process to understand it, decoding the overall meaning when the story is concluded. The icon as symbolic object and the structure as divisional space are turned into the textual image and the literary narrative in storytelling.

Before investigating the role that memory systems play in modern literature, I will look at how the concept of memory has changed over the centuries in order to establish the relevance of my approach for literary texts that, unlike medieval narratives, do not consciously employ memory systems as literary tools.

Chapter 3

Modern Memory Concepts
Neuropsychology and Literary Theory

In the 1920s the Soviet psychologist A.R. Luria encountered the newspaper reporter Schereschewsky whose memory seemingly "had no limits".[1] Over the following forty-odd years he performed many tests with this extraordinary man, who came to be known as S., and documented not only the vast capacity of his memory, but also the techniques he used for memorisation. It became clear that S. relied extensively on the technique of association: visualising what he heard or read, and placing the items in settings which helped him organise them. Hence a table of numbers would be visualised on a blackboard in a grid, or a list of items placed along backgrounds on a walk through Moscow. The technique was not one he had learned from the ancient art of memory, despite resembling it in many aspects. It was a logical progression from his natural, involuntary way of 'seeing' everything he heard, instantly, including every sound (*synesthesia*) – often to the detriment of his comprehension of the concept as a whole.

When asked by Luria to recall a list of words fifteen or sixteen years after the initial memory experiment

S. would sit with his eyes closed, pause, then comment: 'Yes, yes ... This was a series you gave me once when we were in your apartment ... You were sitting at the table and I in the rocking chair ... You were wearing a gray suit and you looked at me like this ... Now, then, I can see you saying ...' and with that he would reel off the series precisely as I had given it to him at the earlier session.[2]

By recalling his environments in detail, by placing the participants against the correct backgrounds and visualising particular aspects of their apparel, the full memory is restored. S. is the modern version of the classical Simonides, the presumed inventor of the art of memory, who also recalled information by returning in the mind to the setting where the event took place and relying on the organisation of this picture to release the correct items from memory: relying on backgrounds and images.

The case of S. shows that the ancient memory palace system is based on natural memory functions which create images in the mind in order to aid retention of the information. When S. turned professional mnemonist, earning his living by showcasing his extraordinary memory, he used artificial memory techniques more often. These, however, were merely extensions of those he had used automatically all his life. The rules he developed for his techniques through

---

1   Luria, *The Mind of a Mnemonist*, p.11.
2   Ibid.

experience – through trial and error – very much recall those laid down almost 2000 years before by the author of the *Rhetorica ad Herennium*. For example, when using the journey method to memorise a list of items

> he would 'distribute' them along some roadway or street he visualised in his mind. Sometimes this was a street in his home town, which would also include the yard attached to the house he had lived in as a child and which he recalled vividly. On the other hand, he might also select a street in Moscow. Frequently he would take a mental walk along that street – Gorky Street in Moscow – beginning at Mayakovsky Square, and slowly make his way down, 'distributing' his images at houses, gates, and store windows.[3]

The mistakes he made on recalling the items encountered on this journey were not mistakes of forgetting, but rather of 'omission':

> If S. had placed a particular image in a spot where it would be difficult for him to 'discern' – if he, for example, had placed it in an area that was poorly lit or in a spot where he would have trouble distinguishing the object from the background against which it had been set – he would omit this image when he 'read off' the series he had distributed along his mental route. He would simply walk on 'without noticing' the particular item, as he explained.[4]

In order to avoid such 'omissions', he might place a street lamp near the object to add light to the scene or choose a background which differed in colour from the item to make it stand out more – complying with the rules regulating the choice of backgrounds in the *Rhetorica ad Herennium*.

Although S. was an unusual man with an abnormal memory capacity, his case may yet throw light upon the workings of the brain in general. It is especially apt for my backgrounds-and-images approach as it documents a modern application of the rhetorical system, albeit based on a natural rather than an artificial memory.

We still know little about the exact functions of the brain and the part that memory plays within it, but we have a much better idea than those writing at the time of the *Rhetorica ad Herennium* or when its ideas were adapted for use in the Middle Ages. Since I base my entire theory of literary interpretation on the analogue states of memory processes, defined in the ancient backgrounds-and-images system, and the creative thinking involved in producing narrative in fiction, it is necessary to discover whether current memory theories make the comparison feasible. One question must be asked with regard to our modern understanding of how the memory works: how does classical/medieval memory psychology compare with modern neuropsychology of memory, and is the backgrounds-and-images system still relevant in our new perception of how the memory functions?

---

3   Ibid., p.32.
4   Ibid., p.35.

The most common concept in medieval psychology of how memory works, we recall, is the tripartite division of the brain: according to this model the imagination is located in the foremost cell or part of the brain where sensory input is received and made into images, the middle cell uses reason to judge the validity of these sense-impressions in image form, while the final cell at the back of the head contains the memory where the images representing the sensory impressions are stored for later retrieval (see Ch.1). Today there is no complete consensus about how the memory works, especially since different disciplines use very different methods of investigation: neurology uses the new inventions regarding neuroimaging, 'photographing' the impulses sent out during memory activity; psychology experiments with test persons and researches psychological illness; philosophy evaluates the new discoveries paired with theory which allows for extensive excursions into ontological questions. Often the disciplines overlap, making it impossible to determine which category a given topic falls under.[5] For the sake of this investigation, I will attempt a brief summary – a lay description – of the positions which the first two hold regarding memory functions at the time of writing.

Neuropsychology

Two main schools of thought regarding memory function can be distinguished by the emphasis they place on the memory as either being made up of 'systems' or 'processes'. Those who employ the systems-approach (such as Endel Tulving) explain the memory by attributing particular brain functions to particular areas of the brain (i.e., mapping the brain by isolating the various systems), while those who prefer the process-approach (including Henry L. Roediger) believe that there are "similarities in performance factors across tasks",[6] in other words, that it is not possible to designate specific brain functions to specific areas since a variety of sites are activated during memory processes.

A related argument, but not a direct subcategory of the above, deals with the question how memories are 'stored' and 'retrieved' (although these terms can be misleading, as will be seen). This is the aspect which interests us here. I call the

---

5   Markowitsch lists seven modern methods of cognitive research: "Verhaltensbeobachtung und -analyse, neuroanatomische und biochemische Methoden, Läsionsmethoden, Hirnreizung und Hirnselbstreizung, elektrophysiologische Methoden ("neuro-monitoring"), bildgebende Verfahren ("neuro-imaging") und neuropsychologische Verfahren." Furthermore, he notes that "in vielen Wissenschaftsbereichen konvergieren mit zunehmender Erkenntnis zuvor konträre Ansichten. Hierzu trägt sicher auch bei, dass die Vielfalt der Analysemethoden, mit denen das Gehirn untersucht werden kann, in den letzten Jahren einen enormen Aufschwung genommen hat." This encourages interdisciplinary approaches, such as my method of interpretation that uses concepts of how the memory works as analogues to concepts about the creation of visual worlds in literary fiction. *Dem Gedächtnis auf der Spur*, p.76.

6   Parkin, "Component process versus systems", p.282.

opposed views the 'engram' and the 'pattern activation' views. The engram view is reminiscent of the systems-approach in that it suggests that items to be remembered are stored in one particular place in the brain from which they can be retrieved. It leans on the metaphor of the brain as a computer: information data is input, then stored in a memory cell from where it can be retrieved by following the same route for decoding that was used for encoding during the initial phase of memorising.[7]

Pattern activation, on the other hand, in extension of the process-approach, suggests that it is not the exact location of each individual item which produces a memory, but instead the reactivation of a pattern which was first created when the original memory entered the mind, with all its associations; its context. Hence, when we remember the occupation of a new acquaintance, we don't merely remember the most important details, like his face or his name, but that we sat by the beach when we were given the information, on a white bench with a glass of red wine in our hand, the sun burning on the back of the neck, the light breeze making it a pleasant heat, the smell of the sea, the taste of the wine, the time of day, the activity in the background where a children's circus was putting up its tent and the jovial comment of the fish-vendor who also sold us the wine. All these pieces of information are stored, but not in isolation. Each of them has created a new synapse – a connection that momentarily closes the gap between two neurons. When several of these connections are activated simultaneously, the reactivation of the pattern, that was formed during the original experience, will bring back the entire situation. This is often referred to as a network rather than a storage facility.[8]

PATTERN OR NETWORK

The above does not mean that a systems-led thinker cannot support the pattern activation theory or that a supporter of the engram view cannot be convinced by the process-approach. When judging the outcome of a systems/process debate in an essay collection created for that purpose, Alan J. Parkin points out that he is "not convinced that component process and system theorists are really saying anything radically different" because "both approaches seem to seek the same criteria for establishing their existence by testing for functional independence at task level and looking for neural substrates".[9] He suggests that it is a case of

---

7   The German biologist Richard Semon coined the term 'engram' in 1904 to describes the cumulative encoding and storage of an enduring memory trace. In Markowitsch's glossary the engram is called a *Gedächtnisspur* and described as "[d]as Produkt der erfolgreichen Ablagerung von Informationen of Hirnebene. Die alten Griechen hatten die Vorstellung einer Wachstafel, in die sich die Information eingraviert", *Dem Gedächtnis auf der Spur*, p.179. This is compatible with the attempt to locate remembered items in particular sites in the brain.
8   See, e.g., McClelland, "Connectionist models of memory" which inclines towards the network-conception of memory processes.
9   "Component processes versus systems", pp.285–6.

placing emphasis on one or another aspect of the same argument. It is, therefore, possible to compare their theories to ancient concepts of memory: both modern approaches employ the neural network as a basic principle, which is reminiscent of the backgrounds-and-images system that relies on an interplay of several items located in relation to each other in space.

The greatest difference between the 'old' and the 'new' concepts of memory is surely that the latest discoveries have prompted scientists and theorists alike to turn away from a basic dichotomy of the system, which persisted for a long time, and which still dominates the general perception despite the recent developments within modern research. The simple division of the brain into two parts – be they long-term and short-term memory, the clinical dissection between left and right brain hemispheres or the psychological distinction between episodic and semantic memory – no longer suffices as a model for how the memory works. Although each definition is still valuable for explaining brain functions, they are now seen as part of a much more complex organisational structure. A strict dichotomy of the brain into two areas would obscure the understanding of how it works by oversimplifying the matter.

The tripartite division of the memory in earlier days falls under this restrictive simplifying aspect. But just as it is still helpful to use left and right brain hemisphere outlines as the springboard to more complex considerations about the mind, so the three cells of memory – though not scientifically correct – are helpful general divisions in discussing the subject, especially since the functions attributed to each show many similarities with modern neuroscience. The various faculties fulfil the same functions now as then: they take in sense-impressions, create images through association, use common sense or logic to make decisions or solve problems, and store information and retain it to be retrieved at a later date, to name only some of the functions still under investigation in modern memory research.

A SHARED TERMINOLOGY

This investigation is primarily interested in artificial memory. The physiological mapping of the memory is, therefore, secondary to my topic. To stay within the confines of my argument, I will use discoveries about the workings of the natural memory as an indication of why artificial systems work, concentrating on the lines of memory research that help to clarify the way we structure, visualise and process memories. Specifically, I will look at the techniques that enhance memory by placing images against backgrounds in an ordered sequence, as expressed in the *Rhetorica ad Herennium*. In chapter two I showed how this system could be used to shed light upon narratives by medieval writers. In order to do the same with modern texts (in chapters four and five), I need to establish the validity of the backgrounds-and-images memory technique in relation to our understanding of memory function today. Only if they align can the adaptation of one to the other be successful.

Literary criticism and the science of neurotransmission share a terminology, especially a use of metaphors, that provides the basis for a comparative approach. Douwe Draaisma describes neural function as follows:

> The route taken by a pattern through the [neural] network is determined by the thresholds and strength connections, the mathematical equivalents of the grooves which previous patterns have worn in the network. It is this configuration of grooves that contains the record of experience which has been processed by the network and which is denoted in connectionist literature as 'memory'.[10]

He could as well be referring to the 'route' taken through the artificial memory, depending on the 'thresholds and strength connections' created in the imaginary memory palace which houses the memories, the capacity of which is increased with the regular retracing of the steps along the route: the more often the journey has been taken; the easier the memory is recalled. Already Descartes in the seventeenth century referred to the concept of *facilitation* described above. Facilitation, in the words of the psychologist William James, relates to the fact that "nerve currents propagate themselves easiest through those tracts of conduction which have been already most in use".[11] Or as a teacher of rhetoric from Antiquity would put it: practice, practice, practice. The backgrounds-and-images system relies on the same aspects that strengthen natural memory processes, building on the already existing ability to remember.

The theoretical physicist J.J. Hopfield suggests that a pattern activation network guides memory storage and retrieval. He says that patterns created by synaptic connections through sensory impressions can be called an artificial memory,[12] thereby equating natural and artificial memory. If we compare the terminology used to describe the process of facilitation in Draaisma and James' quotations with language used to describe the artificial memory system set in three-dimensional space, we find that they can be used to describe the main rules of artificial memory: memories are activated (recalled) more easily the more the "tracts of conduction" (memory journeys) have been exercised (traversed in the imagination). The terminology used above to talk about neural memory transmission is largely interchangeable with that of artificial memory. We talk about routes, pathways, circuits and chains when we explain how the memory works in neurological studies as well as in memory systems and both make connections between the individual stages. The memory item placed within a context in the neural network is comparable to the memory image placed within an organising structure, such as a palace or a journey.

---

10   Draaisma, *Metaphors of Memory*, p.204.
11   Discussed in James' *Principles of Psychology*, mentioned by Draaisma in *Metaphors of Memory*, p.204.
12   Hopfield, "Neural networks and physical systems with emergent collective computation ability", mentioned by Draaisma in *Metaphors of Memory*, pp.191–2.

A shared terminology, however, does not prove a shared function. So what does modern neuroscience say to the creation of ordered backgrounds? In general the concept of organising information into manageable bits is emphasised, be it through the limiting of items to be remembered, as in George A. Miller's seminal essay "The magical number 7 ± 2", or through the arrangement of items within a structure, which is often discussed in relation to spatial awareness.

Miller suggests that, for some unexplained reason, the number of items which seem to stick most easily in the mind on average are seven plus/minus two. He, therefore, proposes that larger numbers of items to be memorised should be subdivided, so that no individual group is larger than the number between nine and five which a person finds most effective. We may, for example, end up with seven main categories which each contain seven items, thereby enlarging our memory capacity from seven to forty-nine (7 x 7). He calls this ordering process "chunking", which has entered common memory terminology.[13]

This technique complements the rules regulating the choice of backgrounds in the art of memory. The *Rhetorica ad Herennium* author suggests a signpost at every fifth site to aid retention and emphasises that each person must erect the memory palace according to their own memory capacity, choosing its size and number of individual backgrounds to suit their ability. Interestingly, in many mnemonic lists that use image-to-number associations (peg-words or numerals) examples of those numbering seven abound. This, of course, also has its source in the numerological value of seven, especially with regard to its many religious connotations. But were the significance associated with a number really the determining factor for how often that particular length of memory list was used, then lists of ten (the Commandments) or twelve (the apostles) ought to appear much more frequently. Instead, lists of five, seven and nine occur extremely often – in complete concordance with Miller's proposition.[14]

With regard to the spatial awareness necessary for creating a memory palace, systems- and process-theorists seem to agree that a setting aids recall. In fact, the

---

13   "The magical number seven", p.93. Interestingly, Ebbinghaus, with whom modern memory research is said to have begun in 1885, independently discovered that seven was also the number of items he could most easily remember. His ability to remember, therefore, coincides exactly with the average number of items, despite the fact that he was highly involved in investigations into the topic and had presumably trained his memory by partaking in many memory tests. Mentioned in Draaisma, *Why Life Speeds Up As You Get Older*, p.6.

14   Some reasons for the proliferation of the number seven can be found in Hopper, *Medieval Number Symbolism*, where he investigates its significance as an astrological, Christian, Gnostic, philosophical and Pythagorean number. Its popularity amongst medieval or classical memory practitioners has not been documented. On the basis of Miller's proposition, that seven is the number of items most people find helpful when trying to remember a list of things, such an investigation might reveal that memory techniques had influenced ancient and medieval choices of the number seven.

neuroscientist Edmund Roll writes that "whenever memories are stored, part of the context is stored with the memory".[15] This should not come as a surprise to anyone: we know from experience that one memory rarely occurs in isolation (we may recall a person, the surroundings, the topic of discussion and the atmosphere all at once). It also confirms ancient memory techniques based on natural memory functions that incorporate a context for the memory in order to strengthen it.

Waagner's self-experiment, for which he wrote down his personal experiences in a diary for four years, shows the benefits of including contextual information to increase the chances of recall: he prompted his memory by asking circumstantial questions such as 'who?', 'what?', 'where?' or 'when?' about the events he tried to recall several years after they had taken place. This proved more helpful than concentrating on one specific memory. On those occasion when his memory failed to recall the wanted situation, prompting from others who had attended the same event, and therefore could add further circumstantial details, helped him recover the memories he thought had been forgotten irrevocably.[16] This suggests that an experience which we cannot recall, and which may seem wiped entirely from the memory, merely needs the right kind of stimuli to bring back not only the one specified item or event, but the entire setting in which it was first observed or took place.

The significance of placement is made apparent in experiments relating to spatial awareness and memory in which two groups of test persons are asked to remember a number of items. One group is simply shown the objects lying together in the same spot, while another group views the items spread out across the available space in neatly distinguishable positions. Test persons of the second group show a greater retention of items than test persons who are not given the added spatial condition. This suggests that adding the third dimension to a memory task does, in fact, increase memory capacity.

Tversky writes that the experimental evidence available "supports the view that mental spaces are mental constructs, consisting of elements and the spatial relation among them. Elements may be objects, people, landmarks, regions, cities, and so forth. Elements are coded and remembered relative to each other and relative to reference frames."[17] Not only do we need to think in three-dimensional space in order to improve our memory capacity, the way we organise this space also resembles the physical representation of it in which objects help to measure distances and provide structural organisation, in Tversky's terms reminiscent of a landscape populated by tangible items, including people. She not only describes the artificial memory system, but also an author's creation of an imaginary world – settings (regions, cities) in which characters (people) find themselves relating to

---

15   From *The Brain and Emotion*, (1999), quoted by Nalbantian in "The almond and the seahorse", in *Memory in Literature*, p.140.
16   Schacter, *The Seven Sins of Memory*, p.33.
17   "Remembering spaces", p.364.

each other and the space around them (reference frames), guided by conspicuous images (objects, landmarks).

Baddeley and Lieberman undertook an experiment designed to investigate whether the control process "in forming, manipulating and utilizing images" was spatial or visual. The experiment was partly based on the ancient backgrounds-and-images system. This part of the experiment yielded a secondary result which shows that a relation exists between spatial awareness and memory capacity. In this part of the experiment university students were asked to use the journey method to remember a list of things. They were asked to visualise themselves placing ten objects in ten designated locations on the university campus. Results show that this simple exercise clearly aids memory, and the experimenters conclude that for these kinds of memory test the placement of objects against backgrounds linked by a journey is helpful.[18]

CRITICISM OF THE ANCIENT ART OF MEMORY

Despite acknowledging the potential of the system, Baddeley does not consider it practical for everyday memory purposes. It is somewhat surprising that exactly those scholars who use the ancient art of memory most openly seem to add an emphatic statement distancing themselves from the backgrounds-and-images system. Tversky, when referring to the system as described by Yates in *The Art of Memory*, says that "although remembering locations of places may not be completely effortless or perfect, it is certainly relatively easy", doing away with it as a simple mnemonic of limited value.[19] Baddeley's comment on the value of the system is more openly critical. He writes:

With one or two exceptions [...] mnemonic systems are typically not particularly helpful in remembering the sort of information which one requires in everyday life. They are, of course, excellent for learning the strings of unrelated words which are so close to the hearts of experimental psychologists, but I must confess that if I need to remember a shopping list, I do not imagine strings of sausages festooned from my chandeliers and bunches of bananas sprouting from my wardrobe. I simply write it down.[20]

He is referring to an example he has given earlier to explain the backgrounds-and-images system: to make a mental shopping list, Baddeley writes, you should imagine yourself distributing the required items throughout your house; this will then enable you to recall them at the shop by mentally walking through your house, encountering each required item in turn.

This description, as well as the critical comment above, occur in the chapter on mnemonics and mnemonists which suggests that Baddeley, like many previous critics of the architectural memory system, relates the technique to ostentatious

---

18   Baddeley, *The Psychology of Memory*, pp.231–2.
19   "Remembering spaces", p.365.
20   *The Psychology of Memory*, p.369.

memory feats, to a 'showing off' which in effect is merely a parroting of collected pieces of information and, hence, too complicated to be helpful in everyday life. Its helpfulness in everyday life confines itself to the "learning of strings of unrelated words which are so close to the hearts of experimental psychologists", writes Baddeley, having a good-humoured go at his peers who use that approach. Baddeley fails to make the connection between spatial mnemonics and creative thinking, possibly because he applies the skill to short-term rather than long-term memory: a shopping list only requires the use of the short-term memory. This omission seems to be based on his assumption that memory systems are only useful in instances when things to be remembered cannot be written down in a list. He is here pointing to Yates' statement that mnemonics lost their usefulness with the disappearance of the oral society – a proposition which has been convincingly disputed by Carruthers since (see Ch.1).

Coincidentally, some psychologists use the mnemonic practices in their works, praising their effect without acknowledging that that is what they are doing. Daniel Schacter, for example, uses the basic mnemonic principle of "chunking" and association through peg-words to structure his entire work. *The Seven Sins of Memory* takes its title from the breakdown of the topic, the organisation of which is described by the author as follows:

[I had] brought together everything I knew about memory's imperfections and attempted to impose some order on a vast array of lapses, mistakes, and distortions. I generated a variety of unsatisfactory schemes for conceptualising these diverse observations, but eventually hit on a way of thinking that helped to make everything fall into place.

I propose that memory's malfunctions can be divided into seven fundamental transgressions or "sins" [...] Just like the ancient seven deadly sins, the memory sins occur frequently in everyday life and can have serious consequences for all of us.[21]

Not only does Schacter use the number seven – the 'magical' number which experiments have proven to be the number of pieces of information most easily remembered – he also links his seven categories of forgetting to the seven sins, which are perfect for creating very vivid mental images. He even uses a simile: memory sins are like the seven deadly sins as both 'frequently occur in everyday life and can have serious consequences'. Schacter has, indeed, found a perfect categorisation for his information that can serve as a powerful memory aid to his readers. If one were to go further and link each item from one group with one from the other, using the ancient art of memory for adding items to an existing list by combining the images invoked by both (for example, the Christian sin of Anger with the mnemonic sin of transience, or the sin of Pride with absent-mindedness), a visual world would appear that contained the memory failures in a memorable way.

---

21 *The Seven Sins of Memory*, p.4. Schacter's seven categories are: transience, absent-mindedness, blocking, misattribution, suggestibility, bias and persistence. See Ch.4 for the relevance of these sins for literature.

Another example is Suzanne Nalbantian's chapter regarding neuroscientific developments. It is entitled "The almond and the seahorse" rather than 'the amygdala and the hippocampus' – the two distinct areas of the brain said to be primarily involved in memory processes.[22] Nalbantian uses the figurative description of the brain regions, based on the Greek/Latin origin of the words which were chosen because they correspond to their shapes: they resemble an almond and a seahorse respectively. She prefers the image-based expression to the language-based one. Readers of her book may be gripped more easily by a visually led concept than by a scientific one because her topic is literature which anyway exploits the ambiguity and 'vividness' of words. The doubling effect she creates (brain section and corresponding visual image) kick-starts the reader's imagination and provides a head start on the theme. The images become memory hooks, or peg-words which stand out because they unexpectedly pair seemingly incompatible physical shapes to the subject-matter. Nalbantian here follows the rule regulating the choice of memorable images which says that they should be as striking as possible in order to activate the memory and be retained the best.

Modern critics of the ancient system follow in a long tradition of those who posed accusations against it from the start. Thus Quintilian believed it needed simplifying and was often used for ostentation alone, limiting its purposefulness;[23] Erasmus and Francis Bacon argued that the work involved in creating the memory palaces and mnemonic structures far outweighed the benefits of the system.[24] However, defenders of the practice, such as Cicero who used it extensively in his legal debates, propose that it is laziness alone which makes the system inefficient – with enough dedication and practice, the system itself would presents no burden to the memoriser.[25]

Most critics agree that memory-for-words is less efficient than memory-for-things (see Ch.1), related to the fact, as Schacter writes, that "memory improves when people generate sentences or stories that tie together to-be-learned information with familiar facts and associations."[26] Although a conclusive explanation has yet to be found, experiments have clearly shown that this is the case.[27] Everything indicates that the backgrounds-and-images system can be an effective artificial memory aid because it mimics the physical memory processes. Particularly as they are understood within the pattern activation school of thought: the spatial awareness which creates a three-dimensional space; the context which

---

22   Ch. 8, in *Memory in Literature.*
23   *Institutio Oratoria,* XI, ii, 23–6.
24   Spence, *The Memory Palace of Matteo Ricci,* pp.12–13.
25   *De Oratore,* II, lxxxvii, 356–60 and Blum, *Die antike Mnemotechnic,* p.162.
26   *The Seven Sins of Memory,* p.26.
27   Tversky mentions work done by Paivio (1971) and Shepard (1967) in "Remembering spaces", p.364, while Draaisma points to Paivio's concept of "dual coding" where a cooperation between verbal and visual, i.e., between two associative processes, strengthen memory capacity, in *Metaphors of Memory,* pp.16–17.

enhances memory through pattern activation; the power of images over words; and the "chunking" of information into separate, manageable bits.

To see how this is related to literature, I will look at memory experiments in which the test persons were presented with a *story*, rather than with mere words on a list, to test what is remembered and how this memorised matter is retrieved.

Neuropsychology and Storytelling

In his 1932-book *Remembering* the psychologist F.C. Bartlett presents his findings after an experiment involving the memorisation of an Indian folk tale, *The War of the Ghosts*, which the test persons were asked to recall fifteen minutes later, and then at differing intervals varying from months to years. The evaluation of this material produced a list of the six most characteristic changes made to the story during recall. They are presented as follows by Baddeley:

1) *Omissions.* Not only are details omitted but also features of the passages that do not fit in with the subject's prior expectations. The supernatural element in *The War of the Ghosts* was frequently omitted by Bartlett's subjects, who tended to find it puzzling and illogical.
2) *Rationalisation.* Subjects would sometimes introduce material in an attempt to "explain" incongruous features of a passage [...]
3) *Dominant details.* Certain features of the passage often become central and appear to serve as an anchor point for the rest of the passage. [...]
4) *Transformation of detail.* Words and names are often changed so as to become more familiar (e.g., *canoes* may become *boats*).
5) *Transformation of order.* The order of events may change considerably, although this is much more likely in a descriptive passage than in a well-structured narrative. Narrative material in general tended to be better recalled than descriptive passages.
6) *Importance of the subject's attitude.* In trying to remember a passage, the first thing the subject tends to recall is his attitude toward the material. "The recall is then a construction made largely on the basis of this attitude, and its general effect is that of a justification of the attitude."[28]

The above suggests that, when reading a story, the memory does not remember facts according to a purely technical system, but is highly influenced by the reader's personal experience of the text. The 'omissions', the first point on Baddeley's list, which occur on recalling the short story are predictable since we do not expect that almost anyone can recall a story word for word with all the correct information intact. The fact that the more incongruous features – which do not coincide with the reader's perception of the world – are also likely to be omitted shows that an editing process takes place while we are reading. It could be said that what we recall of a story very much depends on what we have chosen to read into the story on first encounter in order to make it more acceptable or understandable.[29] Our memory hooks onto the thoughts we have while reading

---

28   *The Psychology of Memory*, p.12.
29   Maurice Halbwachs describes this experience in relation to re-reading a childhood favourite: "The book seems to lack pages, developments, or details that were there when we first

rather than onto the words in the text. They have to be transformed into personal experiences in order to be memorable. This also explains points two and four: rationalisation and transformation of detail. Rationalisation happens because certain changes can make a text seem more logical, while transformation of detail (like changing the word *canoes* to the word *boats*) clarifies the image: it is easier to imagine something that is already familiar, than expend energy on creating a wholly new image to comply with the concept of an unfamiliar object.

The third point regarding dominant details – where particular features become anchors for the text – relates to the idea that memory requires spatial awareness. By emphasising the features that stand out most clearly within a text, the rest can be organised around it. The feature becomes a signpost, leading the reader on to the next dominant detail, following a route like that of a memory journey. An easy self-test is trying to recall a book read some time ago. Commonly, only particular scenes, remarkable characters or very vivid descriptions spring to mind around which the rest of the narrative then seems to reveal itself if time is spent lingering over the remembered details.

The creation of dominant details seems to be a natural memory process which helps anchor the memory to a few strong points which then allow the remaining memories to cluster around them. To use Miller's term, a kind of chunking takes place: by choosing a few strong categories under which further items can be stored, the capacity of the memory is extended. Rather than remembering a long string of bits of information, which can confuse by its sequential sameness, the memory recalls its content by chunks. The transformation of order, point five, relates to this same spatial awareness: a reorganisation of the events takes place because a clear arrangement structures the information and so aids recall.

The conclusion reached by Bartlett in the thirties and revived by Baddeley in the late seventies is reminiscent of recent research undertaken by literary critics into cognitive psychology. Susan Lohafer, for example, suggests that a natural chunking of a story takes place (using Miller's memory term), based on her theory of preclosure – of possible earlier end-points of a story. She argues that each reader brings to a text a natural "storyness" which makes the reader intuit possible closure points, what Bartlett might call dominant details or anchor points, since they have the same effect on the reader: to bring them up short and make them take special note of what happens.[30]

---

read it; at the same time, additions seem to have been made because our interest is now attracted to and our reflections focused on a number of aspects of the action and the characters which, we well know, we were incapable of noticing then. These stories moreover seem less extraordinary to us, more formulaic and less lively. These fictions have been stripped of a major part of their prestige: we no longer understand why and how they once communicated to our imagination such an uplift." *On Collective Memory*, pp.46–7.

30   Lohafer uses the fascinating results of her reading-for-preclosure experiments as a literary tool of interpretation. It is closely linked to my own aim when combining cognitive psychology

Bartlett's most important point – number six, about the reader's attitude towards the text – emphasises that it is not the text itself, but how it is experienced by the reader that determines how it is remembered. This was already implied by point one about 'omissions'.[31] When a book we have read is mentioned, we may not recall many details at once, but we usually recall whether we enjoyed reading it or not, whether it was a positive experience, a hard slug or a necessary evil done as preparation for a class on literature. And the way we feel about the book will colour the way we recall it.

In fact, Bartlett bases his experiment on the assumption that the memory is activated by the reader's "active search for meaning rather than the passive response to the stimuli presented by the experimenter".[32] He distances himself from the memory work of Ebbinghaus, whose seminal work *Über das Gedächtnis* (1885) by many was seen as the starting point of modern memory research. Where Ebbinghaus avoids any form of association and mnemonic aids during his self-tests in order to make the outcome as clinical as possible (according to Bartlett with little success), Bartlett emphasises exactly this subjectivity of the person as a main factor in creating lasting memory. He calls it the "effort after meaning" in which any perceived item is immediately connected to others already contained in existing schemata in the mind, thereby making sense of them.[33] According to the conclusions that Bartlett draws from his tests, the search for meaning obviously has an important function in interpretation and will fundamentally influence our reaction to anything we hear or read.

As mentioned in my introduction, the contentious topic regarding literature and meaning is clarified by distinguishing between the author's intended meaning, whether consciously or unconsciously incorporated, and the reader's extrapolation of significance from the text, to use Hirsch's dichotomy.[34] Generally, I assume

---

and literary criticism. She, however, combines her findings with text definition – attributing each consecutive ending to a genre. By the sequence in which they appear in the story, she attempts interpretation – with success. It is noteworthy that many of the preclosure points chosen reveal a congruence with dominant details and changing backgrounds relevant for my backgrounds-and-images approach: among them she lists "changes of space / time / condition" and "natural-event terminals" which in the architectural memory system would indicate a change of background, and "image recursion" that clearly are dominant details that are repeated to aid the structure of a text. Lohafer even calls these points "signals", which supports the idea that they are included for the cognitive activity involved in the act of reading. *Reading for Storyness*, p.27.

31   See Chapter 4 for my reference to Lecan and his perception of reality. It emphasises that we perceive ourselves, and the world we live in, through what is reflected back at us. Simultaneously, whatever we encounter will always be registered as a reflection on ourselves. This is relevant to literary interpretation and will become part of my approach when considering Angela Carter's text.

32   *The Psychology of Memory*, p.4.

33   *Remembering*, p.44.

34   This is explained by Hirsch in "Meaning and significance", in *The Aims of Interpretation* and *Validity in Interpretation*. See also my Introduction.

that the one true meaning the author incorporates in the text can never absolutely be determined: it may not even exist. However, meaning becomes part of a text during its creation and without it there would be little sense in interpreting stories. Furthermore, there may be as many meanings as there are readers (to paraphrase a relativist view) – every reader finding their own significance in a text – but, unlike Hirsch, I see no problem with the ever-changing condition of this meaning, reverting to the medieval idea, expounded by Anselm, that any interpretation of a text is only a further building block in the ongoing discussion about it: an ever-expanding concept of what a text may mean (see Ch.1).

Bartlett's reading experiment, and his belief that all reading includes the "active search for meaning", clearly relates to the idea of Hirsch's 'significance'. It is the reader who initiates this search, finding his or her own personal significance within the text. Whether the reader thinks he is able to find the one true meaning or not is not important, for he still tries to 'understand' the story, to make sense of it. To do so he relies on personal experience. Even if we aim to take an objective approach, our personal preferences, experiences and attitudes will always form part of our reaction to a text because we always relate new information to what is already extant in our memories. The reader's extrapolated meaning of a text is, therefore, always tinged by the subjective experience.

Schacter's assertion that the memory works better when the items to be remembered are somehow linked with 'familiar facts and associations' is extended by Bartlett. He includes the idea of creative thinking since, as Baddeley puts it, human memory creates structures during the process of comprehension "which involves integrating new material with existing structures".[35] He explains further that "Bartlett suggested that our knowledge of the world comprises of a set of models or schemata based on past experience. When we attempt to learn something new, we base our learning on already existing schemata".[36]

This concept of integrating new material into existing structures is fundamental to the instructions given by Hugh of St Victor to his pupils in the Middle Ages: he urged them to ensure that the mnemonic structures he taught them were learned by heart and embedded so securely in the mind that new information could effortlessly be added to them, enriching the group of related items already located there. He formulated the conclusion reached many centuries later by modern-day memory researchers. Artificial memory requires a great deal of practice and a strong commitment to the task of memorising as it is a voluntary assistance to the natural memory. Reproducing the mechanics of the memory artificially naturally requires more physical determination than is involved in its natural function.

---

35   *The Psychology of Memory*, p.355.
36   Ibid., p.13.

From the importance of the structure into which new elements can be integrated, we now move to images, using metaphors to explain the effectiveness of storing images rather than words in the memory. During an experiment Raynolds and Schwartz presented test persons with eight short texts. One group was handed stories with literal endings, while the other group had stories the conclusion of which was phrased in form of a metaphor. The test showed that those persons who read the metaphor ending retained the conclusion better than the people from the other group who read the literal ending. Furthermore, the metaphor-ending group could recall more details from the story itself which had been identical for both groups.[37] Draaisma comments that "[t]he authors think that metaphors enable one to set the process of reproduction in motion more easily and to pursue it for longer," i.e., metaphors seem to kick-start the memory and to keep it activated. Draaisma explains this phenomenon by referring to Paivio's concept of dual coding. Paivio argues that the cooperation of language-based and image-based memory (left and right brain hemispheres respectively) aids recall because the more abstract language-based memory item can be attached to the image created through the metaphor. "With an image we immediately have a set of relationships. Unlike sequentially processed verbal information, these relationships are a simultaneous given". The metaphor "function[s] as a conceptual peg on which the more abstract term can be hung".[38]

An experiment testing the memorability of words versus images was undertaken by Sachs who, in the 1960s and 70s, gave test persons passages of text to read. Alterations were then made to the texts and the test persons were asked what had been changed: "most of the syntactic information had been forgotten almost immediately, in contrast to the semantic information [i.e., the content] which showed very little forgetting".[39] The pronounced effectiveness of the image over the word, as shown in many experiments, makes the long-standing bias towards the assumption that memory functions are entirely language-based seem inexplicable. As Baddeley points out, even a simple word like 'cat' has so many associations pertaining to all five senses (how it looks, feels, smells and sounds – maybe even tastes) as well as to our personal experiences with cats. It gives this word cumulative significance of all the cats we have know (a generic memory), so that the storage of the *word* 'cat' in a computer-like system would need an extraordinarily large amount of subcategories to even come close to the meaning we attach to the word.[40] An *image* of a cat with all its associations and within a

---

37   Draaisma, *Metaphors of Memory*, p.16.
38   Ibid., p.17.
39   Baddeley, *The Psychology of Memory*, p.117.
40   Ibid., p.355. Attempts to create computer programmes using language-based systems to copy memory functions have quickly proved incompatible, because the complexity necessary to arrange even the simplest of factual information soon becomes too confusing and extensive to be physically viable. Draaisma clearly states the inappropriateness of the 'computer as memory'

larger context that comprises all three dimensions of the 'real' world (as opposed to the linguistic one) can in an instance produce the meaning of the word 'cat' in all its facets and connect it to any other words we hear at the same time.

The danger with creating images to represent words is not so much that they will not spring to mind when wanted, but that they do so in an excessive way which confuses the issue by its multifariousness. For an example we can return to S., Luria's test person with the exceptional memory mentioned at the start of this chapter. Although the automatic recall of memorised items by using visualisation techniques gave him an extraordinary ability far beyond that of most people, exactly this vivid recall impaired S.'s ability to grasp "the simple idea of the thing", as he put it himself.[41] What he meant was that the images which were called up unbidden as he heard the words of a sentence would be so dominant that they would often obscure the meaning they were meant to convey. For example, the simple sentence 'The work got under way normally' gave him trouble:

I read that 'the work got under way normally'. As for *work*, I see that work is going on ... there's a factory ... But there's that word *normally*. What I see is a big, ruddy-cheeked woman, a *normal* woman. Then the expression *get under way*. Who? What is all this? You have industry ... that is, a factory, and this normal woman – but how does all this fit together? How much I have to get rid of just to get the simple idea of the thing![42]

Whenever he was told a story, already the first few words would create an entire context: the words that followed might therefore not fit into the imagined setting. Persons with an average memory capacity will constantly be able to adapt the mental image, making a meaning available rather than creating an entire world of possible associations which all exist at the same time. S. was not able to do so:

I was read this phrase: 'N. was leaning up against a tree ...' I saw a slim young man dressed in a dark blue suit (N., you know is so elegant). He was standing near a big linden tree with grass and woods all around ... But then the sentence went on: 'and was peering into a shop window.' Now how do you like that! It means the scene isn't set in the woods, or in a garden, but he's standing on the street. And I have to start the whole sentence over from the beginning ...[43]

Furthermore, the images would be so strong that if a word or name from a previous story turned up in a later one the image produced would, the second time around, be identical to the first instance of its occurrence. A porch in one story might mean that in a following story which also contained the setting of a porch

metaphor: "The fact that the human brain does not operate as a location-addressable device, does not run through indexes, and does not form categories on the basis of explicit criteria, only comes as a surprise to theoreticians who had accepted the computer metaphor too subserviently."
Metaphors of Memory, p.206.
41   Luria, *The Mind of a Mnemonist*, p.128.
42   Ibid.
43   Ibid., p.112.

the characters entering this setting from either story would meet in S.'s imaginary, ultra-visual world. It seems that the effort and determination that must go into creating a memory palace is part of the safety apparatus in our minds which controls the visual imagination, making it support the actual meaning contained within the image-producing words: the meaning is "the thing!"

CREATIVE THINKING

Memory experiments that focus on literary texts suggest that visualisation can enhance memory function. So far we have taken as a given that images play a prominent role when reading a text and trying to comprehend it. But is this actually the case? Are images definitively involved in creative thinking?

Aristotle famously wrote that the soul never thinks without a mental picture and Thomas Aquinas declared that we cannot understand without images. Both take for granted that mental images are key to cognitive activity. It has remained the traditional approach to cognitive psychology over the centuries, but for some time now questions have been asked attempting to determine whether images are *necessary* for thought. The question has been raised with regards to creativity, discovery and problem-solving in particular and has thrown up more questions than decisive answers. The results of various tests and experiments, although not conclusive, throw some light upon the fascinating question of *how* we think.

There can be no disagreement about that images *can* be part of thinking. In general, people do experience mental images on a regular basis. It is more difficult to say what these images are like. The disagreement amongst cognitive psychologists regarding the role and function of mental images in thought processes may to some extent stem from a lack of definition rather than from incompatibility of evidence. Daniel Reisberg and Robert Logie distinguish between the mental image and the picture, using them comparatively, seeing where they differ and where they have communalities in order to understand the mental image better.[44] Rudolf Arnheim suggests that mental images need not be exact replications of the real object. They can instead be made up of "significant detail" that represents the whole; for example, "a briefcase held by an arm" may represent a jurist, as it did for one of Koffka's test persons who described this mental image.[45] "This sort of incompleteness is typical of mental imagery," writes Arnheim, "it is the product of a selectively discerning mind, which can do better than consider faithful recordings of fragments." To him this is "a positive quality, which distinguishes the mental grasp of an object from the physical nature of that object itself".[46]

He also says that mental images can appear to be seen as out of the corner of an eye: we know what it is but the details are blurred, colourless or distant and

---

44   "The ins and outs of working memory", p.39.
45   "The images of thought", p.105.
46   Ibid., p.107.

sometimes even "perceived as present but not visible". The conclusion Beverly Roskos-Ewoldsen, Rita E. Anderson and Margaret Jean Intons-Peterson reach is that images can have several forms. "Images range from conceptual images (e.g., intentional thought) to spatial images to mental pictures (e.g., experiential sensation), with spatial images occurring more frequently than either conceptual images or mental pictures."[47] Deborah Chambers adds that the traditional distinction between mental pictures and propositions (abstract thought) is misleading because they are not mutually exclusive and can work in combination.[48] They all agree that whatever form the image takes it *can* be helpful for creative thinking and problem-solving; whether images are *necessary* for thought remains unresolved.

Michel Denis suggests that images may not be "the *core* of thought processes, but rather a potential *medium* for them".[49] He is referring to the symbolist and conceptionalist traditions: the first suggests that we think in symbols (that is, in mental images) and the other believes that we think in abstracts that result in images. Intons-Peterson, who is interested in the interaction between imagery and creativity, asks what comes first when we think: the word or the image? She does not find an answer to this question, but concludes that "the evidence suggests some independence between two types of creativity, one primarily verbal and the other, primarily spatial" (spatial using images in three-dimensional space).[50]

Although all researchers above take different approaches to the complex question of the role that images play in creativity or problem-solving, they agree that images *can* occur during cognitive activity and, when they do, that they aid understanding, comprehension and creative thought. Whether the images are perceptual or pictorial, whether the word or the image comes first and whether the image is tool or result of thought – although extremely thought-provoking questions – is secondary to my investigation.

The question relevant here is whether mental images *can* play a role in creative thinking and whether they can be helpful when they do. Since both questions are answered in the affirmative by every writer considered here, regardless of approach or remaining reservations, it seems acceptable to state with some confidence that the backgrounds-and-images system can be a helpful tool in cognitive processes. Furthermore, the emphasis on the effectiveness of structure and framework – usually referred to as the "reference frame" – shows that the three-dimensional setting required by the memory palace is indeed a help when trying to comprehend an idea, so Denis, Reisberg and Logie, amongst others. And the spatial image is the type of image that occurs more frequently than any other type, according to Roskos-Ewoldsen, et al.

---

47   "Imagery, creativity, and discovery", p.317.
48   "Images are both depictive and descriptive", p.95.
49   "Imagery and thinking", p.104.
50   "Imagery's role in creativity and discovery", p.31.

Having answered the question whether images play any part in creative thinking, the relation between creative thinking and literary texts must now be established. An author uses creative thought when inventing stories, holding a mental image of some kind in the mind before putting words on a page. The reader, too, engages in creative activity since the words must be converted back into ideas in order to make sense.[51] A transition takes place which involves creative thinking. The question of 'what comes first: the word or the image?' takes on a different meaning when asked in relation to the writing process. With regard to the reader, it is clear that the words come first and the images follow. The case of the author is more complex. Depending on the type of mental activity which initiates the mental process, the author converts abstracts, images or ideas as part of thought into words that exist in thought before they are written down as visual words on the page. The reader then inverts the process. Where the author changes insubstantial ideas to substantial words, the reader takes 'tangible' words on the page and converts them into intangible ideas.

The cognitive psychologists above suggest that the employment of images is helpful for creative thinking. It follows that readers would benefit from attempting to visualise what is read. Not because the reader replicates the original images produced by the author at the point of invention and composition, but because mental images allow for a wider perspective. Roskos-Ewoldsen et al. conclude that "what appears to be the most important for the creative process is to be able to transform information from one code to another – for example, from verbal to imaginal and back again – so as to gain multiple perspectives on the task at hand [...]".[52] Despite being based on psychological results – and care must be taken when transposing these insights onto artistic subjects – the findings suggest a great deal about analogue processes within the arts: memory is involved whether we deal with cognitive tests or with literary texts. The psychological discoveries have extensive consequences for literature. They question how far the author can stimulate the reader to reconstruct the original reference frame, and to what extent the reader can stimulate the creative imagination in order to approach a visually led comprehension of the text.

The ability to express the same idea in various mediums is emphasised as paramount to understanding, and the visualisation of texts certainly belongs here. It puts the onus on the reader: not only to engage with the text, but actively to convert words into images because the act itself, of decoding or recoding the subject, increases the ability to comprehend.

---

51   As the above shows, one could argue about how this happens, what kinds of image are involved in the process and whether there may not be instances where there are no images at all. I accept that there may be instances or individuals who do not rely on mental images, but will concentrate on the cases where images do play a part and will refer to these (documented as the most common) instances.

52   "Imagery, creativity, and discovery", p.324.

It seems authors have always been aware of the potential of images, employing iconography and metaphor as visual aids and settings in three-dimensional space as reference frames in order to guide the reader towards a fuller understanding of the text. This is particularly true of medieval authors, as was seen in chapter two. Kolve refers to this intentional use of visual clues when he writes about Chaucer's work that he saw

imagery [...] as an iconographic possibility of narrative action itself. Chaucer was not a 'painterly' poet; his iconographic descriptions are swift, spare, and concerned only with the essential. [As in the Dido scene in *The House of Fame* discussed above.] But they are descriptions, and they invite a certain activity in response. The degree of their indeterminacy – their lack of inessential specification – indeed facilitates iconographic recognition, for it is the outline and notional content of an image that ultimately relate it to other images in this powerful way [...][53]

Reminiscent of Arnheim's idea of the mental image as sometimes consisting only of 'significant detail', Kolve suggests that it is exactly the "swift, spare" descriptions and the concentration on "the essential" which makes the iconographic clues so powerful. Images do not have to resemble 'the real thing', as it would 'look' in real life; instead, these images contain the core idea in essential parts which therefore invite comparison, association and creative thought. Kolve, too, emphasises the active involvement of the reader, whose understanding is aided when it picks up on iconographic clues along the way. These help to create an extensive world into which the new story is placed, relating it to things beyond the text and thereby to larger questions, ultimately encouraging creative thinking.

The intentional inclusion of visual aids into the text is not solely a medieval or antiquated writing technique. The following chapters will clearly show that modern writers avail themselves of similar methods. They may call them by different names, but the encouragement to the reader to take an active part and to use images to create a three-dimensional setting for the story abound.

Neuropsychology and Literary Criticism

Several branches of literary theory touch upon the concept of the interplay between the author and the text, the reader and the text and between the author and the reader. They include phenomenology, reader-reception and reader-response theory, hermeneutics and historicism. They all assume that there are meanings to be found in the text and that these reside with either the author, the reader or with both, rather than with the text itself. It is this interaction, whether between person and text or between author and reader, which is a prerequisite for the validity of my theory: the author's memory processes are embedded in the text and by revealing these, meanings can be deduced.

---

53   *Chaucer and the Imagery of Narrative*, p.363.

The literary theories referring to this concept are too numerous and too varied to be sketched here – and, furthermore, would emphasise the theoretical aspects whereas my aim is to find concrete textual adaptations of memory concepts to show the practical gains of my theory. I have chosen three examples from literary criticism which exemplify the appropriation of memory theory into literary theory in various ways. Suzanne Nalbantian ascribes the influence of certain types of memory function to texts of particular literary periods, John S. Rickard uncovers mnemonic aids intentionally incorporated into Joyce's *Ulysses* and Renate Lachmann sees intertextuality as the memory of a text in her interpretation of works by Russian poets. Although their approaches are very different, they have in common that they use aspects of the architectural memory system as part of their approach when interpreting literary texts.

SUZANNE NALBANTIAN

The book *Memory in Literature: From Rousseau to neuroscience* relates specific developments in memory research to literature written at the time and shows how the two influenced each other. Nalbantian starts in the nineteenth century with the 'era of dynamic psychology'. In many ways, this was the birthplace of modern memory research with William James as one of its most important proponents. She then covers memory topics such as autobiographical memory and emotion by looking at Rousseau and the Romantics; she looks into how writers like Baudelaire and Rimbaud use sensory stimuli to express recollection in their works; relates the engram idea to the memory trigger as employed by Proust in the famous madeleine-scene; considers associative memory in Woolf, Joyce and Faulkner; automatism and aleatory memory amongst the surrealists; and describes how modernist writers like Nin, Borges and Paz see memory as an expression of the subconscious, and the mind as a labyrinth of passageways and language. The final chapter contains a concise description of the latest developments within neuroscience at that time.

Nalbantian's approach is exemplary in that it very clearly shows how any theory of memory can be employed to interpret literature, and her individual case-studies prove that the physiological and psychological perceptions of how the memory works have influenced writers in these periods. A forerunner of this approach is Aleida Assmann's seminal text *Erinnerungsräume* which, however, is very culturally orientated: she makes similar comparisons between the concept of memory and the literature written at one given time. Both are restrained by limiting themselves to the time-frame in which memory theory and literature overlap. While Assmann is interested in the cultural aspects of memory and how the collective memory has influenced writing, Nalbantian approaches the text from a more hermeneutical angle. I have therefore chosen to use Nalbantian's investigation of Virginia Woolf's novel *To the Lighthouse* in order to show a practical employment of memory concepts, as it comes closest to my own proposed practice of literary interpretation.

In Nalbantian's chapter on associative memory Virginia Woolf's novel *To the Lighthouse* is interpreted by using the memory principle of association as outlined by William James. The man who coined the phrase 'stream of consciousness' not only gave name to the narrative technique based on memory function used by Woolf in several of her works, but also reflects her use of figurative language. James describes the process of remembering in architectural terms:

> We make search in our memory for a forgotten idea, just as we rummage our house for a lost object. In both cases we visit what seems to us the probable *neighborhood* of that which we miss. We turn over the things under which, or alongside of which, it may possibly be; and if it lies near them it soon comes to view. But these matters, in the case of a mental object sought, are nothing but its *associates*. The machinery of recall is thus the same as the machinery of association, and the machinery of association, as we know, is nothing but the elementary law of habit in the nerve-centres.[54]

As mentioned above, James is a strong forerunner of modern neuroscientific ideas about memory and his insights are as relevant today as they were innovative then. His metaphor of *searching* a house, of *visiting* places or *neighbourhoods* to locate remembered items, is closely related to the system of backgrounds and images and he makes the rule of association the defining factor of the process – Nalbantian writes that he "focuses on an interior landscape of mental objects".[55] Woolf, too, when speaking about memories, uses landscapes and architectural references to explain the experience: she describes the memory of her mother, who died when Woolf was thirteen, as placed "in the very centre of that great Cathedral space which was childhood", using an established memory *summa*, the cathedral, to symbolise this time-delineated space.[56] When referring to the past in general, she says, "I find that scene-making is my natural way of marking the past": she marks scenes by placing landmarks in the landscape of the past.[57]

A talent for scene-making seems to be paramount for a writer to succeed and Woolf's novels certainly show evidence hereof. That they also refer to the process of memory is abundantly clear in *To the Lighthouse* (as in *Mrs Dalloway*) where a memory of the past "is completely linked to the perception of place".[58] Not only are particular memories linked to particular places, but they also become memory images, memory triggers and landmarks by which the reader can orientate him or herself, they guide the reader through the story: the kitchen table, visualised in the branches of a tree near the summer house, is the memory image which symbolises Mr Ramsey's abstract work to Lily (21); the pattern on the tablecloth becomes the memory trigger which enables Lily ten years on to recall the solution she hit upon

---

54   *The Principles of Psychology*, vol.1, p.654.
55   *Memory in Literature*, p.21.
56   Quoted in *Memory in Literature*, p.79.
57   Ibid.
58   *Memory in Literature*, p.85.

for finally completing her painting;[59] and the lighthouse of the title "which has been associated with the nurturing Mrs Ramsey figure"[60] becomes a landmark in the unfolding tale, the return to which supplies a fixed point and a centring force of the narrative, recalling the main theme. Nalbantian calls the drawing Lily finally completes after a ten-year absence "the memory painting": the landscape painted on it – the view from the summerhouse which includes the lighthouse – represents a memory landscape: Lily has "transfer[ed] her recollections of her friend Mrs Ramsey into a painting which would prefer her memory forever".[61] Here a landscape (in a painting) becomes the physical receptacle of a memory – a complex and many-layered memory of one person: her character and life.

Nalbantian compares the tripartite structure of the novel to the well-established three steps involved in the memory process: the taking in, the storage and the retrieval of memory items. The three parts of the novel's plot correspond in sequence and function to the three memory steps. Part one contains the events at the summerhouse, experienced firsthand by the characters (the first step or 'take in'). The second part covers the ten years in which the summer house lies desolate, holding in readiness all the items and places needed for a return to the summer holiday mood (the second step or 'storage'). The third and last part sees the return of some of the characters to the summerhouse, where they are reminded of Mrs Ramsey, who has died in the intervening years: the familiar surroundings recall her vividly to those present, aided by the surroundings, by the backgrounds against which she lived part of her life (the third step or 'retrieval').

The memory triggers and physical landmarks which appear in the third part are aspects of the tripartite concept of how the memory works. Woolf has written a novel that exemplifies this process. The neurological concepts are backgrounded and become the vehicle for the story, helping to uncover its meanings. When Woolf mimics the memory process, she provides a psychological angle on Lily's problem of how to recall the true essence of a person and to portray this memory in a physical abstract. Her answer is to use a symbolic landscape which contains the right landmarks, situated in the right place, in relation to each other (moving the tree!) – thereby mirroring the memory landscape that exists in her head: the memory space.

---

59   Lily first sits at the table when "[i]n a flash she saw her picture, and thought, Yes, I shall put the tree further in the middle; then I shall avoid that awkward space. That's what I shall do. That's what has been puzzling me. She took up the salt cellar and put it down again on a flower in pattern in the tablecloth, so as to remind herself to move the tree". Ten years on, Lily remembers this incidence: "When she had sat there last ten years ago there had been a little sprig or leaf pattern on the table-cloth, which she had looked at in a moment of revelation. There had been a problem about a foreground of a picture. Move the tree to the middle, she had said. She had never finished that picture. It had been knocking about in her mind all these years. She would paint that picture now." *To the Lighthouse*, p.79 and p.141.

60   *Memory in Literature*, p.1.

61   Ibid.

From the concept of association which helps Nalbantian uncover the memory processes incorporated into Woolf's novel, we move to mnemonics, the artificial memory aids which Rickard argues Joyce uses as a literary tool in *Ulysses*.

In the fourth chapter of *Joyce's Book of Memory: The mnemotechnic of "Ulysses"*, Rickard perceives the book as developing "its own memory, a textual repository of words, phrases, objects, and sounds charged with power by the associations they carry on a number of levels of memory".[62] He shows that Joyce, who was greatly interested in memory systems and familiar with several memory treaties, employed mnemonics in his novels to give a structure to the text. Joyce's mnemonic principles are informed by the cultural background of his day, where a "contra-Darwinian tendency [...] would subsume chance into design and chaos into telos".[63] From this Joyce developed the idiosyncratic interaction between chance and destiny where coincidences are destiny's signposts, indicating a preordained direction. This is incorporated into *Ulysses* through the characters' involuntary memory. An object, an encounter or a word calls forth associations which lead a character to his next step: not coincidentally; but because they are charged with a collective power which guide all mankind.

The manipulation of Joyce's characters' memories is overtly done and allows the reader into their minds, not merely by being privy to their thoughts, but also by being shown how these thoughts come about. Rickard writes that

in Joyce's mnemotechnic memory triggers – symbols or images that stimulate involuntary memory on the parts of Stephen and Bloom – gain their power to evoke the past not only through associations with the past life of the individual character responding to the mnemonic stimulus, but also through shared associations [...] and through a larger, cultural – in effect, universal or collective – network of associations that increases the numinosity or charge of the symbol, even though the characters themselves may not be aware of these associations.[64]

What Rickard calls the 'universal or collective network of associations', apart from being a form of cultural memory, can be traced back to the Renaissance forms of occult memory systems in which emblems and signs were seen as containing compressed knowledge which would be available to the person who internalised (i.e., memorised) those images. The memory concepts he finds embedded in the writings of Joyce employ the same features that are at work in Woolf's *To the Lighthouse*, such as memory triggers, landscapes and association, but the underlying ideas are the hermetic ones of the Renaissance.

Joyce uses this memory concept as a literary tool, creating meanings and connections on a supernatural level between his characters. As readers, we can comprehend these instances as the intervening hand of the author; in Stephen

---

62   *Joyce's Book of Memory*, p.118.
63   Ibid., p.120.
64   Ibid., p.129.

Dedalus and Leopold Bloom's universe they become unexplainable phenomena of cross-fertilising memories – they pick up on wayward associations which link them together on a mental level which they themselves are not aware of. In a sense, here we see Joyce interfering in the story, 'playing God'. Usually we are not shown this aspect of the author's work. In a fictionally created world it is always the author who takes on the role of God the Creator, deciding the fates of his characters, but usually this aspect is blended out in order to lend authenticity to the story. Joyce uses the involuntary memory function of his characters as a plot-device to move the story along. And this plot development, which provides the characters with motives for their actions, is based on the technique of a collective network of associations, a sharing of memories which makes the characters inhabit not only the same physical world, but also the same mental one.

Rickard's most extensive investigation into the integration of memory triggers as plot-devices in *Ulysses* occurs in his interpretation of the fox riddle in the "Circe" section. He counts it "among the most powerful, polysemous, resonant, and subtle symbols in *Ulysses*, operating as triggers to involuntary memory throughout the text", their "meaning" depending on "the psychic charge they carry".[65] He traces words that appear in the riddle, such as 'fox', 'cock', 'bell' and the number 11 with all its numerological implications, to show how these words attract to them more and more meaning as they are repeated in the text in various circumstances, becoming repositories for particular aspects of the story, more comprehensive the further we progress into the narrative.

These powerful associative memory triggers do not, however, consist of highly mystical, many-layered or highly symbolic items. Joyce prefers simple, everyday objects to perform this task, such as a potato in *Ulysses*[66] or a door handle in *A Portrait of the Artist as a Young Man*.[67] Rickard suggests Joyce's "awareness of mnemonic potential of trivial or ordinary objects and places may have been heightened by Tommaso Campanella's *City of the Sun* [,] a copy of which Joyce owned". He goes on to quote Yates in the *Art of Memory* as arguing that this Renaissance Utopian work

could be used as an occult memory-system through which everything could be quickly learned, using the world "as a book" and as "local memory." The children of the sun City were instructed by the Solarian priests who took them round the City to look at the pictures. The pedagogic method of the highly occult Solarians, and the whole plan of their City and its images, was a form of local memory, with its places and images.[68]

Joyce takes up the Renaissance idea of the city as a memory map which is clearly linked to the ancient art of memory with its backgrounds and images. Rickard

---

65   Ibid., p.146.
66   Ibid., p.154.
67   Ibid., p.142.
68   Ibid.

points out that this mnemonic system, described by Yates in her book on memory and reworded by Rickard as "an imagined correspondence of place and image that trapped or held memory for the rhetorician until it was needed", would "serve well as an analogue for the way that Joyce embodied mnemonic power throughout his text in the objects, sounds, and language that makes up the city of Dublin".[69]

However, in Joyce's works particular geographical details are more prominent than the overall representation of a setting, as stated by Richard Ellmann:

other novelists are [...] much more likely to present a city in reconstructable form. Joyce offers no architectural information, only places to bump elbows, or to lean them, to see out of the corner of an eye, to recognise by a familiar smell. The city rises in bits, not in masses.[70]

This, again, can be related back to Joyce's use of memory processes. To him places need not be physically presented by their exact coordinates or constituent parts. He uses metonymy in which a corner, a door or a particular spot fixes his attention and represents each specific background. He forgoes the overall map of the city for its individual features which carry intense memory-led images. In architectural memory terms, Joyce takes for granted the building in which he places his specific backgrounds in order to emphasise the images placed against them. When a Joycian character wanders the streets of Dublin, the organisational aspect of the journey does not matter. Often characters are led from place to place, 'finding' themselves in unexpected quarters from where they are brought to the next by association, inspired by the memories called forth through their presence in that particular spot.

The structural function of the associative memory triggers is not always obvious to the reader, and it seems that Joyce did not intend to show his hand openly. Jacques Mercanton recalls that Joyce told him "[t]he hallucinations in *Ulysses* [...] are made up out of elements from the past, which the reader will recognise if he has read the book five, ten or twenty times".[71] This (hopeful!) statement shows that the novel itself is build up on logical memory processes. The suggestion of five to twenty read-throughs necessary to pick up on this either makes Joyce an extremely optimistic writer with regard to the stamina of his readers, or indicates, rather, that the reader need not necessarily realise the presence of these internal references to comprehend the story. Joyce does not mean the reader to see the seams – how the text is put together – but, instead, uses the internal references as structural aids.

Rickard takes Joyce's section headings, a spatial memory aid, to be directly related to the ancient art of memory and again refers to the backgrounds-and-images system as delineated by Yates. He compares the 'Circe' heading for the section in which Stephen Dedalus and Leopold Bloom confront their pasts head-

69   Ibid.
70   Ellmann quoted by Rickard, p.142.
71   *Joyce's Book of Memory*, p.2.

on for the first time with the ancient technique of using Gods as classifying rubrics under which a vast amount of memory associations can be stored: a form of mental heading for a large network of associations which was common practice in Antiquity. Joyce, too, uses the name of a goddess as his heading and assimilates under it a vast array of associated concerns. The Circe heading covers the myriad problems that the main characters have with women in the narrative, while referring back to Homer's *Odyssey* and the concept of transformation, implying the change that takes place within Dedalus and Bloom in this section.

Rickard's approach greatly draws on the art of memory as described by Yates in her book *The Art of Memory*. He has taken Yates' theoretical and historical approach and turned it into a practical application to be used on literary texts. He shows, unquestionably, that the ancient art of memory with its rules regulating the conception and application of backgrounds and images holds great potential for literary hermeneutics. Rickard has proven that Joyce consciously appropriates memory systems adapted from Antiquity and uses them as a structural device in order to design his story and to move it forward.

Like Lachmann, who I comment on below, he sees the text itself as a repository for memory, as a storage facility akin to those traditional psychology refers to. But he also sees the backgrounds-and-images system as analogue to Joyce's writing technique: the memory system helps to explain *how* Joyce has put his book together. This insight leads Rickard to say that Giordano Bruno's memory theatre (adapted from the backgrounds-and-images system), "where a deep structural organisation of powerful symbols can focus and direct powerful forces", is the blueprint for how Joyce "designed the 'Circe' episode"; namely, "as a theatre of involuntary or spontaneous memory".[72]

The inspiration for my investigation also came from reading Yates' *The Art of Memory* and, just like Rickard, I have attempted to apply the theories to actual texts, using the memory systems as tools for interpreting literature. Rickard's approach differs from mine in that he pinpoints the exact inspirational sources for specific memory-related aspects in Joyce's text to prove that these were intentional, that the author knew of the systems and worked out a technique for incorporating them into his work. I am not interested in locating the actual source of an author's memory-related concept. Instead, I see an inherent connection between artificial memory that creates images to aid recall for rhetorical purposes, and poetic imagination which creates an imaginary world full of images for the reader to interpret as the narrative unfolds in three-dimensional space.

---

72   Ibid., p.166.

114

Lachmann asks the critical question in her introductory chapter to *Memory and Literature* which concerns us here: how does mnemonic and poetic imagination interact? "Are these parallel processes mirroring, or commenting on, one another?" She answers the question by inspecting what they have in common:

Is it not the case that literary iconography always appeals to mnemonic iconography, that the image bank of literature is the same as the image bank of memory, or, put in another way, that their image-producing activity of memory incorporates poetic imagination in itself?

If we accept the notion that poetry participates in the mnemonic knowledge of imagery in the same way that mnemonics has assimilated the (lost) original legacy of the poetic perception of the world, then we may surmise that, through mnemotechnics, elementary achievements of imaginative remembering have been pragmatized—inasmuch as these achievements, as acts of memory, serve as the basis of all acts of writing.[73]

Lachmann's close association of memory and writing, like mine, is based on the concept of the ancient art of memory, particularly the backgrounds and images as presented through the Simonides story by Cicero and Quintilian. Her answer to the above question is to use the aspect of intertextuality as the combining factor between memory and literature, seeing intertextuality as the memory of a text in its cultural setting. Her approach to the architectural memory system concentrates on the conceptualised transference of memory from mind to text, from architecturally organised memory images to words written on the page. These perform the same function in a book as the backgrounds and images do in the imagination. She writes of "a transposition of the memory spaces and their images to the outside – so that the *locus* becomes a writing surface, and the memory images become letters", when commenting on Leonardo da Vinci's aphorisms.[74]

She employs Stefan Goldmann's interpretation of the Simonides story as ancient myth-narrative. We recall that Simonides was the only survivor after the roof of Scopas' banqueting hall collapsed, crushing everyone in the room. Simonides was able to identify the individual mangled bodies because he could remember where each person sat at the table. Lachmann undertakes a symbolic reading of the text in which "the dead stand for the past" and where "the catastrophe consists in the experience of forgetting", symbolised through a break: the collapsed walls. She returns to the idea that the text is transformed into a memory storage facility when she writes that "the *tabula* of the banqueters becomes a *tabula rasa*", the erased tablet where the written word has been removed from the slate just as the guests have been removed from the table when the building collapsed, seeing it as a metaphor for forgetting.[75]

Lachmann points out that Cicero "makes this interplay between script and image, *gramma* and *eikon* [portrait], place and tablet, architecture and book, into

---

73   Lachmann, *Memory and Literature*, p.14.
74   Ibid., p.3.
75   Ibid., p.6.

his central argument".[76] But unlike many writers before and since, she does not see the demise of the ancient memory systems in this transference. She sees it as being integrated into the art of writing: "writing technique replaces ritual" in Cicero's discussion while the underlying memory process remains the same.

Lachmann equates individual features of the architectural art of memory with aspects of the writing process, both as macrocosm and as microcosm. "On the one hand, these texts sketch out a space of memory and enter the memory space existing between texts; on the other hand, they construct an architecture of memory into which they deposit mnemonic images based on the procedures of *ars memoriae*."[77] In the macrocosm (or external, inclusive view) texts themselves become the *loci*, each text a *locus* which is relevant in relation to the other texts, retaining its images in the spaces created between them; in the microcosm each individual text creates an imaginary world with places, backgrounds and related image. The first instance is most clearly linked to Lachmann's topic since it is the interplay between texts that provide the fertile ground for intertextuality. The second instance, with each individual text containing a fictional setting (a city in Lachmann's examples), comes closer to my theory in that a written text incorporates its memory architecture visually by location. In this case "the city appears as a *locus*, as the sum of *loci* where the *imagines* [images] of stories, cultures, and experiences have been deposited".[78]

However, Lachmann extends the concept to its full cultural context in that she incorporates the collective memory, the collective human store of signifying images: any city, whether based on a real one or wholly invented, is a *clavis universalis*. Thus the often depicted Petersburg "is an imagined world, as a universe in which all cultures, all contrary and heterogeneous mythological elements are contained, the mnemonic city Petersburg is a *clavis universalis*; it is not only the world but also the book of the world".[79] As such it holds the key to the understanding not just of the particular situation presented in the book, but of the entire world.

Lachmann, here, returns to her concept of the text as memory: the *book* of the world. She highlights the cultural significance of a fictionally represented city that incorporates within it all cultures and all aspects that a writer wants to bring to it; not a realistic representation of its typology. Hence, she refers to "Dostoevsky's phantasmagoric urban landscape", says "Bely's memory theatre is the labyrinth of the city" and "Nabokov's memory theatre is a metaphoric (Gnostic) space, a prison that stands for the fraudulent image of the world".[80] Lachmann sees each fictional city or setting as an expression of cultural memory (exposed through its

76   Ibid., p.9.
77   Ibid., p.15.
78   Ibid., p.19.
79   Ibid., p.20.
80   Ibid., p.19.

intertextual content). She interprets the physical descriptions of the place as a manifestation of the intangible, emotional landscape that the characters live in. She uses images placed against backgrounds to show how authors mirror the emotional world of the characters in the actual surroundings they inhabit. But this is a minor aspect in her concept that "the memory of a text is its intertextuality".[81] She uses the art of memory as a metaphor to explain how intertextuality works within a text.

Although Lachmann, of the three critics I've discussed, comes closest to describing the angle I take on the subject, like Nalbantian and Rickard she keeps returning to memory aspects openly at work in the text – the city is here a storage space for literary memory while the entire text is a storage space for cultural memory. In my approach the backgrounds are actual fixed points in the process of storytelling, as they are fixed points when preparing to write a story, when recollecting it, bringing it to order and giving it meaning during the process of creative thinking, which precedes the process of creative writing.

CONCLUSION

All three critics, Nalbantian, Rickard and Lachmann, have proven that memory processes, mnemonic features and memory systems like the backgrounds-and-images system can be helpful tools for interpreting literary narrative. None of them, however, go beyond the investigation of memory aspects consciously incorporated into the text or of instances where the theme itself is memory. They halt before the next step which no longer focuses on *how* memory is presented or dealt with by the author under investigation, but instead concentrates on *what* the memory structures embedded in the story through the author's memory processes can reveal about the text.

J. Hillis Miller writes in his introduction to *Charles Dickens: The world of his novels* (1958) that "in literature every landscape is an interior landscape, just as each imaginary man or woman is also a figure in the writer's own private world of perception or memory, longing and fear".[82] Not only does he express the concept underlying the phenomenological approach of the Geneva school of theorists to which he belonged, he also describes the theory that informs my investigation. Miller then, as I now, "presupposes that each sentence or paragraph of a novel […] defines a certain relationship between an imagining mind and its objects".[83] He uses this approach in his interpretation of Dickens to reach his goal, which is "the exploration of the imaginative universe of Dickens, and the revelation of that presiding unity hidden at the centre, but present everywhere within his novels and partially revealed there in the embodied disguises of particular characters, actions,

---

81   Ibid., p.15.
82   Miller, *Charles Dickens*, p.x.
83   Ibid., p.ix.

interiors, landscapes, and cityscapes".[84] Where Miller's aim is to capture the entire world of Dickens' imagination by relating his entire canon to the world he lived in, catching "the inner structure of the writer's spirit",[85] I will use the same approach, but be satisfied with an outline of the author's thought processes, embodied in the structuring and imaging of the narrative's "characters, actions, interiors, landscapes and cityscapes".

This is what the next two chapters aim to do. Neuroscience and psychology suggest that the principles of the ancient memory systems hold good today, that memory function is related to spatial awareness, that the way we remember relies on three-dimensional networks of association rather than on individually stored items, and that we retain images better than words and recall them more easily when they appear in an ordered configuration. Draaisma points out that

thinking about processes in memory has been a constant and constituent part of philosophical reflection; doctors in particular, but also theologians, physicists and writers have contributed to theories of memory, and if one pays attention to the metaphors of memory, one is struck more by continuity and consensus than by revolutions or a sudden start in 1885.[86]

Although memory research has developed immensely in a short space of time, the fundamental ideas remain the same. The adaptation of the classical memory system used to enhance the orator's skill in Antiquity, though changed in application, is still relevant to the question of how the memory works and, therefore, how we 'see' things that exist only in the mind.

Only a limited number of attempts to interpret literature based on memory processes have been made by literary critics. Those who have, and especially the three mentioned above, show that there is a vast deal to be extricated from the interaction between memory and literature. In the following chapters I will look at English and US novels to investigate how backgrounds are used as structural features and how images become vehicles for meaning in literary texts.

---

84   Ibid., p.x.
85   Ibid.
86   *Metaphors of Memory*, p.4. 1885 is the date when Ebbinghaus wrote his pioneering work of empirical research into memory function, *Über das Gedächtnis*.

Chapter 4

The Modern English Novel
Salman Rushdie and Angela Carter

This investigation aims to discover whether the memory process, expressed through the concept of backgrounds and images, can be used as a hermeneutical tool. The previous three chapters have striven to show a) the origin of mnemonics and memory systems, b) the mostly conscious implementation of these in medieval literature and c) how memory and literature have been connected in modern subjects such as psychology, neurology and literary theory. The following two chapters no longer aim to show how memory and literature have been brought to bear upon each other in the past; instead, my theory is applied to modern literature. My theory posits that the creative process of the author becomes embedded in the text in the form of backgrounds and images which spring from the author's three-dimensional mental construct. An identification of these in the text enables the reader to attempt a reconstruction of the author's visual landscape. I will test this theory by analysing chosen texts to show how the rhetorical memory palace can become a tool of interpretation. In this chapter I will concentrate on backgrounds and images in relation to two modern English writers: Salman Rushdie and Angela Carter.[1] Before going on to the interpretation of these texts, a brief look at some fundamental changes regarding the perception of memory in modern literature will be helpful.

UNRELIABLE NARRATION AND MEMORY

Rushdie and Carter follow in a long tradition of authors whose narrative voices are not so much representations of an ultimate authority, as examples of human narrative duplicity: what in modern times has been termed *unreliable narration*. The term was coined by Wayne C. Booth in *The Rhetoric of Fiction* (1961). It has come to cover a vast array of narrative voices and seems to defy exact definition. Ansgar Nünning attempts to clarify the term by determining which signals are given within the text or extratextually to indicate that an unreliable narrator is at work, in order to create a basis upon which these various voices can be discussed.[2] He questions whether a distinction between the untrustworthy and unreliable

---

1   The Bombay-born author Salmon Rushdie is here listed as an English writer: despite his mixed heritage, both social and literal, he has influenced British literature to an extraordinary extent and spent many years, including those of his education, in England. Furthermore, he was a resident of England when he wrote *Midnight's Children*, the main text under discussion here, which confronts British and Indian culture. The fact that Rushdie can also be classed as a post-colonial author merely emphasises fundamental concepts of multiplicity and identity within his writings, which forms part of my discussion in this chapter.

2   *"Unreliable Narration* zur Einführung".

narrator (*der unglaubwürdige und der unzuverlässige Erzähler*, terms suggested by Renate Hof in 1984) brings clarification. He argues that they are two vague terms which merely obscure the case further; instead, he lists features that indicate that unreliable narration is involved. One of the main features are inconsistencies between what is narrated and what actually seems to be the case. These can be consciously or unconsciously incorporated by the narrator, be initiated by self-deception or by an attempt at reader-deception, or the narrator can openly acknowledged that facts have been falsified. Accordingly, the tone in which these inconsistencies are presented varies greatly, from serious to sarcastic and from guilty to teasing.

Both Rushdie and Carter enjoy creating inconsistencies through the narrative voice and continually urge circumspection – the reader shouldn't take anything at face value. Their inconsistencies are intentionally incorporated in order to create uncertainty and to break down the authoritative voice of the narrator. One aspect which determines the reliability of a narrator is how far the memories which form the basis for a particular story can be trusted. Nünning includes the failings of memory in his list of signals internal to the text, under a point that covers such aspects as "eingestandene Unglaubwürdigkeit, Erinnerungslücken und Hinweise auf kognitive Einschränkungen".[3] He thereby places memory loss between, on the one hand, the honest admittance of the narrator's unreliability and, on the other, uncontrollable cognitive limitations, clearly classing memory as an unreliable faculty. Nünning suggests that memory can be a strong indicator of unreliability in narration since it is not controllable and spans a huge field of topics, from unreliable memories to neurological instances of memory loss and mental illness that affects memory function.

The narrator's faulty memory is a common literary topos. In the Middle Ages memory, despite acknowledging its fallibility, was considered to be a relatively controllable faculty which made possible creative, theological and academic thought. In modern times memory is mostly referred to in its unreliable capacity. With the application of psychological theory to literary criticism, the way the narrator's mind functions has been emphasised. In particular, the narrative voice often shows aspects of faulty memory and is presented as unreliable – not necessarily because it tells downright lies or because it misunderstands a situation (as is the case with dramatic irony), but because the narrator cannot be certain that her memory serves her well. One of the greatest changes, with regard to how the topic of memory is dealt with in medieval and modern texts respectively, is the shift from the emphasis on remembering to that of forgetting. The narrator's mind can play tricks on her, and readers are often shown the experience of *trying* to remember, rather than the act of reproducing literary truths of seemingly infallible remembrances.

---

3   Ibid., p.28.

Daniel Schacter divides the various aspects of faulty memory into seven categories, calling them the seven sins of memory (see Ch.3). They are: transience, absent-mindedness, blocking, misattribution, suggestibility, bias and persistence.[4] All seven appear frequently in modern literature and influence the perception of a text. Four of the sins are generalised aspects of memory and have played a part in literature throughout the ages, although they can be linked to specific modern genres. Thus the sin of transience, i.e., of forgetting past events through the passage of time, is the most common experience and hence part and parcel of relaying human activities realistically. Absent-mindedness – being unable to recollect certain events because we were not paying attention at the time – is frequently employed in comedy, most stereo-typically in the portrayal of the preoccupied professor or the ditsy blond. Blocking – not being able to remember something we should know, stored somewhere in the memory, but at that moment not accessible (amnesia or the blocking of one vital bit of information, e.g., a secret code) – is a helpful tool in creating suspense within the thriller genre. Finally, persistence – the opposite of forgetting, where a traumatic experience is relived again and again – is used to document cultural and social problems through trauma.

The sins of memory most of interest here are those of *misattribution*, *suggestion* and *bias* because they underline the unreliability of memory – features employed extensively in narrative to influence the relationship between reader and text. *Misattribution* can be explained by an example from Mary Antin's autobiography *The Promised Land*. In the opening paragraph of chapter five, "I Remember", she explains that she will use only her own "broken recollections" of her childhood rather than relying on stories told her by her parents: "I want to string together those glimpses of my earliest days that dangle in my mind, like little lanterns in the crooked alleys of the past".[5] Apart from using architectural terminology to describe the organisation of her memories, she is also aware of the unreliability of these "glimpses", adding, "I have not much faith in the reality of my first recollections". The reason she nevertheless chooses this route is explained in the following passage which is a clear example of misattribution: on recalling the grandfather's house in which she was born, Antin particularly remembers one window with blue sash curtains and a view onto a narrow, walled garden filled with deep-red dahlias. Onto this description is added the following corrective paragraph:

Concerning my dahlias I have been told that they were not dahlias at all, but poppies. As a conscientious historian I am bound to record every rumour, but I retain the right to cling to my own impression. Indeed, I must insist on my dahlias, if I am to preserve the garden at all. I have so

---

4   *The Seven Sins of Memory.*

5   *The Promised Land*, p.79.

long believed in them, that if I try to see *poppies* in those red masses over the wall, the whole garden crumbles away, and leaves me a gray blank. I have nothing against poppies. it is only that my illusion is more real to me than reality. And so do we often build our world on an error, and cry out that the universe is falling to pieces, if any one but lift a finger to replace the error by truth.[6]

Replacing poppies by dahlias in her memory was unintentional, and the mistake only discovered when others pointed out this error to her. However, to Antin it is not the correct recalling of details that matters, but the memory image and the emotions and circumstances attached to it. In Carteresque and Rushdian style she claims that the "illusion is more real [...] than reality". Although she ironically calls herself a "conscientious historian", she realises that only the false memory picture contains the true emotional history of her childhood – were she to replace it by a new and correct image, the essence contained within the image would be lost and the memory along with it. By admitting to her unreliable memory, Antin, paradoxically, becomes more trustworthy because she openly admits her fault.

The sin of *suggestibility* is best know from situations where leading questions produce predictable, but incorrect answers, for example in a police interview. The unintentional influencing of witnesses is something that police psychiatrists take great care to avoid by creating strict guidelines for questioning.[7] Fiction, in contrast, heavily relies on the intentional influencing of people's memories. George Orwell makes it the pivotal feature of his novel *1984* where the party slogan "who controls the past controls the future: who controls the present controls the past" encapsulates the working methods of the totalitarian state of Oceania. Suggestibility is used to brainwash its citizens into the mind-set which enables the ruling class to stay in power. In less extreme form, suggestibility can be used by authors to direct the reader's judgment and possibly lead them into drawing specific conclusions about a situation or a character. In a sense, every author uses suggestibility because the way the story is told will lead the reader in a certain direction, and the extent to which it is incorporated into a text says a great deal about the author's ambitions.

Bias, and particularly hindsight bias, is an unintentional falsifying of memories that happens because we cannot ignore what we already know. It influences how we perceive and ultimately memorise new experiences that are automatically compared to, and linked with, already existing memories. One of the ways in which writers exploit bias is by hinting at the outcome of a process which is still underway, or at events yet to take place which will colour the way we perceive a current situation. 'Giving away the plot' is a common technique amongst authors who either want to capture the reader through anticipation of the upcoming event, or who want to add another layer of meaning, another perspective by preparing the reader for the situation at hand.

---

6   Ibid., p.81.
7   Schacter, *The Seven Sins of Memory*, p.119.

Authors have always experimented with the inclusion of memory faults in their texts, especially in the form of unreliable narration. Carter points out that the concept of the unreliable narrator has become a cliché: "[p]eople babble a lot about the 'unreliable narrator' – as in Salman Rushdie's *Midnight's Children* – so I thought: I'll show you a really unreliable narrator in *Nights at the Circus!*"[8] The protagonists Saleem and Fevvers, discussed below, certainly fall into this category. They exemplify not only the naivety that lies in trusting a narrator blindly, but also the comedy inherent in these duplicitous narratives.

The unreliability of narration is equal to the unreliability of memories: both require a framework within which their reliability can be tested. Nünning rejects as impracticable, even untenable, Booth's suggestion that the 'implied author' should be the reference point for deciding whether a narrative is reliable. Nünning argues that the definition of an implied-author depends on moral or ethical discrepancies between the narrator's and the author's world views: it is therefore impossible to pinpoint. Instead, he suggests that any inconsistencies should be sought between the narrator's posited view and reference frames that are brought to the text by the reader. Nünning refers to Monika Fludernik's observation that "[r]eaders actively construct meaning and impose frames on their interpretations of texts just as people have to interpret real-life experiences in terms of available schemata".[9] According to this concept, Nünning concludes, readers "'entnehmen' […] dem Text nicht einfach Informationen, sondern sie konstruieren selbst Bedeutungen unter Rückgriff auf kognitive Schemata und lebensweltliche Erfahrung".[10] Such a framework would, therefore, be helpful when staking out a horizon, to use Husserl's term (see Introduction), against which the narrator can be qualified.

Nünning is indirectly referring to the memory concept described in chapter three: new information is always related to already existing information in the memory, adding to and updating existing memory patterns in the brain. A story told by an unreliable narrator seems to require a technique analogue to the memory process which creates frameworks within which the narration can take place. These reference frames are the three-dimensional spaces within which the backgrounds and images (settings and symbolic objects or events) are placed in order to make sense of them.

The concept of the memory palace with its reliance on backgrounds and images can be used as a framework to investigate what unreliable narrators are expressing. Since we cannot rely on their words alone, we must resort to the imaginary landscape they set their stories in, create frameworks within which they can be assessed and interpret the images they populate it with.

---

8   Haffenden, *Novelists in Interview*, p.90.
9   Quoted by Nünning in "*Unreliable Narration* zur Einführung", p.26.
10   "*Unreliable Narration* zur Einführung", p.26.

Salman Rushdie – Expanding Views

Salman Rushdie writes that his novel *Midnight's Children* became to him "a book about the nature of memory". He explains: "I thought I would be doing the Proust act [...] of bringing back the past as if it had not been away. I believed that the filter of memory would be removed, so one could get to what it was like if you didn't have the distortions of the filter. And then I just became much more interested in the filter".[11] Rushdie's 'filter of memory' is related to recalling the past. The filter distorts the past through what Schacter would call misattribution, and Rushdie often deals with memory in relation to this 'sin' in his novel. To him the "nature of memory" is that it is unreliable. But rather than deploring this fact, it becomes integrated into the way the narrator Saleem tells his story and that of the 1000 other midnight's children. Reminiscent of the attitude Antin takes to misattribution, the overt incorporation of the unreliability of Saleem's memory adds to his trustworthiness: even though memories may be slightly amended or even completely false, they represent a more truthful memory than a correct image would because it is a true representation of what Saleem 'saw' or what his memory held on to when he first experienced the situation. While writing his memoirs in the pickle factory where Padma works and looks after him (their dialogue frequently interrupting the story and producing a framework for the novel), Saleem explains that the truth he is aiming to capture in his memoirs is

[m]emory's truth, because memory has its own special kind. It selects, eliminates, alters, exaggerates, minimises, glorifies, and vilifies also; but in the end it creates its own reality, its heterogeneous but usually coherent version of events; and no sane human being ever trusts someone else's version more than his own. (211)[12]

This confrontation between memory and history, between memory and truth is played out openly throughout the novel. The aspect of misattribution, which stands between each of the two pairings, manifests itself most strongly in Rushdie's incorporation of mistakes into the text. He explains in an interview that he prepared to write the novel by spending a long time

excavating my memory and the memory of other people. And when there were errors in the remembering, I found I quite liked that, because I didn't want to write something that had journalistic truth but rather something that had a kind of remembered truth. And of course memory does play those tricks. For instance – this is something that Indian readers catch at once – at one point Ganesh is described as having sat at the feet of Valmiki and taking down the *Ramayana*, which of course he didn't. There are a lot of mistakes like that: they are consciously introduced mistakes. The texture of the narrative is such that it almost depends upon being an error about

---

11   Chaudhuri, "Imaginative maps".
12   All references are to the Vintage, 1995 edition of *Midnight's Children*.

history; otherwise it wouldn't be an accurate piece of memory, because that's what narrative is, it's something remembered.[13]

By using the verb 'to excavate' (and other references to memory as a kind of archaeology[14]) Rushdie employs the same phrase that Sigmund Freud uses to explain how he gets at a hysterical patient's hidden memories: by excavating them "layer by layer towards the trauma hidden beneath the hysteria".[15] Although not interested in laying bare hysterical trauma, Rushdie works on a psychological level when he uses the memory to find out what really lies beneath. But where Freud aims to uncover the 'true' experience which would heal the patient, Rushdie, although also aiming to offer solutions for recovery, is not interested in the 'truth' behind the memory, but rather in the truth which it may express: 'a kind of remembered truth', as he writes, which is more truthful than reality itself.

He qualifies this by explaining that "that's what narrative is, it's something remembered". Rushdie here equates narrative with memories and, by extension, the act of writing with the process of remembering. He makes the connection which is fundamental to my thesis: that the memory processes of the author build the foundation for the narrated text. Michael Reder comments on this interplay when he writes that "[m]emory mimics the artistic process".[16] To include the final step of the literary creative process, that of putting ideas into words, the comment must be inverted: the artistic process mimics the memory. Any text is an imprint of the author's mental work that went before. Rushdie's connection between narrative and memory is based on the contemporary realisation that memory is faulty by nature. He says, "of course memory does play those tricks", accepting it as a natural component of the memory process; hence the mistakes, which he stresses "are consciously introduced", embrace the unreliable memory as a literary tool, employing it to make the narrative more, not less truthful – paradoxically more realistic through its errors.[17]

Rushdie's example of an intentionally incorporated memory error is preceded by the line: "this is something that Indian readers catch at once". What about non-Indian readers? During an interview Rushdie is asked whether he ever worries that "using so many culturally specific references" would mean some readers wouldn't

---

13   Chaudhuri, "Imaginative maps".

14   A comparison also used elsewhere, e.g., in "Imaginary homelands", p.12.

15   Draaisma, *Metaphors of Memory*, p.9.

16   "Rewriting history and identity", p.240.

17   Of course, it also excuses any mistakes unintentionally incorporated in the text. Since these are 'sincere' errors, they help to make the text even more truthful, because the author himself is subject to this uncontrollable aspect of narrating. However, it should be noted that Rushdie has admitted that some unintentional mistakes found their way into his novel. In "'Errata', or unreliable narration in *Midnight's Children*" he gives examples of such sincere mistakes. Initially he tried to have these corrected, but later decided to leave them in exactly because they were mistakes caused by a faulty memory – in this case his own. The essay is published in *Imaginary Homelands*, pp.22–5.

understand what he was trying to say. Rushdie's unambiguous answer is "No". He explains that he uses them "as flavouring" and goes on to give an example of how American Jewish writers like Philip Roth may use Yiddish, "and sometimes I don't know what they're saying. [...] It's fun to read things when you don't know all the words," he adds, showing that the multitude of references and hidden clues are only a seasoning for the book.[18] When Rushdie describes the culturally specific references as flavouring, he lifts his narrative into the realm of the senses and, appropriately for *Midnight's Children*, to that of taste. Much of the novel deals with sensual experiences to portray a "remembered truth" rather than a journalistic one.[19] Sensory stimulus activates memory intensely and immediately, particularly stimuli involving smell and taste. These dominate in *Midnight's Children*, both in Saleem's loss and subsequently intensified sense of smell, and in the pickle factory where the narrator Saleem writes his memoirs. He is surrounded by flavours and tastes and even compares the thirty chapters of his narrative – one for each year of his life – to thirty jars of pickle, each with its specific sensual definition.

COLLECTIVE MEMORY

Beyond the comprehension of sensual memory, Rushdie also touches upon collective memory. When asked whether his creation of multilingual words in *The Moor's Last Sigh* is an attempt at reproducing the actual language spoken in India, Rushdie answers:

Oh that's just made up. [...] What I wanted was not to reproduce Indian speech absolutely, but to create a family and its verbal habit. Every family has its own words for things, its own phrases. [...] There is that verbal habit, or family vocabulary, but there is also the habit of storytelling; every family has stories about itself. You could argue, in fact, that the collection of stories a family has about itself is actually the definition of the family.[20]

Rushdie describes the collective memory of a family, the shared memory which makes them a social unit, links them together, undeniably, and creates a sense of belonging. Something he physicalizes in *Shame* when Rani embroiders several shawls depicting family memories, mainly shameful ones (191–5). This is a somewhat spiteful, if understandable action on Rani's part, implying that an individual's actions will affect every member of the family. Within the topic of cultural memory a family provides individual identity within a small group, but also serves as a microcosm for the identity of a nation – the topic that Rushdie

---

18   Salon Interview, "When life becomes a bad novel". Rushdie obviously delights in adding inconspicuous pieces of information to his texts. These include mnemonic games; for example, he composes an acrostic poem at the beginning of *Haroun and the Sea of Stories*: the first letters of each line spell out the name of Rushdie's son.
19   I intentionally use the term 'sensual' (rather than 'sensory') to express the involvement of the emotions when recalling incidents by using the senses.
20   Salon Interview, "When life becomes a bad novel".

returns to again and again in his work. But as Reder points out, "[w]hen Rushdie speaks of 'memory' [in *Midnight's Children*] he is speaking not of cultural memory or national consciousness but of individual memory".[21] Although the family creates part of an identity, the individual is not defined by the family. A variety of influences will make members of the same family perceive events experienced together in very different ways. The emotions and mental images (the memories) that spring from these experiences are disparate and individual. Family, in Rushdie's novels, frequently implies a limiting of the personal identity rather than a helpful definition of the self.

RUSHDIE'S LEITMOTIF – BARTLETT'S ANCHOR POINTS

One structural way in which Rushdie consciously incorporates memory features into the text is by providing reference points in the form of recurring images or dominant details. These can serve as 'anchor points', to use Bartlett's term (see Ch.3). Rushdie refers to this as his 'leitmotif'.[22] With regard to *The Satanic Verses*, Rushdie has been said to "knit together the various threads of the novel by introducing a host of cross-references, repeating the names of characters, catch phrases, and images in a complex network of allusions and echoes".[23] This is not only true of *The Satanic Verses*. In relation to *Midnight's Children*, Rushdie himself mentions the hole in the sheet and the spittoon as leitmotifs,[24] but one could also mention the concept of snakes and ladders, the image of leaking and facial features like big ears and noses. Todd Kuchta makes the leitmotif of the finger and the hand the topic of his essay. He concentrates on instances of their appearance to set up the major topics of the novel. It could be argued that he, incidentally, uses the backgrounds and images system, investigating how the images (the leitmotif of the finger and the hand) develop across various backgrounds and drawing conclusions about the entire novel from this.[25]

In a novel like *Midnight's Children* that constantly jumps between time periods (the writer sitting in the factory at the present date recording his family history over three generations), an anchor point like the silver spittoon or the finger and the hand helps the reader to knit the story together. The recognition of the item not only provides a brief rest for the mind, which is constantly

---

21   "Rewriting history and identity", p.226.
22   Rushdie's choice of the word "leitmotif", to explain this technical feature, relates creative writing to musical composition. See Kuchta, "Allegorizing the Emergency" and Noakes, "Interview with Salman Rushdie". Rushdie also speaks about the "third movement" instead of the novel's third part and describes its structure as working "symphonically". Noakes, "Interview with Salman Rushdie", p.16 and p.25. It emphasises that Rushdie experiences the creative process as a coming together of intricate patterns, an interweaving of sounds, related to the "tuning fork" that helps him find the right words to express an interrelation of ideas through associations. See below.
23   Brians, "Notes for Salman Rushdie", p.87.
24   Noakes, "Interview with Salman Rushdie", p.14.
25   "Allegorizing the Emergency".

bombarded with new, often striking images and ideas; it also encourages us to remember what happened last time we encountered the same object. It divides the story into particular sections (or chunks) which help us to think about it in its entirety rather than merely in its overwhelming detail. Kuchta quotes Rushdie's explanation of how his leitmotif works: "objects or phrases which in themselves have no meaning [...] form a kind of non-rational network of connections in the book".[26] It is non-rational because the object is an instruction to stop and take stock rather than a message in itself. It resembles the creation of a memory network pattern, where the interaction between several individual memory traces will produce the actual memory. The leitmotif builds up the pattern of the story and creates a comprehensive picture of the whole.

As well as objects, Rushdie uses names as anchor points, using their associative powers to create a connection between various parts of the story. Rushdie writes that "[i]t is impossible to overestimate the importance of names. I think they affect us much, much more profoundly than we think. [...] I take enormous amounts of care about naming. It is probably the thing I agonize over most".[27] In *Midnight's Children* the name of Sinai (main character Saleem's surname) is explained in detail with all its associations and meanings (304–5). Rushdie comments upon it, saying that he only realised some of the meanings along the way and that they fitted perfectly:

It's in a way a discovery that you've got the right name when suddenly you look at it and you find all the resonances in it that you want. A surprise, because you really haven't consciously put all that in. Then you also know that your 'tuning fork' is working properly. Because when it is, then everything you think of is right. Then you think of something out of nowhere, and it fits perfectly. I think this is kind of commonplace about writers' experiences when they're going well. Literally everything they pick up seems to be connected – open a newspaper, they find something they want to put in a book. They pick a book off the shelf, they find a solution to the problem they're thinking about. It's a kind of magic that happens when it's going properly: you create a kind of magnetic field and everything conforms to the shape of your magnetic field.[28]

What Rushdie refers to here is the writer's experience, the state of mind he finds himself in when things are going well, when his "tuning fork is working properly". He is describing the open, free-flowing state off mind where images can move in and out amongst the existing memory schemata. The magnetic field seems to symbolise the greatest capacity for association – when, in the right state

---

26   Ibid., p.206.
27   Chaudhuri, "Imaginative maps". It is important to Rushdie that readers realise these connections exist, so that they become aware of the associations inherent in a name. This can be seen, for example, in the glossary at the end of *Haroun and the Sea of Stories* in which names of places and people are explained. However, this is principally a children's book. Adults are usually not given this help in his other novels; here, the explanations are contained within the text itself, to be uncovered by the reader.
28   Ibid.

of mind, it is possible to find connections between practically any two things and make them relate to each other.

IMAGINARY LANDSCAPES

This magnetic field is compatible with an imaginary landscapes that provide backgrounds against which images can be place in a structured, three-dimensional setting. Rushdie's awareness of these landscapes is apparent in the title of his essay collection *Imaginary Homelands*. In one of the essays Rushdie equates the job of the writer with that of a cartographer:

What one is in the business of doing is *mapping*. One of the paradoxes that [*Midnight's Children*] deals with is that India may be an ancient civilisation but it's also a new country. One of the things you have to do with new countries is to draw maps of them. That's one of the things that the book was an attempt to do. And that's one of the things writers can do for readers, provide them with *imaginative maps*. And then you can put yourself on the map. If the book is something that means something to you, then what you're doing is seeming to describe the place you know in which you can see yourself. (my italics)[29]

This passage suggests the way Rushdie sees his profession as a writer and his relationship with the reader. When he speaks about drawing maps of the "new country" that India became, he obviously does not mean that he draws lines on a piece of paper to indicate its exact layout or to determine the borders of the country. Although the topic is fuelled by political confrontations, the India he is in the process of mapping is the one that manifests itself not through borders and segregated areas, but through its people, its ideas and varied human experiences. The imaginative map he draws is one clearly linked to the physical country; but its anchor points, its backgrounds and images are not. Instead, the intangible landscape is structured by a collection of scenes played out against specific backgrounds which bring out the images placed against them. The author places himself amongst these scenes, these islands of events which all link up, positions himself to show how he fits into this new landscape. Rushdie points out that this is "one of the things writers can do for readers, provide them with imaginative maps". These maps are both imaginative in that they have been invented by the author and because they are the foundation for the imagined world an author can help the reader create in his own mind.

Unfortunately, the interviewer did not follow up this thought-provoking answer. It would have been interesting to elucidate what Rushdie meant by the author "describe[ing] the place [he] know[s] in which [he] can see [him]self" only if the book "means something to" him. This comment implies two things about Rushdie's writing technique. First, it suggests that the 'realism' which the text conveys to the reader does not rely on it *being* real, but on it being *meaningful* to the author – because only when the place and situation described takes on a reality

---

29   Ibid.

for the author in *his* mind will it be able to convey a sense of reality to the reader. This coincides with Bartlett's memory experiment which suggests that readers approach a text guided by a search for meaning. The memories created during the reading process are inspired by the perception of the text during this search, rather than by the actual words on the page. The second thing Rushdie's comment implies is that this 'realism' shows itself (literally) to the author, who seems to describe a place he knows although it is wholly invented, because he can *see* himself in that place. Rushdie very clearly describes the condition of having an imagined landscape in his memory, a three-dimensional vivid space into which he can place himself. The realism of this mental image determines how great the effect on the reader will be because it manifests itself in the text.

With Rushdie's references to 'place', 'seeing' and 'mapping' in the mind, we are firmly within the subject (and terminology) of architectural memory systems. The author describes the creative process in terms which could be taken over directly to speak about memory processes that use backgrounds and images. He doesn't make the direct connection because he is describing his experience of writing, which is analogue to the internal memory process that produces the constructed mental world. Rushdie actually invites us to enter his world, to pick up the pointers (the anchor points) and clues to the internal landscape that he has created and seen in his own mind.

TYPICAL BACKGROUNDS

Looking at Rushdie's use of place, it quickly becomes apparent that his various settings easily develop into three-dimensional, vivid images in the reader's mind, reminiscent of the basic outlines which constitute the memory palace.

Rushdie's backgrounds stand out amongst those of other authors in the way they seem to expand. Often they are vast, sometimes metaphysical spaces which despite their limitlessness or shape-shifting component create strong images in the mind. He often uses an amalgamation of directions and associations that build up a picture encapsulating an unlimited space (an oxymoron) which contains within it the universal setting for a specific confrontation. When he does describe a clearly defined limited space, for example the washing chest in Saleem's family home or the magic basket of Parvati the witch, it usually conveys a sense of bondage, suffocation or restriction.

Particularly many opening scenes present the reader with a wide space rather than a clearly defined limited area. We first encounter the eponymous Moraes Zogoiby of *The Moor's Last Sight* in a "dark wood" – a setting with strong symbolic value. However, this description is straightaway qualified by the words "that is, upon this mount of olives, within this clump of trees, observed by the quizzically tilting stone crosses of a small, overgrown graveyard" (3–4). Hence the first impression the reader is given of the background is a metaphorical one – a dark wood – in which meaningful, psychological or frightening things are usually acted out, but here immediately pulled back from the otherworldly realm to mundanity by the comment that the graveyard lies "a little down the track from the Ultimo Suspiro gas station". Despite the ironic repositioning of the character in the everyday world, the 'dark wood' has established itself in the reader's mind and has created a background which adds significance to the scene.[30]

In *Shame* the first line provides a shape as a lasting memory image: "the border town of Q., which when seen from the air resembles nothing so much as an ill-proportioned dumb-bell" (11). The dumb-bell shape also contains a metaphorical element which gives the setting (the background) its context: the city divided into two barely linked parts. The house itself in which the non-hero Omar Khayyam lives with his three mothers is an ever-expanding, ever-changing space where even whole rooms seem to move around. In the final chapter of the book "the house had actually expanded, it had grown so vast that it held within its walls every place in which [Omar] had ever been" (275). The formerly restrictive home, because Omar was not allowed to leave it, has now become a representation of his own memory – containing every place he had ever been. The building here becomes a metaphor for the memory itself, using the various rooms as a metaphor for the faculty of memory and the capacity of storage.

In *Haroun and the Sea of Stories* we also encounter an entire city in the first paragraph, but this city is described in purely emotional terms: Alifbar, "the saddest of cities", by "a mournful sea, full of glumfish", with mighty factories which manufacture sadness and produce black smoke that covers the city. The landscape image we are given here relies entirely upon the feelings generated through its description and hence we have an emotional landscape into which the characters are placed.

In order to create his extraordinary backgrounds against which the stories can be played out, Rushdie sometimes moves heaven and earth – literally. In *The Satanic Verses* the entire first chapter is acted out in midair: the two main characters Gibreel Farishta and Saladin Chamcha tumbling through the air towards London below, after the aircraft they travelled in from Bombay was torn apart by a terrorist bomb. The background is clearly allegorical, representing the Fall (underlined by the exploded plane's name: Bostan – one of the two Islamic gardens of paradise).[31] Suspended during their elongated fall (time stretches to accommodate their conversation) the characters are clearly defined as opposites in their attitudes towards being immigrants in England. The backdrop of the Fall from Grace presages the metamorphoses both will undergo: Gibreel the 'sinner' turns into an angel (like his namesake the archangel) complete with halo, but is ultimately destroyed by his own religious zeal, while Saladin, who always tries to do what is right, grows horns and turns into a demon. They become part of the

---

30   On recalling the opening scene for this chapter, I was, in fact, convinced the dark wood was the actual setting, only to realise on rereading the section that the image that had stayed in my memory was the metaphorical and not the physical one.

31   Pointed out by Höfele in "Wasteland sprouting", p.42.

allegory, representing the equally incorrect demonisation and elevation of Indian immigrants in England. As Brians writes: "Rushdie makes concrete" the popular literary term 'demonization' by "turning Saladin [...] literally into a demon".[32] The term 'literally' appears frequently in my discussion of Rushdie's and Carter's texts because both often reveal the meaning of popular terms by making them concrete. They do this by taking metaphor literally, which is also an effective way of creating a memory image: of inspiring the visualisation of a concept.

By using one of the Four Elements as the background for his opening sequence in *The Satanic Verses*, Rushdie creates an imaginary space which, even though it is translucent, evokes a strong image in the mind. The respective demonisation and elevation of the characters (the metaphysical metamorphoses) is appropriate when seen against the airy background of the fall to earth. Against this intangible background the characters stand out even more and are defined by the act of rushing through the air, the earth looming ever larger below them. By freeing the characters from any kind of (tangible) physical setting, the reader's mind is also freed from placing the characters within a defining space. What *does* define them are the emotions which accompany them on their crazy tumble towards earth and the sense of being suspended in time and space, on the point of a great change – which (in true Rushdian style) is not the expected one of a sudden and deadly contact with the ground.

Despite their remarkable and often surprising qualities, these settings are very naturalistic; Rushdie's backgrounds are not fantastical. There are no twirling houses, palaces resting on blocks of ice or impossible scenery. What makes these settings so very remarkable is the way Rushdie presents them: they expose the significance of the characters who populate them. He provides a very vivid and easily imagined, naturalistic setting against which unusual events or people are portrayed. In the combination between setting and image, in their interaction or effect upon each other lies the clue to a scene's meaning. Rushdie provides the features necessary for a well-functioning memory palace. But he, of course, doesn't describe it as such. In an interview Rushdie mentions Charles Dickens as someone from whom he learned how to use backgrounds most effectively. He says that Dickens "manages to pull off the trick of having an incredibly meticulously naturalistically observed background, and then to project against that a completely surrealistic foreground".[33] This is also true of Rushdie's work: it is a regular feature of settings in *Midnight's Children*. I shall look at three very different scenes in the novel to examine exactly how Rushdie uses naturalistic backgrounds to project various images onto them in order to enhance the conflict played out against them.

---

32   Brians, "Notes for Salman Rushdie", p.87.
33   Noakes, "Interview with Salman Rushdie", pp.29–30.

Salman Rushdie's *Midnight's Children* tells the story of Saleem Sinai and his family, starting with grandfather Aadam and ending with Saleem's own death by disintegration at the age of thirty-one. Saleem is born in Bombay at midnight on the day India achieves its independence and is exalted from birth as a symbol of the new country's progress. Attempting to live up to this ideal proves his downfall despite his, and the other 1000 midnight's childrens' various supernatural powers. Saleem's struggle to understand his own role in history underlies the entire book. However, this is not a historical novel or a *Bildungsroman*. Numerous unexpected turns are taken along the way, extraordinary characters introduced and questions about history, politics and identity are intermingled to present an intensely colourful world in which there are no simple answers.

Background 1: A Kashmiri valley
One of the Four Elements again plays a major part in the opening scene of *Midnight's Children*. This time, Earth:

One Kashmiri morning in the early spring of 1915, my grandfather Aadam Aziz hit his nose against a frost-hardened tussock of earth while attempting to pray. Three drops of blood plopped out of his left nostril, hardened instantly in the brittle air and lay before his eyes on the prayer-mat, transformed into rubies. Lurching back until he knelt with his head once more upright, he found that the tears which had sprung to his eyes had solidified, too; and at that moment, as he brushed diamonds contemptuously from his lashes, he resolved never again to kiss earth for any god or man. This decision, however, made a hole in him, a vacancy in a vital inner chamber, leaving him vulnerable to women and history. Unaware of this at first, despite his recently completed medical training, he stood up, rolled the prayer-mat into a thick cheroot, and holding it under his right arm surveyed the valley through clear, diamond-free eyes. (10)

Before looking at the way Rushdie uses prolepsis to increase the reader's awareness of the topic under discussion, I will focus on the background, the setting for the scene, to discover whether it will yield meaning.

We are in Kashmir on a freezing spring morning. A young man has unrolled his prayer mat across the frozen earth, looking onto a valley that is just coming out of winter hibernation. We may assume a traditional Muslim at his traditional prayer ceremony in his homely environment. Against this predictable and very naturalistic background we find enacted a predictable ritual, which is interrupted in a surprising manner. It is at this point that the imagery and metaphors become unusual. Blood turns to rubies, tears to diamonds – all Aadam's humanity freezes, his emotions laid on ice. Aadam has been infected by his surroundings, has taken on the cold that imprisons the natural features of the landscape. But instead of melting into the background by becoming like it, Aadam completely turns away from everything it symbolises; namely, Islam and obedience. He loses his faith and gains a vacancy within instead, making him vulnerable to women and history.

A woman who proves this assertion appears in the following chapter, but history is presented in the very next paragraph when the valley is described:

The world was new again. After its winter's gestation in its eggshell of ice, the valley had beaked its way into the open, moist and yellow. The new grass bided its time underground; the mountains were retreating to their hill-stations for the warm season. (In winter, when the valley shrank under the ice, the mountains closed in and snarled like angry jaws around the city on the lake.)

In those days the radio mast had not been built and the temple of Sankara Acharya, a little black blister on a khaki hill, still dominated the streets and lake of Srinagar. In those days there was no army camp at the lakeside, no endless snakes of camouflaged trucks and jeeps clogged the narrow mountain roads, no soldiers hid behind the crests of the mountains past Baramulla and Gulmarg. In those days travellers were not shot as spies if they took photographs of bridges, and apart from the Englishmen's houseboats on the lake, the valley had hardly changed since the Mughal Empire, for all its springtime renewals; but my grandfather's eyes – which were, like the rest of him, twenty-five years old – saw things differently … and his nose had started to itch. (10)

Aadam with his 'altered vision' (11) sees beginnings, expansion and possibilities in the surrounding landscape: the background for his new-found outlook is one that is full of promise. But in the immediately following paragraph this hopeful interpretation of the landscape is seen to be faulty because it will change and incorporate landmarks of the troubled times ahead – of the Indian/Pakistani conflict. Rushdie introduces the concept of time to the landscape, projecting a different foreground onto the "meticulously naturalistically observed" background (to use Rushdie's own phrase), and employs it in order to create an atmosphere of uneasy expectation, a worry that Aadam's hopefulness will not be met. This one paragraph encapsulates the conflict between the past and the future in a country where the Mughal Empire and the Kashmiri situation are played out against the same background, thus containing within it the conflict of what was and what is to come without solving it.

If we move from this wide perspective and zoom in on the insignificant event which initiated the process, we can see that the background description informs our understanding of the event. As Rushdie himself points out in an aside: "[t]he tussock of earth, crucial though its presence was as it crouched under a chance wrinkle of the prayer-mat, was at bottom no more than a catalyst" (11). The tussock is a catalyst for the plot, a technical device to materialise a mental change, as much as it is a catalyst for the consequences Aadam draws from the incident. Only one page later we encounter the same episode again. This time we are given a very detailed account of the circumstances as well as the reason for Aadam's extreme reaction. We are told that Aadam was having an internalised argument about Christianity versus Islam. He was recalling discussions with fellow students during his five-year visit to Heidelberg while, distractedly, mumbling the words of the prayer and mechanically producing the movements involved. His frame of mind leads him to overlook the tussock hidden under the prayer mat and to blame the tussock for the incident, by extension seeing it as a wilful assault upon him by his religion. It brings to eruption the inevitable outcome of his argumentative mind-set: Aadam rejects his faith which leaves a "hole in him, a vacancy in a vital inner chamber".

By moving from the enclosed, iced-up Kashmiri valley with a traditional scene played out against it (the prayer) to the internal landscape in Aadam's head – filled with an entirely different world, the German university town, with differing viewpoints – we are experiencing the confrontation between the Eastern Muslim and the Western Christian. We have progressed from the seemingly simple, prejudiced idea of a typical Muslim in Kashmir to the complex person whose internal landscape is not mirrored by the external one. It is in this that Aadam's conflict lies. He cannot combine the two: his external and internal worlds clash and the tussock is an excuse for avoiding this problem and instead blaming an innocent piece of earth for his actions.

By describing this scene twice, once from the outside; once from the inside, Rushdie orchestrates the way the reader absorbs it into the memory. He influences how the image is produced in the imagination. While Rushdie recounts the incident for the second time – in more detail, explaining exactly what thoughts went through Aadam's head at exactly which part of the prayer – the reader already knows the outcome: that soon Aadam will make the profound decision of turning his back on the ritual he is currently performing and all that goes with it. This very much colours the way the scene is read. What is at work here in the memory is called hindsight bias. If the memory-sin of misattribution is the one that most informs Rushdie's conscious integration of how the memory works, then the memory-sin of bias is the one that lies behind his frequent use of prolepsis. Bias, and especially hindsight bias, is the way existing knowledge influences or distorts any new experiences, or memories created from these experiences, because we will always compare new information with already existing material and assimilate the new one into the existing framework or schemata.[34] When an author supplies forward-looking information (when he gives away the plot) he is priming the reader's mind for that particular event, which will then be approached from the angle instilled into the reader's memory on first encounter with the episode. In many instances the first account is meant to be enticing – making the reader keen to read on – and is therefore often mysterious and open-ended, hinting at some exciting or surprising event.

In Rushdie's case the approach is somewhat different. As Brians points out, Rushdie "routinely refers to events to come as if they were already known".[35] This complicity with the reader, the presenting of dramatic events through mere fact, as if recounting a well-known incident, means that the anticipation lies not in the revealing of the plot, but in answering the more profound question: why? Rushdie guides the reader's thoughts in the right direction. Instead of getting distracted by

---

34   See the introduction to this chapter on 'bias'; or Schacter, *The Seven Sins of Memory*, p.138.
35   "Notes for Salman Rushdie", p.6.

circumstances, the reader looks for reasons within the protagonist's internal dialogue – ironically set against the automatic repetition of the securely stored words of the prayer. Rushdie's use of bias is very effective. He is well aware that he can influence his reader to look at a situation in a certain way by exploiting the way the mind works. He does so by portraying the main protagonist Aadam, the embodiment of a large topic, against a background which helps clarify this view by introducing symbolism and the effects of time to the setting. When Aadam collides with the tussock, it literally hits him that he can't go on the way he has done so far. The confrontation between two cultures experienced during his stay in Europe has left him with a new outlook which means he cannot simply settle back into his old life. Aadam, in this simple incident, embodies the enormously complex problem of culture clashes.

Josna E. Rege writes that *Midnight's Children* "celebrates the creative tensions between personal and national identity",[36] and this scene is a very intense personal experience which is sparked by questioning national identity. Aadam is no longer defined by the fact that he is Kashmiri born. This produces creative tension because it challenges Aadam to discover his new identity. This early episode in the novel introduces the basic conflict which will be investigated throughout the book – moving ever further away from the initial simplified dichotomy between 'them' and 'us'.

Rushdie certainly exploits the "creative tension between personal and national identity" in his work, as Rege suggests. He "celebrates" this tension *because* it inspires creativity, imagination, multiplicity and variety. His characters come to life exactly because of the tension they live under. In the episode described above it is the vast topic of religion that encourages Aadam to break out of his constricting identity and to gain a new one – unfortunately, he is somewhat overwhelmed by the task. As with all Rushdie's creative tensions, this one isn't solved by a clean bipolar structure which keeps a healthy balance. This is not Muslim versus Christian, East versus West; it is a much more complex form of identity. As Rege further remarks: "sparks fly between the private and public realms, making artistic fireworks where there had previously been deadening dichotomies".[37] A look at Rushdie's use of backgrounds shows that he is never satisfied with the presentation of opposites or parallels.

Background 2: The Pioneer Café
Aadam is caught between cultures and religions (a basic introduction to the topic of personal versus national identity); his daughter Amina and former son-in-law Quasim in the following episode are caught between the private and the public realms. This is another scene which confronts personal and national identity, but on a very different plane.

---

36   "Victim into protagonist?", p.250.
37   Ibid.

In book two Saleem's mother Amina drives to the Pioneer Café in Bombay for a secret assignation with Quasim Kahn – her first husband with whom she lived in hiding underground. He then fled from politically motivated persecution but kept writing love-poems to his soon-to-be ex-wife. Saleem has hidden himself in the boot of the family's Rover ("the vehicle of maternal perfidy") to discover where his mother goes on her sudden shopping trips which always occur after the frequent 'wrong number' calls to their home. On arrival he climbs out of the boot of the car, unseen, and follows his mother to the café, through the dirty window of which he observes the loving encounter between Amina and Quasim (or Mumtaz and Nadir, as they were when they last were united). Their romance expresses itself merely through their "dancing hands" and the Bollywood imitation of sensuality: a kiss on opposite sides of the same drinking glass. It poignantly mimics the Bollywood actress Pia, Amina's sister-in-law, who starred in a film that caused an uproar due to this daring use of symbolic eroticism (142).

This brief interlude, this very personal and private scene of constrained emotions is packed with references to Saleem's adolescent and somewhat skewed morality and curiosity, the constraints of Indian social morality and how political involvement encroaches upon personal relationships. The theme of the Indian film industry and party politics is established along with the background. As the car approaches the café, we are entering the northern zone which contains "tenements and fishing-villages and textile-plants and film-studios". We are clearly in the working class district of the city that is unfamiliar to middle class Saleem, who immediately stands out through his attire. The Pioneer Café is a microcosm of the area, a place where film-studios come scouting for extras for the day's filming, while every lunchtime it becomes "a notorious Communist Party hangout" – both sets of people with their "different set of dreams" (216) which makes the café itself "a repository" for these dreams (215).

The setting is saturated with Bollywood references: "Through the dirty, square, glassy cinema-screen of the Pioneer Café's window, I [Saleem] watched Amina Sinai and the no-longer-Nadir play out their love scene; they performed with the ineptitude of genuine amateurs" (216–17). A detailed description follows in "extreme close-up" where "hands enter the frame" but are afraid to touch, and where faces are seen "jerking away all of a sudden in a cruel censor's cut … two strangers each bearing a screen-name" who "act out their half-unwanted roles". Amina and Quasim are caught up in a bad film, controlled by rules set up by the elusive censor of society's morality, adhered to by the two in a pathetic imitation of Bollywood films.

Bollywood cinema is used extensively as a metaphor in the novel, presenting Bombay as a factory that produces unrealistic films in the world of which viewers find escape from their difficult lives. Pynchon, too, uses mass media as a reflection on modern society's escapism into a false world, emphasising the subversive influence the medium has on a seemingly willingly manipulatable population, but the US setting gives it completely different overtones (see Ch.5).

Rushdie equates his own writing with the process of making Bollywood films when he directs the view of the reader by saying "we cut to a long-shot" (33) or when he indicates the passage of time by pages of a calendar flying off at ever increasing speeds (346). *Midnight's Children*, too, presents a fake world, created to extract a certain reaction from the reader, presenting a parallel universe where people and events are invented. However, the further we move into the book, the more this world of illusion is fragmented, shattered into smaller and smaller pieces, giving the reader more and more detail. Rushdie uses the metaphor of the cinema to explain the sensation of being too close to something and therefore not able to comprehend it, and then turns it on its head. "Suppose yourself in a large cinema," says the narrator in *Midnight's Children*,

sitting at first in the back row, and gradually moving up, row by row, until your nose is almost pressed against the screen. Gradually the star's faces dissolve into dancing grain; tiny details assume grotesque proportions; the illusion dissolves – or rather, it becomes clear that the illusion itself *is* reality … (165–6)

The Bollywood-inspired setting forms the basis for Amina and Quasim's emotional conflict. On the surface it looks like a scene from a film, but the more details we are given – the closer we get to the screen – the more we realise that the illusion *is* the reality. "Reality is a question of perspective," says the narrator (165). What to Saleem, observing the scene through the cafe's window (the cinema screen), appears to be a lewd, cheap re-enactment of cheesy Bollywood love turns out to be the truthful and complicated love of Amina and Quasim.

The political setting, like the Bollywood one, takes on a very personal aspect in the way Quasim's political association affects their relationship. To Amina the term 'communist' has an entirely private significance: when she hears the word she blushes, "politics and emotions were united in her cheeks" (216) – associations with the colour red unite in her personal experience of love, shame and politics since Amina does not associate political images with the word, but instead her secret love for Quasim. Nadir/Quasim the "official candidate for the official Communist Party of India", nicknamed Quasim the Red, is still restricted in his personal expression of his feelings through the conventions he lives by. The politician Quasim, however, deviates from the earlier comment on his 'kind'; the politicians "for whom all alternative versions of the world are threats" (217). Hence 'the politician' as an abstract figure in Rushdie's generalised comment clearly falls under the popular perception that politics is narrow-minded and the individual politician pursues only his own goals. But Nadir/Quasim, the poet/politician is a hybrid – a non-abstract, a human being who can contain binary oppositions within his character. What defines him is not so much that he is a communist or a secret lover, but his compassionate yet ineffectual character. A hapless idealist, who picks his alliances rather badly when we first encounter him in the book, he is forced underground and emerges a couple of years later under a different name to work for the cause of Communism. Despite being Amina's great love, he is the same lanky-haired, unsuccessful man he was before, who will "narrowly fail to win his seat" in the upcoming election (222). His political officialdom (emphasised by the repetition of the word "official" in the one line of description) is undermined by his inofficial status with regard to the love for Amina (an inversion of their earlier situation where his political involvement made him hide in a cellar while his marriage to Amina was acted out – but also failed in the end).

The Pioneer Café, the repository of dreams for aspiring film-stars and up-and-coming Communists alike, is not pioneering anything so much as pointing out the lack of pioneering spirit amongst its visitors. The grubbiness and cheapness of the place (with its dirty glasses, neon lighting and plastic table-covers) is an extreme opposite to the dreams spun there. There is also the ironic reference to the colonisers of India in the café's name: those individuals who, for better or worse, came to bring progress to an entire country, making the scene a private and public confrontation of cultures, established against a strained historical background, growing out of religious as well as political, social and cultural conflicts. At this point in the book the colonising pioneers have left India to independence and a new pioneering outlook is needed.

India's entire history is entangled in this very personal and private encounter between Amina and Quasim; but not because they are particularly involved in it or because this is a pivotal moment in the novel. Through every scene in the book runs the mixed history of India, of East and West, in the global sense as well as the Pakistani/Bangladeshi conflict. The name of the café, the Bollywood music playing in the background and the political orientation of the lunch-time visitors – all this is part of the story not because the historical elements are to be brought into the foreground, but because each character is made up of all of these aspects, stands in a personal relationship to them, whether trivial, profound or accidental, and can only be understood as entire beings through these relationships. As Saleem repeats again and again, "[t]o understand just one life, you have to swallow the world" (109). A person is not a limited entity, but is influenced and connected to everything around it. People are 'leaking' into each other, to use one of Rushdie's favourite images. People absorb everything that goes on around them and adapt it to fit their world-view, created from their experiences. Unfortunately, they are not always able to give it a Bollywood ending.

Background 3: The purgatorial jungle
The third episode, taken from book three, expresses the tension between national and personal identity through the psychological effects of actual warfare on four young men. In the jungle sequence the tension is created in the conflict between external and internal warfare. The external conflict is caused by the chaos and horrors surrounding amnesic Saleem (now the 'snifferdog' for the Pakistani army, called the buddha) and his three soldier-boys (Ayooba, Shaheed and Farooq) during their active participation in the war between East and West Pakistan in

1971. The internal conflict is based on psychological chaos and horrors which befall the four characters during their timeless stay in the rainforest. Here they are visited by ghosts who accuse them of past crimes and make them face up to the horrors perpetuated on others by themselves. The three Pakistani Muslim soldiers must face facts in the jungle. What seemed an idealistically viable career during preparation for the fighting, an abstract idea in relation to the history of the nation, becomes a personal affair when the effects of actual wartime events take hold upon the boys. Just like a European fairy tale forest, the East-Pakistani rainforest is a way into the unconscious, an encounter with the unspeakable self – the true identity hidden under layers of external definitions, including national, religious and political ones.

The narrator explains what he wishes to achieve by reporting the jungle passage: "I hope to immortalize in pickles as well as words [...] that condition of the spirit in which the consequences of acceptance could not be denied, in which an overdose of reality gave birth to a miasmic longing for flight into the safety of dreams" (360). The reality of the war makes the four companions wish to escape into dreams. But instead of providing an escape, the dreams only help materialise the consequences of their acceptance of the situation they found themselves in. The re-enactment of past events in the mind become even more crushing than physical actions seemed at the time – a 'punishment' which cannot be evaded. The development of personal identity is here propelled forward by national identity – but it has a different meaning for each individual, and the historical events experienced together unleashes in each of them, in the not so still moments of contemplation in the jungle, aspects of their characters and effects them in various ways. Although they share a national identity, even a very similar recent history, they experience and digest it very differently.

The background Rushdie provides for this conflict has strong political as well as religious overtones: the "labyrinthine salt-water channels" along which they initially make their way through the jungle in the rowing boat are "overtowered by the cathedral-arching trees" (360) that populate it. After a night of seemingly endless rain the trees appear to have grown even taller and produce from Shaheed the comment that "the birds at the top must have been able to sing to God" (361). The jungle itself seems to hold spiritual powers which appear to promise solace at first, but turn into threatening aspects, especially when the Hindu temple dedicated to the goddess Kali, in which the four (Muslim) companions every night encounter and have sex with four mysterious young women, turns out to be an illusion and the final instance of the jungle playing with their minds: "[t]he last and worst trick of the jungle, that by giving them their heart's desire it was fooling them into using up their dreams, so that as their dream-life seeped out of them they became as hollow and translucent as glass": the buddha (that is, Saleem) calls it "a depredation worked on [the] imagination" (367).

In an interview Rushdie calls the jungle chapter the "descent into hell",[38] and it is a veritable purgatorial experience for the four of them. The greatest danger to these four characters is not the harsh environment of the jungle (they learn to live in it) or even the psychological self-confrontation (which helps them individually to 'grow up' and the buddha to regain his memory); it is the loss of their dreams, of imagination, that is the real danger. Without an 'inner life' the outer one becomes meaningless and the person fades away, becomes translucent like the insects and fruits of that jungle. Historical facts make up a person's identity; their hopes, dreams and imagination sustains it. Without this there is no life.

Consequently, to succour their dreams and imagination, they must return to reality, to the world of facts and figures, of history and politics. There is a link between the two which means that in isolation both would fail, while their interaction sustains life and shapes individuality: an individuality which is fed by many oppositional aspects. In the jungle scene Muslim boys go through Catholic purgatory which climaxes in a Hindu temple during a war for independence between two parts of the same country divided by a country of independence; physical and mental strength is tested by modern psychology as well as traditional superstition in a subtropical environment with aspects of Christian church architecture. Nothing is ever either just the one or the other in this book.

IDENTITY AND THE LOSS OF SELF

Saleem regains his memory during the jungle episode: his personal history. But he does not remember his name until some time later when Parvati the witch calls him by it at a chance encounter in the magicians' ghetto (379). But the return of his name does not augur a greater self-knowledge, as the jungle experience does for Ayooba, Farooq and Shaheed. Saleem is drawn back into the perception that he is instrumental in India's history. Rushdie breaks with conventional norm: the main protagonist of a story traditionally goes on a journey of self-discovery which increases self-awareness and a growing ability to judge himself. But it becomes clear that Saleem, despite his many extraordinary experiences, withdraws more and more into his world, which becomes ever more unrealistic.

Rushdie says that without book three (which includes the jungle sequence and concludes the entire novel) *Midnight's Children* would have been "a kind of *Bildungsroman*".[39] The final book, however, shows that Saleem's development is not linear or progressive in the traditional sense. It describes Saleem's developing delusion about his personal involvement in national identity. Saleem has been defined by an allegory from birth: Prime Minister Jawaharlal Nehru's letter, sent to congratulate him on having been born at exactly the moment of India's independence, marks him as "the newest bearer of that ancient face of India" and states that his life "will be, in a sense, a mirror of our own" (122). Saleem takes

---

38   Haffenden, *Novelists in Interview*, p.239.
39   Ibid.

this allegory seriously, identifies with it, equates his self with India's history, and this informs his entire outlook on life. The supposed meaning of his life has been handed to him and has made a search for identity superfluous. Saleem literally falls apart trying to live up to the definition of this self. He shatters the frame the allegory imposes upon him. It reveals that the novel cannot be read as a simple allegory on Indian history. Or rather, it could be read as such, but this would diminish its significance. Rushdie himself points out that he avoids using straightforward allegory because

[a]llegory comes very naturally in India, it's almost the only basis of literary criticism – as though every text is not what it seems but only a veil behind which is the real text. I quite dislike the notion that what you are reading is really something else. [...] Although the book contains [...] large allegorical notions, it tries to defuse them.[40]

Reder sees *Midnight's Children* as "a parody of an allegory that reveals the potentially repressive use of allegorical representation and readings".[41] Metaphor serves Rushdie's style and message much better because it is fluid, like his ideas, settings and images. In Ron Shepherd's words, Rushdie "insists on mistaking metaphor for reality, metaphoric meaning for actual meaning".[42] In the first paragraph of *Midnight's Children* Saleem's birth is described: he is born at midnight on August 15th 1947 in Bombay at exactly the same moment as India's independence. Saleem says that he was "mysteriously handcuffed to history" (9). The author here proposes that Saleem is locked into history, that his life, and therefore his identity, is determined by the events that unfold around him. At this point national and personal identity can be understood to be one and the same. As we progress through the novel, we see that this connection between Saleem and Indian history, which so easily can be read allegorically, becomes more and more tenuous: Saleem's own explanations for his direct responsibility for historic events (like the Emergency, the language riots, etc.) become ever more fantastic and unbelievable. (For example, Saleem says with comic hubris that he was "beginning to take [his] place at the centre of the universe", 126). We realise that Saleem's own importance is build on very dangerous ground at the latest when we are told that the two generations preceding Saleem, which we've been following for over 100 pages, are not his real ancestors at all because he was switched at birth. The early assertion that we can understand Saleem if we understand his ancestors and the times he grew up in is sorely tested when almost nothing we've been told turns out to be true.

The final image of the book shows Saleem literally disintegrating amongst masses of people celebrating India's independence of thirty-one years. Saleem

---

40   Ibid., p.243.
41   "Rewriting history and identity", p.232.
42   Quoted by Reder in "Rewriting history and identity", p.232.

stated this outcome as fact from the very beginning – his most unbelievable assertion turning out to be his most truthful. Now Saleem is falling apart into more than six million pieces (at the time Rushdie wrote the book the approximate population of India), "a broken creature spilling pieces of itself into the street" (463). Trying to identify with the nation has torn Saleem apart; his personal identity cannot survive being equated with the nation. There are as many versions of history as there are people retelling it – Rushdie conveys forcefully through the image of Saleem's fragmentation – and, therefore, there are just as many truths. The 'remembered truth' is more real than reality itself, according to Rushdie. Nationality and everything related to it (such as politics, religion, history, society and culture) informs our understanding of the world. As soon as we are part of a particular group of people, in the case of nationality defined by geographical limits, we share experiences, a collective memory which naturally influences the way the world is viewed.

Rushdie stresses that our identity need not be based on these specific influences alone because our personal and emotional responses to all aspects of nationality are ultimately a choice: collective or communal memories feed our imagination, our dreams; but how far we accept these is up to us. The destructive last scene contains the hope that it is possible for an individual to escape from collective thinking in order to draw independent conclusions about the world.

CONCLUSION

In his novels Rushdie chooses locations (backgrounds) which, looked at close up, dissolve into individual pixels, like a cinema screen. As the three scenes inspected above show, settings in *Midnight's Children* are generally not used as allegorical frameworks for one specific reading of the text. Rather, they expand the possibilities of meaning expressed by the actions played out against them. I've said in chapter one that allegorical writing is analogue to the architectural memory system. But if we try to apply the backgrounds-and-images system allegorically to *Midnight's Children*, we fail. When Rushdie says that he "quite dislikes the [typically Indian] notion that what you are reading is really something else," he suggests that the story is *not* an external structure which is the "husk" of an inner "matiére" (see Ch.1), merely a framework for the meaning. The story *is* what it seems. We must take the unbelievable elements seriously: they do not stand for "something else" in a true allegorical fashion.

It becomes apparent that allegorical analysis of *Midnight's Children* fails when attempting to interpret the novel by means of personification: Saleem is *not* India! Furthermore, there is no allegorical palimpsest-reading (there are not so much layers of meaning or chains of images as diversity of interpretation) and the map Rushdie draws of the countries (India, Pakistan and Bangladesh) is not a traditional allegorical map, leading a person through a symbolical landscape like the maps in *Piers Plowman* (see Ch.2). Unlike Carter, who relishes creating levels of meaning through allegorical interaction of ideas (see below), Rushdie avoids the clear-cut structure that comes with it. He emphasises disintegration, constantly changes identities (even of landmass) and is interested in the concept of people 'leaking' into each other. Boundaries are vaguely drawn and frequently redefined. His ideas expand like his backgrounds. They are snapshots of specific events, but simultaneously contain the entire world. The characters portrayed against these expanding backgrounds are not archetypes or symbols of something else, but idiosyncratic pieces of the puzzle that is humanity. At once unique and one amongst millions.

Rushdie avoids traditional norms, attempting to inspire a unique outlook. With regard to *The Satanic Verses* Rushdie writes that "*Mélange*, hotchpots, a bit of this and a bit of that is how newness enters the world".[43] This is said in relation to the mixing of cultures through immigration which Rushdie embraces. He welcomes this "newness" by which others feel threatened. It is this *mélange* which also informs the novel *Midnight's Children*. It is a hotchpots in which the backgrounds of amalgamated ideas, linked together by recurring images, enables a progression of ideas not confined by the form in which they are presented.

Angela Carter – The Stage and the Swan

I remember everything.
Yes.
I remember perfectly.
[…] I must write down all my memories … since, after all, I remember everything

These are the confident first lines of Angela Carter's novel *The Infernal Desire Machines of Doctor Hoffman*. But only four pages later the same narrator says, "I cannot remember exactly how it began" (15). According to Brian Finney, "[m]emory is part of the bewildering contradictory nature of the art of narration" in this surrealist novel.[44] This kind of discrepancy, these contradictory statements that occur within only a few pages of each other, shows how the memory faculty can be used to establish uncertainty through the unreliable voice of the narrator. Pointing out inconsistencies within the narrative comes top of Nünning's list for textual signals of unreliable narration. He defines these instances as "explizite Widersprüche des Erzählers und andere interne Unstimmigkeiten innerhalb des narrativen Diskurses".[45] Carter clearly signals to the reader that an unreliable narrator is at work and thereby increases the reader's sensitivity towards other such instances. However, in *Doctor Hoffman* we are dealing with an addled mind rather than an intentionally manipulative voice. This becomes clear as we progress through the story. Faulty memory and forgetting are emphasised in much of

---

43   "In Good Faith", p.394.
44   "Tall tales and brief lives".
45   "*Unreliable Narration* zur Einführung", p.27.

Carter's work; here it is used to characterise the protagonists and to add a sense of ambiguity to the text. General references to the common failings of memory, such as 'as far as I remember' and pointing out that certain things are forgotten, occur frequently in Carter's texts. That she is interested in the more character-revealing aspects of memory is apparent when Carter coins the word 'misremembering' in *Wise children* to emphasise that it is not a loss of memory, but an unreliable memory we are dealing with. This opens up the possibility of probing far more complicated psychological states of mind.

ARTIFICIAL MEMORY

Beyond these references to failings of the natural memory, Carter also shows an awareness of the workings of artificial memory in her use of spatial awareness, memory metaphors and the power of images which surge through all her work. We've already encountered the city as a memory map in Chaucer's *Troilus and Criseyde* (see Ch.2). Carter, too, refers to the memory map when she says *Doctor Hoffman* "began as an inventory of imaginary cities".[46] Each new city in the novel is indeed given functions which produce the perfect background for the events that take place within it; thus, each new city establishes the parameters of the protagonist Desiderio's new state of mind, reminiscent of the personifications of the mental faculties which did the same for Will in *Piers Plowman*. By using the word 'inventory', Carter links the imaginary cities to the storage facility of memory that uses an inventory, an overview of specific items placed within a given space. It is a way of structuring her narrative which is reminiscent of the pilgrimage genre: each station (in this case each city) along the way containing a specific significance and a particular place in the order.

In *Nights at the Circus* the journalist Walser discards his factual reporting style and for the first time turns his hand to imaginative writing. His topic is the description of a city: "I am inventing an imaginary city as I go along" (97),[47] he comments as he puts together a rather romantic and lyrical description of St Petersburg – but a St Petersburg of which he has seen only the dilapidated back alleys he creeps along to remain unnoticed.

As Lachman writes in her book *Memory and Literature*, the city described by an author is never the real city because it is suffused with the author's own cultural imprint (see Ch.3). The St Petersburg in Carter's novel is only one of many possibilities, reflecting the views and perceptions of the author. Carter uses the city to represent various characters' personal development through the way they react to it. In Walser's case it shows a break from his typical behaviour, but also one that encourages a false, wholly illusory picture of the town, predicting that Walser's change from pragmatist to romanticist ultimately confuses him and is merely an emotional stage in his development.

---

46   Haffenden, *Novelists in Interview*, p.95.
47   All references are to the Vintage, 1994 edition of *Nights at the Circus*.

On a smaller scale, architectural structures also form symbolic backgrounds for events in Carter's novels. They are directly linked to the concept of memory when the character Dora in *Wise Children* writes that "[t]here was a house we all had in common and it was called, the past, even though we'd lived in different rooms" (226). Carter, like Virginia Woolf (see Ch.3), compares the past to a building. Here it is a regular house rather than a Cathedral because there is nothing reverent about Dora's memories. The house distinguishes itself from most of Carter's settings in being so realistic. More often than not her buildings add a layer of meaning to the text, sometimes "in order to build up a picture, almost unbearable in its nightmarish intensity". For example, "the Borden house itself [in "The Fall River axe murders"] takes on the surreal quality and distorted perspective of an Escher engraving".[48]

This is Carter's speciality: to use circumstantial settings to emphasise the inherent meaning and thereby create an atmosphere which draws the appropriate emotional response from the reader. However, sometimes her settings which are so specifically chosen and so thoroughly fashioned to aid comprehension are overlooked by the reader. An example is Tristessa's glass house in *The Passion of New Eve*. Carter intended it to represent "an image of a certain kind of psychic vulnerability [...], indicating something quite specific about the nature of illusion and of personality". The hall of immortals, in which wax works of famous dead Hollywood film stars are laid out, "was intended to say something about representations, but readers seemed to think that it was all just part of the fantastic decor of the house".[49] Carter is often mistakenly read as a sensationalist author but, as the quotation above shows, settings are another artistic tool she uses to place the events in a larger context; not merely ostentatiously fantastic spaces used to capture the reader's imagination. Carter incorporates relevant and meaningful settings in her novels because "there's a materiality to imaginative life and imaginative experience which should be taken quite seriously".[50] The materiality is made apparent in her imaginative writing through the importance she places on the detail of location, and her images are just as significant.

The strength of her imagery-painting and scene-setting is partly derived from the way she employs spatial awareness in the text and then appropriates it to create a comic picture, as in the scene in *Wise Children* when the twins Nora and Dora visit the theatre with their Grandma for the fist time and see their father, also for the fist time. Upon spotting him in the seats a level above them "Grandma rose up and raised her hand, she pointed: If you'd drawn a line straight form the end of her finger up into the dress circle, it would have landed on the nose of a man" who turns out to be their elusive father, Melchior Hazard (55). Several things are accomplished by this simple image: we are aware that the father is elevated above

48   Gamble, *The Fiction of Angela Carter*, p.160.
49   Haffenden, *Novelists in Interview*, pp.86–7.
50   Ibid., p.85.

his children – a symbolic representation of his feelings for them – while the comic picture of a line drawn across the open space from the stalls to the dress circle, hitting the nose of a man, clearly expresses the Grandmother's opinion of him. She ridicules him by openly making a connection between the two parties, breaching the gap metaphorically produced by the distance within the theatre. It is an accusation that is made in comic form which points out that the comic figure is the father – whose nose is punched by an imaginary accusatory beam sent out unceremoniously from an aggrieved old woman's pointing finger.

NIGHTS AT THE CIRCUS

For the purpose of this thesis, I will concentrate on Carter's novel *Nights at the Circus* to discover exactly how she uses backgrounds and images to convey meaning in her texts. *Nights at the Circus*, set in the last months of the nineteenth century, tells the picaresque story of the Cockney aerialist Fevvers, who is purported to have wings, and the young American journalist Walser, who follows her tour with the circus to St Petersburg as an undercover journalist where he gets a job as clown. When the train that takes the troupe to their next destination breaks down in the Siberian tundra, all but Walser are taken by outlaws: he ends up in a small village as the Shaman's apprentice. After further adventures Fevvers is reunited with Walser in the shamanic hut. The question asked throughout the novel deals with Fevvers' physique – 'is she fact or is she fiction?' – i.e., does she really have wings with which she can fly? By deconstructing gender roles and stereotypes in their various manifestations throughout the book, we end with the happy coupling (in both senses of the word) of Fevvers and Walser, the New Woman and New Man; not in the traditionally happy ending of a marriage, but starting into the new century (the twentieth) with hope for the possibility of developing a new role for man and woman alike.

TYPICAL BACKGROUNDS

Nights at the Circus is a journey displayed against clearly defined backgrounds – three geographical places which contain various clearly defined settings: the seedy dressing room, the brothel and the "museum of women monsters" in London; hotel rooms, the circus arena and the Grand Duke's palace in St Petersburg; and a female detention centre, a shabby musical conservatoire and a shamanic den in Siberia. Carter offers an extraordinary array of settings which are an imaginary delight in their vivid glory of description. Her settings, so three-dimensional in their detail, yet so strangely foreign, have influenced the attributes that describe her work as variously Gothic, grotesque and fantastic and are partly responsible for classing her work in the magic realism genre. Carter's strength is to create an intense atmosphere through her settings that are extremely vivid, yet never so overpowering that they get in the way of the story. No setting ever appears coincidental or merely sufficient. Rather, it provides the exact background which aids the events played out against it and truly becomes a vehicle for the story and a clue to its meaning. Carter's many asides undermine, contradict or comment on a chosen setting and thereby draw attention to the added level of information they provide. Simultaneously, her critical, comical or subversive references to the style she uses prevent too narrow readings of the scenes.

It is difficult to settle on one scene for specific attention, even with an eye to obvious connections with the architectural art of memory, as all contain within them the terminology, structural coherence and three-dimensional imaginative existence that are fundamental to the memory system. Carter says, she chose the picaresque mode because within it "people have adventures in order to find themselves in places where they can discuss philosophical concepts without distraction":[51] the background determines the action. The questions whether Fevvers is fact or fiction is taken up continuously. It lies at the heart of *Nights at the Circus* and works as a specific example of the philosophical question Carter poses in all her novels: what is real and what illusion? The backgrounds Carter uses in this novel to compare reality and illusion usually set them in opposition, but at the same time expose the artificiality of such a strict dichotomy. Thus the brothel where Fevvers grows up is a place that pampers to men's sexual needs, but also a hotbed of feminist ideas in the form of the prostitutes' progressive hobbies which foretell the jobs that became available to women in the wake of the suffrage movement at the beginning of the twentieth century.

Another setting in *Midnight's Children* that contains a wealth of material for investigation is the circus itself:

What a cheap, convenient, expressionist device, this sawdust ring, this little O! Round like an eye, with a still vortex in the centre; but give it a little rub ... instantly, the circus ring turns into that durable metaphoric uroboric snake ... the wheel whose end is its beginning ... O! of wonder; O! of grief. (107)

Carter ridicules Walser's lyrical, metaphysical contemplations which show him still in his romantic phase. Walser's pompous interpretation of the setting is immediately contrasted by an actual event in the circus ring. Lamark's Educated Apes invert the human hierarchy of subordination during an unobserved rehearsal: they persuade Walser to strip naked (except for his dunce's hat) to aid their secret anatomy lesson. Here, the apes clearly are the superior beings, and Walser's example of human speech (requested for didactic purposes by the ape professor), the quotation from *Hamlet* "What a piece of work is man", takes on very ironic overtones in this setting: with Walser as the representative of the human race, what a strange, naive and ridiculous piece of work is man! Carter uses the traditional circus setting which, in her own words, "is always a microcosm"[52] and turns this entire world up-side down. This setting, with its implications of an

---

51   Ibid., p.87.
52   Ibid., p.89.

inverted world picture, relates to Bakhtin's concept of carnivalisation: the literary convention of mixing sacred and sublime elements with profane and ridiculous ones in order to overthrow the culturally accepted hierarchy and, thereby, give prominence and power to normally unheard voices. Carter herself writes about the "carnival-like proceedings" that take place in the circus ring (146), and calls Buffo, the head clown, the "Lord of Misrule" (175) in accordance with the carnivalesque tradition.

Paulina Palmer interprets this carnivalesque scene not so much as released mirth, but as "representing the violence which is rife in a male-dominated culture" where the circus ring "becomes an effective symbol of the patriarchal social order".[53] Carter does indeed adapt Bakhtin's carnivalesque concept, but Palmer's patriarchal reading of the passage seems somewhat constrictive. Carter appears to question the concept of carnivalisation itself. As Marina Warner writes, Carter understood perfectly well "the limits of merry-making [,] the power of the carnivalesque to contain rather than to release".[54] Carter told Lorna Sage in an interview that the aim of the carnival is that it "has to stop. The whole point about the Feast of Fools is that things went on as they did before, after it stopped."[55]

The inversion of social hierarchy is only a safety valve to ensure the security of existing structures. This is also made clear in *Nights at the Circus* when Buffo, during the circus act tellingly entitled 'The Feast of Fools', attempts in earnest to kill Walser, who is dressed as a chicken. The audience responds with laughter, not realising that they are witnessing an attempted murder. The clown's tragic fate is that he can tell the truth, but that no one will take him seriously: Carter calls it his "ambivalent blessing" (152). The circus setting is chosen to invert society and show its failings, regardless of which segment of society it suppresses, be it through patriarchal rule or general human arrogance. Underlying the entire scene is an acknowledgement that the carnivalesque freedom is only momentary because the lid is quickly replaced in order to retain the status quo.

Carter explains that the middle section of the book that contains this episode "is very elaborately plotted, like a huge circus with the ring in the middle, and it took me ages tinkering with it to get it right".[56] Carter uses a spatial image (a huge circus) while plotting the novel, with clearly ordered locations (the ring in the middle). She relates the structural complexity of her thinking to the physical places, mixing the actual locations in the text with the way they are connected. The circus becomes a form of memory palace which embodies all the aspects of the macrocosm it reflects. While wandering through the Siberian tundra, Lizzie (Fevvers' foster-mother and confidante) philosophises about their picaresque adventure which, according to Carter's comment above, invites such thoughts.

---

53   Quoted in Gamble, *The Fiction of Angela Carter*, p.141.
54   "Angela Carter: Bottle blond, double drag", p.254.
55   Ibid.
56   Haffenden, *Novelists in Interview*, p.89.

She concludes that the circus troupe "constituted a microcosm of humanity, [...] an emblematic company, each signifying a different proportion in the great syllogism of life. [A] little band of pilgrims [taught] lessons [on their] journey" (279). By comparing the colourful, often brutal and certainly worldly company to pilgrims on a spiritual journey, Carter lifts the discussion into the realm of allegory.[57] However, the allegory she implements here is not reverential of social systems, but represents the world through rather reprehensible beings.

Compared to the most famous example of literary pilgrimage, the *Canterbury Tales*, the social groups represented here are not stereotypes. Carter does not adopt the contemporary social structure which was Chaucer's starting point, which he then commented on and criticised. Carter shows us the strangeness of society, of human variety, and also suggests that everyone would fit into this motley crew of weird and wonderful performers. Where do *we* fit? With the American money-grubbing opportunist Kearney, the circus proprietor? The romantic and slightly mad Walser? The freak Fevvers with wings? The philosophical Lizzie? The brutal brawn-no-brains strong man, Lamark? Or maybe with the animals? The dangerous and menacing yet beautiful tigers, the intelligent mute apes or the prophesying, almost-become-a-meal pig Sybil? By presenting the circus as a microcosm of society, Carter provides a strange portrait of it, affording us a different look at something that has become pedestrian in its representation in the arts, inverting it in carnivalesque fashion to expose its ordered surface as hiding a multitude of uncontrollable aspects of human nature.

SURREALIST INFLUENCES

Creating strange new ways to look at the world is deeply rooted in much of Carter's work. The question of what is real and what an illusion is very much the inspiration for Carter's style of writing. She has often been linked to surrealist concepts and particularly to later theorists influenced by them, such as Jacques Lacan. The surrealist idea that art is a lie – it cannot tell or represent the truth because it is a construct of impressions, always at one remove from reality – lies at the heart of Carter's art. Language is equally inadequate to describe the world and the self because words are merely the signs used for the things themselves (Ferdinand de Saussure's 'signifier and signified'). For Lacan, the oneness with reality we feel as children is lost when we learn words and images. They displace 'the real' (*la réelle*), because they are at an imbalance with it. Language and images, therefore, carry us away from *la réelle*, but since we have once experienced it, our lives are driven by a desire to recapture it.

This concept is clearly taken up by Carter in her novel *Doctor Hoffman* where Lacan's 'desire' is personified by the character Desiderio who is torn between two masters: on one hand, the Minister of Determination, a scientist "in the process of

---

57   Carter clearly acknowledges her allegorical orientation. She says, "as a medievalist, I was trained to read books as having many layers". Ibid., p.87.

tabulating everything [he] can lay [his] hands on [in] the sacred name of symmetry"; on the other, the metaphysical scientist Doctor Hoffman (modelled on the surrealist Breton) who frees things from their confining definitions in order "to establish a regime of total liberation". He has "populated the city with analogies … for the sake of liberty" in a revolutionary attempt to gain freedom for the mind (45). Because Desiderio initially is not affected by the impossible changes taking place, some critics have taken this as an indication that Carter with this novel turns her back on surrealism. But the surrealist revolution begun in the first chapter is the starting point for Desiderio's personal development and it ultimately enables him to see the world in a different light.

The surrealist belief that truth is to be found in the gaps between reality and illusion, at the edges of meaning, is picked up by Carter: "all the elements that are available [to imaginative writing] are to do with the margin of the imaginative life, which is in fact what gives reality to our own experience, and in which we measure our own reality".[58] To obtain meaning from Carter's texts, we must look for any gaps that appear at the margins of her narrative. This clearly informs the imaginative landscape she creates for the reader and gives a specific and unusual structure to her architectural memory palaces, something I will look at below when considering the scene at the Duke's palace.

The technique to engender these gaps in writing is to use "puns, allusions, jokes, logical contradictions [and] language games"[59] because they require the reader to look beyond the words themselves to the meanings and associations they contain. Carter's writings overflows with oxymorons, twisted sayings and word games. Her aim is not to create something new, but to look at the world and make it appear in a new light, so that it is seen anew. "Surrealism didn't involve inventing extraordinary things to look at, it involved looking at the world as though it were strange," she says in an interview.[60] By making the reader think about reality and illusion, she creates the possibility of seeing the world as strange, thereby opening up gaps through which the world can be seen anew.

These gaps between reality and illusion, hidden in the language, can be uncovered by deconstructing the text. In other words, by "tricking language into saying what can't be said": another aim of surrealist artists.[61] Although Carter uses and refers to literary techniques frequently in her work (for example when the clown Buffo deconstructs himself in the circus ring, physically as well and mentally – an example of Carter taking metaphor literally in the same way that Rushdie does), she simultaneously shows the limitations of these techniques and plays with the expectations readers may have with regard to them. Asked to

---

58   Ibid., p.92.
59   Davis, "Lacan and deconstruction", 10.4.
60   Haffenden, *Novelists in Interview*, p.92.
61   Davis, "Lacan and deconstruction", 10.4.

explain herself while wandering lost through the Siberian tundra in *Nights at the Circus*, Fevvers says:

'Look, love,' I says to him, eventually, because I'm not in the mood for *literary criticism*. 'If I hadn't bust a wing in the trainwreck, I could fly us all to Vladivostok in two shakes, so I'm not the right one to ask questions of when it comes to what is real and what is not, because like the duck-billed platypus, half the people who clap eyes on me don't believe what they see and the other half thinks they're seeing things.' (244, my italics)

She is "not in the mood for literary criticism" – a provocation typical of Carter. But she is not rejecting literary criticism either. Carter shows that Fevvers is well aware of how her persona can be interpreted, and sometimes too much interpretation can obscure the simple facts. Fevvers, with a strong tinge of Carter's own voice, cuts through the symbolism and mysticism and tells it as it is: "I could fly us all to Vladivostok". No question: Fevvers *has* got wings, *can* fly and is too tired and dispirited to keep up the pretence of uncertainty and mystique with which she normally surrounds herself. Only when she encounters the Shaman does she regain the strength to be unique because the Shaman makes "no categorical distinction between seeing and believing. It could be said that, for all the people of this region, there existed no difference between fact and fiction; instead, a sort of magic realism." (260) The 'magic realism' – again an employment of a literary term used to express an idea by making something known seem strange – is both employed to ridicule the Shaman's naivety, but also to applaud his mode of existence because it opens up a realm for an alternate reality. This is reminiscent of Rushdie's approach to reality and is the reason why both fit into the magic realism genre: they credit illusion with truth and doubt reality. Magic realism opens up those surrealist gaps in reality through which a form of 'truth' can be teased out.

BLURRING THE EDGES

One specific scene in *Nights at the Circus* shows particularly well how Carter creates these gaps through which reality can be gleaned. Here she uses "puns, allusions, jokes, logical contradictions and language games" to make the world seem strange. She takes two backgrounds and fuses them at the edges to introduce the aspect of transition, which the reader seems to experience rather than merely observe. In this instance her memory palace is constructed in such a way that the backgrounds are linked together, like a chain where the individual parts reach into each other. This replicates the rhetorical practice of linking memory images through interaction to aid movement from one to the next. Carter's backgrounds are interlinked in this way and the effect it has on the reader is extraordinary.

The scene referred to takes place at the Grand Duke's palace from which Fevvers, after realising the Duke intends to keep her in his collection forever, barely escapes. Fevvers, tempted by the promise of valuable presents and despite the bad premonitions of foster-mother Lizzie, goes to dine with the Grand Duke in his palace. Here she finds an ice-sculpture of herself, slowly melting, an automated orchestra playing soulless music and a collection of Faberge eggs, each containing miniature items symbolic of the capture of Fevvers – the last a cage still empty, awaiting its prey. Realising the Duke's intentions, Fevvers turns his sexual arousal against him through a "deep instinct of self-preservation" (191), and controls him by bringing him to ejaculation and thereby facilitating her own escape. The relevant passage starts with a description of the Faberge egg the Grand Duke has ordered particularly for Fevvers:

It was white gold and topped with a lovely little swan, a tribute, perhaps, to her putative paternity. And, as she suspected, it contained a cage made out of gold wires, with, inside, a little perch of rubies and of sapphires and of diamonds, the good old red, white and blue. The cage was empty. No bird stood on that perch, yet.

Fevvers did not shrink; but was at once aware of the hideous possibility she might do so. She said goodbye to the diamond necklace down below and contemplated life as a toy. With oriental inscrutability, the automatic orchestra laid down the geometrics of the implausible and, by the thickening of his member, the movements that now came of their own accord, by his panting breath and glazed eye, Fevvers judged the Grand Duke's time was nigh.

Then came a wet crash and clatter as the ice-carving of herself collapsed into the remains of the caviare in the room below, casting the necklace which had tempted her amongst the dirty supper things. The bitter knowledge she'd been fooled spurred Fevvers into action. She dropped the toy train on the Isfahan runner – mercifully, it landed on its wheels – as, with a grunt and whistle of expelled breath, the Grand Duke ejaculated.

In those few seconds of his lapse of consciousness, Fevvers ran helter-skelter down the platform, opened the door of the first-class compartment and clambered aboard.
'Look what a mess he's made of your dress, the pig,' said Lizzie. (192)

In those last sentences Carter creates the illusion of a shrinking Fevvers who escapes in a miniature train in what Finney calls "one of Carter's most brazen instances of narrative manipulation in the book".[62] An experience of disorientation and an actual sensation of shrinking is conveyed to the reader. Carter makes this fantastical proposition of the shrinking Fevvers believable by the way that the backgrounds and the images placed against each are intertwined and linked to the senses. A closer look at the relevant sentences reveals how Carter accomplishes a metamorphoses from one setting to the next by using a few choice words that mould the images created, so that they affect the reader in this specific way.

The first indication we get that something irrational is about to happen is in the use of the word 'mercifully': the ice-sculpture below has collapsed, the diamond-necklace has submerged and Fevvers realises the true danger of her situation, so "[s]he dropped the toy train on the Isfahan runner – *mercifully*, it landed on its wheels". Why mercifully? How can the position of a miniature toy train have any influence on the outcome of Fevvers' situation? Although not able to answer this question at that point, the toy train takes on a mysterious significance and is placed on its wheels – in the imagination – ready for action. Paired with the

62   Finney, "Tall tales and brief lives".

carefully chosen word 'runner' to describe the piece of Eastern carpet with its synonymous meaning (to do a runner), the scene is prepared.

In the second part of the sentence the train comes alive, personified by the noises accompanying the Duke's sexual climax: "with a grunt and a whistle of expelled breath, the Grand Duke ejaculated". When these noises are taken to describe either the train or the Duke only, they are a mixture of realistic and symbolic noises: a train that whistles is perfectly normal, whereas grunting and expelling breath are prosopopoeial noises; the Duke's grunting and expelling of breath are physically correct, while a whistling noise, although imaginable, has a symbolic meaning. Since they appear intertwined in the same phrase, these sounds create an image in our imagination, which tells us much more than the bare physical facts. The associations of a train coming alive through heavy breathing and grunting noises and of the Duke reaching boiling point and whistling like an old-fashioned kettle takes metaphor literally. The Duke's engine is running at full steam and the train won't stop until it has reached its destination – and this pressure cooker tension is Fevvers' salvation.

Through the mixing of images, by supplying sense impressions that combine the two elements (train and Duke), the metamorphoses has already begun. And the following line completes it: "in those few seconds of [the Duke's] lapse of consciousness, Fevvers ran helter-skelter down the platform, opened the door of the first-class compartment and clambered aboard."

Carter states very clearly that the described actions take place "in those few seconds" – which makes it impossible in real time. But time has been manipulated previously by Fevvers (the old clock of Father Time, for example). She seems to hold some power over it which enables her to stretch it sufficiently for her own benefit. However, it is also the "lapse of consciousness" attributed to the Duke that the reader seems to experience: we ask, how did we suddenly get here, to the train on the platform? And the only train we know of is the miniature toy-train we've just seen plump down on its wheels at the feet of the protagonists, and which had inscribed on its side the name of the train Fevvers intended to catch all along – the Trans-Siberian Express. Our reason, which reaches for the nearest solutions first, combines the two images we've just been given: a miniature train and an escaping Fevvers at the train station.

For it to work, Fevvers must needs be reduced to a size fitting for the world of miniature, so she shrinks. And we've been given ample examples by Carter earlier in the chapter to prepare us for this event, both in her by-the-way comments regarding diminishing objects and, mainly, through the detailed description of several of the Faberge eggs, peeling away outer shell after outer shell and all ending in a minute object representative of Fevvers in one way or another. Furthermore, an atmosphere of unease accompanies the entire scene, from Lizzie's bad premonitions to the sense of foreboding and the symbolic overtones of a melting Fevvers – we have been prepared for something dramatic to happen.

The speed with which the final transformation ultimately takes place, in merely two lines, demands quick thinking by the reader: an ability to continuously adapt the picture just established in our imagination in order to accommodate the new one. This also heightens the sense of urgency, intensity and disorientation which mirrors Fevvers' emotions in her situation. Carter infiltrates our imaginary memory palace, where the scene is depicted by removing the background before the images are replaced. She creates an overlapping of memory spaces which produces a confusing collage through the gaps of which the impossible becomes possible. Only with the encounter of the down-to-earth Lizzie and her practical, unflappable attitude ("Look what a mess he's made of your dress, the pig") in the train compartment do we return to real time. We have a sense of having escaped from a nightmare. The entire chapter has been wonderfully crafted to lead up to the climactic moment and the final paragraph – returned to the relative safety of the train – is a relief from tension, not just for the Duke and Fevvers, but also for the reader who has been taken on this image-making tour-de-force.[63]

---

63   An earlier example of the seamless intermingling of backgrounds comes from Charles Dickens' novel *Our Mutual Friend*. Here an intermingling of impressions provides a highly effective emotional surge. Eugene Wrayburn has followed his love Lizzie to a remote country setting, has just met her in the evening light. As he wanders back along the river, pondering this new emotion inspired by Lizzie, he is brutally hit over the head by his jealous rival Headstone, who dumps him in the river and leaves him to die. This unexpected event breaks into the calm, reflective mood and is described as follows:

[Eugene] had sauntered far enough. Before turning to retrace his steps, he stopped upon the margin [of the river], to look down at the reflected night. In an instant, with a dreadful crash, the reflected night turned crooked, flames shot jaggedly across the air, and the moon and stars came bursting from the sky.

Was he struck by lightning? With some incoherent half-formed thought to that effect, he turned under the blows that were blinding him and mashing his life, and closed with a murderer, whom he caught by a red neckerchief – unless the raining down of his own blood gave it that hue. (682)

Initially, the reader is placed squarely in the "ever widening beauty of the landscape", experienced by Eugene on arrival. It is made almost magical because people seem to float above the ground: they are immersed breast-high behind hedgerows. Dickens draws a memory map, mentioning locations: the village, river, boat, bridge, grazing sheep and haystack. They paint a clear picture and relax us into the sensitive philosophical contemplation about love. Into this clearly defined space breaks the brute force of Headstone, mad with love and capable of murder. The night Eugene sees reflected in the river's water turns "crooked" and "the moon and stars [come] bursting from the sky". Dickens describes what Eugene experiences physically at the very moment when he receives the brutal blow and thereby simultaneously shows his world collapsing.

Although Dickens and Carter both make this complete transition in a couple of sentences and both use the events to mirror emotional states, Dickens always remains in naturalistic settings. Eugene's distorted view of the picture in the water can be read as traditional symbolism: the falling moon and stars represent the end of the world and the flashes of lightning depict the flashes of pain he feels. Carter uses imagery and setting in a less traditional way. She incorporates comedy into this serious episode and uses images that are unusual and require a good deal of wakefulness on the reader's part. Dickens' transitional episode is a symbolic description of an emotional state; Carter's metamorphoses takes place on another level. By including the impossible and strange (the shrinking and the time contraction) surreal gaps appear that can confer a new viewpoint.

The background which most clearly depicts Carter's recurrent confrontation between reality and illusion is the stage: whether a puppet-theatre in *The Magic Toyshop* or a film set in *Wise Children*, carnivalesque ones in the form of grotesque tableau or the circus ring in *Nights at the Circus*, mythological ones in *The Passion of New Eve* and *The Infernal Desire Machines of Doctor Hoffman* or merely dramatised private homes in *The Passion of New Eve* and *Wise Children*. The main association with all of the stages is one of pretence and illusion. The stage with its proliferation of symbolic meanings and diverse associations contains the key to the theme which pervades her entire canon: each life is a performance of a myriad of roles. And each setting, in turn, repeats the question: what is fact, what fiction? – both in real life and in the arts. The film set of Shakespeare's *A Midsummer Night's Dream* in *Wise Children* is a straightforward employment of such a setting. The wood "was twice as large as life. Larger" (124). It was made of stiff materials that clank in the blast from the wind machine. Everything is artificial. We are placed squarely in the world of the money-making factory that is Hollywood where the exaggerated scenery appears uninspired and cheap. Dora expresses her disappointment in the set:

What I missed most was illusion. That wood near Athens was too, too solid for me. […] This wood, this entire dream, in fact, was custom-made and hand-built, it left nothing to the imagination. [...] It was all too literal for me. (125)

Dora's expectations are not met because she bases her ideas of the stage on childhood memories. To her and Nora the theatre should be an imaginary space, a static background against which wonders are portrayed and magic can be performed. This magic, that takes place in the mind alone where an active imagination is all-important for it to happen, is lost in the three-dimensional landscape of the Hollywood film set because it attempts to materialise the magic. As Dora says, it leaves no room for the imagination. And by materialising forms of magic (by playing with size, movement and sound) the set loses its ambiguity, thereby allowing for only this one exact image to be created. The film set is 'fake', not because it is made from cardboard, metal and manipulated by a wind machine – in that sense the theatre is even more fake – but because "it left nothing to the imagination".

The farcical intensity of the last night party is a climax of the book and has all the makings of the final act of a Shakespearean comedy: the disguises, marriages, revelations of family-relations, mistaken identities and the appearance of the surprise person. It is a scene filled with references, indications and barely hidden meanings where real life interferes with stage-pretence and true events are more theatrical, require more make-up and acting, than actual film-takes have done.

It was a strange night, that night, and stranger still because I always misremember. [...] I distort. [...] I no longer remember that set *as* a set but as a real wood, dangerous, uncomfortable, with real, steel spines on the conkers and thorns on the bushes,[...] as if Hollywood were the name of the enchanted forest where you lose yourself and find yourself, again; the wood that changes you; the wood where you go mad; the wood where the shadows live longer than you do. (157–8)

The film set takes on the function of a fairy tale wood where people go into the enchanted forest to experience change – like a psychoanalytical adventure into the subconscious. Dora comes out the other end having altered her picture of what stage magic is all about. The wood has now magically become a real wood and, paradoxically, she realises that what seems most fake is sometimes most real, while reality is often an illusion – and we are back to Carter's favourite theme.

If the stage/film set has lost its ephemeral magic, it has opened Dora's eyes to see that all of existence is an act. She realises that the existence of her father, the famous actor Melchior Hazard, is entirely staged: Dora comments on his private home, saying that "he was a player to the marrow so he lived in a permanent stage set" (95). The culmination of this state of affairs is reached at Melchior's 100th birthday party in his home. The entire section is described as if it were a theatre performance in the way that Melchior has staged himself and in the language employed. Thus "a thrill ran through the room. Something *unscripted* is about to happen" (206); Melchior's brother Peregrine arrives unannounced "to *upstage* his own brother" (207); Melchior's first wife, Lady A., "pushed herself backwards [in her wheelchair], as if she were trying to roll *offstage* back into the *wings*" (209); while the very modern second ex-wife of Melchior's, Daisy, wonders "who held the *mini-series rights*" for the very entertaining spectacle performed here (216, my italics). Dora comments, "I could have sworn that the curtain came down, the lights went up and there was a standing ovation". But Nora tells her otherwise, and furthermore, "it would have been discourteous of that audience to applaud" (216) the magnificent family performance which is so successful exactly because it is real.

Carter's preferred images, as her favourite type of background, are related to the question of reality and illusion, particularly when looking at Carter's interest in gender roles. Carter has been quoted as saying "that in the 'real' world, to be a woman is to be in drag".[64] She is referring to the constraints conventions put upon people, and that women in particular 'dress up' in order to fulfil the expectations of what a woman should be. In *Wise Children* this 'drag act' is extended to include both genders and all classes, stating that everyone tries to play the part that is expected of them rather than admitting to idiosyncrasies that actually make them who they are. This concept goes back to Lacan who, in Culler's words, argues that "the self is constructed by what is reflected back: by a mirror, by the mother, and by others in social relations generally".[65]

64   Webb, "Seriously funny", p.204.
65   Culler, *Literary Theory*, p.114.

Melchior's character is entirely informed by the perception of others and he consequently turns his entire existence into a performance. But also Dora is vulnerable to these reflections. On the night of the party she has sex with her uncle Peregrine and sees herself reflected in his eyes. In that moment a suppressed memory returns: she remembers having sex with Peregrine at the age of thirteen on a day trip to Brighton. The reflection of herself in his eyes brings back this memory because in it she sees not the image of her seventy-five-year-old self, but a memory of how Peregrine saw her all those years ago. The way he sees her shapes her self-image, making her feel thirteen again.

A similar incident occurs in *Nights at the Circus*. Towards the end of her journey Fevvers encounters her newly realised love Walser and confronts him for the first time, but he has lost his memory:

In Walser's eyes, she saw herself, at last, swimming into definition, like the image on photographic paper; but instead of Fevvers, she saw two perfect miniatures of a dream.

She felt her outlines waver; she felt herself trapped forever in the reflection in Walser's eyes. For one moment, just one moment, Fevvers suffered the worst crisis of her life: 'Am I fact? Or am I fiction? Am I what I know I am? Or am I what he thinks I am?' (290)

Throughout the book Fevvers has defined herself by the way she can make other people perceive her. Walser, in his capacity as journalist, initially reflected back the image she intended to created of herself. With Walser's mind temporarily gone, so is her identity. This is emphasised in the constant repetition of the personal pronoun 'I', indicating the danger in letting a projected identity overshadow the sense of self. Her outlines waver, she is no longer sure who she is and she finally asks the question that is usually posed by others about her: is she fact or fiction? This conundrum has kept her in business, enabling her to remain interesting. Now, with no one to reflect back her identity, she loses her sense of reality. At that crucial moment people enter the room, and by taking on her artist persona in front of them, she regains her sense of self. They now reflect back her image: in their reactions she can recognise herself.

Fevvers has invented herself, but this state of ambiguity is hazardous and it takes an effort of will to uphold it. This is seen as a positive will of invention, however, and one that propels her into the freedom to be unique and different. Carter's view of identity clearly differs from Lacan's. Carter uses his idea – that each person identifies with what is reflected back at them – but argues it is possible to influence this reflection. She empowers Fevvers, giving her the ability to reinvent herself by choosing *how* she wants to be seen.

One of Carter's most obvious figurative presentations of being restrained by expectations is the image of Leda and the Swan, employed in several of her novels. This image has often been related to Carter's statement that she is "in the demythologising business".[66] By following the image of Leda and the Swan and

---

66   "Notes from the front line", p.71.

its development throughout *Nights at the Circus*, it is possible to discover just how Carter goes about her demythologising business. In the novel she takes the subject of Leda and the Swan and makes it part of the story's structure. It recurs at important points of the narrative in different stages of deconstruction. By following this development and paying special attention to the backgrounds against which the image is placed, it becomes apparent how Carter takes the myth apart and thereby breaks the mythical spell it may contain, simultaneously confronting and subverting its message.

Carter, unlike Rushdie, uses allegory very openly in her novels. She points out in an interview that her thinking when creating a story-line is highly allegorical, creating straight comparisons by allocating particular symbolic meanings to places, persons or events. She says, "I do put everything in a novel to be read – read the way allegory was intended to be read, the way you are supposed to read *Gawain and the Green Knight* – on as many levels as you can comfortably cope with at the time".[67] Carter expects the reader to pay attention, consider what is read and attempt to make sense of it, interpreting specific instances on as many levels as possible. Her reference to the medieval text *Gawain and the Green Knight*, which belongs firmly to the allegorical genre, shows that she expects her readers to engage the creative faculty in the way that medieval readers had to. As was shown with regard to medieval texts in chapter two, the reading of allegory involves memory processes to a large extent. Carter not only describes her work as allegorical, she also uses medieval literary techniques, including those involving artificial memory, when she places images in an ordered literary structure, thereby creating imaginary spaces, bringing the classical art of memory to bear on modern literature.

The classical and medieval images upon which allegorical texts from the Middle Ages are based may have disappeared from the current collective memory, and instances of these in texts can be difficult to comprehend. However, each new era creates its own collective memory: a collation of new images, of old images and of some that are a combination of both where traditional symbols have been developed and incorporated into modern concepts. Although Carter resurrects the allegorical mode and uses traditional imagery, she also adapts it for the modern readership. Her images and ideas are accessible through modern-day symbolism, taken from politics, literary theory and popular culture. An excursion into the world of Carter's works with this in mind renders meanings from its settings and images. With Leda and the Swan Carter takes an 'old' image which she combines with a new reading, adding new pictures to the existing memory images conjured up by the story in order to change the old perception and demythologise it.

In *Nights at the Circus* the character of Fevvers is fundamental to the imaginary depiction of Leda and the Swan. Carter writes that the impetus for Fevvers' character came from Guilliaume Apollinaire's metaphor which describes the

---

67   Haffenden, *Novelists in Interview*, p.86.

advent of a new kind of woman "who will have wings and who will renew the world".[68] By taking this metaphor literally, Carter creates a character who can fly (who has wings) and imagines what the consequences might be. Carter's first reaction to Apollinaire's sentence was: "[h]ow wonderful [...] How terrific". But then she thought, "[w]ell no; it's not going to be as easy as that. [...] Really, how very, very inconvenient it would be for a person to have real wings, just how really difficult".[69] It is this contradiction of the real problems and the wonderful possibilities caused by the wings that Carter investigates in her novel, and she depicts it as a physical as well as a mental struggle. Although Fevvers very much is her own person throughout, exercising her right to be different, paradoxically she has always been confined by her chosen role or by the background she was displayed against. As Carter puts it: "[e]ach time she encounters a mad scientist Fevvers gets away, and each time she loses a little more of herself – until finally she turns the tables on the last one, the Shaman, who is in any event the most sympathetic".[70] These encounters are often accompanied by a representation of the Leda-and-the-Swan image.

Direct references to the image in painting and poetry (particularly to Titian's painting and Yeats' poem) appear throughout the book. A traditional reading sees Leda overwhelmed by the beauty and majesty of the swan (lecherous Zeus in one of his several disguises) and, as Yeats implies, Leda ought to be honoured by his attentions. Carter, however, sees it as a mythologised and idealised image of rape. This is apparent in one of Carter's earlier books. In *The Magic Toyshop* the father of the family makes his orphaned niece Melanie act out the part of Leda on his puppet-stage. The swan is a large puppet on strings menacingly manipulated by the uncle. Nicole Ward Jouve writes that "[t]he trope is a patriarchal powertrip. Uncle Philip's swan has neither knowledge nor power [as professed in Yeats' poem]. He is cardboard, and creaking machinery. Only Melanie's fear makes him overwhelming".[71] Already here Carter uses the example to "demot[e] the myth",[72] showing that it is the victim's fear that facilitates the subordination.

In *Nights at the Circus* Fevvers makes her first attempt at flight, her first attempt at 'taking wing' in Ma Nelson's brothel where she grows up. Despite being kept out of direct contact with the punters, Fevvers compromises by showing herself off half-naked as a statue of the Winged Victory. Although the stance suggests strength and beauty, it is a man-made image, underscored by the picture of Leda and the Swan hung in the parlour above the fireplace. It is from this fireplace that Fevvers first tries out her wings. She manages to hover in the air for a brief moment, but is symbolically still held back by the constraints of her

---

68   Atwood, "Running with the tigers", p.119.
69   Katsavos, "An interview with Angela Carter", p.232.
70   Haffenden, *Novelists in Interview*, p.88.
71   "Mother is a figure of speech", p.154.
72   Ibid., p.155.

given role: the fear makes her a victim and manacles a confident attempt at flight. She still takes on the role of the victim (of Leda) rather than the powerful swan who takes what it wants. Finally, it is from the roof of that house that she manages her first proper flight through the night air, revealing that she does not fit into any category of woman depicted in the house below, be they whore, suffragette or mythical Leda and her subservience. But she takes aspects of all of them with her on the journey. Her uniqueness gets Fevvers a position in Madam Schreck's "museum of women monsters" where she shares her fate with other women exhibited in titillating tableaux. Her individuality is displayed as a freak of nature alongside, amongst others, a midget, a woman with a cobwebbed face, a sleeping beauty who is awake for only a few minutes each day and a woman with a second pair of eyes instead of nipples. Here she first meets Mr Rosencreutz who later buys Fevvers from Madam Schreck, has her brought to his home and intends to sacrifice her in a ceremony to bring him eternal life.

In front of an alter, imitating the high priest and mumbling metaphysical nonsense, Rosencreutz is ready with the knife. Fevvers recognises the ramblings for what they are and in a humorous aside comments:

[t]his is some kind of heretical possibly Manchean version of neo-Platonic Rosicrucianism, thinks I to myself; tread carefully, girlie! I exhort myself. [...] I try a dollop of his excellent Stilton, pondering as I savour it the baroque ecleticism of his mythology. (77)

She has seen through his self-deluded pseudo-mythology. But it is only when he accidentally happens upon Fevvers' real name, Sophia, while listing a number of goddesses, that she realises the seriousness of her situation. Until now she has indulged in the luxuries of comfort and food, but with the mention of her real name she stops her performance as the adored and powerful goddess and realises that she is merely a woman after all, again revealing the dangerous but also exciting gap between others' reflections of her person and her own identity. However, she does have the power of her wings and flees from this scene, flying out through the open window, naked and vulnerable, and escapes back to her foster-mother, Lizzie. Although she is still the victim, her wings enable her to escape from capture; but she has a habit of putting herself in situations where the same power game is played out again and again.

When she joins Kearney's circus as the aerialist, the mystical flying trapeze artist, she is very much defined by her act. But attempts to classify her fail. Thus she is at one point suspected of being "not a woman at all but a cunningly constructed automaton made up of whalebone, india-rubber and springs" (147) – a forerunner of the lifeless automaton-musicians at the Duke's palace. Fevvers' strength and potency lies in the uncertainty about her person. As long as people speculate whether she is fact or fiction, as long as she can't be classified as either automaton, fraud or freak, she can retain her independence. As Walser cynically comments early on in the book, "in a secular age, an authentic miracle must purport to be a hoax, in order to gain credit in the world" (17). However, in this precarious state of ambiguity, Fevvers is in danger of losing her sense of self.

The Rosencreutz episode is replayed in a different version when Fevvers enters the Duke's palace in St Petersburg – the scene described in detail above. Here the coat of arms above the door (a unicorn goring a knight) recalls Rosencreutz's coat of arms, the phallus rampant. The Duke, like Rosencreutz, sees Fevvers as an object which can give him pleasure, but only by injuring her. The obvious sexual connotations of Rosencreutz' coat of arms is only implied in the Duke's emblem. He is a collector of *objet d'art* and his interest lies in the unique (the unicorn). But combined with it is a brutality and destructive aspect that Fevvers encounters on her visit to the palace and realises almost too late.

The swan theme recurs in the Duke's scene both through the ice-sculpture (by cliché a swan) and the miniature swan in the Faberge egg. The ice-sculpture is melting, like a liquid hourglass which counts down the remaining minutes of Fevvers' life. Her chance of empowering herself as the swan (she already has the wings) is slipping away; the constant drip, drip of the melting sculpture an unsettling background noise. The Faberge-egg swan foretells the outcome of Fevvers' experience if she doesn't take action: her uniqueness would simply make her a pretty and expensive miniature trinket. In this situation Fevvers is both Leda and the Swan: one her former victim position, the other the powerful creature she can grow into. Now she turns the lechery expressed in the image against the predator. The ice-sculpture has melted, the time has run out and at the last moment Fevvers chooses to give up the role of victim, of kept woman. She takes control of the situation in a symbolic inversion of the rape, using the sexual desire against the perpetrator himself.

The final appearance of the image at the end of the novel shows how Fevvers has reversed the roles of Leda and the Swan. Aidan Day comments that when Walser and Fevvers finally are united in the Shaman's hut, "Walser and Fevvers, in love, make love with Fevvers on top because of her wings [which alludes to] the rape of Leda [and] inverts the classical stereotype".[73] Fevvers is on top, both physically during sex and mentally after having gone through the many adventures which have been formative for her self-perception. She exclaims: "to think that I really fooled you! [...] It just goes to show there's nothing like confidence" (295). She has fooled even Walser, not only about that her wings might not be real (which they undoubtedly are), but also about being a virgin. She has managed to break free from expectations about her person as a woman and an individual. Confidence has helped her overcome fear, drop the role of victim and become the swan. Her dominance is based on joy and love – she wants a life with Walser that defies the typical happy ending (i.e., no marriage), and the novel ends with an infectious laugh that Fevvers sends out around the world.[74]

---

73   Quoted in Gamble, *The Fiction of Angela Carter*, p.148.
74   This, too, is reminiscent of Bakhtin's interest in the carnivalesque. The idea of the Easter

The recurring setting of the stage and the deconstruction of the Leda myth demonstrate that everyone plays roles, but that each individual can choose their parts. The surrealist angle allows for a new perspective. Carter uses it to create unusual images which provoke unusual thoughts. Carter's aim, as Sarah Gamble succinctly puts it, is simply this: "[s]he wants to make us think".[75]

CONCLUSION

Both Carter and Rushdie clearly use backgrounds and images consciously and in combination to convey meaning. They use the voice of an unreliable narrator to challenge the reader, who must be alert to inconsistencies and ambiguities in the text. Both comment on their own technique with irony and subversion as an invitation to the reader to engage with the text, to become active participants through the reading process and to draw their own conclusions from it. By concentrating on the topic of memory, specifically on backgrounds and images, a broad understanding of the texts is made available. An internal landscape is created, providing parameters for the text and revealing complex internal connections. Backgrounds and images help visualise the story and make the reading of it a more direct experience. An emphasis on the backgrounds and images has, in this instance, resulted in pinpointing abstract concepts which retain their complexity despite having been put into words.

Laughter in medieval times, blasphemous but permitted, is also a form of carnivalesque inversion. Carter, again, realises the limitations of this freedom of expression. But Fevvers' laughter at the end of the novel is an expression of the successful inversion of the roles she has achieved at that moment. This particular inversion of the roles of Leda and the Swan depicts the freeing of both man and woman that results from it. The laughter is spread around the world, just as the hopeful outlook is carried into the new century.

75   *The Fiction of Angela Carter*, p.10.

Chapter 5

The Modern US Novel
Thomas Pynchon and Paul Auster

Two separate and distinctive issues have been under investigation with regard to the medieval and English texts looked at so far: first, how the author presents the concept of memory; secondly, what the backgrounds and images, based on the architectural memory system, reveal about the text. These two questions initially may seem unrelated, but do, in fact, greatly depend upon each other because the way the author perceives memory informs the way that the story's imaginative landscape is created. If the author believes that the memory can be used as a repository for a wide variety of items (as Langland does), the story will reflect this in its structure and amount of detail: the structure may compartmentalise the text, allowing for the individual ideas to be placed within a given space; elaborate detail may be included, because the author expects readers to arrange and store these in their memory as they proceed with the tale. When an author sees memory as a personalised adaptation of the truth (as Rushdie does), the backgrounds will be coloured by the personal attitude of the characters. These backgrounds will not support character description by supplying circumstantial facts, but instead will reflect the characters' idiosyncratic ideas.

Very specific views on memory inform the novels of the US authors that we come to now. By relating these views on memory to memory systems in the text (to the backgrounds and images), we gain a specific angle into each. In Pynchon's novel *Vineland* memories *are* truths, proof of past events. However, these are vulnerable to outside influences and are easily forgotten, adapted or ignored because they are quickly sacrificed for an easier life. This is reflected in the backgrounds in so far that they carry the truth within them, but are overlaid with false meaning – only an active effort will reveal their true meaning by discarding those aspects which distort their original value. The images put against the backgrounds, i.e., the characters, are also obscured by lazy prejudice and must be freed from false identities.

Auster's angle on memory is entirely different from all the earlier examples discussed here. He relates it to the Renaissance cabbalistic idea in which memory systems are attributed with the power to reveal higher truths or hidden meanings. His novel *Moon Palace* is set in a landscape that creates a pattern which, almost mystically, exposes a deeper meaning, employing the metaphysical adaptation of memory to create a literary text. Auster is the only author considered here who relates a specific memory system directly to his writing: he compares the creative process to that of architectural memory. His adaptation of the Renaissance art of memory enables Auster to integrate themes, such as identity and creativity, into a mobile structure that itself comments on the complex concepts of the novel.

Thomas Pynchon – *Vineland*
An Exercise in Remembering

The message in Pynchon's *Vineland* seems to be the age-old admonition: do not forget! Grounded in the belief that the past holds the key to the future, that history can teach and the resulting understanding of the past can influence the future positively, it is reminiscent of the Neoplatonic belief that knowledge is contained within memory, because memory connects us to a higher instance. But Pynchon avoids the sincere approach where the fictional story clings to realistic and easily accessible narrative – where a series of facts is related in order to convince the reader of the importance of the topic. In fact, Pynchon does exactly the opposite. His fictional story entangles the realistic and the fantastical: "[r]ealism [...] and fabulation [...] have equal claims to authority in the text".[1] As David Dickson points out: "the problem for the reader is not so much to suspend disbelief as to find an orientation in relation to the various narrative voices involved".[2] Indeed, the picture is further destabilised by the various, often dubious narrative voices and a constant, usually uncommented and sudden shift between past, present and future. It unsettles the narrative, confuses the reader and does certainly not make the plot easily accessible. Historical facts are incorporated into the text in a way that they at first glance appear secondary to the overall picture; only in retrospect do they reveal their significance as absolutely fundamental to a comprehension of the story.

Several critics have attempted to answer the question why Pynchon has chosen to present his strong political and social views in such an indirect way. Niran Abbas concludes that Pynchon "frustrates our desire for order by ironically disassembling the text and its character", and that "reading Pynchon is a 'subversive experience'",[3] while David Dickson says, readers of Pynchon must "recognize that fiction and truth are two necessary aspects of one and the same reality".[4] Shawn Smith suggests that Pynchon refuses to portray postmodern horrors in "normal" circumstances because it would make them part of everyday life, thereby lose some of the impact of the horrific and to some extent become acceptable.[5] Others point out that Pynchon is simply avoiding narrative conventions because *that* is a construct – reality is always more unbelievable than any invented story: "The truth of the sixties is stranger than fiction", writes Andrew Gordon[6] – or that postmodern society is self-satirising: Pynchon picks up

---

1   Shawn Smith, *Pynchon and History*, p.99.
2   *The Utterance of America*, p.155.
3   *Thomas Pynchon*, p.17.
4   *The Utterance of America*, p.179.
5   *Pynchon and History*, p.3.
6   "Smoking dope with Thomas Pynchon", p.167.

on this and, in effect, presents a more realistic picture of society than so-called realistic writing does.[7]

Simultaneously at work in the text, alongside these possible intentions and inspirations for Pynchon's style, is a heuristic aim – another reason for his choice. By concentrating on the backgrounds and images that make up the author's memory palace, or his imaginary world, I will show how the structure, choice of backgrounds and visual representations of ideas are employed by Pynchon not only to encourage an interactive relationship with the past, but also as an exercise in remembering in the form of an entire novel.

CONFUSING CHRONOLOGY AND PARANOIA

Pynchon's novel *Vineland* covers, loosely, the progress of three generations who lived through significant political periods: the 1930s, 60s and 80s. The Plot concentrates on the middle generation with main characters such as Zoyd Wheeler, Frenesi Gates, DL and Weed Atman, showing how their dreams and perspectives have altered. Zoyd's daughter Prairie's search for information about her absent mother Frenesi runs as a thread through the story. She realises Frenesi's true history which, at the height of her undercover activities as an informant for the government agent Brock Vond, culminated in her involvement in the shooting and killing of the now zomboid Weed. Frenesi's former friend DL helps Prairie in the search for information about her mother and thereby reveals her own past. DL's relationship with the lawyer Takeshi Fumimota runs parallel to Frenesi and Brock's story. They meet when, through mistaken identity, DL performs an eastern death-ritual on Takeshi. She takes him to the retreat of the Kunoichi Attentive Sisters to reverse the effect, and together they end up running a karmic readjustment clinic in the Thanatoid village, inhabited by zomboid beings like Weed. The novel ends in an anticlimactic family reunion: relationships are resolved and an unexpected sense of harmony is established.

The concept of memory is most demonstrably represented in *Vineland* by the Thanatoids, the undead, who have unresolved karmic business: zombies, not able to let go of their memories and intent on revenge. This, at least, is Ortho Bob's definition. It inspires Takeshi's karmic readjustment business-venture in Shade Creek, the Thanatoid village in Vineland. By the end of the story the narrator clearly equates Thanatoids with memory: "What was a Thanatoid, at the end of a long dread day, but memory?" (325).[8] But the Thanatoids are simultaneously personifications of death ('Thanatoid' means "like death, only different", 170) and thus, by extension, memory and death are linked: as long as we remember, we are alive; if we forget, we die.

---

7   William E. Grim, "Good-buy, Columbus", p.160.
8   All references are to the QPD, 1990 edition of *Vineland*.

There is no sense in the book of the New Age emphasis on 'letting go'. Thus Takeshi's "Open Karmology Clinic" (177) does not resolve anything, but rather adjusts the situation; making his Thanatoid clients feel a little better, but not helping them to 'move on' to the finite state of oblivion. There is an undercurrent in the narrative which appreciates the Thanatoids and their refusal to forget, to lie down and die. Memories are like ghosts (or Thanatoids): they haunt the world reminding it of both good and bad. In Pynchon's case, mainly bad. Pynchon's narrative has Thanatoid attributes: it is meant to remind his readers of the past. Shawn Smith writes that Pynchon structured *Vineland* like "a haunted house" (coincidentally using architectural-memory terminology to explain literary space) where the characters are tantalised by "memories of the freedom that they once had but which was stolen from them," and which haunts them.[9]

But Pynchon does not urge a return to the past. As David Cowart writes, *Vineland* is not

the simple-minded exercise in nostalgia some have taken it for. Far from the sour grapes of some bitter ex-hippie, it is a treatise on the direction history has taken, without our having given it much thought. [...] In a single generation [...] America has veered from a liberal to a conservative bias, from the New Frontier and the Great Society to "Reaganomics," from hordes of student demonstrators to whole undergraduate populations majoring in business, from Yippies to yuppies.[10]

Hence, Cowart calls *Vineland* "a condition-of-America novel" in which Pynchon attempts to alert the reader to these changes. The first step towards altering the course of history, depicted in the novel as the direct route to self-destruction with a regime developing totalitarian overtones, is frighteningly reminiscent of Orwell's Oceania in *1984*, the year in which the 'present' narrative of *Vineland* is set. In David Thoreen's words: "*Vineland* is Pynchon's wake-up call to the American voter, who, like Rip Van Winkle and Pynchon's own protagonist Zoyd Wheeler, has been asleep for twenty years."[11]

The force memories are imbued with – that they can awaken an entire nation – might lead the reader to expect a clear structural distinction between the three time zones (past, present and future) to emphasise their interaction. But Pynchon again chooses the opposite. The narrative moves constantly between various pasts and the present, and also includes the odd forward flash. This simple orientational aid of orderly sequenced events – the chronological development – is removed from the equation. Pynchon thereby ignores one of the most basic principles of artificial memory technique; namely, to provide a clearly defined chain of events. Pynchon creates this confusion on purpose and, presumably, does not expect the reader to comprehend these shifts between times immediately: they are much too frequent

---

9   *Pynchon and History*, p.128.
10   "Attenuated postmodernism", pp.11–12.
11   "In which 'acts have consequences'", p.64.

and too unceremoniously incorporated into the text for that. It seems, then, that Pynchon intentionally puts the reader off track. But only on the first read-through.

A second reading of the novel is an entirely different experience. Naturally, every book read for the second time will reveal new aspects and details formerly obscured, because the reader uses hindsight to interpret the text. *Vineland* has this effect to a much higher degree than most books. This has two reasons, both linked to the way the memory works. First, after completing the novel for the first time a chronological order of things automatically establishes itself in the reader's memory – listing the grandparents Sasha and Hub, the hippies Frenesi and Zoyd and Prairie's and Justin's 'presents' consecutively. The events described would be listed according to *when* they happened, i.e., in time, rather than according to the structure of the novel. On rereading the book a section on Frenesi's collaboration with Brock will automatically be placed after her initiation into the 24fps film-initiative, but before the birth of Prairie. Takeshi's Thanatoid karmic adjustment business is seen to follow the footprint incident and the Death Touch encounter with DL, while Justin's clever comprehension of the world, which outpaces his parents Frenesi and Flash by miles (88 and 351), is linked to Frenesi's first marriage, to Zoyd, and to their child Prairie.

The second reason why rereading the novel is such a different experience is that things that seemed fantastical, paranoid or crazy have by now been placed in the correct context and have become reliable. Thus the many secret government agency references, which initially are the strongest points for supposing that the main characters, particularly Zoyd, are somewhat delusional and paranoid, are now seen as entirely truthful and turn out to be the pieces of information most reliable and a driving force behind events. Seemingly laughable events, like Zoyd's annual window jump, become poignant moments of unselfish love (performed to protect his daughter from Brock), while his apparent paranoid hysteria becomes self-preserving necessity, and idealistic philosophising on Frenesi's part turns out to be a fertile ground for re-establishing fascist notions. Frenesi 'the good' turns into the traitor murderess; Brock 'the exploiter' is exposed as a sad cog in the machine of the powers that be; Zoyd 'the loser' is a man struggling for survival, whose cluelessness is natural bewilderment and whose paranoia turns out to be well-founded.

Critics have frequently pointed out that these extraordinary turnabouts in the perception of character are unbelievable, i.e., not grounded in the text. Possibly these critics did not find the time for a second read-through, for during it, realisation dawns that the clues were there all along, but the way they were presented meant the reader didn't take them seriously. Thus Frenesi's change from idealist to informant is clearly documented along the way, explained both in the course of events and in her psychological make-up.

Rereading reveals that what at first appeared as a confusing, often surreal and frequently confounding text is permeated with significance and rationality. Like Rushdie, Pynchon challenges the reader to discover integrated puzzles – what

David Porush calls his "penchant for posing paradoxes and unsolvable puzzles"[12] (although I am not aware of any that are truly unsolvable). These puzzles function as exercises: they train the reader to make connections between things, for example through intertextuality, which extends into popular culture, reminiscent of Carter's texts. Often the puzzles are presented in the form of allusions to be picked up or jokes to be worked out, as in the acronym of the tubal detox centre – National Endowment for Video Education and Rehabilitation – which spells out the sarcastic comment NEVER.

A more elaborate example is Prairie's answer to Brock's stipulation that he is her dad: "But you can't be … my blood is type A. Yours is Preparation H" (376). Pynchon invites the reader to work out the reference by following it with the sentence: "By the time Brock figured out the complex insult […]" As readers we are now encouraged to 'figure out' the reference ourselves, with the additional hint that it is a 'complex insult'. An extra-textual reference to popular US advertisements uncovers the comment as a roundabout way of calling Brock a 'pain in the bud': Preparation H being a popular haemorrhoid product. Another example is the incident when Frenesi discovers little people playing cards (pinochle) under sleeping Weed's nose, only to scatter and disappear when they realise they've been spotted by a freaked out Frenesi. The explanation to this scene lies in the reference at the end of the passage to "the famous worms of song" which are "already playing a few preliminary hands on Weed Atman's snout" (238). They refer to the popular children's Worm Song in which "The worms crawl in, the worms crawl out, the worms play pinochle on your snout" (sung to the melody of a requiem). Here, they imply Frenesi's foreknowledge of, and implication in, Weed's forthcoming death.

Solutions to these puzzles are sometimes obscure, and further hindered by the uncertainty of *when* we are and what to take seriously. But the non-chronological order as confusing structure and the enlightening pieces of information dressed up as crazy notions are clues to the meta-narrative of the novel: they require a rethinking of events in order to reach the correct solution. Not only does Pynchon say that, in order to understand this book, you must constantly revisit what you already know and adapt preconceived ideas to comprehend what is going on; by requesting this intense interaction between reader and text, he is simultaneously exercising the reader's capacity for remembering.

ENTIRELY RELIABLE MEMORIES

Pynchon's reliance on the memory as a powerful tool, which can awaken people to reality, suggests that they must contain some form of 'truth' within them. Consequently, the memories that are recounted in *Vineland* must be reliable – a highly unusual idea amongst postmodern writer, such as Rushdie and Carter. One way of testing the value of the memories presented in the novel is to see whether

---

12   "Purring into transcendence", p.33.

they are individual, personalised memories, or whether they instead are pictures planted in the memory by familiarity with a topic. Initially Pynchon confirms conventional expectations and prejudices, especially of sixties' American hippie-ism: even his characters buy into the popularised clichés. Consequently the characters' recollections ought to be unreliable because the memories were stored by inebriated or drugged hippies with nebulous images of what really took place. Their memories ought to be drug-induced hallucinations, distorted images rather than actual representations of past events. This seems to be supported by Zoyd's much quoted statement that

these acid adventures, they came in those days and they went, some we gave away and forgot, others sad to say turned out to be fugitive or false – but with luck one or two would get saved to go back to at certain later moments in life. (285)

Zoyd is commenting on the birth of his daughter Prairie: one of those moments that are 'saved', i.e., memorised. Taken on its own, this sentence suggests that memories are unreliable, in Zoyd's case exactly because of the drugs which made everything hazy. But this sentence is also extremely unrepresentative of the novel in sentiment and language. It is one of only two instances (as noted by David Dickson[13]) that seem to allow Pynchon's own narrative voice through. Not necessarily the real-life Pynchon, but certainly the omniscient third-person narrator, who here includes himself amongst those reminiscing by using the personal pronoun "we".

The comment appears to be a generalisation of the topic of memory and of how drugs distort, interfere with or entirely wipe out memories, and corresponds to medical science. For this brief moment Pynchon steps outside the *Vineland* world he has created and enters real space and time to emphasise that Prairie's birth is such a monumental experience for Zoyd. The generalisation includes the reader's realistic understanding of how the memory works. It states emphatically that a few of the memories we retain are crystal-clear and shape our view of things because they were born from moments of deep insight.

This neurological truism, correctly depicting the functions of a drug-influenced memory, stands on its own in the novel. Every other mention is qualified in relation to the invented *Vineland* world and adheres to its principles: the rules established by the author and independent of the laws, physical or otherwise, which guide our non-fictional world. The power of memories is never questioned, never doubted. Interestingly, the two most common sins of memory – which according to Schacter are transience (forgetting through the passage of time) and misattribution (a visual image of a memory which turns out to be incorrect) – are entirely absent from the text. Despite Pynchon's comment that many memories from the drugged-out sixties were "fugitive or false" (285), the ones presented in

---

13   *The Utterance of America*, p.156.

the story turn out to be highly reliable. Even seeming confirmations of the unreliability of memories are immediately qualified to give a power to memory that informs the plot, the actions of its characters and the underlying concept which states that memory is power and remembering is a function of conscience: a powerful tool against injustices.

For example, Takeshi hands Zoyd an IOU card and tells him he will remember that he has got it, someday, when he needs it. Zoyd answers: "Not with my memory" (67), i.e., the memory of a spaced-out hippie. He seems to confirm conventional belief of the sixties' flower power generation, strengthening the image Pynchon has built up so far. But his comment is immediately qualified by Takeshi's response: "You'll remember" (ibid). And Zoyd does: later, much later, when he passes the card on to Prairie on a whim and thereby brings about Prairie's encounter with DL. What seems like an eastern medallion with mystical powers is a recurrent literary device in the novel: memory is often the driving force behind plot development, items are imbued with power because they carry a memory imprint. In the novel people *do* remember things correctly and we as readers *can* trust their narratives, especially Zoyd's. He is "the big idealist" who

liked to believe that Hector [the federal agent who comes looking for him] remembered everybody he'd ever shot at, hit, missed, booked, questioned, rousted, double-crossed – that each face was filed in his conscience, and the only way he could live with such a history was to take these chances with his own bad ass, upping the ante as he moved into his late midcareer. (29)

Zoyd, the big idealist, is aware that this is not possible ('*liked* to believe'), but he connects the concept of remembering with conscience, which in this instance becomes the receptacle for memory. It is reminiscent of Neoplatonic idea about memory which classes memory as part of prudence: Zoyd connects remembering with justice, with righting a wrong. Memory is introduced as the purveyor of justice this early in the novel, and the idea becomes more prominent as we continue into the story.

In context, Prairie's damning accusation that Zoyd's memory is like an Etch-A-Sketch sounds more like teenage petulance than a realistic evaluation of the situation. Zoyd, the worried father, calls her at work and asks her to wait for him, fearing she may be in danger. The conversation is as follows, initiated by Zoyd:

"You OK over there?"
"Something wrong?"
"Do me a favor, stay till I get there, all right?"
"But Isaiah and the band were coming to pick me up, we're goin' camping, remember? Sheez, all that shit you smoke, your brain must be like a Etch-A-Sketch."
"Uh huh, don't get alarmed, but we are facing a situation where a quick mouth, even a leading example such as your own, won't be nearly as much use today as a little cooperation. Please."
"Sure this ain't pothead paranoia?"
"Nope and now I think of it could you ask the young gentlemen when they git there to stick around too?" (45–6)

172

Prairie is the teenage daughter who won't let her father tell her what to do, so she uses the hippie cliché to have a go at him. She aligns herself with the reader when she asks whether it is "pothead paranoid" that makes him talk like that. At this point the reader is more inclined to believe Prairie than Zoyd, but as it turns out, Zoyd is very clear-headed and absolutely justified in his fears. Prairie is used by Pynchon to strengthen the wrong impression of Zoyd's paranoia, keeping the ambiguity and tension of the situation alive, and what initially appears as an old head on a young set of shoulders in Prairie's case turns out to be a well-spoken version of conventional teenage petulance.

Looking at the language, it also becomes clear that she has inherited her eloquence from her father, whose language, although colloquial, is intelligent and witty. Zoyd is the grown-up in this instance, and Prairie the teenager who has bought into the mainly media-inspired image of the pothead sixties generation. As Werner Reinhart writes, America's TV culture defines Prairie's "bildliches Vorstellungsvermögen und ihre analytischen Fähigkeiten", limiting her outlook on life and, thereby, on her own father.[14] And Zoyd does little to refute this image. He even answers in the negative when asked whether he is sure he's not simply paranoid: "Nope" is an ambiguous answer which could mean either 'no, I'm not paranoid' or 'no, I'm not sure'. Pynchon leaves his readers unsure of the situation and allows their thoughts to follow the most obvious connections, the most commonly travelled routes in the memory: in this case to the clichéd ideas about hippies. But it gets harder and harder to delude oneself with these worn-out ideas, and the novel becomes harder and harder to understand if we are determined to follow this line of thought.

The memory is pitted against media-age manipulation in *Vineland*. "[T]he ever-dwindling attention span of an ever more infantalized population" (52) is lamented by the night manager of the Pizza place where Prairie works. Stated, as this is, by the "saintly" manager of the Bodhi Dharma Pizza place with its "eightfold pizzic mandala" (51) portrayed in the stained-glass window, one might be forgiven for interpreting this as a typical New Age grudge against modern society. But this sentence encapsulates one of, if not *the*, main concerns of the novel: it combines the dangers of forgetting (the short attention span) and the manipulative medium of television. The latter stops its viewers from growing up and drawing their own conclusions by creating an "infantalized population" which experiences life second hand, believes predetermined conclusions and wishes only for a happy ending, Hollywood-style.

The attention deficit is picked up most prominently by the Kunoichi Attentive Sisters, watched over by the Head-Ninjette Sister Rochelle, already apparent in the title of their community. Rochelle's pointed criticism of DL is phrased in form of a question: "when do we ever see you concentrate, where's the attention span?" (155). DL must learn to be attentive, to concentrate. But, again, the setting is an

---

14   *Pikareske Romane der 80er Jahre*, p.529.

alternative New Age retreat and invites a reading of this instance as an example of New Age spiritualist waffle.

However, by now the attentive (!) reader has become aware that Pynchon does not categorically reject this approach to life which so often is ridiculed in the novel. He even equates the eighties' spiritual interests with sixties' hippiedom. Just as there was some truth and sense in the ideas within the hippie movement, so there are sensible ideas within New Age philosophy. However, just like the hippies, the New Agers do not have the answers either, merely the inspiration for attempting to find answers. They can locate possible starting points, but certainly not the end-point of the journey. The television-induced lack of attention span is countered by the meditational practices of new spiritualism, but which one will succeed in the end is left open to speculation.

DL, whose training consists in increasing her concentration, acts as a mirror to the character of Frenesi Gates. The sub-plot of DL and Takeshi runs alongside that of Frenesi and Brock/Zoyd. While DL is trying to counter her dwindling attention span (or call it memory-function deficiency), Frenesi seems to disappear further and further into the paralysing world of half-forgotten memories. But she does not do so contentedly, and her new outlook on life sits uneasily and uncomfortably with her. When she is an active and spirited supporter of the revolutionary ideals of 24fps (24 frames per minute, the anarchistic film collective), she says that 'they', some unidentified oppressive agency, will never win "because too many of us are beginning to pay attention" (195).

But Frenesi's idealistic concept of 'them and us' proves vulnerable to manipulation. She falls victim to outside influences and instead of paying more attention (having remembered and therefore stored away powerful material), she forgets. When Frenesi is held by Brock at PREP, his camp for enforcing his Political Re-Education Program, she feels herself shiver as Brock approaches. She "tried to cross her arms, hug herself into an invisible shawl or the memory of one she used to wear ... but he was too close" (273). Frenesi herself has been 're-educated' by Brock over time, and has been surprisingly receptive to his influence. Her loss of memory is simultaneously a loss of comfort because she still recalls her earlier convictions, but has sacrificed these. Many critics have seen this depiction of Frenesi's change as unrealistic, but if we see her as representing the American public, she becomes symbolic for the ease with which people can be manipulated, even seemingly intelligent and revolutionary persons with firmly held believes like Frenesi. The "invisible shawl" she tries to remember is a symbol of her lost convictions. Brock's influence means she can't reach it, can't recall it, and can't be comforted. Brock has power over Frenesi because he can manipulate and influence her memories.

In fact, Brock's entire success with PREP depends on this manipulation of the memory faculty. For this purpose, he concentrates on that section of the population that, unlike Frenesi, is most easily manipulable. He does not aim to re-educate (or brainwash) "the tough cookies, long hair and all". Instead he says,

"I'm counting on the other 90%, amateurs, consumers, short attention spans, out there for the thrills, pick up a chick, score some dope, nothing political. Out in the mainstream, Roscoe, that's where we fish" (270). Those "consumers" with "short attention spans" make up 90% of the population according to Brock. If he can manipulate them, the last 10% have no chance. This is a concise explanation of Pynchon's fear of mass crazes, of widespread fashions, embodied by New Age spiritualism and a diet of TV sitcoms.

But it is not new spiritualism or the television media itself which is dangerous: it is the manipulation and sedation of a large section of the population for which it can be used that worries him. And the antidote? To remember: remember what happens in real life, not on the television screen or in the spirit world, because their institutionalisation (indicated most pointedly by Pynchon's use of the capital letter when talking about 'the Tube') brings with it dangers of mass manipulation. Brock calls it 're-education', but it is clear that the concept is far removed from education; the last thing he wants his 'students' to do is to think for themselves.

The fact that Brock realises that there are ten percent of the population that it is harder to re-educate explains his fascination with Frenesi. Many critics have commented on Brock's seemingly unfounded obsession with Frenesi that guides many of his actions in the novel, and have put it down to either an undocumented sexual obsession or a wish to keep controlling her because of the wish to dominate women, therefore also Prairie later in the novel. However, if seen in the light of the scene between Frenesi and Brock at PREP, it seems that Frenesi is Brock's proudest success-story in his campaign to manipulate. He has managed to 'turn' an intensely revolutionary and subversive person, and is not willing to let go of this proof of his power. It turns into an obsession which grows proportionally to his increasing loss of control. His futile attempt at snatching Prairie towards the end of the novel expresses his desperation to regain control.

Although memories have been proclaimed as the tools whereby manipulation can be avoided, their vulnerability is emphasised, as in the instance above. Another, and possibly the strongest indication of this occurs in another much quoted passage. When Zoyd talks to his friend Mucho about the 'good old days', they lament the changes in society. Zoyd retains his idealistic outlook with regard to memory when he states that these cannot be taken from you: "they can't take what happened, what we found out," to which Mucho, pessimistically, replies:

"Easy. They just let us forget. Give us too much to process, fill up every minute, keep us distracted, it's what the Tube is for, and though it kills me to say it, it's what rock and roll is becoming – just another way to claim our attention, so that beautiful certainty we had starts to fade, and after a while they have us convinced all over again that we really are going to die. And they've got us again." It was how people used to talk.
"I'm not gonna forget," Zoyd vowed, "fuck 'em. While we had it, we really had some fun."
"And they never forgave us." (314)

This is the second time in the novel that Pynchon the omniscient narrator shows his hand (according to Dickson[15]). The sentence "This is how people used to talk" is neither Zoyd's nor Mucho's comment on the conversation. We are again taken out of the invented world of *Vineland* and shown the reality of the situation; namely, that television, and popular culture in general, is prescriptive and therefore guides our thinking, leading it into preordained channels. The thinking is done for us, there is no time to actually consider what we see or hear, and attention is diverted to instant gratification and away from critical analysis. Pynchon is here clearly stating that we must not let that happen to us; we must engage our critical faculty when reading his book. By stepping outside the story for a moment, he adds emphasis to this passage, just as he did in the instance recounting Zoyd's reaction to Prairie's birth in order to make a metacomment about the reading of his book. The first time we were told that memories can be extremely powerful; the second that we must work hard to retain them.

Mucho's pessimistic outlook is somewhat softened by Zoyd's idealistic view on memory: he won't forget. This later part of the novel is much more pessimistic about people's ability to use the memory faculty. Pynchon seems to question how far it is possible to withstand the distracting onslaught of popular entertainment and to remain discerning adults in a country that treats its citizens like children in order to suppress them. Pynchon points out the danger of Zoyd's kind of idealism. He is suggesting that we, the readers, may also have let ourselves be manipulated by *his* text. Not only because we may initially have accepted the clichéd pictures and stereotypical characterisations of certain protagonists unquestioningly, but on a much larger scale, because the novel itself, it seems, is a film script. We may ourselves have been 'watching' a movie rather than reading a book – we, too, are willing victims of mass-media manipulation.

In the last (and comprehensive) chapter Hector has a conversation with two film producers who have been roped in to assist him on the film he wants to make about Frenesi's life, maybe even winning her as the director of the film. Thus when Frenesi and her mother Sasha are finally reunited, an understated event which ends with the two women "jitterbugging" together to the hotel pianist's tunes, Hector comments to his producers: "Too bad we can't use it. But screamín, and confrontations, is much better, actresses love that shit" (362). And so do readers, supposedly, because we are surprised by the peaceful reunion which is repeated in all the other instances of previously much anticipated reunions, whether between Prairie and Frenesi, Weed and Frenesi or Zoyd and Frenesi's new husband Flash. Everyone seems to become friends, to put the past behind them and look forward to a harmonious common future. Even DL and Takeshi enter into a loving relationship at the end.

This is an unexpected conclusion to the book. But if we have actually been watching a film, this would not only explain the constant flashbacks, flash-

---

15   *The Utterance of America*, p.169.

forwards and changes of scene. It also explains all the illogical events or inconsistencies in tone and action that are played out in the final chapter, such as Brock's timely withdrawal back into the helicopter which saves Prairie at the last moment (in an ironic inversion of the *deus ex machina*), the peaceful reunion of the main characters and, most of all, the Hollywood-style happy ending, so unusual for Pynchon, with the return of Desmond the dog in open parody of the Hollywood classic feel-good movie *Lassie Come Home*, as commented on by many critics, and the entire novel ending in the uncannily comforting and inappropriate word "home". These are not the values Pynchon has shown in the novel. Rather, they seem to be the values film makers are impressing upon us, the viewers, in order to give us a false sense of security to lure us ever further away from independent and critical thought.

The final reference to memories in the novel emphasises this point. The uneasiness which underlies the otherwise so strangely harmonious reunions is expressed through details of language. Thus Sasha, Frenesi and Prairie, three generations of the same family, are trying to reconnect with each other by connecting up their memories: they sit down "beneath an oak tree, where they would sit and hang out for hours, spinning and catching strands of memory, perilously reconnecting—" (368). But for whom is the reconnecting perilous? It could relate to the insecurity the three women feel on finally meeting up and realising that they 'belong' together. But the choice of words suggests otherwise. Throughout the book memories have been hailed as saviours of justice, thus "spinning and catching strands of memory" should indicate a healthy occupation. The ambivalence is expressed in the verb: 'spinning' is associated with inventing, as in 'spinning yarns', used in *Gravity's Rainbow* to expose the deception of a proposed analytical system.[16]

Are the women inventing memories because a film crew is documenting their reunion and the true memories would not suit the intentions of the film? "Catching strands" implies an interaction between the women based on wishful thinking rather than facts, as in catching at dreams, strands of moonlight. The reunion here is tenuous and carefully approached, to the outside world a personal reconnecting between long-lost mothers and daughters. But maybe we as readers are asked to look beyond the frame created by the novel, to try to see beyond the

---

16   See Bernard Duyfhuizen's "Starry-eyed semiotics" in which he connects the idea of spinning yarns with the misinterpretation of a situation. Slothrop's map in *Gravity's Rainbow* documents his supposed encounters with women – which strangely coincide with the sites where bombs fall. This is taken to mean that Slothrop has an innate sensor which tells him when and where bombs will fall, thereby looking for significance in the seeming coincidence. In the third part of the novel it is revealed that, in fact, Slothrop would "edit, switch names, insert fantasies into the yarns he spun" (360), thereby exposing it as fiction. Duyfhuizen argues that "Pynchon's playful narrator sabotages a particular reading of *Gravity's Rainbow* and the convention of reading in general" (26). This also seems to apply to *Vineland*: the 'spinning of memories' suggests that alternative readings of the scene are encouraged.

'shot' we are offered, the angle presented, to what is actually being played out in front of our eyes. This would mean that the Traverse/Becker clan have also succumbed to manipulation, in which case the novel leaves us with a very dark view of the future.

PASTORAL BACKGROUNDS

One way of discovering what is actually going on in the scene is to consider its setting. Pynchon, the director of this film, has chosen a pastoral setting for the ending. This is highly relevant for its reading. Having looked at the relevance Pynchon attributes to memory – as a powerful yet vulnerable tool of justice – we can now look at some specific backgrounds and images in the novel to discover whether they reveal any meaning. Pynchon says about memories that they can be manipulated when we allow only clichés or prejudice to guide our thoughts. My proposal – an author's concept of memory influences his choice of backgrounds – therefore requires that the backgrounds in *Vineland* must first be cleared of false significances before the true meaning comes to light.

Before going on to the conspicuous pastoral scenes, the most obvious setting of the novel – Vineland itself – must be considered. The title itself urges this reflection and suggests historical depth because the two Vinelands of modern times (the real Vineland in New Jersey and Pynchon's invented one in California – geographically spanning the continent from East to West) are etymologically linked to the origins of modern America: with Vinland, the name given to America by the Vikings, and with the mythological 'Vineland the Good'. This seems to imply a return to the values and hopes associated with these places, of utopian dreams, of abundance and promise, or in M.K. Booker's words, of "[a] New World as a whole [which] originally functioned in the European psyche as a locus of hopeful idealism" and stood for the American ideal of freedom.[17]

The pastoral scenes echo this sentiment in that they, too, reflect a dream of a simpler life in accordance with nature. The novel begins and ends in Vineland and three main pastoral scenes span the entire book. The wedding of Frenesi and Zoyd (38–9), the fantasy picnic (232–3) and the Becker/Traverse family gathering (375 to end) are set in the past, future and present respectively. This contributes to a (false) sense of nostalgia about the sixties, which Pynchon establishes throughout the novel. However, the pastoral scenes, which should strengthen this image, contain aspects which undermine it. As Reinhart writes: "Pynchon stattet 'sein' Vineland zwar zunächst mit den Attributen einer außerentropischen, arkadischen, mystisch-utopischen Enklave aus, um es danach um so nachdrücklicher als eine fragwürdige, ja infizierte Idylle zu demaskieren".[18]

The pastoral scenes have a dream-like quality, typical of the simplicity-celebrating Georgics of classical literature, a genre employed differently in these

---

17   Quoted in Dirk Vanderbeke, "Vineland in the novels of John Barth and Thomas Pynchon".
18   *Pikareske Romane der 80er Jahre*, p.533.

three different settings: in the first instance through Zoyd's hazy memories of his perfect wedding day to a perfect woman, with the world in mystical, peaceful union. This feeling is both drug-induced and inspired by Zoyd's unmitigated love for Frenesi. He is sincerely asking her whether she thinks love can save anyone (an ironic question in hindsight, as Frenesi's marriage to Zoyd derives from her need for a place to hide rather than personal attraction). Not focusing on her answer "[h]e thought, At least try to remember this, try to keep it someplace secure, just her face now in this light [...]" (39). This episode is an anchor-point for Zoyd, who wants to capture his feelings, just as it is an anchor-point for the reader: the intense emotional bliss that pastoral poetry adulates, inspired by natural surroundings and a (supposedly) happy simple life. As we know, Zoyd's honest feelings are not reciprocated, and the pastoral setting turns out to be false.

The second instance of a pastoral scene is the imagined picnic set in the future and attended by Rex (murderer-to-be), Weed (to-be-murdered), Frenesi (instigator of Rex's act and Weed's death) and Prairie (yet unborn, but attending in her 1984 teenage form). It is a flash-forward to a time when the present has become a distant memory that everyone can share and laugh at while recounting it to the next generation. However, it is completely fanciful since Rex will shoot Weed, Frenesi outed as an informant and Prairie motherless – the picnic is hence a pastoral scene of utopian wishes: a deliberate usage of the genre to show the misconception of the idyllic world depicted there.

The full comprehension of this passage is again delayed: we are told of the picnic before Weed's death, at a time when Rex is still willing to help him out of his dangerous situation. Neither does Pynchon mention Prairie by name, she is "some fine-looking young teener", the "pleasant package with the eats" (232), presumably from Rex's point of view because it fits his vocabulary and thinking. And it is the first mention of the gun in Rex's fringe-bag – only later do we find out that Frenesi planted it there, instructed by Brock to do so. This scene, therefore, set "beneath some single low oak out on an impossible hillside, with sunlight, and the voices of children" (ibid) is as impossible to understand as the scene itself is impossible, both because the future will turn out quite differently and because the background seems to be taken from an idyllic, Georgic romance. As the narrator points out a few pages later in a cynical comment immediately following Weed's murder: "He [Rex] would not after all be lucky enough to sit under that oak on that dreamed hillside someday with a miraculously saved Weed Atman, in some 1980s world of the future" (246). This comment recalls the picnic and in hindsight much of its meaning is revealed.

The comment not only looks backwards to the fantasy picnic, it also looks forwards to the third pastoral setting, the annual Becker/Traverse family gathering in the forests of Vineland. By the time this third setting is evoked we have met Weed as a Thanatoid and are "in some 1980s world of the future" where a meeting between Rex and Weed would, after all, be possible. Even the oak tree of Rex' pastoral dream makes an appearance in this final section of the book. Rex, however, does not turn up at the family gathering. Had Pynchon meant to suggest that an idyllic reunion – such as that presented in the last chapter – was possible, he would surely have brought Rex back and made his pastoral vision complete. But Rex is left out of the final picture for conceptual reasons, due to his symbolic function in the story, best explained by two character analyses: the first is Weed's identification with memory and death, the other Rex's close associative link with REX 84: Reagan's 1984 Readiness Exercise.

Rex Snuvvle, graduate student, Porsche-lover (literally), secret correspondent of Trotskyite Paris exiles and trigger-finger, plays a relatively minor part (first mention p.207) in the gallery of Pynchonian characters in *Vineland*. Nevertheless, he is the person who performs the pivotal act of the entire novel – the shooting of Weed. As Weed so precisely states during the family gathering: Rex is "only the ceremonial trigger-finger, just a stooge..." (366). Although he shot the gun, he was only a link in the chain of events. Weed follows this chain backwards: "Used to think I was climbing, step by step [...] toward a resolution—first Rex, above him [Frenesi], then Brock Vond, then—but that's when it begins to go dark, and that door at the top I thought I saw isn't there anymore, because the light behind it just went off too" (ibid).

The trail may have gone cold for Weed, but we as readers can follow it further back. Not through the individuals in a chain of command, but through associations presented in the text itself. The most obvious link is the name Rex. In retrospect the story runs on two levels simultaneously: the personal and the political. On the personal level, where recognisable individuals tell their private stories from own points of view, Rex is the lynchpin in a network of personal experiences. His irreversible act of shooting Weed changes the lives of everyone involved. On the political plane Rex is the code-name for Reagan's Readiness Exercise in 1984 around which all other political aspects seem to revolve: according to Pynchon, another metaphorical trigger-finger, but one that luckily was not engaged.

Pynchon's political orientation is very clear, and his criticism of Nixon's and Reagan's governments are intense and specific. He highlights certain events during Reagan's leadership which culminate in the secretive organisation of an exercise preparing for national crisis situations – it eroded civil liberties and brought the US to the edge of a dictatorship in which "the United States was one auto-pen signature away from martial law."[19] REX 84, just as Rex in 1984, is the central act which, unlike Rex the human, is stopped just before it is too late.

On the personal plane this is depicted when Brock is unceremoniously hauled back inside the helicopter from which he so (un)threateningly (like "Death From Slightly Above", 375) converges on Prairie, because "Reagan had officially ended the 'exercise' known as REX 84" (376) and thereby withdrawn Brock's unusual authorisations that he had exploited for personal gains. It could be said that Rex

---

19   David Thoreen, "The president's emergency war powers", p.791.

plays a major role in the final scene of the novel in his symbolic guise as trigger-finger, the REX of the political plane: the near-submission of a nation through manipulations that is based on dubious legal prowess, as Pynchon indicates, by extending the Fourth Amendment and constructing a reason for claiming that the US is in immediate danger – a position the US has been in continuously since WW2, according to all following US administrations.

Pynchon has shown the reader on the political plane, through the REX 84 example, how laws amended for exercises can lead to actual infringements of civil rights, and has imposed this idea onto the personal plane to make it more directly comprehensible. Had Rex and Weed been brought together at the family gathering and been reconciled, it would have implied approbation for Rex's act – by parallel the political situation as well.

But Pynchon is not out for revenge, as supposedly are the Thanatoids. Weed is asked by Prairie at the family reunion whether he wants to find Frenesi to get his revenge, for "he was, after all […] still a cell of memory, of refusal to forgive, sailing like a conscious virus through the population, seeking her out" (365). Weed shrugs and says: "As a Thanatoid one's reduced to hanging around monitoring the situation, trying to nudge if you don't think it's moving along fast enough but basically helpless and, if you give in to it, depressed, too" (ibid). Weed, as the personification of memory, is not here for revenge. Instead he is "a conscious virus" constantly reminding "the population" of his existence. He is "monitoring the situation", reminding us of the real situation whenever things aren't "moving along fast enough." Even Weed's name expresses the Thanatoid strength: you cannot kill him, cannot get rid of him; he keeps coming back. Ambiguously, his name could, furthermore, be translated as 'marihuana breath', incorporating the danger of forgetting into the urge to remember. Memories are the guardians of justice, reminding us that things are not right. They are not meant to inspire reprisals, but are instruments to get things moving. Phillip Gocheonour points out that in *Vineland* "[m]emory serves, not as the anchor bringing everything to rest and revealing the truth of history, but rather as the means of destabalizing history and bringing injustices before us".[20]

URBAN BACKGROUNDS

The novel's pastoral scenes are contrasted by urban scenes. A general look at Pynchon's choice of background reveals that much of the action is played out against everyday backgrounds, such as motel rooms or down-market housing. These often merge into each other. Although the various motel rooms where Frenesi meets Brock or Weed are individually described, they do not normally stand out as easily distinguishable settings – a way of expressing the regularity of these illicit meetings and thereby the extent of Frenesi's collaboration with Brock.

---

20   "The history written on the body", p.179.

The greatest contrast to the pastoral scenes is produced through the detailed description of the city of Columbus, where DL hides (133–4). According to Grim, the episode uses the actual topography and demographics of the real Columbus to the last detail. Grim argues that, from the position of the waterside Pizza place to DL's job in a vacuum-cleaner factory, and from the percentage of Japanese businesses to the centre for computer technology, each background element, which so accurately describes DL's situation, is factual.[21] The setting of Columbus is an example of what Bernard Duyfhuizen calls Pynchon's "meticulous concerns for the interrelationship and dislocation between character and locale" where he "exploits [...] location by filling it with detail".[22]

The depiction of a real town in all its detail, which so extraordinarily fits the situation (Pynchon must have borrowed Rushdie's tuning fork, see Ch.4), is an antipode to the pastoral dream-like settings. This is urban living: fast, electronic and economy-led. Pynchon is presumably depicting a typical American town, the real New World, choosing the city of Columbus for its name to connect it to the theme of American pastoral gone wrong, where the machine has invaded the garden; both the prairie (hence Prairie's name also usurped by modern culture in the surname Wheeler) and the paradise Columbus apparently had discovered. When DL chooses Columbus to hide, she, like those following in the wake of Columbus, is seeking a new start. But just like the new inhabitants of America, she is exposed by the New World where God is a computer and where the Vineland of plenty is an Arcadian dream only.

THE MEMORY MAP

The large-scale setting, the map of the United States spanned from coast to coast by the two Vinelands which delineate it both geographically and historically, reveals large-scale concerns. A detailed look at how Pynchon creates three-dimensional settings in relation to memory uncovers more specific concerns. Mark D. Hawthorne writes that the settings in *Vineland* "provide keys to character development and thematic content",[23] and one way to read the settings is to investigate memory structures embedded in the text through the settings. In addition to the memory map – an obvious structure to focus on in *Vineland* as the instance of Columbus above shows – I will look at architectural structures and examples of the memory journey.

The topic of maps and memory is introduced by Takeshi reading a map when searching for the road to the Retreat. He internalises the map, memorising it in order to forestall any unwished-for encounters with those trailing him: "he'd handicapped the alternate routes and imagined changes of plans associated with each", a paranoia-born precaution which shows that his mind works on an

---

21   "Good-buy, Columbus".
22   "Starry-eyed semiotics", p.1.
23   "Imaginary locales in Pynchon's *Vineland*", p.77.

imaginary three-dimensional plane, approaching the journey like "an all-day hard-edged video game, one level of difficulty to the next" (161). The comparison between memory techniques and computer technology is Pynchon's way of updating memory metaphors and bringing them into the postmodern era. The accompanying 1s and 0s stand for impersonal digits that can be used to control people's lives (as in Frenesi's case, 71), but also as the wood which obscures sight of the trees (as when Prairie wonders whether it is not in the spaces between them that the really important information lies, 114, or Rochelle's emphasis on knowing "the exact spaces between things", 111). Porush writes that

[i]n the Pynchon mythography, the whole nexus of conceits—communication systems, codes of hidden meaning, technologizing of the Word, the reduction of options, the alliance between tech and Death ...—all resolve into the image of flashing electronic gateways, meant to imitate the shining paths (neurons) of the human brain.[24]

He alludes directly to the metaphor that compares memory and the computer, using visual descriptions of how the brain works to express it. Pynchon seems to inhabit the space which remembers when he uses the metaphor – using the memory therefore means entering a space and finding one's orientation amongst the items located there.

As we have seen in the case of Columbus, the city map, an extension of the general map, plays a large part in the novel. The more abstract references most clearly link it to the memory process. When Zoyd explains his mind-travels to Prairie, which he uses to search for Frenesi, he describes the frustration of not being able to get his bearings by saying, he tries "to read signs, locate landmarks, anything that'll give a clue, but—well the signs are there on the street corners and store windows—but I can't read them. [...] there's something between it and my brain that won't let it through" (40). One of Pynchon's many references to mind-travel, this example uses memory-technique terminology, looking for 'signs', 'landmarks', 'clues' and placing them on a map made out of architectural and topographical features, such a street corners and store windows, but Zoyd can't 'read' these signs with his "third eye".

The something interposing itself between the image and the brain is the same something that interferes with memory images, and Zoyd's dream journey can be compared to a faulty artificial memory system. The instance can be interpreted either as a true transcendental connection with Frenesi or as pure wishful thinking on Zoyd's part. Either way, the attempt at visualising the landscape, the surroundings Frenesi lives in, expresses the intensity of Zoyd's feelings for Frenesi. It emphasises the importance of the three-dimensional setting and the dormant power that resides within it, an example of which are the native *woge* spirits who inhabit the Vineland coast.[25]

---

24   "Purring into transcendence", p.40.
25   Pynchon's description of the *woge* – pre-human creatures to whom the native Yurok-

Zoyd's dream journey also expresses the common human urge to frame events in order to make them more understandable:

The smartest kid Justin ever met, back in kindergarten, had told him to pretend his parents were characters in a television sitcom. 'Pretend there's a frame around 'em like the Tube, pretend they're a show you're watching. You can go into it if you want, or you can just watch, and not go into it.' (351)

Extraordinary advice from a very young boy. Pynchon is referring to the fixation with television that permeates the text, and the analogy suggests itself in a world where TV shows and reality intermingle constantly. TV culture is so ingrained in society that already at kindergarten-age children limit and control external influences and thereby distance themselves from the world's chaotic reality. But it is also a way of coping. By putting a frame around his parents and the scene in front of him, Justin gains distance and thereby the space in which to choose which role he wants to play in the situation, if any at all. However, we can not completely disengage: objectivity is impossible. The distance may help to map out the scene, but the act of mapping the scene tells us more about the mapper than about the scene itself. As the character Wood in *Mason & Dixon* says:

the map is *about* the world in a way that reveals, not the world – or not *just* the world – but also (and sometimes especially) the agency of the mapper. That is, maps, all maps, inevitably, unavoidably, necessarily embody their author's prejudices, biases and partialities.[26]

Robert L. McLaughlin comments that Wood "recognizes that the means for knowing the world are inseparable from the means of representing that knowledge".[27] By framing something, mapping it, it is made comprehensible or controllable. When Pynchon uses a map, it is not to delineate the ground, to guide the reader in one direction. On the contrary, his maps point out the divergence of a map and its possible readings. Maps as exact palimpsests don't work. The most prominent example appears in *Gravity's Rainbow*. Here Slothrop's map is

---

Indians turn for guidance – shows that the power of memory resides within the landscape: these *woge* "withdrew [...] into the features of the landscape, remaining conscious, remembering better times, capable of sorrow and as seasons went on other emotions as well". They become the memory of the place, anchored to particular points. And "[e]verything had a name—fishing and snaring places, acorn grounds, rocks in the river, boulders on the banks, groves and single trees with their own names, springs, pools, meadows, all alive, each with its own spirit" (186). In Langland-fashion a memory map is created that retains memories. Memory and landscape are clearly linked in Pynchon's imagination. In the context of the novel the landscape is a metaphor for memory storage. It is also an analogy for the way a country's history does not disappear, but is perpetuated in the physical surroundings. It highlights a distinction that needs to be made between settings as nostalgic reminiscences of idealised pasts and powerful backgrounds for a comparison between the past and the present.

26   Quoted by McLaughlin in "Surveying, mapmaking and representation in *Mason & Dixon*".
27   Ibid., p.179.

misread by both the protagonists and the reader – Pynchon using it to point to the ambiguous readings that can be made of his text.[28] Maps, therefore, are both positive, because they allow an overview and a greater comprehension of things, yet simultaneously contain the danger of altering the subject-matter depicted, in a way that limits its relevance, or by attempting to impose a pattern on a subject that is not classifiable. It becomes necessary to learn how to read these maps, and that is part of Sister Rochelle's function: she teaches how to interpret 'space' and is, therefore, related to the idea of memory as an architectural structure, as a veritable memory palace.

ARCHITECTURAL MEMORY

Metaphors that compare memory to a building occur in *Vineland* when Prairie searches the computer for information about her mother and is "led room to room" (114) through the computer's memory, and when the houses in Brock's and Zoyd's dreams (275/374) are used to symbolise the subconscious. The most unusual use of memory architecture occurs when Prairie and DL encounter Sister Rochelle in the Kunoichi Retreat's Coffee Lounge: Rochelle, holding

a mug of coffee in her hand, slowly emerged [...] from invisibility. It seemed to [Prairie] that this must be a magical gift. She learned later that Rochelle had memorized, in this room, all the shadows and how they changed, the cover, the exact spaces between things ... had come to know the room so completely that she could impersonate it, in its full transparency of emptiness. (111)

This passage contains many features of the memory palace: the architectural setting, the minute familiarity with the space, the organisation or "exact spaces between things", the relationship between light and dark and the concept of memorising itself. Sister Rochelle exemplifies the disciplined practitioner of artificial memory. Her memory palace is so familiar she can "impersonate" it. The items to be remembered (the shadows) and the reason for remembering them (to attain invisibility) are, however, decidedly incompatible with traditional aims of artificial memory. This is because ancient memory techniques and ancient eastern philosophies converge in the figure of Sister Rochelle.

Throughout the book references to eastern philosophy, meditational practices and astrological predictions are presented ambiguously: on the one hand, they represent the ridiculous 1980s New Age fashion spreading through the Western World (and affecting people like Nancy Reagan whom the passage on astrology and politics (262) clearly refers to),[29] creating a mindless obedience to unfounded magical notions about easy means to solve life's problems. This idea is ridiculed architecturally in the stained-glass eightfold pizzic mandala of the Bodhi Dharma Pizza restaurant where Prairie works (51). The mandala does not aid a spiritual

---

28   See note 16 above on *Gravity's Rainbow*.
29   David Thoreen, "The Fourth Amendment and other inconveniences", p.220.

escape from the physical world because it calls "attention to the body and its needs rather than to block out such things".[30]

On the other hand, certain meditational aids seem helpful and some predictions turn out to be true and serve as potent symbols of Pynchon's warnings (such as Brock's star sign that accurately foretells his future activities), and some eastern philosophies bear fruit (such as DL and Takeshi's karmic agreement to counteract DL's delayed Death Touch consequences). Sister Rochelle sits squarely between these two positions. As the Head-Ninjette, she embodies the spiritual way, but at the same time she is highly critical of people it attracts who expect instant enlightenment. Hence her comment to Prairie on being asked how she achieves invisibility: "Takes a serious attention span [...] Common sense and hard work's all it takes. One of the first of many kunoichi disillusionments—right, DL?—is finding that the knowledge won't come down all at once in any big transcendent moment" (112).

The heavy-smoking, coffee- and alcohol-drinking Rochelle is unexpectedly earthbound. Her message is: if you want something, you've got to work for it. The retreat teaches "disillusionment": disengaging from illusions and attempting to see reality through personal experience and effort. This could be advice given to a student of artificial memory: this skill cannot be used as a magical short cut to understanding either, but requires hard work, common sense and the much lamented "serious attention span".

Into this architectural memory space Pynchon introduces the element of time, which confuses the situation. The structure of the novel is made less accessible because the plot moves freely between past, present and future, while the physical memory palace Rochelle inhabits changes by the minute. She must remember how the shadows alter every moment in order to perform her (seemingly pointless) vanishing act. But Rochelle is a teacher of the technique, not of the content, and each of her appearances in the text serves as a guide to the process which must be attempted to reach *dis*illusionment.

Rochelle's allegories of Eden (166) and Hell (382-3) are three-dimensional orientational maps, a way of positioning oneself in order to get the best view of the situation. Martin Klepper calls Rochelle "eine feministische Deuterin"[31] with regard to the map of Eden. However, she does much more than add a feminist interpretation to the story of the Fall: she provides Takeshi with an alternate way of thinking. Eden is a mind map she creates to help him understand the position DL is in. Hell, again a mind map drawn for Takeshi, inverses the traditional concept of Heaven and Hell, allowing for an inverted reading of the symbolism and inviting an up-side down view of the world, depicted in spatial form.

Rochelle's maps underline that there is no divine justice, no superior instance that will even out the balance in the end, as the Emersonian quotation, read out

---

30   Elaine B. Safer, "Pynchon's world and its legendary past", p.58.
31   *Pynchon, Auster, DeLillo*, p.236.

during the family gathering in the last chapter, suggests. Susan Strehle points out that "[a]ccording to Sister Rochelle, justice is created by and on earth, rather than soaring as a transcendent given in Heaven and Hell. It is a human longing, not something established with the order of the universe".[32] Pynchon uses maps of Heaven and Hell, not to anchor right and wrong, punishment and reward in a landscape of virtues and sins (see Langland, Ch.2), but to show how these maps can be misread as expressions of a fictitious universal order. Justice is a human longing, and one which humans can see fulfilled by remembering. Sister Rochelle is the wise instructor who first tells us how to create spatial awareness (by concentration and hard work) and then how to apply it to deal with specific situations (by mind-mapping them).

THE MEMORY JOURNEY 1: THE CHAIN

Pynchon establishes maps for his readers as backgrounds, as guides to the concerns of his story. His characters are placed against these backgrounds, and their movements within the three-dimensional spaces are further indications of the themes under investigation. The memory journey, structured by the movement through space, is the ideal system to access their meaning. As one major topic of *Vineland* is remembering, it is only natural that memory systems, like the memory journey, should be present in the text. However, it is extraordinary how exactly Pynchon's memory images recall those from classical systems.

Beyond the traditional metaphor that sees memory as a journey into the past (as a "spin in the time machine", 147), Pynchon also employs the memory chain: the simplified version of the journey method. He follows the journey of Takeshi's IOU card as it goes "into a pocket, then another, into a long sequence of pockets, wallets, envelopes, drawers, and boxes, surviving barrooms, laundromats, doper's forgetfulness" (67), until Zoyd finally hands it to Prairie, who then benefits from it because it brings her to DL's attention. This chain of events (and three-dimensional places) shows a certain fatalistic belief that things go on a destined journey and turn up again at the required moment.

The second instance shows what happens when the chain is ignored: after Weed's shooting "[n]obody attempted to trace the path of the gun. It was almost a supernatural term in the story—a creature that appears only so that the deed will be done, and then vanishes. No sign-out form, no log entries, no ballistics tests or serial numbers..." (243). Connecting up the individual links in the chain would have led back to Brock. It again suggests that nothing exists in isolation, and that everything leaves a trail that can be followed to reveal the truth.

The idea of a chain of events is contained in the novel in more general forms too; for example, through the three pastoral scenes which, linked up, form a basic structure for the novel, or in the suggestion that personality traits are passed from one generation to the next, such as Frenesi's passion for light which she seems to

---

32   "Pynchon's 'elaborate game of doubles' in *Vineland*", p.115.

have inherited from her father, or the fascination with men in uniform passed down from her mother and possibly further to Prairie. The individual links in Pynchon's memory chain are particularly conspicuous: they are depicted as crossings between worlds.

THE MEMORY JOURNEY 2: CROSSINGS

As many of the characters are constantly on the move, it is surprising how few scenes are actually played out during travel. Those that happen 'on the go' usually pertain to action sequences (DL freeing Frenesi from Brock's camp; Prairie, DL and Takeshi's flight from the retreat) or transitional episodes where a change takes place (Zoyd taking baby Prairie to Vineland for the first time via the Golden Gate Bridge; Brock's journey to Hell). Actual journeys, like those referred to above, are related to the concept of interconnectedness; to cause and effect. Interestingly, it is neither the place of departure nor the destination that is emphasised, but the transition between two realms or distinct areas, even between two worlds. Shawn Smith points out that already the family name Traverse emphasises the act of crossing over.[33]

The transfer between two worlds is perceived by the protagonists as a physical crossing. Weed describes the feeling upon leaving each of his many dentist appointments (brainwashing sessions initiated by Brock or his peers to undermine Weed's leadership role at the college) as going "back across a borderline, invisible but felt at its crossing, between worlds" (228). In this case the two worlds are the fabricated one installed into Weed's mind during his dental visits – a world which produces long stretches of memory loss (the manipulators covering their tracks) – and the real one which, due to whatever images have been established wrongly in his mind, leaves Weed ever "less sure about anything" (ibid). This manipulation of memories creates false anchor points for an entire world picture. The difference between these worlds is "felt" by Weed, an experience taken in through the senses and related to the "pain inflicted, pain withheld, pain drugged away, pain become amnesia" which creates strange memories through sense-impressions.

The parallel to this horrific crossing between worlds is Brock's transfer from the world of the living to that of the dead. With what appears to be poetic justice, Brock, the supposed instigator of Weed's awful experiences, crosses a threshold into another world from which, however, there will be no return. After Brock's failed attempt to kidnap Prairie, having had his special authorisation revoked, he steals a helicopter, crashes in the Vineland forest and is picked up in his new Thanatoid state by Vato and Blood, who take him to the crossing into Hell. Here the transfer point is symbolised by the river. Vato recounts the Yurok tale "about a man from Turip [...] who lost the young woman he loved and pursued her into the country of death" (379). The story, which includes Illa "who ferries the dead across the river", relates to the classical river of death (Styx) with its ferryman

---

33   *Pynchon and History*, p.125.

(Charon) and should alert Brock to his coming passage into Tsorrek, the land of death. Instead he asks whether the man from Turip got back the woman – showing his preoccupation with Frenesi. By then "the Ghosts' Trail [...] was already chest-deep", Brock sinking ever deeper into the other world. In cynical imitation of Weed's dental visits, Brock now sees a man approaching who "carried objects in his hands that Brock couldn't make out clearly" (ibid) – reminiscent of Weed's instruments of torture – and accordingly is told that these are implements that will be used to remove his bones prior to crossing the river.

These unpleasant crossings between worlds are contrasted by those which promise a greater understanding or that reconnect a person to original, spiritual knowledge – or so it seems at first. When Zoyd takes Prairie to Vineland as a baby, she watches the passing countryside through the bus window, apparently having a particular connection with the typical Vineland redwood trees, "in a very quiet voice talking to them. [...] It seemed now and then as if she were responding to something she was hearing [...] as if this were a return for her to a world behind the world she had known all along" (315).

Zoyd's suspicion of Prairie's supernatural connection with something beyond his comprehension goes back to his reaction to her birth when he first looked into her eyes and thought: "oh God, God, she knew him, *from someplace else*" (285) – a common experience for new parents, but to the slightly hazy (drugged) Zoyd that moment and "this look from brand-new Prairie [...] would be there for [him] more than once in years to come, to help him through [...]" (ibid). It is Zoyd's first contact with another world – the real world – one he hasn't really noticed so far. When he takes Prairie to Vineland for safety, he is again brought into contact with the real world through Prairie's connection with it. When Prairie is ill a couple of years later, looking at her father "with dull hot eyes, snot crusted on her face, hair in a snarl, and croaked, 'Dad? Am I ever gonna get bett-or?' [...] he had his belated moment of welcome to planet Earth, in which he knew, dismayingly, that he would, would have to, do anything to keep this dear small life from harm" (321). The world he first glimpsed in the eyes of his newborn daughter, and then during their journey to Vineland, has become his world at last. With a realisation of his love for her, he accepts responsibilities beyond his own person.

Like Angela Carter, Pynchon is interested in the crossing between two places, but where Carter leaves the crossings on the edges of her scenes and makes the experience of crossing from one to the other concise and intense, hoping to expose the gaps that lie between the scenes to allow for another view of the world, Pynchon places the crossing between two places at the centre of a scene and lingers there. It is not a clearly defined break which comes as somewhat of a shock, as in Carter's case, but rather a slow merging of lines, a dissolution of boundaries, which happens almost mystically, leaving the reader uncertain of exactly when the line was crossed. Pynchon emphasises that the different worlds he describes are superimposed on each other: they exist at the same time. It is tempting to say that one represents the real world while the other is an illusory one, but that would be to gravely oversimplify Pynchon's intent.

The palimpsest method Pynchon employs here, reminiscent of that used in medieval writing (see Ch.2), is adapted to suit his purpose. He superimposes one background on top of the other in memory-chain fashion that also links the various associations together, but he simultaneously dissolves the boundaries between them. In classical memory-practice a clear distinction between each image is vital. By merging backgrounds, Pynchon presents a confused picture – one that doesn't allow for clear thinking. He mirrors the mental processes of a population that doesn't bother to clarify ideas, which allows false images to be created. Only by stripping back the superimposed images can the actual image be found. Pynchon's backgrounds contain these confusing layers (superimposed images), but a little circumspection reveals what actually lies at their heart.

Even Zoyd's crossing into the real world, that is, out of his science-fiction and drug-inspired reality into the world of responsible parenting, contains negative aspects. Zoyd only "dismayingly" realises that he "would have to" look after his daughter. This could be read as selfishness on Zoyd's part, but it rather seems to relate to the pastorally depicted family reunion. The family is the centre of the last scene, depicted as an ultimately harmonious structure that carries and supports its members because they 'belong'. But isn't this exactly what authoritarian agencies wish their subjects to believe? And believing in the sanctity of family is equated with believing in the old American Dream of freedom, in a happy ending. It seems that the main characters have finally bought into this dream, seduced by the ideal of family unity, and become respectable citizens. In other words, Pynchon's trust that the general American public can be woken up, can be made aware of the true situation their country is in, has rather diminished by the time the novel ends and all its characters have succumbed to the comfort of 'belonging'.

Pynchon contrasts the pastoral vision with urban reality to expose the real situation. The dream of freedom has been replaced by a reality of "the American government's repression of its people" where "[t]he American culture preempts dissent; Hollywood and the Tube even weakens people's intellect and powers of resistance".[34] The landscape presented by Pynchon is not so much a dream turned nightmare as a desperate attempt to wake up from this nightmare.

The urgency with which Pynchon expresses his concerns suggests that he believes that there is hope of escaping the nightmare; at the same time he is aware that the deterrent for doing so is enormous. People cling to old dreams, go backwards rather than forwards and escape into apparent safety in social structures, which means that responsibility is removed. The family is such a structure: it dulls the sense of urgency. Pynchon does not seem to offer any solution on how to deal with this paradox of the family as both necessary and dangerously dulling.

---

34   Dan Geddes, "Pynchon's *Vineland*", p.1.

The meaning contained in the backgrounds and images of the novel is not straightforward although the message is. "Do not forget" can easily be mistaken as an instruction to hark back to better times. Pynchon qualifies the statement by showing what happens when idealism overpowers realism. By expressing his meaning so ingeniously, however, it could be said that Pynchon greatly reduces the dissemination of his ideas because readers may not understand what he wants to convey so urgently – or, as surprising as his idyllic ending, one might conclude that Pynchon believes his fellow Americans could be nudged into consciousness; that monitoring the situation may be enough to inaugurate change.

Paul Auster – *Moon Palace*
Renaissance Mysticism

This investigation set out to test my theory that memory systems can be applied to literature to aid interpretation. Each new text under consideration and each chapter has held encouraging results, but has also meant that elements of my theory had to be modified in order to become practicable, or even had to be discarded as false assumptions. The vagueness of theory with which I began has made way for actual practical steps of interpretation. Now that I have reached the final text, *Moon Palace* by Paul Auster, it seems appropriate to undertake its interpretation according to the individual steps revealed during my investigative journey.

A detailed account of the theory and practice involved is set out in the Conclusion. Suffice for now to state the four steps to be taken towards an interpretation of Auster's novel. First, discover Auster's concept of memory in general (related to other works in his canon) and in particular in *Moon Palace* (by considering direct references to memory and instances where the memory function is involved). Secondly, establish what kind of background Auster employs and discover how his ideas of memory influence the way these spaces should be read. Thirdly, investigate background-connections to approximate an overall structure of the text by identifying which memory systems Auster employs most frequently (from the six systems listed in chapter 1). Finally, analyse the backgrounds as the vehicle for the story and the images as the elements containing a possible meaning of the text, taking into account the information gathered during the three preliminary steps. These four steps should lead, purposefully, through the text and to a comprehensive interpretation of it.

Step 1: Auster's concept of memory
Step one, looking at Auster's angle on memory, has turned out to be extremely fruitful since he, of all the six authors considered, most prominently and unambiguously links memory to a particular school of thought: the Renaissance cabbalistic adaptation of the classical memory system, using backgrounds and

images to create a mystical connection with an instance of higher knowledge. In his novel *Moon Palace* Auster's main character Marco Stanley Fogg refers directly to "the memory systems of Cicero and Raymond Lull" (107), and to the most famous exponent of them in the Renaissance, Giordano Bruno (85).[35] He further links the concept of memory to the classical system by attributing a blind man's extraordinary ability of locating every book in his huge collection correctly to a Lullian-like feat of memory prowess. Effing, the blind man, reflects that "[y]ou can't study those things […] It's a talent you're born with, a natural gift" (107–8). This emphatic rejection of the effectiveness of artificial memory and commendation of natural ability is representative of Effing's character and will be taken into account later. A look at Auster's first prose work, *The Invention of Solitude* about the death of his father, and in particular the second half, "The Book of Memory", which contains several references to the ancient memory systems, suggests Auster opts for neither one of the views on artificial memory systems he has attributed to his characters Fogg and Effing respectively.

THE RENAISSANCE ART OF MEMORY

"The Book of Memory", an autobiographical attempt at expressing the myriad thoughts of a brief moment in text, to a large extent turns into an investigation of the function of memory in writing. It is interspersed with various references to exponents of the art, including quotations from Cicero's *De oratore* which rephrase the text of the *Rhetorica ad Herennium* with regard to the system of "places and images" (what I translate as backgrounds and images). However, a closer look reveals that Auster's knowledge about the subject seems to derive exclusively from Frances Yates' seminal text *The Art of Memory* – the book that in part inspired my own theory. Thus, the quotations used are taken from that book (i.e., they are Yates' own translations), the inclusion of obscure memory personages, such as Cosmas Rossellius, are taken directly from that text and, most importantly, the emphasis on Giordano Bruno and the Renaissance approach in general equals the emphasis in Yates' book.

Auster's interest in the Renaissance art of memory expressed in this early work is reflected in several of his following novels and suggests that the concept of Renaissance memory systems became integrated into the his thought processes. However, the system is presented ambiguously in "The Book of Memory" and used as a character-descriptive device in *Moon Palace*. Fogg brings up the topic ("I once asked [Effing] if he was familiar with the memory systems of Cicero and Raymond Lull", 107). The reference serves to stress Fogg's pseudo-intellectual ostentation: he is knowledgeable, but only superficially so. He makes the crucial mistake of assuming that memory systems were created by Cicero himself (a common misconception rectified in Yates' book and therefore presumably known

---

35   All references are to the Faber & Faber, 2004 edition of *Moon Palace*.

to Auster) and the false assumption that Raymond Lull's memory systems could in any way be adapted to help the mental cataloguing of a book collection.

Although this helps the understanding of Fogg's character, it also throws up the question whether Auster is actually aware of the specifics of the art. If the mistakes are incorporated intentionally, why does Auster choose inconspicuous ones that only specialists will pick up on? It may be irrelevant for the novel whether Auster is aware of these mistakes, since they suit the character so perfectly.[36] But it does suggest that Auster himself is not primarily interested in the exact history of the art, but rather in the possibilities of artistic expression it provides. This gives us an idea of how he approaches his writing in general; namely, not by being a stickler for facts (unlike Pynchon), but by presenting established concepts in a new light. With the Renaissance cabbalistic art of memory, he had found fertile ground for adaptation and reinvention.

In contrast to Fogg, Effing comments that good memory stems from natural ability alone, rather than from artificially appropriated systems. Auster thereby makes him echo Yates' tone of voice. In *The Book of Memory* Yates questions whether anyone other than naturally gifted people can employ the artificial memory techniques from Antiquity to great advantage. She believes, just like Effing, that it is a natural gift, a talent which certain ancient rhetoricians possessed and extended for their personal use only. Again, this does not seem to represent Auster's own viewpoint; his reliance on, and fascination with the subject belies such a view, as shall be seen later.

Both characters in *Moon Palace* employ the concept of artificial memory to further their public image: Fogg to impress his equally ostentatious employer; Effing to establish his independence. The latter's statement, that memory prowess is a natural gift, clearly attaches to himself the label of a natural talent, associated with genius, which is how he surely would like to be seen. Effing's distrust in the ancient technique also underlines that he is not reliant on a system. This coincides with his self-obtained freedom outside the social system, his ability to regenerate without outside assistance. He relies entirely on his natural gifts (see below). However, in typical Auster fashion, this statement is straightaway qualified by Effing's teasing adage, added "in a sly, mocking way" (108), when he intimates that his apparent memorisation of the book collection is based on a trick: that he moves the books at night when Fogg doesn't notice, or maybe uses telepathy. Effing presents himself as the gifted, but unpredictable teacher who questions every explanation or sense of order and avoids the kind of cataloguing intelligence that the memory system stands for in Fogg's mind. "[N]ever take anything for granted" is his advice, and that is what Fogg, and the reader, should take to heart as they progress through the story.

---

36   It could even be argued that blunders or mistakes can make a narrator more trustworthy, because his fallibility makes him human, as Rushdie points out in relation to his very unreliable narrator Saleem Sinai. See Ch.4.

Auster shares neither of his two characters' views about the memory system; his is a much more abstract approach. Auster uses the concept to investigate the craft of the writer, considering how the idea of backgrounds and image influences, or can be used to describe, the creative process. He ties them together by combining time and space as the two fundamental aspects of writing – both on the physical and the imaginary plane. Most references to memory systems bring with them a twofold image: that of the writer sitting in a room to create an imaginary three-dimensional space, and that of the writer placed in time, creating a linear narrative which manipulates time by simultaneously stretching the moment into narrative and eliding history by bringing the past into the present.[37]

The art of memory, whether in its original classical form or in its Renaissance re-examination, allows for this twofold representation because it is based on backgrounds and images: it is based on space, whether a room, a palace or an imagined landscape, and on the function of memory that collates items spread out over time. It is apparent that Auster's approach has some similarities with my analogy between the memory process and the writing process. But how does Auster implement this knowledge in his work? Two aspects need to be looked at: for simplicity's sake I'll call them history and creativity.

---

[37]   In an interview with J. Mallia, referring to "The Book of Memory", Auster explains how the passage of time is incompatible with the writer's art: "in some sense everything that happens in [memory] is simultaneous. But writing is sequential [...] So my greatest problem was in trying to put things in the correct order" (*The Red Notebook*, p.107.) Hence the episodic, stream-of-consciousness style.

In *Moon Palace* Auster also shows awareness of this incompatibility and overcomes it by employing a natural memory function. In "The Book of Memory" Auster writes that memory is "the space in which a thing happens for the second time" (87); it actually 'happens' again. Thus, according to Auster, a memory is not merely a secondary projection, but an actual occurrence. It is so powerful because it "awakens us to the illusion of time", as Steven E. Alford writes. ("Chance in contemporary narrative", p.118.) In literature, time is always an illusion because time is manipulated to suit the story. Practically, Auster uses the amalgamation of a first experience and the memory of it to create parallels between people or events; thus, although Fogg's personal relationship with Effing is strained at the best of times, he feels that Effing is "a kindred spirit". He explains: "Perhaps it started when we got to the episode about the cave. I had my own memories of living in a cave, after all, and when he described the loneliness he had felt then, it struck me that he was somehow describing the same thing I had felt" (179). It seems as if his experience of the cave 'happens again'. By experiencing it anew, with the time factor removed, Fogg is able to make an alternative reading of it. By repeating a similar experience and changing the outcome (from senseless wiping-out of the self to reincarnation through an involuntary struggle for survival) Auster uses the memory of one event to influence the perception of another. A new insight is possible if time is taken out of the equation when memorising two separate events. And Fogg's encounter with Effing does do exactly that: he lets Fogg see his past in a different light, lets him re-examine his notions.

It has often been noted that Auster acknowledges his Jewish heritage in his novels, but never demonstrably so. Although he emphasises the importance of remembering the history of Judaism, and particularly the atrocities of the Holocaust, he does not drive it home with a sledge hammer. This is relevant to my study because the concept of memory plays a significant part in Jewish culture. Auster connects the art of artificial memory to the Jewish memory culture which is said to function by "sanctifying the present by linking it to the past";[38] combining them to create the imaginary space within which his various literary ideas can be presented. *Moon Palace*, approached with this concept of the mystical power of memory in mind, reveals a great deal about the author's angle on the topics.

Moon Palace tells the story of Marco Stanley Fogg's encounters with two men: Thomas Effing and Solomon Barber. They turn out to be his grandfather and father respectively. Both die either before or shortly after this revelation is made, and the two deaths are main thresholds on Fogg's journey of self-discovery. This journey covers Fogg's time as a student at Columbia, who attempts to exclude himself from society by living on nothing, ending up in a cave in Central Park where he nearly dies from malnutrition and ill heath, only to be saved by his friend Zimmer and girlfriend-to-be Kitty at the last moment. He takes a job as a personal companion and assistant to the blind and wheelchair-bound Effing, whose life-story he takes down from dictation, and stays with him until his self-inflicted death by pneumonia. The planned trip with his father, to discover the cave in the desert where Effing reinvented himself, is interrupted when Barber dies of the consequences of an accident provoked by Fogg. Alone again, Fogg sets out on the trip, only to find that the cave and surrounding area has been flooded. He then has his inheritance money stolen and, resourceless and orphaned for the second time, undertakes the long walk to America's West Coast where, looking across over the ocean to China, at the end of the novel he contemplates the possibility of a new beginning.

Examples of 'memoria' in *Moon Palace*, in the sense of memory as remembrance, first and foremost bring the past into the present to comment on questions of identity, reminiscent of the way that Jewish religious rituals are an act of bringing past events into the present to show that scriptural events are still relevant for us today. In the novel these are personal instances of remembering which are important not so much because they maintain an awareness of the past, but because they help Fogg understand who he is here and now. In most instances it is a negative memory, sometimes even traumatic. Fogg, for example, concludes that Effing's death on the first of November, the day of the dead and the day of remembrance, is "appropriate" (96) emphasising the importance of remembering

---

38   Stephen Fredman, "How to get out of the room that is the book", p.16.

his death, not so much as a reverence to Effing, but as a reminder to himself of what he has learned from it. Another instance is the interpretation of the Blakelock painting *Moonlight* as "a memorial, a death song for a vanished world" (135). Here the painting is seen as a manifestation of a dark past which has far-reaching consequences for the present in that the idealised cultivation of the native American land is a false idyll which has led North-America into humanitarian decline. Fogg's memory of standing at his mother's grave and "putting a stone on top" is made relevant for the here and now because this traditional symbolic action manifests the loss of the mother figure and the consequences her absence has had on Fogg's view of his self.

But *Moon Palace* isn't merely a memorial text which helps the main character Fogg find his identity by relying on the past to reveal his true identity. In fact, Auster hints at the danger of such an approach. Early on in *Moon Palace* Fogg instructs the reader on how to 'read' his life. Referring to the 1968 student uprising at his university, he says, "[m]y own history lies in the rubble of those days, and unless this fact is understood, none of it will make sense" (25). This suggests the text is a traditional autobiographical narrative where events of the past have moulded the character of the narrator. Furthermore, it states the belief that history affects each individual, that human beings are moulded by the society they belong to. It suggests that memory is the agency which can bring the past into the present and explain why things are the way they are, and that the narrator of autobiography describes personal experiences, using memory in the sense of 'memoria' in order to reveal his true identity.

However, the narrative situation suggests a less straightforward reading. The narrator's retrospection allows the reader an insight into Fogg's mentality, and instead of a reliable narrator we discover a self-deluded, pseudo-intellectual young man unable to give a truthful account of himself because he is still very much in search of his identity, and because the parameters he has staked out for himself to discover it are constantly shifting.

On the one hand, the ambiguous sentence appears to be a sincere instruction to the reader to take the past into account when attempting to understand Fogg's character. On the other hand, it urges the reader to look behind the voice, to 'never take anything for granted', in Effing's words. The statement is preceded by Fogg's declaration that he does not intend to "discuss any of that here" (the student uprising), for "[e]veryone is familiar with the story of that time, and there would be no point in going over it again" (24–5). Surely, there would be a point if it helped clarify Fogg's story, especially as his history lies in the rubble of those days. To Donovan this "omission" of background information brings "frustration" to the reader. I, personally, was relieved not to have to trawl through pages of student politics in the words of a pompous student (i.e., the character of Fogg at the time) and, furthermore, believe this not to be Auster's intention with the passage anyway.

Donovan's assumption that the reader's supposed frustration is "compounded by Fogg's insistence that this negligence is actually metonymy, that his personal experience of penury, naïveté and abstraction can be substituted for the larger canvas of the sixties",[39] concisely describes the sense of self-importance which makes Fogg equate History with *his* story. Rushdie's main character Saleem's statement – he can only be understood if his family history, going back several generations, is known – was entirely discredited with the revelation that Saleem had been switched at birth and the ancestors we had been following had no influence on his genetic make-up. Rushdie uses this to emphasise that each personal history is individual and that independence within history (be it familial or national) is possible (see Ch.4).

Auster never refutes the importance of family history. The concept of personal history is here used to show Fogg's state of mind – to indicate the conceptualising process he is undergoing. The flourish of the words ("my story lies in the rubble of those days") appears narcissistic and is an ironic comment, implying that this is a retrospective glance at a younger self. Furthermore, the choice of the word 'discuss' when Fogg talks about his own past ("I am not planning to discuss any of that") implies that he looks back on his younger self as 'a case', and the text he is writing as an analytical study; a clinical distancing from that younger self. The discrepancy between the perceived self and the actual narrating self shows that a distance in time allows for analytical comment, and the self-irony should warn the reader not to believe young Fogg's statements unquestioningly.

The statement – if we know Fogg's background, we understand him – is furthermore ironic because it is not in the rubble of the student-uprising-days, but in the rubble of his own defunct family history that his story lies. It is in these personal relationships, or the absence of the same, that we may begin to understand the person that Fogg is, and why he is struggling so hard to make sense of the world around him, jumping from theory to theory and never finding any peace of mind until the end.

The novel is clearly divided into Fogg's mental phases: from the pseudo-intellectual who nearly eliminates himself by depending on thoughts alone he then enters a phase of spiritual development, feeling "a need to purify" himself with "almost religious fanaticism" (71) which enables him to take on Effing and live in his small room which he calls a "monk's cell" (104), finally to reject it in favour of the mystical rules of coincidence and synchronicity. Klepper points out that the three phases are predicted by Fogg's three names relating to famous explorers (Marco Polo, Henry Morton Stanley and Philias Fogg), tellingly with the name from literary fiction appearing at the end. "Damit wird ein *Entwicklungsprozess* symbolisiert dessen Ende in der Fiktionalität nicht 'Unwirklichkeit', sondern 'Selbsterfindung' bedeutet."[40] When Fogg says that his "own story lies in the

---

39   *Postmodern Counternarratives*, p.90.
40   *Pynchon, Auster, DeLillo*, p.285.

rubble of those days" (25), he is at the beginning of this explorative journey, and like Will in Langland's *Piers Plowman* (see Ch.2), he must begin by discovering and re-examining truisms and clichés in order to create a foundation upon which to build. As the protagonist's three names suggest, the foundation in reality leads to the positively portrayed ability to invent oneself (*Selbsterfindung*) for which one would need true creativity.

CREATIVITY

It could be said that history is treated as ambiguously as memory in *Moon Palace*, because history is presented as both restrictive and informative, depending on how it is employed. This makes sense because memory is the key to history. Time, the structure of history, is malleable (as Auster's experience with writing shows, see note 37); memory, the time-keeper that segments the past into retainable chunks, works in various modes as well. In the creative mind the obstacle of time can to some extent be overcome by positioning it in a three-dimensional space: the imaginary landscape of an author's narrative.

The memory-as-space image, derived from the architectural memory system of Antiquity that Auster refers to in "The Book of Memory" and again in *Moon Palace*, no longer bears any resemblance to the ancient art of memory, but offers an image for Auster that serves as an elucidating abstract of the topic of writing. He remodels this image and extends it to outline a space for the act of literary creation and so uses the mystical aspect of Renaissance memory art to explain creativity; hence, his reference to "the head as a dream palace" (32) rather than a memory palace. Although Auster's stories are very much played out three-dimensionally in his mind, they are no longer part of a neurological memory function, but part of his inspiration which is as mysterious as are dreams.

In an interview with Irwin, having just asserted that "[n]othing in any of my books means anything", Auster concludes that "if you're able to tell a story that resonates with the same power it has for you, it's almost as if it's coming out of your dreams".[41] This implies that great writing is the ability to communicate from one's subconscious, inadvertently putting something on paper that the reader picks up on, but which even the author doesn't know the origin of. It is a form of value judgment upon the art of writing that distances it from a conscious skill of conveying ideas, and moves towards a mystical, alchemical reaction that happens when a writer is able to describe what he 'sees' without having to offer any explanation.

In *Moon Palace* the insubstantial inspiration is contained within 'a dream palace', in a physical building that gives some form of structure to the content. This is clearly related to the architectural system and the spatial awareness necessary for creative imagination. The emphasis on the Renaissance adaptation of the system as a mystical capacity for understanding the world aids his own

---

41   Paul Auster, *The Art of Hunger*, p.330.

interest in language and the ability to describe what he sees, i.e., to communicate insubstantial ideas that come from his imagination. This to some extent coincides with modern memory concepts. So Rudolf Arnheim writes that "[t]heoretical concepts are not handled in empty space" in the memory, but may instead be "associated with a visual setting".[42]

The way Auster rephrases the function of the classical art of memory shows how he has adapted the original idea for his own purpose. "The Book of Memory" begins in the style of a 'note to self' with a brief summary of the topics the author intends to write about, and also how he intends to structure the text. The fifth paragraph reads:

> To follow with a detailed description of classical memory systems, complete with charts, diagrams, symbolic drawings. Raymond Lull, for example, Robert Fludd, not to speak of Giordano Bruno, the great Nolan burned at the stake in 1600. Places and images as catalysts for remembering other places and images: things, events, the buried artifacts of one's own life. Mnemotechnics. To follow with Bruno's notion that the structure of human thought corresponds to the structure of nature. And therefore to conclude that everything, in some sense, is connected to everything. (80)

The chain of thought presented here, from memory over identity to connections, is one that also appears in *Moon Palace*. Every time one of the three topics is mentioned, the other two seem to be referred to as well. The big step that Auster takes in the quotation above is to connect the places (or backgrounds) and images of the architectural memory system to a collection of items that represent a person's life: "the artifacts of one's own life". The system is altered to aid, not universal knowledge, but individual understanding of identity. The Renaissance system, which was originally used to uncover mysteries about the world, has focused in on a much smaller universe – that of the self. 'Human thought' holds the key to unravelling this secret because it resembles the "structure [read 'hidden meaning'] of nature", exposed by the way things are connected. How is the author going to expose these connections? The answer comes in the following paragraph:

> At the same time, as if running parallel to the above, a brief disquisition on the room. An image, for example, of a man sitting alone in a room. As in Pascal: 'All the unhappiness of man stems from one thing only: that he is incapable of staying quietly in his room.' As in the phrase: 'he wrote The Book of Memory in this room.' (ibid)

The combination of memory, identity and connection has shifted to incorporate the effect this has on the work of the writer. The image of the man sitting in a room is one Auster returns to again and again, naturally, as this is his personal experience of space, but also because it is an image that incorporates all the aspects he is interested in. He repeatedly refers to it in "The Book of Memory", as he announced he would, so that it is "running parallel" to the idea of the memory

---

42   *Visual Thinking*, p.111.

palace. He writes, for example: "memory as a place, as a building, as a sequence of columns, cornices, porticoes" (86) and straight away relates this ancient concept to a metaphysical reading of it: "[t]he body inside the mind, as if we were moving around in there, going from one place to the next, and the sound of our footsteps as we walk, moving from one place to the next" (ibid). The outer walls of the memory palace, the building in which items to be remembered are situated, are replaced by the walls of the mind itself, inside which we are walking (the unfortunate plural conjuring up a busy memory palace), and the sense of seeing is aided by the sense of hearing, adding the footsteps as an eerie sound effect. Auster re-establishes the ancient idea that memory palaces, created as three-dimensional images, can be traversed in the mind. The discrepancies with the original system are explained by the intention of the passage, which is to describe the sensation, in fact, to perform the act of the storyteller: to describe a situation so that it resonates with the reader. This is something rhetoricians of Antiquity would not have been interested in, but the Renaissance exponents of the art began to incorporate it in order to heighten the sense of entering a different world.

The concept of the mind as a spacious memory palace is extended a little later to describe the sensation of being a writer toiling away in solitude in order to put words on a page: "Memory as a room, as a body, as a skull, as a skull that encloses the room in which a body sits. As in the image: 'a man sat alone in his room'" (93). This is just one example of many throughout the text that encourage the parallel between memory systems and the writer alone in his room, creating new worlds. Auster's view on memory, then, is greatly influenced by the three-dimensional classical concept of backgrounds and images; in its Renaissance reincarnation as a way to inspire knowledge. He does not copy the Renaissance concept, but instead develops from it his very own foundation on which to situate his main concerns as a writer, placed in space and time, in search of identity and connections, aided by personal history and mystical creativity.

Step 2: Backgrounds and their significance
Having established how Auster understands and uses memory in his literature, we must now ask what that tells us about the backgrounds he has chosen for his novel. Firstly, it seems we must always look for several ideas at once (memory, identity, creation, connection). Secondly, ideas surrounding these topics should never be taken at face value, for they are often presented ambiguously. I will look at backgrounds in particular and the concept of 'space' in general to see how this understanding helps us interpret the novel.

THE SIGNIFICANCE OF THE PHYSICAL SETTING
Like Pynchon, Auster's backgrounds contrast the urban with the pastoral, modern society with founding father ideology. But unlike Pynchon's pastoral scenes Auster's are not visions of Georgic idylls, but rather of the open frontier, the desert with its own laws where nature's roughness dictates man's existence.

Interspersed throughout the novel are desert scenes and references to mostly open spaces in which the characters confront their own limitations. This is very much in keeping with traditional American pastoral literature, and Effing's adventure into the West (the traditional direction for journeys of self-discovery) enables him to establish a new identity, frees him from the past and, in a sense, reincarnates him. He is symbolically born again from the womb of that landscape in the Gresham brothers' cave.

Where Effing experiences regeneration through his encounter with the natural landscape, Fogg, in a post-American-Renaissance attempt at escaping *Walden*-like into nature, fails miserably. This is because he has chosen for this purpose the cave in New York's Central Park. For Fogg the cave is not so much a womb as a tomb in which he approaches physical extinction without the least chance of resurrection. This was already implied by the previous background, Fogg's apartment, which he intentionally dehumanised by emptying it of all furniture (symbolic for his interaction with the intellectual world as boxes of books were used to furnish the place), and which was compared to a coffin (44).

Central Park, the paradoxical "man-made natural world" (61), does not accommodate Fogg's regeneration because it is enclosed in an urban setting, as Christian Seidl explains. In order to regenerate, it is necessary to return to a prelapsarian state, one that exists outside capitalism and its economical confines (both Effing and Fogg lose their money before they can regenerate) because only then can true creativity unfold – creativity: the key to personal regeneration. Since the "urban frontier", which Fogg encounters during his attempted escape inside the city, only imitates the original frontier, nothing truly new can be created.[43]

Seidl, unwittingly, uses the backgrounds-and-images system to interpret the novel *Moon Palace*. He first compares settings (backgrounds) of two kinds of frontier that are then linked to the events played out against them (the images): the original cave in the deserts of Western America and the urban frontier established in pockets of nature within the city are linked to what Effing and Fogg experience in these disparate settings. Seidl concludes that Effing's successful cave adventure allows creative freedom and takes this to be the determining aspect necessary to achieve regeneration. The setting that makes this possible is the one which leaves society behind completely; for an original frontier can not be imitated.

THE SIGNIFICANCE OF SPACE

These frontiers, represented by the comparison of two cave settings and the events played out in connection with them, are given a further dimension when another comparison is taken into account: that of the inner versus the outer space. Since Seidl has undertaken the work of looking at the backgrounds in the novel with such clarity and insight, I turn to the more abstract backgrounds presented in the form of space.

---

43   "Regeneration through creativity".

As Steven Weisenburger points out, the narrator of *Moon Palace* is driven "Inside, into landscapes of metaphysical obsession", an Inside in constant conflict with the Outside.[44] The novel's title already suggests such a confrontation since the moon planet exists in space, the final frontier, while the structurally defined architectural building, the palace, is the outer shell for an inner space. A palace dedicated to the moon suggests that the moon can be encountered within these architectural confines, but the mind struggles with such an image. The palace of the moon must be bursting at the seams, just as the inside space in *Moon Palace* the novel constantly seems to strain at the outside or structure which tries to confine it. I will return to the role and the myriad significances of the moon later, and begin by asking what the palace as structure of an inner space may signify, keeping in mind that it ought to be connected to three themes: memory, identity and creativity – probably presented ambiguously.

The palace of the title has its architectural manifestation in the novel as the Chinese restaurant Fogg frequents and that can be seen from his apartment in a gap between two buildings. The mystery of the East that it seems to promise is not fulfilled (or at least not initially accepted by Fogg, since he rejects the mystery of love offered by his Chinese girlfriend Kitty Wu). The limited view from the room suggests something enticingly close, but not accessible. As long as Fogg identifies with his New York existence, the Moon Palace will always be present in stone, but its secrets will not be revealed. This is implied by the fact that the restaurant Fogg visits has little in common with the associations its neon-light sign, seen from Fogg's apartment, inspire.

When Fogg is vegetating, half starved in his apartment, the sign of the restaurant inspires an intense, almost hallucinatory contemplation: "the words *Moon Palace* began to haunt my mind with all the mystery of an oracle" (31), Fogg writes. Initially, an oracle without answers. Amongst the associations which he spins from the words – clearly linked to the actual restaurant through the immediately preceding reference to Chinese food – is the dream palace: "Chinese food and my empty stomach; thought, as in food for thought, and the head as a palace of dreams" (32). Here, again, we have the parallel topics of memory, identity and creativity, brought together in the image of thoughts that feed the human being. In this instance the palace refers to confinement and the inner space in general (it is related to internal activities such as eating, thinking and dreaming) and to the particular aspect of the inner working of the mind: the memory and the imagination.

Physical spaces comment on the character's mental space. While Fogg lies in his empty apartment with the inhibited view of a neon sign, trying to pair down his life to see all the connections more clearly, he is actually limiting his view: the vast array of thoughts, the chains of thought that resemble an analyst's association test, reveal that Fogg is grappling with the concept of meaning, of connections.

---

44   "Inside *Moon Palace*", p.130.

But rather than helping him out of a confined space, these thoughts allow only for one direction, to the man-made plastic sign of promise which is all that urban life can offer, and which signifies a very non-mystical Chinese restaurant; not an oracle which holds the key to the mysteries of life.

Auster says that he "never made a conscious decision to write about space", but in hindsight realises that "when the characters are most confined they are most free".[45] Regarding Fogg's mental state, both in his first apartment and in the cave, this is a strange statement. Fogg's thoughts may roam more freely than before, but they are hunger-induced and almost drive him mad. When he is most confined, he is also most imprisoned, and this state of mind nearly kills him. Thus when he continuously shrinks his existence until it becomes a mere presence in a small, empty room, his thoughts taking over the space vacated by the things Fogg sells off bit by bit, it does not free him. Although the space he inhabits is filled with thoughts and includes the image of "the head as a dream palace" (32), these images are not able to help him break free.

The danger that Fogg encounters when trying to live on thoughts alone is made apparent when the room is compared to a coffin (44). When the room is exchanged for the cave in Central Park, during the last days of Fogg's mental and physical disintegration, it seems that merely the material of the walls that line his coffin are exchanged from man-made brick to natural stone. Thus, in Fogg's case the more confined he is, the less free he becomes. Other descriptions of enclosed spaces can be read similarly, such as Barber's body, which is compared to a prison, and being most confined means certain death to Barber.

However, not all confined spaces signify the same thing. A comparison of the two caves reveals their opposing influence: for Effing regeneration and rebirth; for Fogg near death. It is therefore not the physical confinement that frees Auster's characters. But even when Auster refers to mental spaces, these do not present freeing experiences for his characters. The mental space Fogg inhabits while in his room, and later in the cave, certainly is not freeing. Other instances of mental spaces in the book seem to suggest the same.

THE MEMORY PALACE 1: MENTAL SPACES

To look for instances where characters experience freedom, the term must first be defined. Is it the freedom to *do* something or freedom *from* something? And how is it expressed? By jumping around ecstatically in an open space, or by sitting down quietly to enjoy a sense of inner peace? Effing uses the term 'freedom' to express a rebirth of the mind. During an encounter with his idol Tesla, who looks right through him "[a]s though I didn't exist", Effing realises "that my life was my own, that it belonged to me and no one else. / I'm talking about freedom, Fogg" (142). Freedom in *Moon Palace* must be contrasted to the restrictions imposed upon persons by the life they lead, here by a capitalist, urban society. A sense of

45   *The Art of Hunger*, p.327.

freedom from it is rarely experienced by Auster's characters, but Effing seems to suggest that freedom is there for the taking because the restrictions need not be accepted; after all, one's life is one's own. Freedom is here not connected to a physical environment, but to a mental space.

The mental space is described variously in *Moon Palace* and most tellingly when attempting a connection with another person. When Fogg systematically reads his way through the large amount of books uncle Victor left him, Fogg discovers that he can read them box-wise in the order they were acquired by Victor and in which he also read them, because his uncle would buy a book, read it and place it next to the previously read book, eventually packing them into the boxes in that same order:

Each time I opened a box, I was able to enter another segment of my uncle's life, a fixed period of days or weeks or months, and it consoled me to feel that I was occupying the same mental space that Victor had occupied – reading the same words, living in the same stories, perhaps thinking the same thoughts. (21)

The sharing of a "mental space" is one of the most intimate images that Auster creates. This allows Fogg to exist in a consoling world of thought. The physical is conspicuously absent. There is a mental space in which two people can connect, but only after the fact, and only at a distance. Furthermore, the correct order is only detectable box-wise, because the order of the boxes is unknown and the connection episodic – an attempt at reconnecting with limited success.

"Books became a refuge" to Barber, "a place where he could keep himself hidden – not only from others, but from his own thoughts as well" (233). Finding solace in the mental space created by stories seems to be hereditary: neither father nor son can connect directly and therefore do so mentally instead, finding peace of mind by creating a mental space, albeit one that offers temporary escape and not a true freedom. This is also true in relation to the grandfather: as Effing tells Fogg his life-story, the grandson "began to live inside that voice as though it were a room, a windowless room that grew smaller and smaller with each passing day" (179). Interestingly, this instance tells us more about Fogg than Effing. Unlike Barber and Fogg, Effing *can* create mental spaces, he *can* communicate his experiences so that the listener uses his words as springboards into a three-dimensional landscape. For Fogg it is a very different experience. It is not calming or freeing, but suffocating and intensifying, because the nearing of the conclusion also is the nearing of the end of Effing's life, and a drawing in of Fogg into this world which brings the two people closer together: a time when he will have to leave the mental space and enter the intimacies of the real world.

Auster's characters seem to search for, and find, temporary freedom in a mental space – in a world populated with thought alone – which is situated inside the mind. This can be compared to Auster's claim that the mental space affords the writer the greatest freedom, even if he is physically confined to the room.

However, this mental space can be a peaceful haven from a confusing and hurtful world or a boundless space for creative imagination. As the earlier quotation from Pascal reveals, "[a]ll the unhappiness of man stems from one thing only: that he is incapable of staying quietly in his room."

The writer's predicament is taken up again and again in Auster's novels, notably in *Oracle Night* and *Travels in the Scriptorium*, the latter an abstract metanarrative about the simultaneously freeing and imprisoning mental space the writer inhabits when he invents imaginary worlds in his room in self-imposed isolation.[46] In both novels, as in *Moon Palace*, the mental space is not sufficient because human beings long to leave it, to venture out and interact with others. But this brings with it an uncomfortable, often distressing confrontation with the self and others. Nonetheless, the mental space can only be a short-lived escape into freedom, for it will always be infringed upon by the physical space.

THE MEMORY PALACE 2: THE ROOM

Actual rooms in *Moon Palace* are influenced by the mutually dependent inner and outer spaces and thereby reflect on the writer's experience of space. The rooms usually contain 'a body', often "a man sat alone in his room" in imitation of the writer. In Fogg's case this is highly appropriate: he is called "the author of his own life" (7) and goes by the initials MS (manuscript) as an expression of the writer's power to create his own life and identity. The same topic is dealt with extensively in the stories of *The New York Trilogy*, particularly in "Ghosts" where

---

46   In *Oracle Night* the narrator, who is a writer, disappears when he creates his narratives – his wife walking in on an empty room despite the fact that the writer has been continuously at his desk. Ultimately this disappearance into an imaginary world becomes extremely dangerous, and only by a confrontation with reality does the writer avert a great personal tragedy: the murder of his wife. It shows a development in Auster's writing that emphasises a reconciliation with life, a possibility of forgiveness. The novel's violent ending inaugurates a new acceptance of life and a positive engagement with reality. However, the emphasis on the power of words remains, since it is suggested that the texts written by the narrator have a direct influence on the events taking place around him: only after tearing up his detailed documentation of how he imagines his wife's infidelity to have played out does the situation resolve itself. And, in accordance with this belief, the narrator does not refer to the subject again, realising that his words would ruin all that is good about their relationship.

Travels in the Scriptorium concentrates on the mental aspects of the writer's job, depicting it as a highly debilitating, disorienting and frightening condition. The aging author has lost his memory and is visited by characters from his novels (familiar to readers of Auster's own work). The story breaks off when the author picks up a manuscript documenting the events of that day – in exactly the same words as *Travels in the Scriptorium* itself began – frustrating the author and sending him to bed, presumably to awaken the following day to repeat the experience. The novel takes up all Auster's favourite themes of the writer in the room, the power of words, the significance of things, the problem of identity and the analogue states of memory and creativity, but he does not develop them any further. Auster has written himself into a room without leaving an opening through which he can exit, suggesting that he has pushed the topic as far as it will go. He has become "the man sat in a room", miserably trapped there.

the image of a man sat in a room is again related to the role of the writer in the act of creating an identity. Fogg is writing the account of his life – we are reading it – so he is a man sitting alone in a room bringing the past into the present, arranging his thoughts, his memories, in a landscape to explain who he is. This suggests that he has achieved a sense of creative freedom by now. But as we proceed with the story, we realise that conveying one's thoughts to another is not a simple task. Effing already has the skill necessary to communicate (he has had his creative regeneration in the desert) whereas Fogg must still gain those skills, and Effing is the obvious teacher.

Successful communication depends on things being described in such a way that others can form their own mental images. Effing's blindness requires that things are described to him, and this becomes part of Fogg's job. On his walks through New York Effing requests ever clearer descriptions of the things they encounter, and Fogg learns how to truly 'see' things for the first time. Fogg discovers that the fewer words he uses, the better: "the more air I left around a thing, the happier the result" (119). 'Space' therefore becomes a concern when words are linked to images, since Effing must create an image from Fogg's words.

Klepper writes that Fogg slowly realises "daß es nicht um die Dinge selbst geht, sondern um die Erweckung ihrer Vorstellung, um ihre Konstitution im Geist".[47] This is also the writer's job: to take emphasis away from the things themselves and instead see them as tools to awaken their image in the mind. Fogg learns how to become creative by seeing things as starting points rather than ends in themselves, and he needs to leave space around them in order for this to happen. Auster says that "[t]he text is no more than a springboard for the imagination" [...] because "the mind [...] creates images based on memories and experiences".[48] Words are things which serve an end; namely, to spark off memories that allow the reader to create an imaginary world.

Auster comments on this writing technique when he discusses how much description should be incorporated into a fictional text. In *The Red Notebook* Auster writes:

The possibilities are infinite. [...] Is the novelist's job simply to reproduce physical sensations for their own sake? When I write, the story is always uppermost in my mind, and I feel that everything must be sacrificed to it. All the elegant passages, all the curious details, all the so-called beautiful writing – *if they are not truly relevant to what I am trying to say, then they have to go.* It's all in the voice. You're telling a story, after all, and your job is to make people want to go on listening to your tale. (112, my italics)

Auster clearly relates the art of writing to the oral culture – suggesting that the reader tells the story to himself by reading it. He emphasises the importance of readers producing their own images, their own imaginary visual world; the

---

47   *Pynchon, Auster, DeLillo*, pp.292–3.
48   Paul Auster, *The Red Notebook*, p.140.

author's text merely provides the "springboard" into this world. His statement that "everything must be sacrificed" to the story and any irrelevant descriptive details "have to go" explains why it is so important to Fogg to leave space around the things he describes to Effing: in order for him to be able to visualise them, he needs a space into which he can place them.

Fogg undertakes the description of a room, and comparing his method to Auster's statement above is very revealing. When Effing is dying, Fogg describes to him the room he lies in, "using the methods I had developed on our walks". This "seemed to give him [Effing] immense pleasure" (213). But as Effing weakens, Fogg's descriptions become more detailed, more intense, to the extent where he says, "I mined the limits of that space until it became inexhaustible, a plenitude of worlds within worlds" (214). Fogg desperately takes over more and more of Effing's part in the process by creating ever more space for the images in order to prolong Effing's life. It suggests that the life force that is slowly but surely slipping away from Effing is sustained by the power to imagine. But this imagination must have its foundation in reality, in things that connect the inner space of the mind with the outer space of the world. For it seemed "as if merely to take one's place in the world of things was a good beyond all other" (ibid).

This also seems to be Fogg's goal: to take his place in the world of things. But to do so he must know what these things are in order to place himself amongst them. One further room description explains this connection. In "The Book of Memory" the narrator A. describes an encounter with the writer Ponge, who is able to recall in great detail an apartment which he had only visited once for a few hours. This initiates a strong reaction:

He realized that for Ponge there was no division between the work of writing and the work of seeing. [...] Memory, then, not so much as the past contained within us, but as proof of our life in the present. If a man is to be truly present among his surroundings, he must be thinking not of himself, but of what he sees. He must forget himself in order to be there. And from that forgetfulness arises the power of memory. (148)

Auster, once again, combines the themes of memory, identity, and creativity. Identity is related to finding one's place amongst the things of this world (or more actively 'taking' it, in Fogg's words). Creativity is the ability to create images from words, and words from things, which enables one to 'see' the space into which one fits. Memory runs parallel in that the Renaissance art of memory provides the structure for these ideas: the three-dimensional space, the backgrounds and the images. The memory prowess of Ponge, tapping into memory feats from Antiquity, is empowered with the ability to gain access to the mysteries of life. Ponge's memory feat "struck A. with all the force of a supernatural act" (148), repeating his ambiguous attitude towards the artificial art of memory by elevating it to the level of mystical insight and equating it with a writer's skill. The fact that the *writer* Ponge uses his memory to describe things in such detail allows this insight. Auster equates 'seeing' with 'writing' and suggests that the sense of sight is as fundamental for memory work as it is for the art of writing: he implies that the processes are analogue.

This passage also explains Auster's preoccupation with objects. It is a recurring topic in his novels, from Stilman the collector of broken items who attempts to create a new and true language in "City of Glass" by defining objects he finds in the streets, to Fogg's attempt at describing the surroundings to a blind man in *Moon Palace*. Andrew Addy relates this to "Auster's concern with language as memory, and memory and imagination as identity".[49]

In the convergence of these elements (memory, identity and creativity), the most confined space (the mind) produces the greatest freedom. When the mind is engaged in this way, the mental space, used to fashion an imaginary world so strongly connected to the real world, becomes a blueprint for the space into which the self can be placed and identified. This leads to an understanding of the text as a search for identity through mental agility and imagination, and the creativity involved in this process parallels the craft of the author, the craft of creating a character, a self, in the sense of being the author of one's own life.

Step 3: Background connections

Having looked at backgrounds and the use of space in general, I now turn to step three: discovering how these backgrounds are connected in order to reveal a possible structure of the text. This is done by discerning which memory systems are embedded in the story, and what the patterns they create tell us about the way the author organises his thoughts.

The topic of connections is always linked with the theme of coincidence and chance in Auster's writing. Coincidence and chance also underlie the final phase of Fogg's development in the novel: he stops searching for the meaning contained within the connections he sees between various object or ideas and instead accepts them as unfathomable. Just as Ponge's memory feat is elevated to a "supernatural act" by A. and thereby given meaning through its connection to a higher instance, Fogg acknowledges that, although a myriad of connections exists, he cannot use these to structure the world, suggesting that an order of some sort *does* exist, but cannot be discovered. This, once again, resembles the Renaissance art of memory, which also combines the search for order with memory training, so as to achieve a mystical understanding of the order of things.

No simple structure can be imposed upon a text, such as Auster's, which simultaneously encourage a search for connections and undermines any form of order that apparently derives from it by emphasising the mystical. One way of approaching a structural analysis without distorting the text is to consider which memory systems have been employed in the creation of the novel. By far the two

---

49   "Narrating the self", p.157.

most conspicuous systems are wordplay (related to the alphabet- and number-systems) and the memory map.

MEMORY SYSTEMS AS LITERARY PATTERNS 1: WORD ASSOCIATION

The unknowable order of things that Fogg accepts at the end of the novel is reflected in the way the story in *Moon Palace* is held together; namely, through an enigmatic network of associations which encourages an almost mystical reading of the text. This network centres on the much berated, because according to many critics over-elaborated, symbol of the moon. In fact, moon references are only inordinately frequent in the first chapter (15 instances).[50] Auster calls the moon image his "touchstone", which is similar to Bartlett's "anchor point" or Rushdie's "leitmotif".[51] It is a recurring image which helps to hold the novel together in the mind. Its employment in the first chapter would be excessive, were it used merely to make absolutely sure it stands out to every reader in all its associations. But it is simultaneously a device for showing Fogg's preoccupation with finding meaning in everything, intellectualising life, which is indicative of his mental decline: it's the crazy time for Fogg; his 'lunatic' phase. When this concludes, the moon image occurs only infrequently and always alongside the implied warning about over-interpretation, because it refers back to Fogg's initial lunatic period.

The moon functions as a magnetic field in the Rushdian sense. It is conspicuous that the language Auster uses to explain this condition is so reminiscent of Rushdie's when he describes what happens when a writer is successful in his work. Auster says, a story has value if it resonates with the same power for the reader as it does for himself, giving it a mystical origin; Rushdie talks about the practical job, about a writer who finds "all the resonances" in a chosen name when the "tuning fork" of the writer is working properly. Although he calls it a form of "magic" when it works, he acknowledges that it is the author who "creates a magnetic field" by choosing the right words – Rushdie's magic is the reward for the technical and creative skill of selecting words and images that have power to communicate the idea. Auster attributes his magic to a higher instance: he suggests that more is at work than man can fathom when literature resonates with other people, when a connection is established to be felt, but not explained.

The emphasis on supernatural, mysterious connections is upheld throughout. Memory plays a large part since this is the brain function that allows us to see these mysterious connections by removing the aspect of time from the equation (see above). Steven Alford comments that "memory is important [to Auster]

---

50   Ch.2 has three moon references, Ch.3 has two, Ch.4 has six (but this deals with Blakelock's painting *Moonlight* and naturally would have many references), Ch.6 has nine (but five of these are examples of bad writing in the synopsis of the intentionally appalling novel *Kepler's Blood*) and Ch.7 has three.
51   Auster uses the word "touchstone" in an interview to describe the function of the moon in *Moon Palace*. *The Red Notebook*, p.151. For Bartlett see Ch.3, for Rushdie, Ch.4.

because it allows us to hold up two seemingly non-simultaneously, yet *eerily* linked events and see them in their atemporal connectedness".[52] In other words, Auster perceives memory as a tool with which to see connections between things, not hindered by the intervention of time. The way Auster initially presents these connections mystifies the situation rather than revealing its meaning. The glimpses into the mysteries of the universe Auster seems to offer through describing these connections by wordplay and mixed metaphors are mysteries of his own making: he wills them into being. It is the writer at work, creating a structure within which he can present his story which does not distract from the important issues. Alford's essay on Auster's preoccupation with chance and fate convincingly argues that the contradictory evidence Auster presents for his theories suggests that Auster implies that he "possesses a type of gnostic or mystical insight that permits him to know something that he claims is outside knowledge". After all, Auster suggests that "the world's operation is a mystery and beyond our understanding",[53] yet, somehow, he alone is able to convey this unknowable operation to us.

Auster clearly cultivates the mysterious narrative element, and his figurative terminology certainly creates a level of mysticism about the universe he describes. One of the most common ways Auster incorporates this into his texts is by introducing paradoxes into his imagery. Another is to take a common phrase, substitute the usual verb for another, and straightaway a sense of something new and original is created.[54] This wordplay adds a dimension to the text which makes it both addictive reading, but at times also frustrating, because the deeper insight they seem to promise does not materialise.

This frustration seems to be consciously created by Auster by his many open endings, hinted-at answers and rephrasing of clichés. The reader is taken on the same emotional journey that the characters must experience, and these frustrations make up part of it. The individual steps must be understood and the relevant connections forged in the mind before it is possible for the character (and the reader) to move on. In the case of Fogg it is the expectation of being able to make sense of the world around him and himself by seeing connections and meaning in everything which forms the first frustration. Initially Auster encourages the reader to search out all the connections along with Fogg, even suggesting that this search will be rewarded. The reader draws conclusions similar to Fogg's which, at the next turn of events, are discarded as misconceptions.

---

52   "Chance in contemporary narrative", p.116.

53   Ibid., p.118.

54   Commonly, verbs are sequentially replaced in an idiom or in a set phrase to create new images, or a metaphor is created by attributing unusual or implausible actions to subjects, such as: "The world bounced off him, shattered against him, sometimes adhered to him" in "The Book of Memory", p.7. In typical Auster fashion this image is reused in other texts, for example in *Oracle Night* in the sentence "The world would bounce and swim before my eyes", p.1.

This is why Auster's texts can seem naively self-important. Auster seems to reinvent the wheel by ignoring literary theory and philosophy that have dealt with concerns for decades which are presented as new revelations in his novels, like Saussure's signifier and signified or Heidegger's model of knowable objects.[55] John Zilkosky comments on a similar situation in *The New York Trilogy* where "[i]t is as if Auster's 1986 detectives had not yet discovered the literary theory of 1968. They must learn all over again, step by step, that the author is a construct, a false endpoint of reading". Zilkosky thus explains this rehashing of ideas as an element in Auster's attempt to investigate "the concept of authorship itself".[56] Statements that are made with great conviction and backed up by intellectual evidence (factual, experiential or literary) ensure that the reader experiences the same development as the character; that the text 'resonates' with the reader rather than merely describes the progress.

MEMORY SYSTEMS AS LITERARY PATTERS 2: THE MEMORY MAP

Auster clearly has a traditional perception of memory as linked to the imagination and the consequent creation of mental pictures. This link between memory and the imagination is apparent in Fogg's and Victor's childhood games; thus, they "developed a game of inventing countries together, imaginary worlds" (6) of which Fogg even drew maps – two-dimensional representations on paper of the three-dimensional places in the memory – a concept Auster returns to in an interview with McCaffery in which he equates the imagination with a continent.[57] This concept is closely related to the map as a memory system, and Auster's awareness of this system is clearly stated in "The Book of Memory". Here he compares a walk through Amsterdam to memory diagrams in the shape of city maps, as used in the Renaissance art of memory.

The cityscape, as a way of mapping memory function, appears in several of Auster's earlier novels, amongst them *In the Country of Last Things*, *Moon Palace*, *The Music of Chance* and in all three *New York Trilogy* stories. However, attempts at mapping the city to derive meaning from its pattern is presented as

---

55   For example, Heidegger's claim that "A broken hammer is more of a hammer than an unbroken one" (Terry Eagleton, *Literary Theory*, p.56) is clearly related to Auster's preoccupation with naming objects and defining their meaning by their actions. This suits the idea behind Stilman's collection of broken objects in "City of glass" and also the discussion about the umbrella – an item that returns in its broken condition in *Moon Palace* during the discussion about what things really are and how best to describe them.
56   "The revenge of the author", pp.64–5.
57   *The Red Notebook*, p.126. The quotation is as follows: "If you think of the imagination as a continent, then each book would be an individual country. The map is still quite sketchy at this point, with many gaps and unexplored territories. But if I'm able to keep going long enough, perhaps all the blanks will eventually be filled in." The act of mapping the imagination clearly refers to an act of creative writing and a way of attempting to 'get the whole picture', to see everything in connection by laying it out in front of the mind's eye.

fruitless in these novels, the author again adapting the Renaissance concept for his own purpose. With regard to *The New York Trilogy*, Richard Swope interprets the protagonist Quinn's attempt to 'read' the map of the city – he translates Stilman's New York paths into individual letters – as a misguided belief that "the world is a text laid bare before the eyes of the master reader".[58] It is misguided because a gap always remains between the space mapped out and what it represents: the map-maker (even if unaware of his act, as in Stilman's case) is not identical with the map-reader. Instead of attaching meaning to the Stilman-map, we should use it to read Quinn, the map-reader, because his attempt at interpreting the map reveals his concerns. This coincides with Pynchon's approach: he points out that a map reveals more about the mapper than the space it delineates; any interpretation of a map is simultaneously an interpretation of the mapper (see above).

Swope links the idea of mapping spaces with the search for identity that also informs much of *Moon Palace*. In *The New York Trilogy* the space in which events occur is ever-diminishing, until it is reduced to one simple room: in "City of Glass" Quinn's slow disappearance, in conjunction with the available space in his notebook, takes place in an empty room – the person extinguished along with the physical space. Swope concludes that the room inside the head "represents an impenetrable ontological limit inside which lies an insoluble mystery. The self remains a final locked room to which the detective has no key".[59] That is, the self is unknowable: the mental space inside the head has become a prison.

While everything in *The New York Trilogy* draws towards this encroaching and unknowable space, *Moon Palace*, although concerned with the same theme, presents it in a more spacious light: it is no longer 'the locked room', but 'the memory palace' we deal with, expressed both in the palace of the title and the 'palace of dreams'. Although Fogg, like his predecessors Quinn, Blue and the author of "The Locked Room", is drawn towards a locked room, creating this annihilating space in his New York apartment, it is no longer the end of the story. The self is still unknowable, but it is no longer so desperately self-destructive. The map, which so far has only led the map-reader into ever diminishing spaces, has now opened up. By introducing the unknowable aspect of a mysterious order into his text, Auster presents a more hopeful outlook, an acceptance of the unknowable which encourages a positive, active engagement with life, as expressed in the novel's (unusual) hopeful ending. The map, too, has extended. It begins as the map of New York into which Fogg fits his life, and by which he defines himself. But at the self-destructive climax of this map-reading, he learns how to read the map differently. And he does so by leaving it behind.

By the end of the novel Fogg has reached "the end of the world" (298). But as Reinhart points out: "Fogg erlebt nicht das Ende einer Welt, er steht am Rand

---

58   "Supposing a space", paragraph 3.
59   Ibid., paragraph 31.

einer Welt".[60] He stands on the edge of the world, and I would add, on the edge of the map of America. He has travelled beyond the original American frontier that helped Effing, and finds his very own frontier that he can cross into something new. He knows that the panoramic space of the ocean he sees in front of him reaches "clear to the shores of China" (298). With the reference to China and the moon rising above Fogg, Auster brings the mystical concept of the East and the moon back into the equation, suggesting that the false promise of the neon sign has been replaced by real promise.

Fogg has come as far West as he can, following the call of the original frontier, and has been rewarded by a new frontier, this time with the real East and the real moon. "This is where I start," Fogg says, "this is where my life begins" (ibid). This promising ending can be explained by the fact that the protagonist manages to escape the meaning-laden map he tried to impose on his life without losing the sense of a mysterious order that feeds his creativity – for the story of his life, his MS, gets written: we are reading it.

The structure of *Moon Palace* comprises an extensive interweaving of associations, a network of connections which offers no secure structure, but whose energising centre is the symbol of the moon. The traditional map of America (the symbolic westward movement of the questing individual) is turned in upon itself with the attempt to reconstruct the frontier cave in New York city. Its failure means that the traditional map stands, but as long as Fogg remains within its limits, he can't move on; only when he comes to its edge and prepares to leave it does he find regeneration.

Step 4: Image and interpretation

This leads us directly to the fourth and final step of my investigation: the final interpretation with particular emphasis on the meaning contained within the images. I am adhering to Bartlett's principle that all reading is a search for meaning because we will always try to make sense of what we hear (see Ch.3). By looking at how images are employed in *Moon Palace*, we can discover how they may help us in a search for meaning and thereby towards an interpretation. While considering step three – discovering how the backgrounds are connected to uncover a possible structure to the novel – I have naturally already begun to interpret the text: 'connection' can be synonymous with 'meaning'. But as the text itself warns us not to rely too much on the meaning contained within connections, it seems appropriate first to look for advice within the text on how to interpret it. And *Moon Palace* offers the reader several guidelines on how to interpret it by clearly describing instances where Fogg is called upon to interpret works of art. In particular, this concerns the painting *Moonlight* and Barber's fictional novel *Kepler's Blood*.

---

60   *Pikareske Romane der 80er Jahre*, p.251.

Moon Palace emphasise the traditional belief that we can communicate great ideas and personal truths through the creative arts. The most obvious example is the case of the Blakelock painting *Moonlight*. Effing's extensive instructions on how Fogg is to view the painting – as an exercise in learning how to 'see' things by concentrating on the sense of sight and using the memory – is presented in an intense, almost ritualistic form. Effing's taste for overdramatisation informs the tone, but it also neatly suits Fogg's youthful and intense search for meaning. Furthermore, it aids the creation of a supernatural atmosphere, one which places the act of interpretation in the metaphysical sphere, thereby linking it to Auster's emphasis that creative arts are inspired by a seemingly mystical process. So already the preparation for viewing the painting combines the physical awareness of reality with a mystical understanding.

Having closely followed Effing's instructions, having arrived at the museum, Fogg gives a detailed interpretation of *Moonlight*, which includes the sentence:

I did not want to make any wild, symbolic judgments, but based on the evidence of the painting, there seemed to be no other choice. (135)

This sentence continues the ambiguous combination of intense reality and mystical comprehension. For what are "symbolic judgments"? Judgments are made, based on the value of something: is it good or bad, right or wrong? Wild judgments usually are best avoided. But how does one judge something symbolically? This phrase is a mixture of a value judgment and an interpretation to extract meaning by looking at symbols. The first half of the sentence, "I did not want to make any wild, symbolic judgments", implies that the narrator does not want to be taken for a pretentious art critic who overstretches symbolic readings in order to judge what is good or bad. However, he is still going to do exactly that since he has "no other choice" – an odd statement as there are always several ways to approach any piece of art.

This comment indicates the great power Auster attributes to works of art for demanding something from the viewer. The piece of art itself initiates the interaction that takes place. William Dow writes that Fogg's lesson is to learn exactly this: that "perception is precisely an intuitive concept originating from the object itself, present itself in its meaning".[61] The union that the work of art and the viewer enter into is one guided by the object in question – it does something, it demands, leaves no choices. It is powerful and draws the person into its confines.

This power is also attributed to other art forms, such as dance. When watching Kitty's dance performance, Fogg comments: "[d]ancing was utterly foreign to me, a thing that stood beyond the grasp of words, and I was left with no choice but to sit there in silence, abandoning myself to the spectacle of pure motion" (93).

61   "Never being 'this far from home'", p.194.

Again, he has no choice, the art extols its power over him. That the art of writing naturally is included amongst these powerful arts is emphasised by Effing's declaration, after his paints run out while painting in the desert, that "he found that writing could serve as an adequate substitute for making pictures" (168); the artistic form of self-expression which his own son Barber and grandson Fogg will turn to later, and which Effing turns to in the end by proxy when he dictates his words to Fogg.

But the statement – Fogg bases his reading of *Moonlight* "on the evidence of the painting" – is rather strange. What evidence does he refer to? The actual appearance of the painting (its layout, theme, colour scheme and objects depicted) surely is not evidence of anything except of itself. The word 'evidence' attributes definite powers of proof to the painting. The *painting* makes Fogg choose one specific form of interpretation, one that is wild (emotional rather than logical), symbolic (associative rather than literal) and which requires a value judgment.

Fogg's interpretation is that the "picture was meant to stand for everything we had lost. It was not a landscape, it was a memorial, a death song for a vanished world" (135). This is not a 'wild' interpretation, but a very logical one. Neither is it a 'judgment', but an interpretation. Only the 'symbolic' factor has been used quite collectedly and serenely, finding meaning in the painting rather than making a value judgment, as he suggested at the beginning he would have to.

The sincerity with which Auster has Fogg undertake the interpretation is not in doubt: it is "a reading of *Moonlight* that Auster originally published (with slight variations) in a 1987 issue of *Art News*".[62] Interestingly, in that article Auster also concludes that "any reading of the canvas must involve 'wild, symbolic judgments'" (ibid). The phrase is therefore not particularly chosen to represent Fogg's very unusual encounter with the painting, but a direct adoption of Auster's personal sensation and conclusion when writing a professional piece of criticism. Fogg's experience, therefore, replicates Auster's own mystical access to art.

Fogg's access to art can be broken up into "vier sukzessive Interpretations-schritte" according to Reinhart: 1) the discovery of the internal landscape; the internal space, 2) the idyll-ising of this space, 3) art as a space for preserving not realised utopias and destructive harmonies and 4) art as a means for self-assertion and for establishing subjectivity and identity.[63] These four steps are conceptually linked to an interpretation that is based on the use of spaces and images: highly architectural and, not only through the terminology, analogue to ancient memory systems that use spaces – that use inner landscapes – as the backgrounds for communicating meaning.

This is another instance where the memory palace technique has been adapted and incorporated into Auster's writing, expressed in metaphysical rather than linguistic terms. Fogg's personal experience of the painting is now stored in his

---

62   Steven Weisenburger, "Inside *Moon Palace*", p.138.
63   *Pikareske Romane der 80er Jahre*, p.228.

memory, which enables him to recall it in the solitude of his own room and to re-imagine it. This creative act of reimagining provides the key to the painting's interpretation. Before relating this method of interpretation to the novel *Moon Palace* itself, I will look at the other instance of interpretation: Barber's novel *Kepler's Blood*.

INTERPRETING THE NOVEL

Although the concept of judgment and interpretation in art are intertwined in Fogg's comment on the *Moonlight* painting, the question about art's meaning is dealt with concisely and clearly at a different part of the novel: "The true purpose of art was not to create beautiful objects" (maybe not a deep insight, but a suitable preface to Fogg's later encounter with the painting in the museum). "It was a method of understanding, a way of penetrating the world and finding one's place in it" (166). It is one of the many instances which state that identity can be found by using the creative faculty because it helps us find our place in the world. *Kepler's Blood* is an example of using creativity to find one's own identity, but its appalling style and heavy-handed symbolism suggest that Barber was at an early stage of his self-finding journey when he wrote it.

The way Fogg goes about interpreting the novel suggests not only how Fogg approaches literature, but also how *Moon Palace* may be interpreted. Reinhart explains it as follows: "da der Erzähler [...] nicht nur referiert, sondern auch interpretiert, liefern seine Deutungen gleichzeitig eine Grundlage, nach der sein eigener Text gemessen, bewertet und interpretiert sein will."[64] Thus, while Fogg acknowledges the low quality of the writing he, nevertheless, perceives the book as "valuable [...] as a psychological document" because "it demonstrates how Barber played out the inner dramas of his early life". He concludes "that Barber's later scholarship was [not accidentally] devoted to exploring many of the same issues", but a continuation of the enactment of his 'inner dramas' (256). Coming very late in the novel, and at a time in Fogg's mental development when the intellectual and spiritual theories are being moulded into the final stance he takes, we can take this statement quite literally. It is a repetition of Fogg's reaction on hearing Effing's tale about the cave:

After a while I stopped wondering whether he was telling the truth or not. His narrative had taken on a phantasmagoric quality by then, and there were times when he did not seem to be remembering the outward facts of his life so much as inventing a parable to explain his inner meaning. (178)

The emphasis is not placed on the truth of the memory, but on whether it represents the true inner meaning. This abstract term is underlined by the definition of the story as a parable and suggests an allegorical reading of the text. During his encounter with Effing, Fogg has learned to look beyond the facts,

---

64   Ibid., p.235.

whether on a painting or in a story, and he is now applying the same principle to Barber's novel. He uses it as a "psychological document" (256), a guide to the writer's identity, his inner meaning by placing him within his writing, amongst the things (or inner dramas) that make up his world.

This approach is perfectly applicable to *Moon Palace* as well. This novel, too, serves as a "psychological document" of "the inner dramas" of the author's past, that is, Fogg's. These are the death of his father, the search for identity which shows itself in an intense form of self-discovery, and the over-employment of the intellect in an attempt to make sense of it all. We can do as Fogg suggests: use the text "as a psychological document" in order to understand the "inner dramas" of his life. Therefore, the narrator automatically becomes the 'case' we study. But the emphasis is on the inner dramas, the inner meaning, the one that is lived in the mind and which is expressed through creative employment of the mind. And since we are told to "never take anything for granted", it seems prudent to consider how these inner dramas are presented by the images Auster uses.

THE MEANING OF IMAGES

Mental images are created from words by association. An author's choice of words should inspire mental images by sparking associations in the mind of the reader. I have referred to Auster's extensive use of wordplay. These simple word games are often extended into complex images. The most prominent example is the moon. It is the associative centre of the novel and holds all the novel's themes in orbit around it. In other words, the moon image at the centre holds together a wide variety of ideas in the form of associated images that inform the structure of the novel.

Other images are more concise and bound to one particular episode. These instances are intensely related to memory as a powerful faculty of the mind. Understandably so, for association is the linking factor between object and memory image, as it is between written word and image. The written word is merely one of the subcategories of object from which a memory is formed in the shape of a mental image. Therefore, the acts of reading and of memorising are analogue, and one can be used to investigate the other. Instances in the novel which relate to memory functions will also tell us something about the writer's art of creating images.

For example, Auster uses the fact that memories are created through the senses to communicate intense reactions and expresses them in writing by linking mental images with sensory impressions. We've already encountered the intense concentration on the senses that clears the mind and aids the memory in Fogg's trip to the museum. Another example is Effing's intentionally disgusting noise made when slurping his soup. This "was so unnerving, so destructive, that I began hearing it all the time. Even now [many years later], if I manage to concentrate hard enough, I can bring it back" (109).

Memory impressions are extended beyond the usual optical field to includes that of hearing – and very effectively, too. The author is aware of the role senses play in the creation of powerful images. He even adds the sense of hearing to his adaptation of the memory palace (see above). Although he can not add sound effects to the novel, he can describe their effect in such a way that the reader can imagine them, to the extent where it is almost possible to hear the slurping noise in the head. It suggests that Auster attributes great importance to the creation of strong, sensual images.

At one point mentally created images are rated above actual objects. Fogg considers the possibility that he may find and view the paintings Effing has painted while in his cave in the desert, paintings Fogg has imagined from the descriptions Effing gave of them: "I was reluctant to let anything disturb the beautiful phantoms I had created. [...] I had dreamt them for myself from [Effing's] words, and as such they were perfect " (226). This contemplation arises when Fogg sets out to discover the lost cave, and his reluctance to find the paintings expresses a fear of being disappointed because the real paintings may not live up to the imagined paintings which are 'perfect' in his mind. It emphasises the power of mental images, related to the Rushdian idea that false memory images can be more valuable than the real thing because the personal emotions connected to them are far more important than their factual correctness. The episode, therefore, expresses how greatly Fogg values his encounter with Effing and places it above factual knowledge – a step in his development where things themselves become catalysts for thoughts, rather than an end in themselves.

Auster is well aware of the tricks the mind can play and employs some of these as literary tools very successfully. For example, he uses them for character description, as in uncle Victor's case: his preoccupied mind and consequent inability to bring anything to a conclusion exploits the common memory sin of absent-mindedness. It creates the basis for the character's lovable, yet distracted personality and explains his life-style and his behaviour towards his nephew Fogg.

The example of the memory sin of suggestibility is used as a plot device, explaining a course of events that would otherwise be unbelievable. When Effing describes his encounter with George, who has come to visit the hermit Tom in the desert, Effing explains the fact that George accepts that Effing – posing as Tom – is indeed the hermit as follows: "Effing's resemblance to the hermit was only approximate, but it seems that the power of suggestion [Effing wearing the dead man's clothes, having grown a beard and living where Tom used to live] was strong enough to transform the physical evidence into something it was not. [Any discrepancies, George accepted as a] product of his own faulty memory" (169–70). It is yet another example of the power of the imagination and an expression of the mind always searching for meaning, trying to make sense of any given situation. The most logical explanation is that George has simply forgotten what Tom looks like. This is the simplest answer, and therefore the one George chooses to believe in.

Auster's attitude towards images is ambiguous. He sees them as extremely powerful, but both as agents to deceive and to clarify. For instance, the narrator in *Moon Palace* describes Barber's longing for stories and information about his late love, Fogg's mother Emily, as a need for "something tangible to carry around with him: a series of pictures, as it were, a photo album that he could open in his mind and study" (241). Mental images are not "tangible", and no matter how real they may appear, the tragedy is that you can't reach out and touch them. The photo album image uses the traditional idea of memory pictures that can become so realistic, they seem almost tangible – in the same way that we can almost hear the soup being slurped, Barber can almost reach out and touch the pictures in his mind, and by extension Emily herself. The mental image and its ambiguous status (both deceptive and real) is here used to show the tragic irony of Barber's position; after all, the most tangible proof of his and Emily's union stands right in front of him in the person of their son, Fogg. His need for an impossible tangible memory shows his inability to make the physical connection with his son. At least at this stage in the story.

Another example of a powerful image is the encounter with Orlando in the streets of New York. Orlando carries a broken umbrella with only the spokes remaining spread out above him to protect him from the non-existent rain. He approaches Fogg and Effing in his wheelchair. They enter into the spirit of the pretence, playing along and receiving the coverless umbrella as a parting gift. This episode influences Fogg so strongly that he comments: "A new set of images had been imposed on us, and we were henceforth cast under its spell" (205). The episode is an instance of great writing: vividly imaginative and powerfully symbolic. It is also another example of Auster creating a mysterious atmosphere. Memory and mysticism are yet again linked, this time by the spell that is cast by the images, preparing the reader for a mysterious coincidence; namely, that Effing manages to catch his death (as he intends) by inverting the situation, using the same object: in the pouring rain he opens the coverless umbrella and exclaims how nice and dry he is under its protection – catching pneumonia and dying from it only weeks later.

It is the claim that the images 'cast a spell' over the protagonists that makes the episode mysterious. The spell that is cast is one of imaginative creativity, the power of the image is celebrated by giving it magical potential. It is placed in the reader's imaginary landscape as a magical anchor point, which singles it out as an important moment in the novel. It is even linked to the central symbol of the text, the moon, in that Orlando could be called a lunatic. But unlike Fogg in his initial lunatic phase, Orlando, like Effing, makes objects bend to his will, rather than letting them rule his life.

Effing's statement, that he and Fogg have "finally done it", have "cracked the secret of the universe" by putting "mind over matter" (208), is a cry of victory. And since Effing previously had reinvented himself and will now determine his own death, he could indeed be said to have cracked the secret of the universe.

Effing wants to die, and by setting mind over matter he does so. Fogg, in comparison, found that he was not able to put mind over matter when he lived in the cave in Central Park. The difference seems to be that Effing uses matter in order to free his mind (in this case the broken umbrella) while Fogg blocks the creative flow through overcrowding and so confuses his imaginative perception of things with the things themselves.

The associations created in this passage through the umbrella, the crazy character of Orlando and Effing's emphasis on 'mind over matter' reach out to the main themes of the novel, while also being linked to the central image of the moon, creating connections between elements of the story which become part of the mobile structure of the novel, held together by the moon's magnetic field. These images point towards themselves, to the power of the imagination and the potential for freedom that lies within creativity.

The two instructions on how to interpret images tell us: first, with regard to the *Moonlight* painting, that a piece of art demands a personal interaction with it which will reveal its meaning because it contains all the clues we need to understand it. Secondly, the novel *Kepler's Blood* suggests that a novel is a "psychological document" because the "inner dramas" of the narrator's life are contained here. Both instructions are given with the proviso not to look for finite answers; hence, it is when Fogg lets go of his need to understand connections between everything and instead trusts in his creativity that the possibility of freedom of mind arises.

CONCLUSION

By the end of the novel, freed from social and economic restraints, Fogg is on the verge of inventing his own identity in accordance with his surname, taken from the fictional explorer Philias Fogg. This lies at the heart of the novel: the possibility of choosing one's own identity in a capitalist and intellectualised society. It is comparable to the concerns pervading Rushdie's novel *Midnight's Children*. But what Auster depicts through the individual's personal struggle for identity, Rushdie approaches through the conflict between a national and a private identity. His concern with the freedom to choose one's identity is a political one, since the adoption of a ready-made identity through the concept of nationality or religion is what empowers national and international conflicts. Being free to choose one's own identity also means being free to choose what to think. And thinking like an individual means seeing other people as individuals, thereby avoiding prejudiced categorisation and an aggressive distinction between 'them and us'.

Although both novels make very similar statements, these are conveyed very differently. The fact that *Midnight's Children* is concerned with global confrontations is reflected in the use of the memory systems employed. The personal experiences of each intimate setting is a microcosm of the larger concerns (the Kashmiri Valley foretells the country's future conflict; the gentle lovers' meeting in the Pioneers Cafe reflects the political and religious conflicts). Settings in *Moon Palace* are centred around the universe that resides within the individual (the caves symbolise possible rebirth of identity; the rooms suggest the mental space enabling mental freedom).

The connections between backgrounds also mirror the different approaches. Rushdie's 'leitmotif', which holds the story together by using recurring objects to link up the disparate settings, are perfectly integrated into the story to serve the greater concerns, while Auster's 'touchstone', the moon, simultaneously is the centre of the novel and the symbol of the theme, comparing the physical to the mental level at every stage of the story.

Furthermore, both Rushdie and Auster employ the memory map for structural coherence. While both favour it for the creation of imaginary landscapes as part of the writing process, they also use it to show how imposed boundaries are restrictive: the maps of India, East and West Pakistan and Kashmir restrict the development of identity and free thought in *Midnight's Children*; the map of America in *Moon Palace* shows that freedom lies in stepping outside this map.

The seven texts investigated here, from the medieval Chaucer to the postmodern Auster, use memory systems very differently. There seem to be as many ways to use memory for hermeneutical purposes as there are novels to be interpreted. In the final text I have attempted a structured approach based on four steps of interpretation which have come into focus during my work with the various texts. I will round off my investigation by pulling together the various approaches into one system, and by explaining my theory and its practical application in which memory systems are used as literary interpretative tools.

Conclusion

This thesis has investigated whether the ancient art of memory, especially aspects of the memory palace, can be adapted to aid literary interpretation. It has revealed the presence of memory systems in three medieval texts, has established the compatibility of ancient memory techniques and modern cognitive psychology, and four modern novels have been interpreted, using ancient memory structures to uncover the author's visual landscape. The process has felt like an experimental voyage, and it now remains to draw conclusions about where the journey has led. Questions that were asked at the outset must be answered. Can memory systems be recognised in modern texts? Are they relevant today? And most of all, do they work as interpretative tools? After a brief outline of the theory that lies behind this investigation follows a definition of its practical application as a hermeneutical method that consists of four steps of interpretation. Finally, I will touch upon the areas of interest related to the topic which had to be left out due to restrictions of time and space.

THE THEORY

My investigation of the interaction between memory and literature is based on the premise that all literature is a form of communication between an author and a reader. My proposition is to offer a mode of reading which enables the reader to approximate the author's original idea by understanding the thought processes that precede the written word; by attempting to replicate the visual world the author has created and stored in the memory. Since the author's words were initially chosen to express a visual world, the act of reimagining it increases the understanding of ideas contained within the text.

At the heart of visualisation lies the ability to remember. A capacity that includes something as simple as remembering the ABC, necessary when creating and reading words, and the ability to link together elements presented sequentially in time; for, what good is a comprehension of individual words of a sentence if the first one is forgotten by the end of a phrase. In Quintilian's words: "[a]ll learning depends on memory, and teaching is in vain if everything we hear slips away".[1] The stronger the story resonates in the reader's imagination, the clearer it remains in the memory and the greater the comprehension *and* the enjoyment.

The onus for activating the memory, and for inspiring lasting images, is usually put on the author. However, the most visual writer will fail miserably if the reader does not engage with the text by using the memory. The responsibility for extracting something from a text lies squarely with the reader. The old adage holds good: the more you put in, the more you get out. Literature can be both

---

1   *Institutio Oratoria*, XI, ii, 1.

entertainment and relaxation, but only offers up its treasures when some energy is brought to bear upon it. Especially the first chapters of a novel or the first verses in an epic poem (the two genres I've looked at) require concentration and an active participation by the reader, asking questions such as: Who is that? Where and when are we? Was that a sincere opinion or are other tones of voice involved? And we need to anchor such and other pieces of information in our memories, so that next time we meet that person, return to that space, encounter that tone of voice, we can link it up and ask questions about what, if anything, has changed.

We tend to rely entirely on our natural memory for holding on to pieces of information. Since memory aids are usually not an integral part of modern teaching methods, we don't have these to fall back upon. But imagine what a few artificial memory aids could do – simple mnemonics – for the details of a story to spread out in front of the mind's eye. The clues to a colourful, detailed and vividly peopled landscape is contained within the words the author puts on the page: through the original choice of backgrounds, images and their arrangement. This ordering of specific images is simultaneously a blueprint of the author's patterns of thought. The reader who pays attention, 'listens' carefully and is quick at linking the created images together gains access to this magnificent world.

My theory, in a nutshell, is that the creative process involved in thinking up a story becomes imbedded in the ultimately written text: the mental construct of the tale, which the author holds in the memory, contains backgrounds and images placed in a defined three-dimensional space (the memory palace of the ancient art of memory). These become the backgrounds and images of the text. By identifying them, it is possible to approximate a reconstruction of the mental image that inspired them, getting an idea of what lies behind the story itself.

THE PRACTICAL APPLICATION

The memory palace, in the rhetorician's employment of the ancient art of memory, is made up of three parts. First, the one confining structure (the outer limits of a space: the palace itself). Secondly, a finite number of sites within that structure, easily distinguishable through setting and organisation (the individual places inside the building: the backgrounds). And thirdly, the various symbolic or significant items, whether persons or things, that are placed individually or in groups in the various sites (the meaning-carrying signs placed against the orientation-creating backgrounds: the images). The memory system functions when the memoriser can walk through the structure (palace) in his mind, from site to site (background to background) in their sequential order, and thereby connect up the signifying items (images) placed here. This facilitates the recall of a memorised sequence of events.

The four steps which make up my hermeneutical method relate to the order and individual points made above, discarding some while emphasising others in order to adapt it for literary analysis. The first point about the memory palace – the one confining structure – can initially be taken as a given because the text itself provides the structure within which all other aspects are contained.

This physical structure which aids the ancient art of memory (the palace) is in my interpretative method replaced by the text's approach to MEMORY IN GENERAL (**step one**). Each literary text investigated in this way will differ; the conceptual framework varies according to the specific angle on the topic of memory. The particular understanding and appropriation of memory within the text is the foundation from which to discover how to employ the following memory techniques and how to interpret their results. An author's particular concept of memory delineates the outer confines of the analytical process.

Specific BACKGROUNDS (descriptions of place in whatever from) are now analysed (**step two**) with regard to their significance implied by the author, and their relevance with regard to the particular concept of memory within the text.

The sequence or ORDER OF BACKGROUNDS is then investigated (**step three**) to reveal any connections, patterns or systems incorporated within the text. Here, again, I deviate slightly from the rhetorical art of memory. Within the traditional memory palace the system employed is very clear: it is the strict journey method leading linearly from one place in the sequence to the next. Without the strict adherence to the sequential order, the rhetorical system would fall apart. In the literary imaginary world no such restraints apply, and various systems may be employed, often in the same text and at the same time. Hence a recognition of specific memory systems is helpful in establishing one or more structures for the text in question.

The final step concerns an in depth look at IMAGES (**step four**), the memory-laden items that go beyond the structure and plot-line of the text and are the receptacles of meaning. This last step comprises the three steps gone before: in combination, all factors produce the final interpretation. The four steps are:

1. The general concept of memory
2. The particular type of background
3. The structural connection of backgrounds
4. The significance of images

The Memory Palace Method

In order to turn the abstract definition of the four steps into practical guidelines for interpretation, each step is explained further by relating them to specific texts.

Step 1. The general concept of memory
When I began the investigation into memory and literature, I didn't expect that the general attitude towards memory displayed in any of the texts would be as relevant as it has turned out. As mentioned in the introduction, I did not choose

the texts for their memory-related concerns. In fact, I was surprised by their fundamental links to the topic. Chaucer's *The House of Fame* naturally would be concerned with memory: fame *is* remembrance. But Chaucer's link to the Italian proponents of the art of memory was unexpected. It was brought to my attention, not by critical writings on the topic, but through Chaucer's detailed description of the palace of Fame that coincides extensively with the ideas behind the technique. Langland's *Piers Plowman* was most prominently linked to memory through the personification of Imagination – the faculty in medieval times clearly linked to the memory – but that rhetorical memory systems were so intrinsic to the structure of the text was a revelation. I had, of course, expected that the art of memory would be reflected in medieval literature: it was still taken for granted as part of an educated person's knowledge. But the extent to which it permeated the texts was surprising and encouraged me to continue in the same vein.

Both medieval and modern authors resort to the topic of memory to enhance their craft. The change of emphasis from medieval texts to modern texts – from memory as an art to the faulty faculty that allows psychological analysis – merely means that the approach has altered; the underlying concerns remain the same. Carter provocatively pushes the boundaries of the unreliability of the narrator. Fevvers in *Nights at the Circus* is a prime example of an author using falsified memory to examine just how far the reader's credulity can be stretched. Rushdie writes that *Midnight's Children* became to him "a book about the nature of memory". To him personal memory is what creates identity. Therefore, a memory made up of prejudice, one informed by external values, is predestined to destroy independent thought. Memory is pivotal to the central theme.

Pynchon's novel *Vineland* emphasises the power of memories to recall a 'true' past that then can be set against one imposed externally, and simultaneously laments the ease with which people let their memories be manipulated. His book is a wake-up call: a call to remember. Finally, Auster's approach to memory in *Moon Palace* is more abstract in that he has completely imbibed the concept of the Renaissance art of memory into his thinking. Using this as a metaphor for the art of writing, Auster offers a specific way into his work.

In various ways, the writers very clearly refer to the concept of memory, some foregrounding it (like Pynchon and Chaucer), others using it as a technique (Carter and Langland) or relating it to history (Rushdie and Auster). But all six authors most emphatically relate it to their job as a creative writer. The analogues between memory processes and storytelling are commented on in one way or another by all of them. Therefore, while an author's attitude towards memory initially seemed secondary, it became the first step towards gaining access to the text. Any reference to memory reflects on the act of writing itself because memory and writing are so closely linked: the author must remember the story in order to be able to write it down, while the narrator is always recounting a story from memory.

When looking for aspects on memory, there are two kinds to look out for: one is the direct comment on memory in the text, the other is external to it. In the first instance, depending on who makes the comment in the text and in which vein it is given, it contains information about how to understand a character. It can be a hint from the author, indicating how far we should trust the narrator: a character who contradicts himself urges circumspection; a character who admits to having relied on a faulty memory is more likely to gain our sympathy than incur criticism for having made mistakes.

The extent of extra-textual references varies greatly. In the case of medieval authors these must be based on circumstantial evidence because they have left few or no observations about their own texts. Education, profession and historical relevance, etc., must suggest in which tradition they were writing. Modern authors tend to leave volumes of written and spoken testimonials behind that can elucidate the topic. Rushdie's interviews and Auster's semi-autobiographical texts alerted me to how deeply they engage with the topic of memory. The exception to the rule is Pynchon. He eschews public appearances, gives very few interviews and writes little beyond the works themselves. In his case, just as in medieval texts, the story must speak for itself, except for the obvious advantage that we react more directly to the text, being his contemporaries. Having said this, in *Vineland* Pynchon points out the danger that lies in this form of assumed familiarity and suggests that we would do well to beware of these kinds of assumptions.

The first step of my method, therefore, collects information on the concept of memory as it is expressed by the author in general and in the text in particular. It moves towards a comprehension of both the author's approach to storytelling and of how characters should be approached.

Step 2. The particular type of background

The second step, looking at the author's choice of background, is a simple exercise that reveals a great deal about the text because it tells us how the author visualises the stories. There are many types of background and many ways of using them, from the naturalistic setting to the highly surreal and from a straight symbolic employment where a landscape represents a specific concept, as in allegorical writing, to an abstract place that functions as a topical location rather than a physical one, such as Langland's use of the various personifications.

When we read any text, we automatically recreate the type of setting the author describes. Our sense of a book – our reading experience – to a large extent derives from this visualisation. It immediately establishes a microcosm of the entire text from which we can expand our thinking. It is an island in the slowly emerging landscape that becomes part of a greater picture as we progress through the story.

The various types of backgrounds, and their style of presentation in the texts under investigation, have revealed very specific aspects about each. Interestingly, but on reflection maybe not surprisingly, the provenance of a work seems partly to determine the type of background. Both US novels, published only one year apart, use the same literary trope (the American pastoral confronted with urban scenes) but they handle these settings, and the social concerns that they highlight, very differently.[2]

Pynchon's pastoral scenes are images of false idyll, reflecting the main theme of the novel which states that people let themselves be lulled into apathy by lazily believing in a Hollywood happy ending. Auster more directly refers to the American pastoral of the so-called first settlers and questions whether it is possible to encounter an open frontier of endless possibilities in modern America. The urban setting, although in both cases reflecting its influence on identity, is extremely different in detail. Auster's New York is constructed from symbols, defined by the person who sees it and thereby part of his identity. Columbus in *Vineland*, in turn, is a very exact description of the actual city. It is the city itself that produces the information Pynchon wants to convey – through its name, through its commercial and social aspects. The world is 'readable' (although with a great deal of humour and scepticism). In Auster's *Moon Palace*, instead, it is the 'reading' of the city (as markedly demonstrated already in *The New York Trilogy*) that reflects Fogg's deluded search for meaning in everything he encounters in New York.

The two imaginary worlds these authors create are visually, technically and experientially very different. Auster's intense, egocentric, minimalist world shows one man confined within spaces, be they rooms, caves or city streets. The only true expansion of the view comes at the end of the book with the panorama of the Pacific; even the desert scenes express a great emptiness within the protagonists rather than an opening up of possibilities. Pynchon's world is one where buildings and confined spaces are somewhat secondary to the scenery. A hidden retreat, overgrown roadways and a monster footprint spring to mind. Some indoor scenes as well, but they tend to be rather specific or unusual; a Tubal detox centre, a room containing the Puncutron Machine and a shopping mall. The central scene of the book, the shooting of Weed Atman, begins inside a sitting room, but tellingly spills out into the street, just as other pivotal scenes move from the inside to the outside, such as Zoyd's annual window jumps. Readers are rarely returned to a location encountered before and must try to keep up with the ever-changing backgrounds: experiencing the intoxication that is Pynchon's writing. Auster's spaces are confining and defining; Pynchon's are expanding and changeable.

Other settings referred to previously are similarly suggestive: whether we take Rushdie's naturalistic settings overlaid with eccentric, sometimes fantastic people and events; Carter's creation of spaces that either encourage philosophical contemplation or, contrarily, immerse the characters in surreal, emotionally charged surroundings; or the settings used by the medieval writers with their

---

2   These two instances are naturally not representative of US fiction. But the fact that the two (very different) texts refer to this common heritage makes a comparison between them especially interesting.

rhetorically inspired choices of buildings, allegorical maps or pilgrim stations. All demonstrate that backgrounds are often simple to identify, carry symbolic value, can be 'read' and vary greatly in their application from author to author.

Step 3. The structural connection of backgrounds
The third step, considering the arrangement of backgrounds, is a very rewarding phase of the interpretation: partly because it attempts an understanding of the text as a whole; partly because it is here that the rhetorical skill, using the art of ancient memory, finds its most practical and significant application.

Having explained the rules governing the choice of backgrounds (*loci*) in the classical art of memory, Yates reflects that:

> what strikes me most about them [the backgrounds] is the astonishing visual precision which they imply. In a classically trained memory the space between the *loci* can be measured, the lighting of the *loci* is allowed for. And the rules summon up a vision of a forgotten social habit. Who is that man moving slowly in the lonely building, stopping at intervals with an intent face? He is a rhetoric student forming a set of memory *loci*.[3]

Although it may not be possible for the modern educational system to reintegrate the classical practice (somewhat romantically described by Yates above), it is easily possible for an individual to engage in memory work, even on a superficial level, and almost immediately reap the benefits.

If we balk at having to create our own memory palaces in which we can store selected pieces of information, as Yates' imaginary student of rhetoric does, we can instead adapt it to strengthen our imaginative faculty and gain instant enjoyment from visualising literary texts. The key element in this process is to keep to the basic rules mentioned by Yates above: arrangement and order, visibility and clarity should determine the images we create in our minds. In literary texts the first part of this process has already been undertaken by the author: the arrangement and order of images is grounded in the text; discovering its underlying arrangement means revealing its underlying structure. It remains for the reader to ensure the visibility and clarity of the images created from the author's words.

CATEGORISATION OF SYSTEMS
In chapter one I listed six categories to cover the vast array of mnemonic techniques from Antiquity: the alphabet- and number-systems, geometric shapes, the journey method, the memory map, allegory and design. Over the following four chapters the individual systems received varying degrees of attention, depending on how appropriate they were for each text in turn. Based on this, I revised my original categorisation and determined on four main categories: the

---

3   *The Art of Memory*, p.24.

alphabet- and number-systems, the journey method, the memory map and the memory building.

For clarity's sake, I decided to set aside the aspect of design, despite its relevance for medieval and modern texts. It is the only physical aspect – visible on the page rather than part of the imaginary structure – and diverges into the entirely separate subject of visual arts. Its importance for interpretation, however, is not in question: its great impact on medieval manuscripts has already been described in chapter one.

Modern texts use design as visual pointers to indicate divisions, and hence organisation of a text, following the tradition of medieval manuscripts. Simple aspects, like the division into sentences, paragraphs and chapters, and the choice or lack of chapter headings are still revealing with regard to what the author expects of the reader's ability to remember.

Printing conventions influence the design of modern texts and it is important to distinguish between an author's intended visual clues and those added by the publisher for editorial purposes. I came across an instance where a critic had attributed great significance to a single asterisk that divided two scenes in Pynchon's *Vineland*. The asterisk segregates the worm-song episode from a flashback of the encounter between Frenesi and Vond earlier that day (239). A pivotal moment in the novel because Weed's imminent murder, symbolically predicted in the first scene, is followed by the episode which reveals that Frenesi will be the one bringing about his death.

However, in my edition a second asterisk is used (on page 8). The position of both asterisks (at the top and bottom of a page respectively) reveals that it was put there by the editor to replace the gap of one line that is usually left between two scenes in a chapter. Since a gap at the top or bottom of a page is easily overlooked, thereby running together two scenes the author wishes to distinguish visually, the solution (although not entirely satisfactory) is to insert an asterisk to point out the change of scene. While writers of manuscripts could influence the point at which a new page would start (by letter size or spacing), mass-published books must conform to a given standard.

On the whole, authors of printed texts tend to avoid all but the most basic visual clues. The use of extra visual signs, such as lines, asterisks, graphs or coloured ink, can appear demonstrative and ostentatious, so most authors rely on the words alone. There are, however, exceptions, such as the famous instance of Lawrence Sterne's *Tristram Shandy*. Here the use of extraneous visual signs is taken to extremes. It emphasises Sterne's opinion that the layout of a book ought to be the author's choice rather than the publisher's; but it is primarily a perfect expression of the narrator Tristram's personality with its inclination towards ostentation and self-delusion, making him a prime example of the unreliable, unintentionally self-revealing narrator.

Design clearly determines the structure of a work, even if it appears in its more restrained form in modern writing. Langland's *Piers Plowman* is a telling example of how disagreement about the visual partition of a work can fuel discussions about its meaning for centuries. Design has here been set aside to concentrate on the memory features included in the imaginary landscape of the text, the central concept of this thesis. From the remaining categories four were incorporated into my method: their application and relevance is considered below.

ALPHABET- AND NUMBER-SYSTEMS

Alphabet- and number-systems lie at the heart of each further memory system discussed, because they bring together the two fundamental aspects of order and association. They play a part in every interpretation undertaken here: most prominently in Langland's *Piers Plowman*, the earliest, most unfamiliar and therefore least accessible text, and in Auster's *Moon Palace*, the post-modern novel with the greatest use of abstract symbolism and therefore not straightaway accessible. Langland's combination of established groupings (the seven deadly sins, the five senses, etc.) relates traditionally associated items from separate systems to each other. It means that various established ideas can be compared, combined and built upon until Langland, ultimately, adds his own link – the Tree of Charity – to the chain of images that make up the familiar mnemonic list. This is an instance where the alphabet- and number-systems provide structures onto which further items can be added to achieve a more complex understanding of a text's concerns.

Auster's employment of the alphabet- and memory-systems ignores the sequential order and instead relies on the associative aspect. He uses one symbol, the moon, around which all the associated items are held in orbit. This makes for a very open structure that lends a myriad of associations equal weight in their relevance for the topic. They are only secondarily linked to each other, able to form new relationships, but all connected to the central symbol. The explanation why two such disparate texts are so responsive to the alphabet- and number-systems may be that their initial inaccessibility is overcome by the simplest of all thought processes: linking and associating.

Having established that alphabet- and number-systems are present in a text, we must ask what they tell us about the way authors imagine their created worlds. Langland clearly is very scholarly in his approach. His readers must have a certain Christian education to be able to follow his ideas. He expects them to apply their logical faculties to the text. The reader is equated with the protagonist Will, who begins his education with simple mnemonics that are then extended, taking in more and more complex memory systems and concepts, moving from simple mnemonics to metaphor, parable, allegory and finally to a spiritual awareness that goes beyond the systems themselves. The key to the text, however, is the comprehension of how to employ the simple list mnemonics upon which everything else is built. The imaginary landscape Langland creates is, therefore, difficult to recreate for the modern reader.

The list mnemonics Langland uses would immediately have sparked images in his contemporaries' minds. They would be placed automatically in an abstract landscape where concepts, such as the sins or the chain of tree images, would exist side by side and could be expanded into larger systems. Since most of the actual physical settings in *Piers Plowman* are symbolical (the first part set in London being the exception), they are not helpful as vehicles for the story. They incorporate meaning and therefore do not work satisfactorily as backgrounds. Instead, the personifications become the secure stations along the way, to which the various meanings, including the various symbolic settings, can be attached. Langland's imaginary world, which we attempt to recreate, requires the mental skill of holding symbolical, figurative images and their significances in an abstract space – a scholar's or philosopher's metalandscape – in order to recreate his thought processes: the abstract stations of the various personifications of mental faculties offer exactly this kind of helpful anchor point.

The case of Auster is very different. The intermingling of a myriad of associations, held together by one defining symbol, demands an entirely different structure for the imaginary landscape. Although his descriptive passages are much more easily visualised than Langland's allegorical or figurative ones, and although we are clearly situated in physical space, the associative centre of the moon defies a definitive order of them. Every physical setting we encounter seems to have at least one, if not more, alternative incarnations. The desert, the cave, even New York appears in several guises, depending on *when* in Fogg's development we are. Just as Auster brings past events to bear on the present, his backgrounds merge into one another. They are not only linked through their position in space, but also through their various appearances in time. This is aided by Auster's minimalist style of writing. He does not emphasise the physical scene his characters inhabit, wherefore a few exact directions suffice for the reader to grasp the idea behind a setting. Leaving "air" around things, as Fogg learns to do, is one of Auster's greatest skills. It allows the reader to 'see' the central core of an episode by simplifying it: the reader does the work and takes the step into the imaginary world. It also means that the concepts, the insubstantial ideas, are foregrounded. The images carried by and in the landscape dominate: the magnetic field Auster has created around the central image of the moon through the use of associations allows these ideas to be seen in their larger context; they are not tied down within a specific structure.

The most basic memory systems, the alphabet- and number-systems, can be extended in order to provide the structure for a complex text. Their simple ruling principles of sequence and/or association provide a way into a text that retains the complexity of its concerns. Allegory, which functions by reading a text on two levels at once, relies on the reader's skill to compare these two levels. This involves the processes of ordering and associating: the processes of the alphabet- and number-systems. Allegory is an instance of how these systems can be applied and is therefore incorporated into this category.

THE JOURNEY METHOD

The journey method is easily explained because it is such an intrinsic part of storytelling and easily observable in narratives. Prominent examples are spiritual journeys experienced through pilgrimage, as in Langland's case, or subconscious journeys, such as that undertaken by the poet in Chaucer's *The House of Fame*. Finding the stations along these kind of journeys is the simplest form of structure present in text. The way these stations are chosen, what they consist of and especially how they are linked together determines how the reader creates the imaginary world. Langland's personified mental faculties are the perfect stations for a spiritual journey, mirroring or anchoring the individual steps that lead towards a greater understanding. Auster's protagonist Fogg's spiritual, or one could say inspirational, journey is a modern example of such a pilgrimage where various stages of insight are traversed during the character's story, a journey typically found in the *Bildungsroman*.

More traditional backgrounds, such as Carter's geographically situated places (London, St Petersburg and Siberia) with their individual and sequential locations, are so strikingly defined that they frame the action to such an extent that it seems as if the fabric of reality bursts open when scenes are linked together. Clear distinctions between places produce clear edges. They allow Carter to pry in between these places or merge them to create physical sensations, shifts in the imagination that restructure the shapes in the mind, opening up gaps into other, new formations – concurrent with the surrealist aim to see the world as strange and thereby gain a new perspective.

The journey method always leads directly to the question of how scenes are connected and, therefore, is the system which reveals a text's structural organisation most openly.

THE MEMORY MAP

The topic of geometry can be integrated into the memory map method since geometric shapes make up part of the map's two- or three-dimensional space. Chaucer's reference to geometry, comparing a poet to a master-builder, relates geometric shapes to the creative imagination, thereby implying the importance of a mental design for creative writing and indicative of his own textual structure. Langland's spiral narrative is an extension of the journey into all direction (not only forwards, but backwards and up as well) and indicates that the journey will revisit concepts on increasingly higher planes of understanding, while Auster's centralised theme (reminiscent of a circle or sphere with a central point) resembles Rushdie's magnetic field of invention, suggesting that a higher power of attraction and association guides the themes of the story. Rushdie's description of the town of Q in *Shame* is the clearest example of a geometric shape: seen from above it resembles a dumb-bell – two circles connected by two parallel lines – that describes the boarders of a map. It immediately sets the scene of division between two camps with brittle communication, later reflected in the story itself. Such isolated instances of geometric figures within texts can explain constellations of relationships, events or topics and are helpful as initial guidelines, which can later be included in the larger picture.

The use of existing cities as maps upon which the events are played out is common in literary fiction, and the chosen texts are no exceptions. Chaucer's legendary Troy may be familiar from its prominence in literature rather than from experience, but the map he draws of it is extremely easy to visualise and links up with previous descriptions of it. Examples of familiar destinations such as London (Langland and Carter), New York (Auster), Bombay (Rushdie) and St Petersburg (Carter) spark off memories in a reader's mind: either from personal experience of those places, or from second-hand visuals (pictures or films), which provides an instant backdrop for the events presented.

Specific landmarks are mentioned rarely in the texts under discussion. When they occur, they suggest a grounding in reality that adds reliability to the tale, as when Walser in *Nights at the Circus* watches Lizzy and Fevvers disappear across Westminster Bridge to the sound of Big Ben's chimes. Tampering with known facts encourages the reader to believe in a world of hidden facts. Placing secret locations underneath familiar landmarks (such as treasures under the Empire State Building or secret government installations underneath the Thames Barrier) is a frequent feature of thrillers and science fiction. It anchors the fiction in reality and gives it credibility.

None of the authors discussed here use familiarity with cities in that way. They do not support conspiracy theories or create fantastic stories with links to reality. No matter how strange the cities appear, their power lies in the fact that they *do* exist. None of the authors attempt an escape from reality, but approach existence more intensely. The sites they create are not fantastical. The few exceptions stand out and carry extra meaning, such as Carter's rotund female correction centre in Siberia: a symbolic place rather than a believable institution, and suitably situated away from familiar landmarks.

Pynchon's very exact reproduction of the city of Columbus is an example of anchoring a story so tightly in reality that we must note that reality can be more extraordinary than fiction. This lies at the heart of Pynchon's novel. The invented Vineland remains a mainly uncharted map since the places visited within it are secondary to the overall impression we get of the area. Maps in Pynchon's novel are clearly there to be read – they contain encoded information – but we must be careful how to interpret them. Rushdie's geographical map of Asia is important because it visualises the fact that the cartography has been done, but the people residing in the various regions are not defined by these boundaries: they still have the potential to be independent.

This is one step on from the linking up of two locations in the journey method. In a memory map all backgrounds are placed in relation to each other. This means going beyond mere plot-line and onto theme, because it requires reflection. The memory must bring the various locations together, several at any given time.

234

The symbolic maps employed by Langland in *Piers Plowman* are the clearest examples hereof. The map describing the way to Truth's castle is an allegory of the right spiritual way: it tells us how to 'do well' through the simplest of symbols. Pynchon uses the idea that landscape conveys meaning when he describes the *woge* spirits that reside in natural features of Vineland, but the didactic aspect has been removed.

In much modern literature the idea of an easily definable right and wrong is eschewed and therefore traditional maps which encourage this differentiation by location (left is evil/right is good) are no longer applicable. Moral tenets are dealt with in greater complexity since the advent of psychological interpretations. The maps of Heaven and Hell that Sister Rochelle describes in *Vineland*, which so clearly hark back to the symbolical maps of medieval didactics, are produced to show their outmoded application as moral indicators. They must be reinterpreted in the light of what we now know about the human condition. The maps drawn by an author reveal the larger themes by indicating how the various situations relate to each other, and by suggesting how to reflect upon the accumulated scenes.

THE MEMORY BUILDING

Initially, I classed the traditional memory palace as a subcategory of the journey method. During my investigation descriptions of actual rooms – the interior of buildings – turned out to be extremely revealing and became a separate category. They can suggest to what extent an author follows or deviates from the rules guiding the architectural memory system by revealing how closely the imaginary landscape resembles that produced by the ancient art.

The first text under consideration, Chaucer's *The House of Fame*, presented the perfect opportunity for investigating buildings described in the text and their suitability as memory palaces. Not being aware of Chaucer's supposed familiarity with the Italian adaptation of the classical art of memory, I was astounded by how much the comparison of the three buildings and the memory palace revealed. In retrospect the topic of fame clearly benefits from its depiction in three types of memory palace because fame equals remembrance: it was an inspired idea to transform it into poetry. Langland intentionally uses buildings as allegorical memory palaces. He links a different virtue to each part of the building, storing all the important aspects in its individual backgrounds, giving them meaning through the associations created with each; for example, the drawbridge that symbolises mercy is the only way to God's Charity that resides in the castle.

In instances where there is no obvious link to the art of memory, descriptions of buildings can still suggest how the author's thoughts are structured. The four modern authors discussed here all describe buildings, and each description is relevant for memory function. In Rushdie's *Shame* Omar's childhood home represents his memory: each room contains past events and Omar, by going from room to room, is able to visit his past. Carter compares the past to a building in *Wise Children* when family history is represented by a building. Here the walls between the rooms symbolise the division between people because the past – the space they inhabit – is not shared. Pynchon uses buildings as an expression of the subconscious (in Vond's and Zoyd's dreams) and very strikingly has Rochelle use a room as a detailed memory locale to show what the memory is actually capable of. Auster's more abstract approach (the room which is both the physical space inhabited by the writer and also the mental space in which an imaginary world is created) is made possible exactly because the memory palace concept is so deeply ingrained in his thinking. Fogg's detailed description of space, when attempting to help Effing create a mental image of his sick room, shows a student of the art of memory at work.

All four authors associate memory function with a building: whether they use it to represent the past (Rushdie and Carter) or the subconscious (Pynchon), or to illustrate the technique of remembering (Pynchon and Auster) or the creative act (Auster). The ancient association between memory and architectural space (the memory palace) has somehow been retained in the imagination, in cognitive structures. Although references to the memory palace have become far from commonplace, the metaphor of the memory as a building still flourishes.

SUMMARY
The third step of interpretation – concerning the patterns made by connections between backgrounds – is conducted in four parts: by looking at 1. ALPHABET-AND NUMBER-SYSTEMS that determine the underlying way the associations are ordered, 2. the JOURNEY METHOD that exposes the type of link between individual backgrounds through the emphasis the author places on them, 3. the MEMORY MAP that sets backgrounds in relation to each other and reveals the theme through the structure that supplies the complete picture and 4. MEMORY BUILDINGS that help confirm the author's general concept of memory and focus on the text's central ideas. Have one or more of these patterns been identified in a text, the foundation for the final interpretation is laid.

Step 4. The significance of images
The final step concerns the images placed against the various backgrounds. When considering the concept of memory in a given text (step 1), the instances are usually manageable and a particular view discernible. Similarly, the individual backgrounds (step 2), although they can sometimes be more effusive, can be analysed according to type. The ordering of these backgrounds (step 3) is more complicated, but with the aid of the chosen memory systems (four in number) they can be identified and analysed.

The images, however, are so all-pervading, so elementary to the text that it is difficult, if not impossible, to suggest types or methods to determine their significance. Few novels contain instructions on how they should be interpreted (the exception is *Moon Palace*), and few concentrate sufficiently on one complex image to allow it to become the focus of an interpretation (Leda and the Swan in *Nights at the Circus* is an exception).

Kolve, helpfully, undertakes an iconographically led classification of images. He distinguishes between three types in the medieval language of signs: the attribute, the symbol and the allegorical figure.[4] His definition of how an image must function in order to benefit from an iconographic reading is particularly useful: he says, these are images that "(1) the tale invites us to imagine and hold in the mind as the narrative action progresses [what I call anchor points]; that (2) are recognizable akin to other images known from other medieval contents, where they bear expressly symbolic meaning [what we may call symbolic intertextuality – this can easily be applied to other literary periods as well]; and that (3) offer an appropriate and illuminating guide to our understanding of something substantial in the tale in which they occur."[5] These are sound guidelines for choosing images to concentrate on in any given text. They are especially relevant for my method of interpretation because they emphasise the associative power of these images and rely on the reader's ability to visualise them.

One of the most often repeated rules governing the ancient art of memory says that persons wishing to memorise something must invent the images themselves. The memoriser should choose the image that naturally springs to mind as an automatic response when something is described – this is necessary for the memory to function most smoothly. A borrowed or second-hand image hinders the process. That is why many of the popular 'how to improve your memory' books that loosely base their method on the ancient art of memory fail. They suggest which images to associate with a subject, listing them in long columns of words or pictures. These books complicate the memory process, blocking the natural memory response by producing additional images that may actually hinder, rather than help the reader. Only when the memoriser relies on her own personal image-creation faculty (the imagination) will the images be forceful enough to linger in the mind and be reactivated at the required time.

Quintilian, when listing the two key aspects of the memory palace system – the backgrounds and images – says about the images that these "we must of course invent".[6] He mentions this as a matter of course, and it is clear from Quintilian's description of the process that there is no doubt that the images must be original to the memoriser for the method to work at all. Cicero writes in *De Oratore* that the images created should be those that have "the capacity of encountering and speedily penetrating the mind",[7] or in a more accessible

---

4   *Chaucer and the Imagery of Narrative*, p.62.
5   Ibid., p.361.
6   *"imaginibus vel simulacris, quae utique fingenda sunt"*, Instituto Oratoria, XI, ii, 21.
7   *"quae occurrere celeriterque percutere animum possint"*, II, lxxxvii, 358.

translation, images that "come to mind and make a quick impression".[8] When describing the episode during which the alleged inventor of the art, Simonides, experiences the helpful aspects of backgrounds and images, the word *fingere* (to invent, imagine, make) often appears.[9]

The seminal text for artificial memory training, the *Rhetorica ad Herennium*, dedicates an entire passage to the importance of inventing one's own images and eschewing ready-made memory lists, or "systems of associating commonplaces with symbols", as Cicero describes them.[10] The *Rhetorica ad Herennium* author strongly disapproves of these lists. His reasons are threefold: he says, first, "among the innumerable multitude of words it is ridiculous to collect images for a thousand", since these thousand words would never suffice or do justice to the multifarious and accurate expressions of a large vocabulary. Secondly, "one person is struck by one likeness, and another by another" because "things seem different to different persons", wherefore everyone "should in equipping himself with images suit his own convenience". And finally, the author compares the teaching of how to use the art of memory to any other kind of teaching, saying that examples are helpful, but in the end the student must learn to apply the process himself: "it is the instructor's duty to teach the proper method of search in each case", for when the *Rhetorica ad Herennium* author teaches "the search for Introductions" to students of rhetoric, he "give[s] a method of search and do[es] not draught a thousand kinds of introduction", furthering the students' creative skills rather than passing on mere facts.[11]

All three points are highly relevant when adapting the art of memory to my method of literary interpretation. Since authors create entire worlds with their imagination, the reader, too, creates ever-new images in the mind and should not be limited to specific ones; hence, a classification of images might limit the variety and therefore vividness of the experience. Secondly, it is a truism that there are as many versions of a text as there are readers of it, for each reader 'sees' their own specific version of the author's imaginary world. Finally, my method does not aim to define texts, to classify specific backgrounds or to equate specific memory structure with specific meanings. I, too, wish to convey a method – the meaning must be sought by each reader in turn.

Interestingly, the author of the *Rhetorica ad Herennium* uses the verb 'to search' when referring to a method whereby a conclusion can be arrived at. It is the same word that Bartlett uses when he speaks about literary interpretation as always being guided by the reader's "search for meaning". The method I propose is also a mode of searching for meaning: a means whereby it is possible to reach an independent conclusion about a text.

---

8   *Institutio Oratoria*, XI, ii, 22; Russell's translation.
9   See, for example, *De Oratore*, II, lxxxvi, 354.
10   *De Oratore*, I, xxxiv, 157.
11   *Rhetorica ad Herennium*, III, xxxiii, 38–9.

The fourth step of my method, the final interpretation focusing on the images of the text, relies on a personal response. The first three steps help to recreate the imaginary world of the author by making it rise up in a three-dimensional shape, determined by the author's words. The fourth step – the significance of the images – is the reader's responsibility, despite being inspired by the author's words. It is from these that the personal interpretation is made. The emphasis shifts in the communication between the author and the reader from the first to the latter between steps three and four. The author is not dead, merely resting after his act of creative invention, having initiated a process that the reader must complete.

TOPICS NOT MENTIONED OR ONLY LIGHTLY TOUCHED UPON
As I write these words it feels as if I am at the beginning of the journey rather than at its end: only now, having researched the topic, tested my theory, developed an interpretative system in four steps and defined these, I feel equipped to prove my method. It would, for example, be fascinating to apply my memory palace method to a non-visual text, or even an entirely factual one, to see what benefits could be obtained from it. Would the attitude towards memory portrayed here, the kinds of backgrounds and their connections, spark off images that enable an interpretation of such texts? I believe they would, but having reached the end of my journey, the questions must remain unanswered.

Many fascinating aspects related more or less directly to my discussion had to be ignored due to the restrictions of time and space. It might, for example, have been interesting to discover whether specific types of text lend themselves more to an interpretation by one memory system than by another, or whether the approach differs with regard to genre or literary period. Lucy Honeychurch's comment in E.M. Forster's 1908 novel *A Room with a View* suggests this might be the case. She says to her fiancé Cecil, "I had got an idea [...] that you feel more at home with me in a room. [...] Or the most in a garden or on a road. Never in the real country."[12] The author implies that specific backgrounds represent specific types of person. A revealing statement, especially when considered in relation to the period in which the novel was written. It might be possible to discover how backgrounds have changed or retained their particular significance over time, and whether their significance changes according to genre.

Many relevant topics could only be lightly touched upon, such as the element of pilgrimage as a specific aspect of the journey method with its extension into procession and other forms of art and architecture. Others are *mappamundi* as a specific form of memory map, in depth research of memory in literary theory, memory tests undertaken with a group of students, data from experiments with eidetics on how colour influences visual perception, a systematic investigation of all memory systems in one text or interviews with memory champions.

---

12   p.125.

One obvious area of interest is the role of memory systems, and memory in general, in education. Urged by orators, taught by medieval teachers and more frequently praised in recent times, the benefit of memory aids for teaching has never been doubted. But the extent to which they can further the creative and cognitive development of students has in most cases been overlooked. Arnheim concludes his discussion about the effects that visual thinking has on learning with this strong statement:

Our educational system, including our intelligence tests, is known to discriminate not only against the underprivileged and the handicapped but equally against the most gifted. Among those capable of becoming most productive in the arts and sciences are many who will have particular trouble with the formalistic thought operations on which so much of our schooling is based, and will struggle against them most strenuously. To what extent do our schools and universities serve to weed out and retard the most imaginative minds? Intelligence test scores and creativity correlate poorly, and the mentally more lively children tend to be a nuisance to their teachers and peers and a liability in class work. These are ominous symptoms.[13]

Since writing this in 1969, great improvements have been made to accommodate the fact that different pupils require different circumstances to optimise their learning capacity. The most prominent probably the distinction between the kinesthetic, the aural and the visual student. My theory is entirely based on the aspect of being able to visualise: to read or hear words and to transform these words into images which come alive in a three-dimensional imaginary world. This may appear counterproductive for those benefiting most from the kinesthetic or aural methods. However, it is commonly acknowledged that the visualisation process aids the comprehension of a proposed idea or situation, and that by far the largest percentage of students is visually inclined. Also, the three methods do rarely appear in isolation and a classification of persons to one category is merely an expression of a dominant mode of comprehension and does not exclude the use of the other two. In fact, a combination of all three seems to produce the strongest effect in the large majority of students, especially for the act of remembering.

Furthermore, the tripartite division of learning methods concentrates on the initial process of taking in new information: merely the first step of remembering. Whether we need to hear the words spoken while sitting quietly in a dark room, whether we need to move around and read out loud what we are trying to learn, or whether we need a basic game to realise the lessons taught, we are only at the first stage of the process. Once this has been accomplished, we still need to encode the information for our brain to store it in the memory, and for this we must use some form of visualisation. We cannot use physical aids, noises or written words: a physical action becomes a visual memory thereof; a noise becomes an abstract image, so that we can 'almost' hear it; words on the page are either seen as words in front of the mind's eye (photographic memory) or translated into iconic images

---

13   *Visual Thinking*, p.207.

in order to be retained in the memory. The second step of learning, the encoding and storing of information, must happen on an abstract level where memory plays a major role. Only then can the third step – recall – function properly.

A memory experiment with students made up of the three groups to test my method of interpretation would give an indication of whether my supposition is correct. Memory tests in general would be highly elucidating. Bartlett's insightful tests involving longer texts rather than mere memory items (letter combinations or individual words) has received relatively little attention since his time, but those who have undertaken these kinds of test have been very successful, such as Lohafer's investigation to determine preclosure points in short stories, mentioned in chapter three.

Finally, it would have been very interesting to collate a large number of quotations by authors on the topic of memory and creativity, memory and writing. The anthologies I came across list general and unrelated comments on memory with little relevance for its influence on the creative work of a writer, or are made by non-fiction authors commenting on the scientific or historical aspects of memory. Since every modern author I've considered remarks directly on the topic, giving an insight into the way they work, a comparison of these statements might suggest which aspects of the memory process are particularly relevant.

Investigating my theory has very much felt like an exploration. I began with a grand theory and an even greater enthusiasm to discover whether the theory might hold. I discovered immediately that 'memory' is a volatile word with a myriad of meanings: before starting literary interpretation, I had to peel back layer upon layer of significance. Some were entirely irrelevant to my topic, others only circumstantially so, and some – although related – complicated matters rather than clarifying them and therefore had to be defined only to be set aside. This suggests that the memory is intrinsically involved in so many aspects of ontological, epistemological and hermeneutical disciplines that the breadth of meaning the word contains is representative of the great relevance memory has in our way of comprehending the world around us.

In this age of communication technology we still struggle to explain how the mind works. Words are still the ultimate tool for communicating ideas. The person who best understands to choose, organise and present words that spark off images will be most successful at conveying these ideas – the person best equipped to receive the words and construct a mental image from them will be most successful at interpreting them. The ancient rhetorical arts may yet hold the answer to many modern puzzles, and a return to some of their successful practices may aid us in our new age of communication by creating a sound foundation for innovative reading and writing.

Bibliography

Primary Sources

Augustine, *De Doctrina Christiana*, ed. and tr. by R.P.H. Green (Oxford: Oxford University Press, 1995) in *Oxford Early Christian Texts*, gen. ed. H. Chadwick.

Auster, Paul, *The Art of Hunger: Essays, prefaces, interviews and The Red Notebook* (New York and London: Penguin Books, 1997).
- *The Invention of Solitude* (London: Faber & Faber, 2005; first pub. 1982).
- *Moon Palace* (London: Faber & Faber, 2004; first pub. 1989).
- *The New York Trilogy* (London: Faber & Faber, 1987; first pub. 1985).
- *The Red Notebook* (London: Faber & Faber, 1996; first pub.1995).
- *Oracle Night* (London: Faber & Faber, 2004)
- *Travels in the Scriptorium* (London: Faber & Faber, 2006)

Boccaccio, *Il Filostrato*, in *Tutte le opere*, ed. by V. Branca, vol.2 (Milano: Arnoldo Mandadori, 1964).

Boethius, *The Consolation of Philosophy*, tr. and intro. by V.E. Watts (London: Penguin Books, 1969).

Carter, Angela, *The Infernal Desire Machines of Doctor Hoffman* (London: Hart-Davis, 1972).
- *The Magic Toyshop* (London: Virago Press, 1992; first pub. 1967).
- *Nights at the Circus* (London: Vintage Books, 1994; first pub. 1984).
- "Notes from the frontline", in *On Gender and Writing*, ed. by Michelene Wandor (London and Boston, MA: Pandora, 1983) 69–77.
- *The Passion of New Eve* (London: Virago Press, 1992; first pub. 1977).
- *Wise Children* (London: Vintage Books, 2006; first pub. 1991).

Chaucer, Geoffrey, *The Canterbury Tales*, tr. by N. Coghill (London and New York: Penguin Books, 1977; first pub. 1951).
- *The Riverside Chaucer*, gen. ed. L.D. Benson (Oxford: Oxford University Press, first pub. 1987).

Cicero, M. Tullius, *De Inventione*, vol.2, ed. and tr. by H.M. Hubbell (London: William Heinemann, 1976; first prnt. 1968).
- *De Oratore*, 2 vols, ed. and tr. by E.W. Sutton and H. Rackham (London and Cambridge, MA: William Heinemann and Harvard University Press, 1967; first prnt. 1942).

Dante Alighieri, *Inferno*, *The Divine Comedy*, tr. by J.D. Sinclair, (New York: Oxford University Press, 1961; first pub. 1939).

Dickens, Charles, *Our Mutual Friend* (London: Penguin Books, 1997; first pub. in 2 vols, 1865).

Durandus, William, *The Symbolism of Churches and Church Ornaments* (New York: AMS, 1973; reprinted from the 1843 London edn).

Forster, E.M., *A Room with a View* (London: Penguin Books, 1990; first prnt. 1908).

Geoffrey of Monmouth, *The History of the Kings of Britain*, tr. by Lewis Thorpe (London and New York: Penguin Books, 1966).

Geoffrey of Vinsauf, *The* Poetria Nova *and its Sources in Early Rhetorical Doctrine*, ed. and tr. by E. Gallo (The Hague and Paris: Mouton, 1971).

Guillaume de Lorris and Jean de Meun, *The Romance of the Rose*, tr. and intro. by F. Horgan (Oxford and New York: Oxford University Press, 1999; first pub. 1994).

Hilton, Walter, *The Scale of Perfection*, ed. by T.H. Bestul (Kalamazoo, MI: Medieval Institute Publications, Western Michigan University, 2000).

Hugh of St Victor, *Didascalicon*, tr. by Jerome Taylor (New York and London: Columbia University Press, 1961).

Joyce, James, *Ulysses* (Oxford: Oxford University Press, 1993; first pub. 1922).

Langland, William, *Piers Plowman*, tr. by E.T. Donaldson, ed. by E. Robertson and S.H.A. Shepherd (New York and London: Norton, 2006).

- *Piers Plowman: The A Version*, gen. ed. George Kane (Berkeley, CA and London: University of California Press, 1988; first pub. 1960).

- *Piers Plowman: The B Version*, ed. by George Kane and E.T. Donaldson (Berkeley, CA and London: University of California Press, 1988; first pub. 1975).

- *Piers Plowman: The C Version*, ed. by George Kane and George Russell (Berkeley, CA and London: University of California Press, 1997).

- *Piers Plowman*, tr. and intro. by A.V.C. Schmidt (Oxford and New York: Oxford University Press, 1992).

- *Piers the Ploughman*, tr. and intro. by J.F. Goodridge (London and New York: Penguin Books, 1966; first pub. 1959).

- *The Vision of Piers Plowman: A critical edition of the B–text based on Trinity College Cambridge MS B.15.17*, 2nd edn, ed. by A.V.C. Schmidt (London: Everyman, 1995).

- *The Vision of William Concerning Piers the Plowman: Together with vita de dowel, dobet et dobest, secundum wit et resoun*, ed. by W.W. Skeat (Oxford: Oxford University Press, 1972; first pub. 1869).

Lull, Ramon, *Selected Works of Ramon Lull (1232–1316)*, ed. and tr. by A. Bonner (Princeton, NJ: Princeton University Press, 1985).

Martianus Capella, "De nuptiis philologiae et mercurii" in *Martianus Capella and the Seven Liberal Arts*, vol.2, ed. by William H. Stahl, tr. by William H. Stahl and Richard Johnson with E.L. Burge, (New York: Columbia University Press, 1977).

Pynchon, Thomas, *The Crying of Lot 49* (London: Vintage Books, 2000; first pub. 1965).

- *Gravity's Rainbow* (London: Vintage Books, 2000; first pub. 1973).

- *Mason & Dickson* (London: Vintage Books, 1998; first publ. 1997).

- *Vineland* (London: QPD, 1990).

Quintilian, M. Fabius, *Institutio Oratoria (The Orator's Education)*, ed. and tr. by D.A. Russell, *Loeb Classical Library* (London and Cambridge, MA: Harvard University Press, 2001).

Rhetorica ad Herennium (Ad C. Herennium; De ratione dicendi), *Loeb Classical Library* (Cambridge, MA: Harvard University Press, and London: William Heinemann, 1968; first pub. 1954).

Rushdie, Salman, *Haroun and the Sea of Stories* (London: Granta Books, 1991; first pub. 1990).

- "Imaginary homelands", in *Imaginary Homelands: Essays and criticism 1981–91* (London: Granta Books, 1992; first pub. 1991) 9–21.

- "In good faith", in *Imaginary Homelands: Essays and criticism 1981–91* (London: Granta Books, 1992; first pub. 1991) 393–414.

- *Midnight's Children* (London: Vintage Books, 1995; first pub. 1981).

- *The Moor's Last Sigh* (London: Vintage Books, 2006; first pub. 1995).

- *The Satanic Verses* (London: Vintage Books, 1998; first pub. 1988).

- *Shame* (London: Vintage Books, 1995; first pub. 1983).

Virgil, *The Aeneid*, tr. by C. Day Lewis (Oxford: Oxford University Press, 1986; first pub. 1952).

Woolf, Virginia, *To the Lighthouse* (London: Vintage Books, 1992; first pub. 1927).

Secondary Sources

Abbas, Niran, ed., *Thomas Pynchon: Reading from the margins* (Cranbury, NJ and London: Fairleigh Dickinson University Press, 2003).

Addy, Andrew, "Narrating the self: Story-telling as personal myth-making in Paul Auster's *Moon Palace*", in *QWERTY: Arts, littératures ans civilisations du monde anglophone*, 6, (Oct. 1996), 153–61.

Alford, John A., "The role of quotations in *Piers Plowman*", in *Speculum*, vol.52, 1 (Jan. 1977) 88–99.

Alford, Steven E., "Chance in contemporary narrative: The example of Paul Auster", in *Bloom's Modern Critical Views: Paul Auster*, ed. by Harold Bloom (Broomall, PA: Chelsea House, 2004) 113–35.

Anderson, M.D., *Drama and Imagery in English Medieval Churches* (Cambridge: Cambridge University Press, 1963).

Antin, Mary, *The Promised Land* (Princeton, NJ: Princeton University Press, 1985; first pub. 1912).

Arnheim, Rudolf, *Visual Thinking* (Berkeley and Los Angeles, CA and London: University of California Press, 1969).

Assmann, Aleida, *Erinnerungsräume: Formen und Wandlungen des kulturellen Gedächtnisses* (München: C.H. Beck, 1999).

Assmann, Jan and Tonio Hölscher, eds, *Kultur und Gedächtnis* (Frankfurt am Main: Suhrkamp, 1988).

Atwood, Margaret, "Running with the tigers", in *Flesh and the Mirror: Essays on the art of Angela Carter*, ed. by Lorna Sage (London: Virago Press, 1995) 117–35.

Baddeley, Alan D., *The Psychology of Memory* (New York, Hagerstown, San Francisco and London: Basic Books, 1976).

Barone, Dennis, ed., *Beyond the Red Notebook: Essays on Paul Auster* (Philadelphia, PA: University of Pennsylvania Press, 1996; first pub. 1995).

Barthes, Roland, *Image Music Text: Essays selected and translated by Stephen Heath* (London: Fontana Press, 1977).

Bartlett, F.C., *Remembering: A study in experimental and social psychology* (Cambridge: Cambridge University Press, 1995; first pub. 1932).

Bennett, J.A.W., *Chaucer's Book of Fame: An exposition of* The House of Fame (Oxford: Oxford University Press, 1968).

- "Chaucer's contemporary", in *Piers Plowman: Critical approaches*, ed. by S.S. Hussey (London: Methuen, 1969) 310–24.

Bloomfield, M.W., *Piers Plowman as a Fourteenth Century Apocalypse* (New Brunswick, NJ: Rutgers University Press, 1961).

Blum, Herwig, *Die antike Mnemotechnik*, in *Spudasmata: Studien zur klassischen Philologie und ihren Grenzgebieten*, 15 (Hildesheim and New York: G. Olms, 1969).

Boitani, Piero and Jill Mann, eds, *The Cambridge Chaucer Companion* (Cambridge: Cambridge University Press, 1986).

Brians, Paul (2004) "Notes for Salman Rushdie: *The Satanic Verses*" [WWW] http://www.wsu.edu/~brians/anglophone/satanic_verses (accessed Oct. 2006).

Bundy, Murray Wright, *The Theory of Imagination in Classical and Medieval Thought* (Urbana, IL: University of Illinois Press, 1927).

Burckhardt, Titus, *Chartres and the Birth of a Cathedral*, tr. by W. Stoddart (Ipswich: Golgonooza, 1995; first pub. 1962).

Burrow, J.A., "The action of Langland's second vision", in *Essays on Medieval Literature* (Oxford: Clarendon, 1984) 79–101; (first pub. in *Essays in Criticism*, 15 (1965) 247–68).

Caldicott, C.E.J. and Anne Fuchs, eds, *Cultural Memory: Essays on European literature and history* (Bern: Peter Lang, 2003).

Camille, Michael, *Mirror in Parchment: The Luttrell Psalter and the making of medieval England* (London: Reaction Books, 1998).

Carruthers, Mary, *The Book of Memory: A study of memory in medieval culture* (New York and London: Cambridge University Press, 1999; first pub. 1990).

- *The Craft of Thought: Meditation, rhetoric and the making of images, 400–1200* (New York and Cambridge: Cambridge University Press, 2000; first pub. 1998).

- "Italy, *ars memorativa*, and Fame's house", in *Studies in the Age of Chaucer*, Proceedings series 2 (1987) 179–87.

- *The Search for St Truth: A study of meaning in* Piers Plowman (Evanston, IL: Northwestern University Press, 1973).

Chambers, Deborah, "Images are both depictive and descriptive", in *Imagery, Creativity, and Discovery: A cognitive perspective*, ed. by Beverly Roskos-Ewoldsen, Margaret Jean Intons-Peterson and Rita E. Anderson (Amsterdam: North-Holland, 1993) 77–97.

Chambers, R.W., *Man's Unconquerable Mind: Studies of English writers, from Bede to A.E. Housman and W.P. Ker* (London: Jonathan Cape, 1939; revised edn 1952).

Chaudhuri, Una, (1990) "Imaginative maps" [WWW] http://www.subir.com/rushdie/uc-maps.html. (Turnstile Press, New York, vol.2, 1) (accessed Oct. 2006).

Clanchy, M.T., *From Memory to Written Record: England 1066–1307* (Oxford and Malden, MA: Blackwell, 1998; first pub. 1979).

Clemen, Wolfgang, *Chaucer's Early Poetry*, tr. by C.A.M. Sym (London: Methuen, 1963).

Coghill, Nevill, "The pardon of Piers Plowman", in *Proceedings of the British Academy*, 30 (1944) 303–57.

Coleman, Janet, *Piers Plowman and the "moderni"*, *Letture de pensiero e d'arte* (Rome: Storia e letteratura, 1981).

Cornoldi, Cesare, Robert H. Logie, Maria A. Brandimonte and Geir Kaufmann, eds, *Stretching the Imagination: Representation and transformation in mental imagery* (New York and Oxford: Oxford University Press, 1996).

Cowart, David, "Attenuated postmodernism: Pynchon's *Vineland*: in *The Vineland Papers: Critical takes on Pynchon's novel*, ed. by Geoffrey Green, Donald J. Greiner and Larry McCaffery (Champaign, IL: Dalkey Archive Press, 1994) 3–13.

Culler, Jonathan, *Literary Theory: A very short introduction* (Oxford: Oxford University Press, 1997).

- *The Pursuit of Signs: Semiotics, literature, deconstruction* (London and New York: Routledge, 2001; first pub. 1981).

Davis, Tom (1995) "Lacan and deconstruction" [WWW] http://www.english.bham.ac.uk/staff/tom/teaching/theories/theorieslectures/lacan/lacanlectures.htm (accessed Oct. 2007).

Denis, Michel, "Imagery and thinking", in *Imagery and Cognition*, ed. by Cesare Cornoldi and Mark A. McDaniel (New York: Springer, 1991) 103–32.

Dickson, David, *The Utterance of America: Emersonian newness in Dos Passos' USA and Pynchon's Vineland* (Göteborg: Acta Universitatis Gothoburgensis, 1998).

Dillon, Janette, "*Piers Plowman*: A particular example of wordplay and its structural significance", in *Medium Aevum*, 50 (1981) 40–48.

Donovan, Christopher, *Postmodern Counternarratives: Irony and audience in the novels of Paul Auster, Don DeLillo, Charles Johnson and Tim O'Brian* (New York and London: Routledge, 2005).

Dow, William, "Never being 'this far from home': Paul Auster and picturing *Moonlight* spaces", in *QWERTY: Arts, littératures ans civilisations du monde anglophone*, 6, (Oct. 1996), 193–8.

Draaisma, Douwe, *Metaphors of Memory: A history of ideas about the mind*, tr. by P. Vincent (Cambridge: Cambridge University Press, 2000; first pub. in Dutch as *De metaforenmachine – een geschiedenis van het geheuge*, 1995).

- *Why Life Speeds Up As You Get Older: How memory shapes our past*, tr. by A. and E. Pomerans, (Cambridge: Cambridge University Press, 2006; first pub. 2004).

Duyfhuizen, Bernard, "Starry-eyed semiotics: Learning to read Slothrop's map in *Gravity's Rainbow*" in *Pynchon Notes* (1981, June 6) 5–33.

Eagleton, Terry, *Literary Theory: An introduction*, 2nd edn (Malden, MA, Oxford, Melbourne and Berlin: Blackwell, 1996; first pub. 1983).

Eliot, T.S., "Tradition and the individual talent", in *Selected Essays* (London: Faber & Faber, 1969; first pub. 1932) 13–22.

Finney, Brian (1998) "Tall tales and brief lives: Angela Carter's *Nights at the Circus*" [WWW] http://www.csulb.edu/~bhfinney/AngelaCarter.html (accessed Oct. 2007).

Foster, Jonathan K. and Marco Jelicic, *Memory: Systems, process, or function?* (Oxford: Oxford University Press, 1999).

Foster, Richard, *Patterns of Thought: The hidden meaning of the great pavement of Westminster Abbey* (London: Jonathan Cape, 1991).

Fowler, Alister, *Kinds of Literature: An introduction to the theory of genres and modes* (Oxford: Clarendon Press, 1982).

Frank, Robert Worth, *Piers Plowman and the Scheme of Salvation: An interpretation of dowel, dobet and dobest* (New Haven, CT: Yale University Press, 1969; first prnt. 1957).

Fredman, Stephen, "'How to get out of the room that is the book?' Paul Auster and the consequences of confinement", in *Bloom's Modern Critical Views: Paul Auster*, ed. by Harold Bloom (Broomall, PA: Chelsea House, 2004) 7–41.

Gamble, Sarah, ed., *The Fiction of Angela Carter: A reader's guide to essential criticism* (Cambridge: Icon, 2001).

Gaylord, Alan T., "The lesson of the Troilus: Chastisement and correction" in *Essays on Troilus and Criseyde*, ed. by Mary Salu (Cambridge: D.S. Brewer, 1979) 23–42.

Geary, Patrick J., *Phantoms of Remembrance: Memory and oblivion at the end of the first millennium* (Princeton, NJ: Princeton University Press, 1994).

Geddes, Dan (2007) "Pynchon's *Vineland*: The war on drugs and the coming American police state" [WWW] http://www.thesatirist.com/books/Vineland.html (accessed Nov. 2007).

Gochenour, Phillip, "The history written on the body: Photography, history and memory in Pynchon's *Vineland*", in *Pynchon Notes*, 32–33, (spring-fall, 1993), 169–80.

Godden, Malcolm, *The Making of* Piers Plowman (London and New York: Longman, 1990).

Goldsmith, Margaret E., *The Figure of Piers Plowman: The image on the coin* (Cambridge: D.S. Brewer, 1981).

Gordon, Andrew, "Smoking dope with Thomas Pynchon: A sixties memoir", in *The Vineland Papers: Critical takes on Pynchon's novel*, ed. by Geoffrey Green, Donald J. Greiner, Larry McCaffery (Champaign, IL: Dalkey Archive Press, 1994) 167–78.

Grim, William E., "'Good-buy, Columbus': Postmodernist satire in *Vineland*", in *The Vineland Papers: Critical takes on Pynchon's novel*, ed. by Geoffrey Green, Donald J. Greiner, Larry McCaffery (Champaign, IL: Dalkey Archive Press, 1994) 154–60.

Haffenden, John, *Novelists in Interview* (London and New York: Methuen, 1985).

Halbwachs, Maurice, *On Collective Memory*, tr. by Lewis A. Coser (Chicago and London: University of Chicago Press, 1992; first pub. in French in 2 vols as *Les cadres sociaux de la mémoire*, 1952 and *La topographie légendaire des évangiles en terre sainte: Etude de mémoire collective*, 1941).

Harwood, Britton J., "Imaginative in *Piers Plowman*", in *Medium Aevum*, 44 (1975) 249–63.

Hawthorne, Mark D., "Imaginary locales in Pynchon's *Vineland*", in *Pynchon Notes*, 30–31, (spring-fall, 1992), 77–90.

Heer, Friedrich, *The Medieval World: Europe 1100–1350*, tr. by J. Sondheimer (London: Phoenix, 1998; first pub. in German 1961).

Hirsch, E.D., Jr., *The Aims of Interpretation*, (Chicago and London: University of Chicago Press, 1976).

- "Meaning and significance", in *The Aims of Interpretation* (Chicago and London: University of Chicago Press, 1976) 1–13.

- *Validity in Interpretation* (New Haven, CT and London: Yale University Press, 1967).

Höfele, Andreas, "Wasteland sprouting: Salman Rushdie's *The Satanic Verses* and the cityscapes of modernism", in *Theme Parks, Rainforests and Sprouting Wastelands: European essays on theory and performance in contemporary British fiction*, ed. by Richard Todd and Luisa Flora (Amsterdam–Atlanta, GA: Rodopi, 2000) 41–54.

Hopper, Vincent Foster, *Medieval Number Symbolism: Its sources, meaning, and influence on thought and expression* (New York: Cooper Square, 1969; first pub. 1938).

Huppé, Bernard F., "'Petrus id est Christus': Word play in *Piers Plowman*, the B-text", in *A Journal of English Literary History*, vol.17 (1950) 3, 163–90.

Inton-Peterson, Margaret Jean, "Imagery's role in creativity and discovery", in *Imagery, Creativity and Discovery: A cognitive perspective*, ed. by Beverly Roskos-Ewoldsen, Margaret Jean Intons-Peterson and Rita E. Anderson (Amsterdam: North-Holland, 1933) 1–38.

Iser, Wolfgang, *The Implied Reader: Patterns of communication in prose fiction from Bunyan to Beckett* (Baltimore, MD and London: John Hopkins, 1974; first pub. as *Der implizite Leser: Kommunikationsformen des Romans von Bunyan bis Beckett*, 1972).

James, William, *The Principles of Psychology* (New York: Dover, 1918; first pub. 1890).

Jones, H.S.V., "Imaginatif in *Piers Plowman*", in *Journal of English and Germanic Philology*, 13 (1914) 583–88.

Jouve, Nicole Ward, "Mother is a figure of speech…", in *Flesh and the Mirror: Essays on the art of Angela Carter*, ed. by Lorna Sage (London: Virago Press, 1995) 136–70.

Kaske, R.E., "'Ex vi transicionis' and its passage in *Piers Plowman*", in *Journal of English and Germanic Philology*, 62 (1963) 32–60.

Katsavos, Anna, "An interview with Angela Carter", in *"T'aint No Sin": Sex and desire in the fiction of Angela Carter* (Ann Arbor, MI: Bell & Howell, 1998) 229–40.

Kaulbach, Ernest N., "The 'vis imaginativa' and the reasoning powers of Ymaginatif in the B-text of *Piers Plowman*", in *Journal of English and Germanic Philology*, 84 (1985) 16–29.

Klepper, Martin, *Pynchon, Auster, DeLillo: Die amerikanische Postmoderne zwischen Spiel und Rekonstruktion* (Frankfurt and New York: Campus Verlag, 1996).

Kolve, V.A., *Chaucer and the Imagery of Narrative: The first five Canterbury Tales* (London and Victoria: Stanford University Press, 1984).

Koonce, B.G., *Chaucer and the Tradition of Fame: Symbolism in* The House of Fame (Princeton, NJ: Princeton University Press, 1966).

Kuchta, Todd M., "Allegorizing the Emergency: Rushdie's *Midnight's Children* and Benjamin's *Theory of Allegory*", in *Critical Essays on Salman Rushdie*, ed. by Keith Booker (New York: G.K. Hall, 1999) 205–44.

Lachmann, Renate, *Memory and Literature: Intertextuality in Russian Modernism* (Minneapolis, MN and London: University of Minnesota Press, 1997; first pub. as *Gedächtnis und Literatur: Intertextualität in der russischen Moderne*, 1990).

Lambert, Mark, "Telling the story in *Troilus and Criseyde*" in *The Cambridge Chaucer Companion*, ed. by P. Boitani and J. Mann (Cambridge: Cambridge University Press, 1986) 59–73.

- "*Troilus*, Books I–III: A Criseydan reading", in *Essays on* Troilus and Criseyde, ed. by Mary Salu (Cambridge: D.S. Brewer, 1979) 109–40.

Lawlor, John, *Piers Plowman: An essay in criticism* (London: Edward Arnold, 1962).

Lawlor, Robert, *Sacred Geometry: Philosophy and practice* (London: Thames and Hudson, 1998; first pub. 1982).

Lohafer, Susan, *Reading for Storyness: Preclosure theory, empirical poetics, and culture in the short story* (Baltimore, MD and London: John Hopkins, 2003).

Loomis, Roger Sherman, *A Mirror of Chaucer's World* (Princeton, NJ: Princeton University Press, 1965).

Luria, A.R., *The Mind of a Mnemonist: A little book about a vast memory*, tr. from Russian by Lynn Solotarof (New York and London: Basic Books, 1968).

MacQueen, John, *Numerology: Theory and outline history of a literary mode* (Edinburgh: Edinburgh University Press, 1985).

Mâle, Emil, *Religious Art in Fance: The 13th century: A study of medieval iconography and its sources* (Princeton, NJ and Guildford: Princeton University Press, 1984; tr. from 9th edn 1958; first pub. in French 1898).

Mann, A.T., *Sacred Architecture* (Shaftesbury, Rockport, MA and Brisbane: Element, 1993).

Mann, Jill, "Chaucer and destiny in *Troilus and Criseyde* and the *Knight's Tale*", in *The Cambridge Chaucer Companion*, ed. by P. Boitani and J. Mann (Cambridge: Cambridge University Press, 1986) 75–92.

- *Chaucer and Medieval Estate Satire: The literature of social classes and the* General Prologue *of the* Canterbury Tales (Cambridge: Cambridge University Press, 1973).

Markowitsch, Hans-Joachim, *Dem Gedächtnis auf der Spur: Vom Erinnern und Vergessen* (Darmstadt: Primus Verlag, 2002).

McClelland, James L., "Connectionist models of memory", in *The Oxford Handbook of Memory*, ed. by E. Tulving and F.I.M. Craik (Oxford: Oxford University Press, 2000) 583–96.

McLaughlin, Robert L., "Surveying, mapmaking and representation in *Mason & Dixon*", in *American Postmodernity: Essays on the recent fiction of Thomas Pynchon*, ed. by Ian D. Copestake (Bern: Peter Lang, 2003) 173–91.

Mensendieck, Otto, "The authorship of *Piers Plowman*", in *Journal of English and Germanic Philology*, 9 (1910) 404–20.

Miller, George A., "The magical number seven, plus or minus two: Some limits on our capacity for processing information", in *The Psychological Review*, 63 (1956) 81–97.

Miller, J. Hillis, *Charles Dickens: The world of his novels* (Cambridge, MA: Harvard University Press, 1958).

Minnis, Alastair J., "Langland's Ymaginatif and the late-medieval theories of imagination", in *Comparative Criticism*, 3 (1981) 71–108.

Moseley, C.W.R.D., *Geoffrey Chaucer, The Knight's Tale: A critical study* (Harmondsworth and New York: Penguin Books, 1987).

- *Geoffrey Chaucer, The Pardoner's Tale: A critical study* (Harmondsworth: Penguin Books, 1987).

Nalbantian, Suzanne, *Memory in Literature: From Rousseau to neuroscience* (New York: Palgrave Macmillan, 2003).

Noakes, Jonathan, "Interview with Salman Rushdie", in *Salman Rushdie: The essential guide*, by Margaret Raynolds and Jonathan Noakes (London and Sydney: Vintage Books, 2003) 10–33.

Nünning, Ansgar, "*Unreliable Narration* zur Einführung: Grundzüge einer kognitiv-narratologischen Theorie und Analyse unglaubwürdigen Erzählens", in *Unreliable Narration: Studien zur Theorie und Praxis unglaubwürdigen Erzählens in der englisch-sprachigen Erzählliteratur* (Trier: Wissenschaftlicher Verlag, 1998) 3–39.

The Oxford Concise Companion to Classical Literature (Oxford: Oxford University Press, 1996).

Panofsky, Erwin, *Gothic Architecture and Scolasticism: An inquiry into the analogy of the arts, philosophy, and religion in the Middle Ages* (New York: Meridian Books, 1957).

Parkin, Alan J., "Component processes versus systems: Is there really an important difference?", in *Memory: Systems, process, or function?*, ed. by Jonathan K. Foster and Marco Jelicic (Oxford: Oxford University Press, 1999) 273–88.

Pethes, N. and J. Ruchatz, eds, *Gedächtnis und Erinnerung: Ein interdisziplinäres Lexicon* (Hamburg: Rowohlt, 2001).

Porush, David, "'Purring into transcendence': Pynchon's Puncutron machine", in *The Vineland Papers: Critical takes on Pynchon's novel*, ed. by Geoffrey Green, Donald J. Greiner and Larry McCaffery (Champaign, IL: Dalkey Archive Press, 1994) 31–45.

Quirk, Randolph, "Vis imaginativa", in *Journal of English and Germanic Philology*, 53 (1954) 81–3.

Raw, Barbara, "Piers and the image of God in man", in *Piers Plowman: Critical approaches*, ed. by S.S. Hussey (London: Methuen, 1969) 143-79.

Reder, Michael, "Rewriting history and identity: The reinvention of myth, epic, and allegory in Salman Rushdie's *Midnight's Children*", in *Critical Essays on Salman Rushdie*, ed. by Keith Booker (New York: G.K. Hall, 1999) 225–49.

Rege, Josna E., "Victim into protagonist? *Midnight's Children* and the post-Rushdie national narratives of the eighties", in *Critical Essays on Salman Rushdie*, ed. by Keith Booker (New York: G.K. Hall, 1999) 250–82.

Reinhart, Werner, *Pikareske Romane der 80er Jahre: Ronald Reagan und die Renaissance des politischen Erzählens in den USA (Acker, Auster, Boyle, Irving, Kennedy, Pynchon)* (Tübingen: Narr, 2001).

Reisberg, Daniel and Robert Logie, "The ins and outs of working memory: Overcoming the limits on learning from memory", in *Imagery, Creativity, and Discovery: A cognitive perspective*, ed. by Beverly Roskos-Ewoldsen, Margaret Jean Intons-Peterson and Rita E. Anderson, (Amsterdam: North-Holland, 1993) 39–76.

Rickard, John S., *Joyce's Book of Memory: The mnemotechnic of Ulysses* (Durham and London: Duke University Press, 1999).

Robinson, Martin, *Sacred Places, Pilgrim Paths: An anthology of pilgrimage* (London: Fount, 1998).

Roskos-Ewoldsen, Beverly, Margaret Jean Intons-Peterson, Rita E. Anderson, eds, *Imagery, Creativity and Discovery: A cognitive perspective* (Amsterdam: North-Holland, 1993). "Imagery, creativity, and discovery: Conclusion and implications", in *Imagery, Creativity and Discovery: A cognitive perspective* (Amsterdam: North-Holland, 1993) 313–28.

Rossetti, W. Michael, tr., *Chaucer's* Troilus and Criseyde *(from the Harl. MS. 3943) Compared with Boccaccio's* Filostrato, *Publication of the Chaucer Society*, Series 1, 44 and 65 (London and New York: Johnson Reprint, 1967; first prnt. 1873).

Rossi, Paolo, *Logic and the Art of Memory: The quest for a universal language* (London: Athlone Press, 2000; first pub. as *Clavis universalis: Arti della memoria e logica combinatoria da Lullo a Leibniz*, 1983).

Rouse, Richard H., and Mary A. Rouse, "The dissemination of texts in pecia at Bologna and Paris", in *Rationalisierung der Buchherstellung im Mittelalter und in der frühen Neuzeit*, ed. by P. Rück and M. Boghardt (Marburg: Rück, 1994) 69–77.

Safer, Elaine B., "Pynchon's world and its legendary past: Humor and the absurd in twentieth-century Vineland", in *The Vineland Papers: Critical takes on Pynchon's novel*, ed. by Geoffrey Green, Donald J. Greiner and Larry McCaffery (Champaign, IL: Dalkey Archive Press, 1994) 46–67.

Salon.com (1996) The Salon Interview, "Salman Rushdie: When life becomes a bad novel" [WWW] http://www.salon.com/06/features/interview.html (accessed Oct. 2007).

Salter, Elizabeth, *Piers Plowman: An introduction* (Oxford: Blackwell, 1969; first pub. 1962).

Salu, Mary, ed., *Essays on* Troilus and Criseyde (Cambridge: D.S. Brewer, 1979).

Schacter, Daniel L., *The Seven Sins of Memory: How the mind forgets and remembers* (Boston and New York: Houghton Mifflin, 2001).

Schmidt, A.V.C., *The Clerkly Maker: Langland's poetic art* (Cambridge: D.S. Brewer, 1987).

- "The inner dream in *Piers Plowman*", in *Medium Aevum*, 55 (1986) 24–40.

Schweitzer, Edward C., "'Half a laumpe lyne in latyne' and Patience's riddle in *Piers Plowman*", in *Journal of English and Germanic Philology*, 63 (1974) 313–27.

Seidl, Christian (2005) "'Regenerating through creativity': The frontier in Paul Auster's *Moon Palace*" [WWW] http://www.fu-berlin.de/phin/phin31/p.31t5.html (accessed Oct. 2007).

Simpson, James, "From reason to affected knowledge: Modes of thought and poetic form in *Piers Plowman*", in *Medium Aevum*, 55 (1986) 1–23.

- *Piers Plowman: An introduction to the B-text* (London and New York: Longman, 1990).

Smith, Ben H., *Traditional Imagery of Charity in* Piers Plowman, *Studies in English Literature* (The Hague: Mouton, 1966).

Smith, Shawn, *Pynchon and History: Metahistorical rhetoric and postmodern narrative form in the novels of Thomas Pynchon* (New York and Abingdon: Routledge, 2005).

Spearing, A.C., *Medieval Dream Poetry* (Cambridge, London and New York: Cambridge University Press, 1976).

Spence, Jonathan D., *The Memory Palace of Matteo Ricci* (New York, Ontario and Harmondsworth: Elisabeth Sifton Books/Viking, 1984; first pub. 1983).

Stokes, Mary, *Justice and Mercy in* Piers Plowman*: A reading of the B-text visio* (London and Canberra: Croom Helm, 1984).

Strehle, Susan, "Pynchon's 'elaborate game of doubles' in *Vineland*", in *The Vineland Papers: Critical takes on Pynchon's novel*, ed. by Geoffrey Green, Donald J. Greiner and Larry McCaffery (Champaign, IL: Dalkey Archive Press, 1994) 101–18.

Swope, Richard (2002) "Supposing a space: The detecting subject in Paul Auster's *City of Glass*" [WWW] http://reconstruction.eserver.org./023/swope.html (accessed Oct. 2007).

Thoreen, David, "The Fourth Amendment and other inconveniences: Undeclared war, organized labor and the abrogation of civil rights in Vineland", in *Thomas*

Pynchon: Reading from the margins, ed. by Niran Abbas (Cranbury, NJ and London: Fairleigh Dickinson University Press, 2003) 215–33.

- "In which 'acts have consequences': Ideas of moral order in the qualified postmodernism of Pynchon's recent fiction", in *American Postmodernity: Essays on the recent fiction of Thomas Pynchon*, ed. by Ian D. Copestake (Bern: Peter Lang, 2003) 49–70.

- "The president's emergency war powers and the erosion of personal liberties in Pynchon's *Vineland*", in *Oklahoma City University Law Review*, 24, 3 (1999) 761-98.

Tversky, Barbara, "Remembering spaces", in *The Oxford Handbook of Memory*, ed. by E. Tulving and F.I.M. Craik (Oxford: Oxford University Press, 2000) 363–78.

Vanderbeke, Dirk (1999) "Vineland in the novels of John Barth and Thomas Pynchon" [WWW] http://www.diss.sense.uni-konstanz.de/amerika/vanderbeke.htm (accessed Oct. 2007).

Yates, Frances A., *The Art of Memory* (London: Pimlico, 1999; first pub. 1966).

Zilkosky, John, "The revenge of the author: Paul Auster's challenge of theory", in *Bloom's Modern Critical Views: Paul Auster*, ed. by Harold Bloom (Broomall, PA: Chelsea House, 2004) 63–76.

Wallace, David, "Chaucer's Continental inheritance: The early poems and *Troilus and Criseyde*", in *The Cambidge Chaucer Companion*, ed. by P. Boitani and J. Mann (Cambridge: Cambridge University Press, 1986) 19–38.

Warner, Maria, "Angela Carter: Bottle blonde, double drag", in *Flesh and the Mirror: Essays on the art of Angela Carter*, ed. by Lorna Sage (London: Virago Press, 1995) 243–56.

Webb, Kate, "Seriously funny: *Wise Children*", in *Flesh and the Mirror: Essays on the art of Angela Carter*, ed. by Lorna Sage (London: Virago Press, 1995) 279–307.

Weisenburger, Steven, "Inside *Moon Palace*", in *Beyond the Red Notebook: Essays on Paul Auster*, ed. by Dennis Barone (Philadelphia, PA: University of Pennsylvania Press, 1996; first pub. 1995) 129–42.

White, Hugh, "Langland's Ymaginatif and Kynde and the *Benjamin Major*", in *Medium Aevum*, 55 (1986) 241–48.

Wilson, Christopher, *The Gothic Cathedral: The architecture of the great church, 1130–1530* (London: Thames and Hudson, 1998; first pub. 1990).

Wittig, Joseph S., "*Piers Plowman* B, Passus IX–XII: Elements in the design of the inward journey", in *Traditio: Studies in ancient and medieval history, thought and religion*, 28 (New York: Fordham University Press, 1972) 211–80.

Nil Korkut

Kinds of Parody from the Medieval to the Postmodern

Frankfurt am Main, Berlin, Bern, Bruxelles, New York, Oxford, Wien, 2009.
144 pp.
European University Studies: Series 14, Anglo-Saxon Language and Literature.
Vol. 449
ISBN 978-3-631-59271-7 · pb. € 26.80*

This book approaches parody as a literary form that has assumed diverse
forms and functions throughout history. The author handles this diversity by
classifying parody according to its objects of imitation and specifying three
major parodic kinds: parody directed at texts and personal styles, parody
directed at genre, and parody directed at discourse. The book argues that
different literary-historical periods in Britain have witnessed the prevalence
of different kinds of parody and investigates the reasons underlying this
phenomenon. All periods from the Middle Ages to the present are considered
in this regard, but a special significance is given to the postmodern age, where
parody has become a widely produced literary form. The book contends
further that postmodern parody is primarily discourse parody – a phenomenon
which can be explained through the major concerns of postmodernism as a
movement. In addition to situating parody and its kinds in a historical context,
this book engages in a detailed analysis of parody in the postmodern age,
preparing the ground for making an informed assessment of the direction
parody and its kinds may take in the near future.

Contents: Functions and Definitions of Parody · Survey of Parody from the
Middle Ages to the 20th Century · Parodies of Texts and Personal Styles ·
Genre Parody · Discourse Parody · Parody and Dialogism · Postmodern Parody ·
Parody and Poststructuralism · Parody and Metafiction · *The Black Prince* (Iris
Murdoch) · *Changing Places* and *Small World* (David Lodge) · *Shame* (Salman
Rushdie) · *Flaubert's Parrot* (Julian Barnes) · *Hawksmoor* (Peter Ackroyd) ·
Mensonge (Malcolm Bradbury)

Frankfurt am Main · Berlin · Bern · Bruxelles · New York · Oxford · Wien
Distribution: Verlag Peter Lang AG
Moosstr. 1, CH-2542 Pieterlen
Telefax 00 41 (0) 32 / 376 17 27

*The €-price includes German tax rate
Prices are subject to change without notice
Homepage http://www.peterlang.de